A Time Such as There Never Was Before

A Time Such as There Never Was Before

Canada After the Great War

Alan Bowker

DUNDURN
TORONTO

Editor: Dominic Farrell
Design: Laura Boyle
Cover Design: Laura Boyle
Front Cover Image: *Brooding Soldier*, Sint-Juliaan, Belgium, Photo by Carolyn Bowker
Printer: Webcom

Library and Archives Canada Cataloguing in Publication

Bowker, Alan, 1943-, author
A time such as there never was before : Canada after the Great War / Alan Bowker.

Includes bibliographical references and index.
Issued in print and electronic formats.
ISBN 978-1-4597-2280-4 (pbk.).--ISBN 978-1-4597-2281-1 (pdf).-- ISBN 978-1-4597-2282-8 (epub)

1. Canada--History--1914-. 2. Canada--Social conditions--20th century. 3. Canada--Politics and government--20th century. 4. World War, 1914-1918-- Social aspects--Canada. I. Title.

FC600.B74 2014   971.064   C2014-902947-0
                                         C2014-902948-9

1   2   3   4   5   18   17   16   15   14

  Canada

Conseil des Arts du Canada **Canada Council for the Arts**

ONTARIO ARTS COUNCIL
CONSEIL DES ARTS DE L'ONTARIO
an Ontario government agency
un organisme du gouvernement de l'Ontario

We acknowledge the support of the **Canada Council for the Arts** and the **Ontario Arts Council** for our publishing program. We also acknowledge the financial support of the **Government of Canada** through the **Canada Book Fund and Livres Canada Books**, and the **Government of Ontario** through the Ontario Book Publishing Tax Credit and the **Ontario Media Development Corporation**.

VISIT US AT

Dundurn.com
@dundurnpress
Facebook.com/dundurnpress
Pinterest.com/dundurnpress

Dundurn
3 Church Street, Suite 500
Toronto, Ontario, Canada
M5E 1M2

Gazelle Book Services Limited
White Cross Mills
High Town, Lancaster, England
LA1 4XS

Dundurn
2250 Military Road
Tonawanda, NY
U.S.A. 14150

Contents

PREFACE

The months following the end of the Great War were a tumultuous, exciting, pivotal, and dangerous period in Canadian history — in the words of humorist and social scientist Stephen Leacock, it was "a time such as there never was before."[1]

A country that had been transformed in less than two decades from a colonial backwater into an industrial, agricultural, and resource powerhouse had found itself part of a titanic world conflict that killed more than sixty thousand of its young men, wounded many more in body and spirit, and engaged the total effort of its farms, industries, people, and families. Canadians had fought for freedom, civilization, the British Empire, and the Kingdom of God on Earth. Victory, they hoped, would usher in a new world of justice and peace in which all things would be possible.

But the war had stressed the many fault lines in this new, unformed country. The relationship between French and English Canada had degenerated to one of open hostility towards each other. Animosity to "foreign" immigrants and others seen as "different" had been unleashed. Three hundred thousand soldiers were coming home, and business and industry would need to provide jobs and compete in a hostile world. Everyone, it seemed — workers, farmers, businessmen, feminists, churches, social reformers, and those excluded from the political and social mainstream — had vociferous demands, impossible expectations, and irrational fears.

The war had a profound impact on Canada. But what happened in the time after the war — the period between the Armistice of November 1918 and the Canadian general election of December 1921 — was also vital in determining what kind of nation would emerge into the 1920s, which of the many changes set in motion would prove permanent, which of the dreams of a better world would be realized, and which would lead only to disillusionment. The new Canada of the 1920s had undergone radical change from the country that celebrated the Armistice in November 1918.

As a result of the war, Canada came of age as a nation, taking its place, somewhat tentatively, on the world stage. Soldiers picked up their lives and struggled to cope with what the war had done to them, while society came to grips with what the war had meant. The great Spanish flu epidemic of 1918 killed more people than the war. Religious faiths, social values, and the very intellectual and moral basis on which the war had been fought, came under challenge. Prohibition outlawed alcohol in the name of moral and social reform, only to unleash a backlash and defiance of the law. Women became citizens and pursued careers, and though their primary role remained that of wives and mothers, they could now draw on professional expertise and state support. Labour and farmers revolted against the domination of Eastern capitalism and Winnipeg saw a six-week General Strike that challenged the political, social, and economic order. Businessmen sought to rebuild the economy in a new world of state engagement, altered trading and financial patterns, and rapid technological change. Artists, intellectuals, and ordinary people sought to define the identity of this new country. French Canadians, immigrants, and excluded minorities advanced different visions of what a truly inclusive Canadian nation ought to look like. All struggled to be accepted into the mainstream of this new nation — some were, and some weren't. By the time it celebrated its Jubilee in 1927, Canada was in in the midst of a new era of prosperity and Canadians could be justly proud of their achievement.

This is a complex story, and to make coherent analysis possible it is told in thematic chapters. But for the people of the time, as the Timeline at the end of this book makes clear, everything was happening at once. They were also viewing events from their own class, gender, regional, ethnic, occupational, and personal perspectives. We will hear the voices of a remarkable cast of characters — labour organizers and agrarian radicals, social reformers, clergymen, feminists, community leaders, businessmen, journalists, scholars, and scientists. But behind them are eight million stories, each important, each unique, of people struggling to adapt to a time of profound change, not always knowing where it would lead, but realizing that their own stories were interwoven with what was going on in the rest of Canada, the British Empire, and North America, in a world turned upside down.

This book is written for the general reader. It flows from the conviction that Canadians need to know and understand our history if we are to be truly aware of who we are, what our country is, and why our experience matters in the world. To do so, however, requires that we leave our own world and enter the world of the past, using evidence, imagination, and the power of language to evoke a different time and place. As L.P. Hartley once wrote: "the past is a foreign country: they do things differently there." We may well find things in that foreign country that will surprise us, things we might wish had been different, things we might want to gloss over, just as we will find much to admire and many people to like. History, after all, is not a morality play, a pageant, nor a Christmas pie from which, like Little Jack Horner, we can stick in our thumb and pull out a plum. We cannot simply judge everything we see by how it measures up to the values of the present time.

For, in the end, our novelist was as wrong as he was right. Our past is not another country — not at least in the sense that Martin Meredith applied that phrase to the transition from Rhodesia to Zimbabwe.[2] It is *our* country, at another time. Canadians in 1919 believed in progress and trusted that their sorrow and sacrifice would lead to something better, even if they did not always know what "better" would be. Their world became ours. Their story is our story.

All Canadians owe an incalculable debt to the many historians whose in-depth research over the past few decades has elucidated different aspects of this period. My personal debt is amply documented in the Notes to this book, which have had to be omitted from the print edition for reasons of length, but may be consulted in the e-book version or at the author's website *www.alanbowker.ca*. If this book whets the appetite of readers to delve further into this wealth of scholarship to learn more about the people and events described here, it will have achieved its purpose.

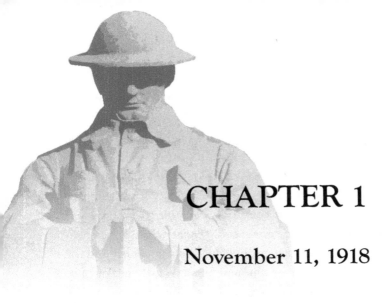

CHAPTER 1

November 11, 1918

Dawn. A dreary sky with morning mist hanging low on the ground. In the Belgian city of Mons, Corporal Will Bird, a Nova Scotian in the 42nd Black Watch, prepares for another day of bloody fighting against German machine gunners. The Canadians of the 3rd Division have dragged their heavy guns through mud and water, outrun their supplies and logistics, and lost over five hundred men in the past four days. Bird has killed three Germans with a rifle grenade and two of his men have been killed by a shell. The men are exhausted, they grumble, they curse everyone and everything. Peace may be near and no one wants to be the last to die. But they are hardened shock troops who do their duty. By 4:30 in the morning they have secured Mons and its eastern suburbs. Now their orders are to pursue the Germans deeper into Belgium.[1]

Since August, the Canadians have been in the vanguard of an Allied offensive that has steadily driven back a stubborn enemy. For four years they had lived underground like rats in gruesome dugouts, tunnels, and trenches, venturing forth at night for brief and bloody raids, enduring snipers and shells, mines and gas, only to be sent, terrified, "over the top" in set-piece battles to be slaughtered in thousands for gains of yards. Now they are moving across open fields, in the sunlight, breathing fresh air, inventing as they go a new form of mobile warfare. "Great days!" writes one of the few officers who have survived four years of war, "and the best two months' war I have ever known, chasing [the Hun] from town to town." But even against weakening resistance, each day brings savage combat that sorely tests the courage of the Canadian soldier.[2]

Canada, Department of National Defence/Library and Archives Canada LAC PA-003592

The Canadians in Mons
Three cheers for Canada! Canadian officers and the civic dignitaries of Mons, Belgium, on the Grand Platz, November 11, 1918. Canadian soldiers have liberated the city; the war is over.

Germany's allies have collapsed. The kaiser has abdicated. The German people are starving and their army's morale has been eroded by influenza, short rations, exhaustion, and socialist propaganda. Germany has appealed to U.S. president Wilson and its envoys have been given safe passage to parlay with the Allied High Command. But Canadian Corps commander General Arthur Currie is certain that unless German military power is "irretrievably crushed," the Allies will "do this thing all over again in another fifteen or twenty years." The enemy must be given no opportunity to regroup, nothing to bargain with. Only total victory will justify the appalling suffering of the last four years, and at last appease the gods of war, already glutted with ten million dead.[3]

But even as Bird and his comrades are getting ready, events in a railway car at Compiègne have altered their lives forever. Currie's morning bath is interrupted by news that an armistice will take effect at eleven o'clock. Orders are sent out to all forward units, though some, like Captain Cecil Frost in Mons, will not get theirs until 10:30. There is still time for men to die. Just outside Mons, Private George Lawrence Price, a conscripted farmhand from Saskatchewan, leaves his trench when a Belgian woman waves to him from a window. A sniper's bullet ends his war at 10:58. "Hell of a note," rages his company commander, "to think that that would happen right when the war's over." "We never even thought about the war being over then, you know," recalls a comrade, "and poor old Price he never knew that it was over. He was just doing his job."[4]

Price has hardly fallen when a far more eerie stillness descends along the line of battle. "All at once everything stopped," recalls one soldier. "And everybody just stood around lookin' at each other ... nobody would believe it." "Nobody yelled or showed uncontainable enthusiasm," recalls Frost, "— everybody just grinned and I think the cause was, that the men couldn't find words to express themselves. I think of the man who every day has his life in danger and who dreams of home more than of heaven itself — suddenly finds that the danger is past and that his return is practically assured — That he has won after personally risking his life — no wonder they couldn't say much — They simply grinned."

Or they sit, dazed and drained, staring at the ruined landscape, at their enemies who are now rising from their dugouts, at each other. Many return to mundane tasks like cleaning harness or polishing brass. Bird has to calm a distraught soldier whose brother was killed the previous day — "for nothing!" A wise officer instructs Bird to take the man away and get him drunk. That night an exhausted Bird will be given a meal and a bath by a Belgian couple who have lost a son in the war. He will collapse for the first time in months into a warm, clean bed. He will awaken to find a frightened German soldier hiding in the house. He will give the man some clothes belonging to the dead son, and he will let him go.[5]

Peace! What is peace but blessed silence and blissful sleep, with "no more horror or death or fear"? Can the bone-weary soldiers contemplate a future beyond the day-to-day obsession with survival? Can they turn their backs on the "friends who lie in battered fields and graveyards of this land," who can now "sleep happy, for the work is done"? Can they begin to think of going home? "I will come back dear, to you all, and for God's sake love me hard," writes one. "I'll need it, and I'll be wild as a hawk, but four years is a long time."[6]

Mons is the place where the Germans inflicted the first major defeat on the British Expeditionary Force in 1914. Now it is Canadians who have set it free. "I had often hoped to be either in London or Paris on this day," writes one Canadian soldier to his family, "but that could never compete with being in Mons, the place where Britain started and ended the war, and to think that our own division had the honour of taking this place." An overjoyed city welcomes the Canadians. "We certainly received a wonderful reception, something that I shall never forget," the soldier writes, "for as soon as we reached the outskirts the people were crowding about us, so that we could not even trot, throwing flowers on us, and in front of our horses on the road, and crying '*Vive les Canadiens*,' 'Long live our deliverers.'" That afternoon Currie reviews Canadian soldiers in the town square, together with the general commanding the British regiment that was the last to leave Mons in 1914, while civic dignitaries watch from the historic city hall. Currie signs the guest book just below the signature of the King of the Belgians, dated 1914. The following day the town will hold a special funeral for the Canadian soldiers killed liberating it, and the place where the Canadians entered Mons will be renamed "Place du Canada."[7]

Three weeks later, General Currie will take the salute at the Bonn bridge as the 1st and 2nd Canadian divisions cross the Rhine in a steady downpour, with bands playing "O Canada" and "The Maple Leaf Forever" — songs that mean little to the German civilians watching silently from the roadside. For most soldiers doing guard duty in the Rhineland, and for the 3rd and 4th divisions, now at loose ends in France and Belgium during a cold, wet winter, the coming weeks will be marked by marching, drills, influenza, and boredom as they wait, and wait, to go home.[8]

Canadians at home have been hearing rumours of peace since October. There have even been some premature celebrations of the end of a war, which, only a few months before, everyone believed would go on for years. Canada has put into uniform more than six hundred thousand men, and a few thousand women, out of a population of less than eight million. It has lost over sixty thousand dead, as well as thousands more maimed in body and shattered in mind. Even the victories of the past few months have cost forty-five thousand casualties. The country is grimly bracing for yet another winter of shortages, casualty lists, and calls for more men, more men, more men. Now, at 2:55 a.m. (EST) on November 11 comes the flash bulletin over the news wire: "It's Over, Over There."[9]

Almost immediately in the cities and towns, factory whistles, church-bells, fire sirens, car horns, and boat whistles sound, newspapers are swamped with callers, people rush from their beds into the streets, sometimes still in nightclothes. A Toronto newspaper reports that "a procession, mostly of women munition[s] workers, paraded Yonge Street, cheering, wildly beating tin pans and blowing whistles. By this time a crowd began to gather all along Yonge Street, motor cars came tearing down street [*sic*], reckless of all speed laws, tooting their horns and awakening the entire city." In Ottawa, a huge electric sign on the pinnacle of the Chateau Laurier, erected a few weeks earlier to sell Victory Bonds, has been altered to flash the single word: "Victory." In Vancouver, twenty-five thousand people gather at Granville and Hastings at one o'clock in the morning, and wounded soldiers stage a pyjama parade in their hospital. In smaller towns, news spreads more slowly, by telephone, by word of mouth, and by the arrival of city newspapers. Saskatchewan farmers light up the skies with burning stacks of straw. In Mahone Bay, Nova Scotia, an effigy of the kaiser is beaten with broomsticks and burned in a huge bonfire.[10]

As the new day unfolds, factories are closed, business is at a standstill, and impromptu parades form — sometimes miles long — of cars, taxis, veterans, workers, women's groups, Victory Loan canvassers, regiments in training, with flags, bands, floats, and tickertape, toilet paper, or whatever else people can find to festoon the streets. In Toronto, a planned Victory Loan parade becomes a victory parade: soldiers march to massed bands, including the U.S. Navy Band led by John Philip Sousa; aircraft fly over in battle formations; and over a hundred thousand people cheer themselves hoarse. "I was a married woman," one Torontonian will recall many years later, "and I was grabbed and kissed a million times that day. It was shocking rather, you know. But everybody was exuberant. You just went crazy." Everywhere dignitaries make endless speeches which no one seems to mind. A strong guard is put on liquor stores where alcohol, though officially banned, continues to be sold "for medicinal purposes." In Kingston, there is a sombre note as the parade is interrupted by the funeral cortege of a returned soldier who has died of his wounds. "Never," recalls a witness, "did the strains of the 'Last Post' sound more poignant than they did as they were sounded as the remains of the departed soldier were laid to rest — on the very day when his sacrifice was crowned with victory."[11]

Churches across the country are packed for services of thanksgiving. Solemn masses are held in Catholic cathedrals. Protestants sing familiar hymns that have kept faith and hope alive: "O God our Help in Ages Past," "Onward Christian Soldiers," "Praise God From Whom All Blessings Flow," as well as "God Save the King." Sermons and speeches proclaim the triumph of the great ideals for which Canadians have fought. They have defended democracy and preserved civilization. Soldiers who took up the gun also took up the Cross, and those who fell are resting in the arms of Christ.

In some places, the celebrations have a less pleasant aspect. In Kitchener, Alderman A.L. Blitzer, an ethnic German, was escorted from his office to the city hall, where he was compelled to kiss the Union Jack, amid the tremendous cheers of the crowd. Evidently this is not regarded in Kitchener as a disturbance. Germans and "foreigners," pacifists, radicals, "slackers," French-Canadian nationalists, and other unwelcome elements might celebrate the end of hostilities and hope for future healing, but if they are wise they keep a low profile on this day. And even as Canadians celebrate, an epidemic of deadly influenza is sweeping the country, taking the youngest and healthiest, including soldiers, nurses, and mothers of young children. In Vancouver, the epidemic is at its height and hundreds will pay for their victory celebrations with sickness and death.[12]

For many at home, like the soldiers at Mons, euphoria will be followed by an unexplainable sense of emptiness. Industrialist Sir Joseph Flavelle, chairman of the Imperial Munitions Board, has done more than anyone to organize production for war, but he has been vilified as a profiteer. He does not join the celebrations, but quietly, tearfully, alone, gives thanks. Many government and business leaders are on the verge of exhaustion, like Finance Minister White who has had to take a rest cure for two crucial months in 1918. For the families of fallen soldiers, joy in victory and solace in sacrifice cannot offset the stark reality that a husband, son, or father will never return. Those whose men have survived will have to wait for their return through another long winter, with no more war work to occupy them.

Lucy Maud Montgomery writes in her journal,

> I am sure no one could feel more profoundly thankful that
> the war is over than I.... And yet the truth is that everything
> seems flat and *insipid* now; after being fed for four years on
> fears and horrors, terrible reverses, amazing victories, all news
> now seems tame and uninteresting. I feel as if I had been liv-
> ing for years in the midst of hell; and then suddenly found
> myself lying on a quiet green meadow stretching levelly and
> peacefully to the horizon. One is thankful — and bored!

The war has wounded society to an almost unbearable level of tension.
Now peace seems, in the words of professor Maurice Hutton of the University of Toronto, like a "long, tedious Sunday afternoon walk." August 1914
is a long time ago, a lifetime ago.[13]

I

That lost pre-war world, innocent and happy in the golden haze of retro-
spect, was indeed a long time ago. Many Canadians cherished the memory — embellished in hundreds of sermons, speeches, and novels — of an
idyllic summer weekend suddenly shattered when the news of war came
like a thunderclap out of a cloudless sky. Clean-limbed young men left their
fields, their vacations, their pleasures, ready to sacrifice all for freedom and
civilization. Opposition leader Sir Wilfrid Laurier pledged a political truce
as long as there was danger at the front. Even French-Canadian nationalist
leader Henri Bourassa seemed at first to support the war. Canadians as one
rose to defend the British Empire and all it stood for.[14]

Like all golden memories this was largely myth. Nineteen fourteen was
a depressed year, and many of the recruits were unemployed men and recent
British immigrants. But the fifteen years before 1913 had been a time of
astonishing growth and change, during which a slow-paced rural society
had been transformed into an urbanized, industrialized, transcontinental
Dominion. The West had been flooded with settlers and was pouring an

amber torrent of Canadian wheat through a network of railways, elevators, and ships to the hungry masses of Europe. Alberta and Saskatchewan had become provinces, and mining, ranching, fishing, farming, and lumbering settlements dotted the mountain valleys and coastal fiords of British Columbia. The mineral and forest wealth of the rugged Canadian Shield was being opened up. Immigrants — four hundred thousand in 1913 alone — had swelled the population from just over five million to almost eight million.

Manufacturing had exploded, fuelled by tariffs, electric power, resource industries, railways, construction, and the wheat boom. Small companies had merged to become giant corporations, which were backed by stable banks and a burgeoning investment industry. Five billion dollars in British capital had flowed into Canada and 450 American branch plants worth $135 million had been established. Iron and steel plants had sprung up in Hamilton, Sault Ste. Marie, and Cape Breton. Service industries like Eaton's department store had begun to define the taste and tap the prosperity of the emerging middle class. Toronto and Montreal had tripled their populations in a decade; smaller towns had become industrial cities; and Winnipeg had become Canada's third largest city. It was a society full of youthful energy, eager to expand, reform and improve, revelling in the promise of its future.[15]

Rapid growth and sweeping change had brought massive problems in their train. "Few persons," wrote economist and humorist Stephen Leacock, "can attain to adult life without being profoundly impressed by the appalling inequality of our human lot." Plutocrats and the middle class alike were uncomfortably aware of the wretched slums, smoky factories, "sweated" female and child labour, and rural poverty that had sprung up. Waves of "foreign" immigrants spoke strange languages and brought unfamiliar customs and religions. The challenge of science to religion, and the impact of rapid change on social relations, values, and customs, threatened to cut Canadians loose from their moorings. Canadian writers like Leacock, Montgomery, Ernest Thompson Seton, and Marshall Saunders looked backward to a more innocent society and celebrated the glory of unspoiled nature. Other commentators looked outward with trepidation at rising social unrest, violent strikes, radical socialism and what they saw as an ugly, perverted modernism in the older societies of Europe and in their neighbour to the south.[16]

The war replaced the fears and doubts that came with change and dislocation with a new and unambiguous moral imperative. It was, in the words of Reverend W.T. Herridge of Ottawa, a war "for the rights of others, not less than for our own. We are fighting for those intangible possessions which are the crowning glory of mankind, and the loss of which would cover earth as with a funeral pall, and wrap it in eternal gloom. We are fighting for the overthrow of impious pride and cruel oppression, and for the final triumph of Truth and Righteousness." In countless speeches, essays, editorials, stories, and sermons, the war became a crusade for Christian civilization against a decadent and tyrannical Germany. It was a call to service, as Christ had been called. "Khaki," said S.D. Chown, general superintendant of the Methodist Church, "has become a sacred colour."[17]

Stephen Leacock

Notman Archives McCord Museum Montreal 11-202933

Indeed, many saw the war, in the words of Andrew Macphail (editor of the influential *University Magazine*), as a sign that:

> Perhaps, after all, God really does know what He is about, and that war, as well as peace, forms a place in His universal design. It is only now that we perceive how dreadful those days of peace were: the whole world sunk in sensuality and sloth, where only the feebler vices and the meaner virtues could thrive in the stagnant and fetid atmosphere; the whole creation perishing in its own exhalation, emanation, and excretion.

The war would burn all this away with the refiner's fire of struggle, service, and sacrifice. "It is not the good in us but the evil that this fire of war is going to destroy," said Toronto historian George Wrong. "When the time of harvest came it was the fruit of the tares that was burned while the good fruit was gathered into barns."[18]

"The world is in agony," University of Toronto president Robert Falconer told his students, "let this agony reach the depths of our nature also, so that it may purge our selfishness. If we shall not be called upon to die or be wounded in the flesh, I hope that we may carry into the revived life of our nation, when it issues from the struggle, the healed wounds of the spirit that will be the sign of the battle in which we have won over again the right to call ourselves freemen in a real democracy." Years of war and mounting slaughter only reinforced this faith. "If there is not a God who is directing this storm then indeed is life a chaos without purpose," wrote Wrong in 1916. "The very awfulness of the upheaval makes us certain of some hard goal to be attained." After two years of war, the golden summer of 1914 had taken on yet another symbolic meaning — an era of materialism, selfishness, and pleasure-seeking, from which, said a character in a popular novel, the trial of war would bring "the beginning of our regeneration." But only victory — absolute victory, whatever the cost — would justify this sacrifice and fulfil God's plan.[19]

Christian idealism, and the Victorian belief that character was more important than intellect, saturated the popular literature that was the

George M. Wrong

heritage of every English-speaking Canadian. A newly literate public devoured swashbuckling adventure tales and clung to the giants of Victorian Romantic literature long after their popularity was on the wane in the mother country. Schoolbooks, magazines, even Sunday school literature, were full of romantic poems depicting great deeds and glorious deaths ("Play up! And play the game!"). Heroic tales from history, adventure stories, studies in character like *Tom Brown's School Days*, and magazines like *Chums* and

Boys' Own, were standard fare for young boys. Religious novels depicting "muscular" Christianity appealed to audiences that wanted morality and faith presented in a simple, convincing way — Canadian Ralph Connor was one of the leaders of this genre.[20]

Canada had a noble mission, as a nation and as part of the greatest empire the world had ever known. Methodist reformer Salem Bland saw the British Empire as a "system that gives to peoples of the most diverse race, colour and civilization peace, unity and freedom." French Canadians like Laurier and Henri Bourassa opposed Imperial centralization, but still saw the Empire as the embodiment of liberty, democracy, and civilization. Others, like Stephen Leacock, yearned for Canada to take on a more central role in a united Empire — "for the greatness of it, for the soul of it, aye for the very danger of it" — and to purge its parochial corruption in "the pure fire of an [I]mperial patriotism, that is no theory but a passion." War provided an opportunity to blend patriotism, adventure, and idealism, and to fulfill the great destiny of Canada.[21]

Canadians were not a military people — certainly not like the Great Powers of Europe that within a matter of weeks could march millions of trained conscripts into battle. In the larger cities of Canada, militia regiments took pride in their fine uniforms, marching bands, drills, mess dinners, polished silver, and the promise of social standing for the officers. But for most Canadians, war was something that happened in far-off places, a glorious, if dangerous, adventure against the "lesser breeds without the law." They saw no need for a standing army or a professional officer corps. There was broad support for Laurier's refusal to be drawn into the "the vortex of European militarism." British journalist Norman Angell, rising Canadian politician and labour reformer Mackenzie King, and many other religious and political figures, believed that Christianity, global trade, and the progress of science and civilization, had rendered European war obsolete. Churches in their annual conferences passed resolutions supporting arbitration, peaceful settlement of disputes, and outlawing war. Labour congresses called on workers to strike in any country contemplating war "so that the workers may see the pitiful exhibition of fighting by those capitalists who seem so fond of it." The Dominion Grange, representing farmers, believed that Canadians should devote "their whole energies to industrial and moral advancements, rather than to the pounding of drums and the clash of arms."[22]

When they had been called on, as in the Boer War, Canadians had proven to be excellent soldiers combining courage, virility, and chivalry. Laurier had responded to the threat posed by the rise of the German navy by creating a Canadian navy, and his rival, Borden, had promised a direct contribution to the British navy. Minister of Militia Sam Hughes had secured increased spending on drill halls and guns, and insisted that "his boys" could lick anybody in the world.

But few Canadians had any idea what modern war really meant. Militia regiments, Boy Scouts, and cadets were popular less because they were military than because they exemplified "manliness." Manliness meant the "animal spirits," strength, courage, and aggressiveness of youth, tempered with Arthurian chivalry, health, clean habits, self-control, duty, and service. Mackenzie King commissioned a statue of Sir Galahad in honour of his friend Bert Harper, who sacrificed his life in a vain attempt to save a drowning woman. Hutton, a cultivated and gentle professor of classics, idealized war as a blood sport played by "brave and straight fighting men, somewhat on a par with brave and straight athletes who play for play's sake, and not to win at all costs, and not for the gate money; who just play up and play the game." James L. Hughes (brother of Sam), superintendant of schools in Ontario, introduced military drill into schools on the grounds that activities that produced straighter backs, healthier lungs, manly bearing, discipline, and courage, were as important to sound education as art, music, kindergarten, or votes for women, which he also championed.[23]

But the celebration of "manliness" had another side. The foremost champions of this Victorian style of masculinity displayed a pervasive sexual uncertainty and a concomitant need for the repression of what might be deemed "unmanly." There was an almost irrational fear that modernism was blurring the distinction between the sexes and sapping the virility of civilization. Hutton advocated military training to counteract the "physical degeneracy and that physical decadence which industrialism continually brings in its train." Macphail was much shriller: "The school-mistress with her book and spectacles has had her day in the training of boys, and sensible parents are longing for the drill-sergeant carrying in his hand a cleaning rod or a leather belt with a steel buckle at the end. That is the sovereign remedy for the hooliganism of the town and the loutishness of the country." Many young men went to war to test their manhood in the greatest contest of all. [24]

II

The outbreak of the First World War brought a quick end to any popular support for pacifism. In the early months of the war, newspapers, speeches, and recruiting campaigns blended all these themes to justify the war as a righteous crusade. Except for a handful of radicals, labour unions endorsed the war and working people enlisted in the thousands. Germans became Huns with no idea of sport or fair play, truth or decency, their *kultur* a grotesque amalgam of dark and twisted ideas, decadent art, and perverted science, with machine-like conformity and lust for world domination.[25]

A spate of novels by leading Canadian authors turned these ideas into popular fiction. The hero, usually a fair-haired, strong-limbed exemplar of Canadian manhood, could be a farmer, preacher, cow-puncher, or logger in an idyllic rural or natural setting, or someone who has lost his way pursuing wealth in the city. In war, he undergoes a journey through darkness, temptation, and pain; and fights for, re-discovers, or preserves his values. He dies in noble sacrifice, or he returns transformed, determined to build a new world in Canada. Speakers and writers like Billy Bishop, who travelled the lecture circuit encouraging recruitment in Canada or drumming up support for the British cause in the United States, depicted battle (and killing Huns) with less idealism and romance, but also portrayed the war as a test of courage and a crusade for Christian values.[26]

By mid-1915, the reality of a modern war was beginning to intrude on these illusions. Canadians rejoiced when their troops beat back the German gas attack at the Second Battle of Ypres, but were stunned by the casualty lists that followed. Still, they clung to an idealistic vision of the war. Newspaper editors, who might have been expected to explore more deeply the horrors unfolding overseas, instead reluctantly accepted censorship, understanding the need to preserve morale — and since reporters and cameras were barred from the front anyway, they had no choice but to rely on official British sources. Virtually none, with the conspicuous exception of *Le Devoir*, questioned the righteousness of the British cause. The war became a succession of distant, unknown place names on whose capture or defence the fate of the world suddenly hung, and its vocabulary the blank prose of government reports and the shrill rhetoric of recruiting speeches.[27]

How *could* the public at home know what life was like at the front? Newspapers relying on censored and second-hand stories, newsreels whose scenes were largely staged, and mock battles at exhibitions and county fairs could not begin to portray its reality. People back in Canada, said war artist Frederick Varley,

> cannot realize at all what war is like. You must see it and live it. You must see the barren deserts war has made of once fertile country ... see the turned up graves, see the dead on the field, freakishly mutilated — headless, legless, stomachless, a perfect body and a passive face and a broken empty skull — see your own countrymen, unidentified, thrown into a cart, their coats thrown over them, boys digging a grave in a land of yellow slimy mud and green pools of water under a weeping sky. You must have heard the screeching shells and have the shrapnel fall around you, whistling by you — seen the result of it, seen scores of horses, bits of horse lying around in the open — in the street and soldiers marching by these scenes as if they never knew of their presence — until you've lived this ... you cannot know.[28]

Even if there had not been military censorship, most soldiers in their letters home had no wish to upset their loved ones with experiences that in any case they could not easily put into words. Instead, they inquired about old friends and recalled old memories, thanked families for gifts, asked for warm socks and underwear, and provided reassurance that they were well. Leslie Frost, a future premier of Ontario, wrote as he prepared for the battle of Passchendaele that "there is really very little to tell. If you follow the newspaper, you will know about where we are and as to experiences, any that I have, I just as soon talk about them when I get home and forget about them when I am here." Bravado was reserved for those comfortably behind the lines or in England. For the front-line soldier, what was most real was the comradeship and shared experience of the trenches.[29]

What was very real at home was the lengthening list of casualties and the sudden devastation brought by the dreaded telegram of condolence. "By each new loss I am made for a time almost speechless," wrote Wrong, who lost a son in 1916.

> The waste, the awful waste, of these young lives, the happiness missed, the years of preparation for life all unfulfilled in achievement, the loss of love, of fatherhood, of the joys of using their matured powers in ripened work! It breaks my heart to think of these bright spirits gone, spirits that have touched mine, to whom I have been able, perhaps, to add some little gift of training and insight.[30]

The only possible response was the stiff upper lip. Doubts about official reports, negative thoughts about the war, and criticism of grand strategy had to be suppressed. John McCrae, a Canadian army medical officer, captured this blend of sorrow and steely determination in his poem "In Flanders Fields," which became, like the poppy, a permanent part of the symbolism and memory of the Great War. The first two stanzas employ almost every cliché of Victorian poetry. But the third is a sudden and heartfelt cry from the dead to the living: keep faith with us, give meaning to our sacrifice, pursue the struggle to final victory.

A new nation was being forged in the crucible of war, a nation that could produce a poet like McCrae and a military victory like Vimy Ridge, that could be the linchpin between the British Empire and the United States, that was ready, in the words of Prime Minister Borden in the aftermath of Vimy, to take its place at the Imperial table and have a voice in the conduct of the war. It was, said Leacock, "a nation of war-workers, every man, in his humble sense, at the front and taking his part." Farmers were growing food for the people of Britain and the armies of the Empire. Urban "Farmerettes" and young "Soldiers of the Soil" were helping out at harvest time. Factory workers justified their high wages by their contribution to the war effort and joined labour unions in unprecedented numbers. Business people believed they were serving the nation by producing efficiently, and Sir Joseph Flavelle urged his fellow industrialists to "send profits to the hell where they belong." All were convinced they were doing their part, and all could hope that the national unity brought by war would bring greater efficiency, better partnership, and fairer distribution of power.[31]

Total war brought women into the mainstream, as mothers and wives of soldiers, as nurturers of families, and as full participants in mobilizing the whole nation. Women took jobs — in munitions plants, in offices, as nurses, and volunteers — with a degree of independence they had never before enjoyed. Nellie McClung's *The Next of Kin* portrayed women doing their duty, sending their men off without tears, comforting each other in their losses, raising children without fathers, carrying on after their husband's or son's death, keeping faith, and being worthy of the sacrifice. The war erased the barriers between home, work, and politics, and made many of the values of women those of society as a whole. Opposition to women's suffrage collapsed, and by the end of the war women had the vote everywhere except in Quebec and Prince Edward Island.[32]

And so, by 1917 the golden summer of 1914 had taken on yet another layer of symbolic meaning. It now stood for an old world of inefficient industrial organization, fuelled by selfish greed, with no national vision and no social safety net. That world had been symbolized by Sam Hughes who, as minister of militia, had tried to conduct recruitment and munitions production in the time-honoured way, through patronage and a network of friends. By 1916, both had become mired in waste, corruption, blatant patronage, and dismal failure to provide the shells and munitions desperately needed by the men fighting for the Empire. In response, governments at all levels began to take on roles that would have seemed fantasy in 1914.

The Imperial Munitions Board under Sir Joseph Flavelle mobilized Canadian industry to produce guns, ships, airplanes, and, above all, shells —

in 1917, one-third of all the shells fired on the British front were made in Canada. Finance Minister White, who had begun the war fearing national bankruptcy, was now spending undreamed of amounts of money, tapping Canadian savings through Victory Loans, and borrowing on the U.S. market to maintain Canadian production and support the British currency. Income taxes, introduced as a temporary measure, would prove permanent.

The Canadian government took on the unprecedented responsibility of caring for the wives and families of the hundreds of thousands of men it had sent overseas, through the Canadian Patriotic Fund, which began as a network of private charities and ended as a virtual arm of the government. By 1918, regulations and boards controlled food, fuel, production, transportation, prices, and wages. Prohibition, long championed by churches and women's groups, became a reality as "the liquor trade" was demonized for wasting grain, sapping the vitality of the nation, and diverting men from their duty. Society would no longer tolerate hypocrisy, incompetence, or profiteering. Hughes was dropped from the Borden Cabinet, followed by Public Works Minister Robert Rogers, whose name had become synonymous with shameless political patronage. When it was alleged that Flavelle's pork-packing company made excessive profits supplying the army, he was vilified as "His Lardship," and a Conservative politician warned Borden that he had never encountered "such wide spread *rage* over any other scandal."[33]

J.S. Woodsworth, a Christian reformer, soon to become a socialist, hoped that the war would produce "a new conception of citizenship, possibly a new conception of religion" led by "men of vision who can point the way and men of devotion who can follow." W.B. Creighton, editor of the Methodist *Christian Guardian*, wrote in 1917 that the war seemed "destined to produce political changes of far-reaching import, and one of them will undoubtedly be a more thorough-going democracy than the world has seen, and if capitalism suffers, as it may, it will be because it has shown itself in this hour of national trial, in only too many cases, to be altogether too intent upon private gain to be truly patriotic." Even the conservative Leacock could advocate a new democracy "inspired by the public virtue of the citizen that raises him to the level of the privileges that he enjoys," and could express a conviction, growing across the political spectrum, that if the state could send men forth to die it should also conscript the wealth of those who stayed behind.[34]

III

But for most Canadians, the war settled into an endless stream of casualty lists, deepening hardship, and relentless anxiety. Prices rose dramatically in 1917, food and fuel were rationed, and there were meatless days, "heatless Mondays," and electricity blackouts. Christmas was bleak, with shortages of coal and other essential goods, and the promise of the worst winter yet. Russia was knocked out of the war, the French army had mutinied, U-boats were sinking ships in the Gulf of St. Lawrence. Nineteen eighteen brought new German offensives, and no one knew if the Americans could get enough men to France in time to stem the tide. People hung on every bit of news, their morale soaring or their spirits crashing with each report, true or false, of defeat or victory. Stress, overwork, and fear were becoming a social pathology among all classes. "The whole country was in flames about the war," one woman recalled. "You couldn't talk about anything else." "This war is slowly killing me," wrote Lucy Maud Montgomery in her journal.[35]

Women faced a constant bombardment of information, propaganda, and appeals. Cook wholesome meals! Conserve food and fuel! Don't hoard! Join volunteer agencies! Above all, don't complain! As rigid social mores became unsettled, they faced prying eyes and tattling tongues. Were they clinging too tightly to their men or letting them go too easily? Were the children they were raising without fathers "running wild"? Should a wife on a Patriotic Fund allowance be allowed to have a drink or any "luxuries"? Or any male company? Were young women who flouted convention being immoral or simply responding to the changed reality of war and the possibility of death? Were visits to a music hall, or a cinema to see Mary Pickford or Charlie Chaplin, or the purchase of a player piano or a Victrola, necessary diversions or betrayals of the brave men overseas?[36]

Men dealt with guilt if they had not enlisted or could not serve. By 1917, recruiters were combing farms and lumber camps, pestering over-age men, fudging medical reports, taking undersized recruits. Pressure to join up had passed beyond messages sent via posters and meetings to shaming and confrontation.

Pierre Van Passen, a Dutch pacifist who had come to Canada to study for the ministry, recalled being accosted in 1916 by a woman dressed in mourning who said she had lost three sons at the front.

"Why do you dare to stand there laughing at my misery? Why don't you go over and fight? Fight, avenge my boys!"

Trying to escape, he claims he was

> immediately surrounded by a mob. A group of business men, who had managed to stay five thousand miles away from where the poppies grow, and who were at that moment emerging from the hotel, gallantly rushed to the woman's aid and forced me to submit, as she pinned a white feather through my coat into my flesh: the badge of white-livered cowardice. The last I saw of her was through a pair of badly battered eyes as she laughingly picked up some of the feathers which had dropped from her bag in the scuffle.

Van Passen joined up.[37]

The dark side of the refiner's fire was a consciousness of sin, of guilt, of divine punishment richly deserved — usually by others. This bred an increased pettiness, crankiness, and sense of grievance against unfair treatment by the authorities, against those not doing their share, or against those who appeared to be benefiting unduly from the war. Farmers needed their sons to stay on the land if they were to grow food, and they resented urban pressure on them to join up. Labour, which was seeing its wage gains eaten up by inflation, bitterly attacked wage controls and the outlawing of strikes as "industrial conscription." The dark side of forging a nation in the crucible of war was authoritarian behaviour, pressure for conformity, intolerance of dissent, and paranoid fear of an enemy within.

By 1917, a large number of discharged soldiers had returned home. Many had been wounded or traumatized by the war. They tried to reconcile their "hero" status with the seeming indifference of society to their problems. They hated unionized workers and "foreigners" who had taken jobs they believed rightfully belonged to them. With discipline reduced and with time on their hands, nursing real or imagined grievances, they were ready on occasion to avenge slights by civilians or arrests of rowdy comrades. Chapters of the Great War Veterans' Association were giving voice to soldiers' complaints, demanding higher pensions, denouncing "slackers" (including "slackers in uniform"), and demanding conscription. Mobs of returned soldiers, with the authorities usually looking the other way, attacked labour and peace meetings. In 1916, soldiers destroyed a dance hall in Calgary on the false rumour that the owner had fired a janitor and given his job to a German. Veterans attacked the Russell Motor Company in Toronto in April 1917 for employing "foreign" internees, and soldiers sent to quell the disturbance initially sympathized with the rioters. In August 1918, soldiers and civilians attacked fifteen Toronto restaurants owned by Greeks, allegedly to protest low enlistment rates among "foreigners" (never mind that Greece was an ally). The following night, two thousand rioters attacked police stations demanding the release of those arrested the previous day. After a few tense days, the arrival of five hundred troops from the Niagara Camp and firm action by the mayor, police, and military officers calmed the situation down.[38]

German Canadians were on the knife-edge throughout the war. Most Canadians managed to distinguish between the Hun and their fellow citizens of German descent. Most German Canadians were treated fairly if they had the good fortune to stay out of the spotlight. But not always. It was one thing to purge Ontario concert programs of "German" music, or to debate whether the settlers of Lunenburg, Nova Scotia, were "Germans" or "loyal Hanoverians." It was another to believe that German saboteurs caused the fire that destroyed the Parliament Buildings in Ottawa in 1916 or an explosion that levelled two-thirds of Halifax in 1917. Sometimes German Canadians were simply convenient targets. In Berlin, Ontario, when the 118th Battalion found it difficult to recruit enough men, soldiers attacked a German club, beat up a Lutheran pastor, and threatened German-speaking councillors. A bitterly fought referendum to change the name of the city was carried by a slim majority of eighty-one votes out of a total of three thousand; and a second referendum (in which only one-third of the registered voters turned out) approved the new name, Kitchener, by a bare majority. This agitation died down once the 118th shipped overseas, but ill feeling continued for years.[39]

But it was the treatment meted out to "enemy aliens," largely Ukrainians from the Austro-Hungarian Empire, that showed how far the war had exacerbated tensions already present in Canadian society. These people had come to settle the Canadian West and had little love for their former rulers. But they remained suspect, less because they were enemies than simply because they were different. At the outset of war, some eight thousand "enemy aliens" were interned in camps across Western Canada and in northwest Ontario. Within two years, most had been released to work on farms or construction sites, or in factories, mines, and hospitals.

J.W. Dafoe, the influential editor of the *Winnipeg Free Press,* spoke for many when he insisted repeatedly that saving civilization and building a nation meant that "Bohunks" must be assimilated. This way of thinking resulted in foreign language schools being abolished in the Prairie provinces. In defence of this, a Saskatchewan Department of Education pamphlet rejected any suggestion the action violated "British justice": "in the presence of a national crisis minorities should yield. Without majority rule our parliamentary institutions become unworkable."[40]

By 1917, it was obvious that German, much less Austrian, plots were unlikely. But late in that year, the triumph of Lenin's Bolsheviks in Russia added a formidable new threat. For some, Bolshevism was, in the words of one Winnipeg worker, a vision of

> equal rights for men and women, no child labour, no poverty, misery and degradation, no prostitution, no mortgages on farms, no revolting bills for machinery to keep peasants poor till the grave, no sweatshops, no long hours of heavy toil for a meagre existence but an equal opportunity for all, a life made worth living with unlimited possibilities for all, aided by splendid machinery to make [the] earth a real paradise where nothing but happiness can prevail.

But for business leaders and government officials, the wave of labour unrest that swept the country in 1918 was a sign that Canada might in its turn fall victim to the social upheaval now sweeping through European societies, allies and enemies alike.[41]

The "Bolshevik" was yet another variant of "the Hun" or "the foreigner." But Bolshevism threatened not only the nation but the basis and stability of the social order. In September 1918, a new category of "foreigners" — Finns, Baltics, and Russians suspected of having Bolshevist sympathies — was added to the Germans, Austrians, Bulgarians, Hungarians, Turks, and Ukrainians already subject to suspicion. Thirteen organizations were banned, and it was made a crime punishable by five years' incarceration to advocate violence to bring about governmental or economic change. As the war was drawing to a close, an Order-in-Council outlawing strikes, and the arrest of many labour and socialist leaders for being in possession of socialist literature or making allegedly subversive speeches, further enraged the labour movement.

This crusading mentality particularly isolated and alienated French-speaking Canada. French-Canadian youth had absorbed many of the ideas of manliness and chivalry that informed their English-speaking counterparts, and the history of New France offered plenty of examples of religious faith, patriotism, heroism, and sacrifice. Most Quebec opinion leaders initially saw the war as a just struggle to defend France and Britain, and hoped that the war would cleanse Canadian society and return it to an older morality. They also welcomed the farm prosperity and industrial jobs it brought. Quebec politicians, led by Premier Lomer Gouin, and most Catholic Church leaders, counselled support for the war and obedience to the law. But public enthusiasm declined sharply when French-speaking recruits found they would have to serve with English-speaking regiments. By 1916, the increasingly shrill, religious-tinged rhetoric of English Canadians, and their growing criticism of the low enlistment rate in French Canada, began to resemble the familiar Orange-Protestant attack on the French language and Catholic religion. The abolition of second-language instruction in Manitoba included French — and this was not an oversight. In Ontario, Regulation 17 restricted the education of Ontario francophone children in their own language.

Henri Bourassa and his newspaper, *Le Devoir*, became the most eloquent voice expressing French Canada's growing opposition to the war. A war in Europe did not concern a people whose roots in North America went back three hundred years, he argued. Young French Canadians should be raising their large families on farms, faithful to the Church. They should defend their homes as they had always done, but they should not be mere cannon fodder for the British Empire. Bourassa feared that the Canada he believed in, an independent nation based on two founding cultures, that valued civil liberties, was being swamped by a tide of war hysteria, imperial hyper-patriotism, censorship, and mendacious propaganda that was dividing its people, weakening its democracy, and threatening its moral and social order. He responded angrily when his cousin, Lieutenant Talbot Papineau (who was really more American than French Canadian), wrote an open letter urging French Canadians to fight for civilization in France. "To speak of fighting for the preservation of French civilization in Europe while endeavouring to destroy it in America, appears to us an absurd piece of inconsistency," Bourassa replied. Outside Quebec, Papineau was deemed to have got the better of the exchange. English Canadians mourned when Papineau was killed. They denounced Bourassa as a traitor. But any action against him would have made Bourassa a martyr.[42]

Henri Bourassa

Library and Archives Canada C009092

IV

All these stresses and conflicts were brought to a head by the conscription crisis, the formation of a Union government, and the general election of 1917. Following a visit to the front, Borden had committed Canada to fielding an army of five hundred thousand men. This was an impossible target — ten thousand new recruits a month would be required as replacements alone and recruitment was drying up. There was a manpower shortage for the farms, mines, forests, and factories. But Borden, along with most of English Canada, was unshakable in his determination that the war must be won at any cost, and this meant conscription. In May 1917, Parliament passed the Military Service Act, with twenty-five English-speaking Liberals, but only four French-speaking Conservatives, voting in favour. French Canadians were adamantly opposed, as were a minority of English Canadians. Many men had family responsibilities, farmers needed their sons on the land, and many workers saw conscription as an attack on unions. Conscription was the very negation of what Canada was supposed to be fighting for.

The political truce of 1914 was disappearing. Elections had been postponed in 1915 by mutual consent. Borden would have lost any election fought on his record, and Laurier would have lost any election fought on winning the war. In 1917, Borden approached Laurier proposing that they form a coalition government to implement conscription, an offer Laurier could never have accepted. Many English-speaking Liberals now abandoned their party, and Borden proceeded to form a Union government comprising Conservatives, conscriptionist Liberals, and representatives of labour and farmers, with virtually no ministers from French Canada.

The gulf between the two founding colonial peoples of Canada had now become profound. Dafoe wrote to a correspondent in Quebec that French Canadians were "the only known race of white men to quit." They could shout all they wanted about their grievances, but "when we demonstrate, as we shall, that a solid Quebec is without power, there may be a return to reason along the banks of the St. Lawrence." Hume Wrong, who would become a leading Canadian diplomat, wrote to his brother from the front that he would "welcome a little military activity in Quebec. My C.O. and I have arranged a little punitive expedition to consist of a string of cars armoured

Dupras & Colas, Library and Archives Canada C000694

Sir Robert Borden

with boiler plate and armed with Lewis guns." Alphonse Verville, a Liberal-Labour MP from Montreal, returned the favour by telling the House of Commons that "organized labour will do all it can against conscription," and that French Canadians "are prepared for civil war."[43]

The election of December 1917 was a bitter, ugly fight — and it was rigged. In an unprecedented violation of constitutional principles, Canadian citizens from enemy countries who had come to Canada since 1902 were disenfranchised (along with pacifists and conscientious objectors). The wives, widows, mothers, daughters, and sisters of soldiers overseas were allowed to vote. Soldiers overseas were also permitted to vote, and to have their votes directed to any riding they wished. An Order-in-Council promised farmers that their sons would not be conscripted. Though a few Socialist candidates opposed conscription, labour was not yet able to mount a coherent opposition. Laurier's Liberals swept every seat in Quebec, but they won only thirty seats in the rest of the country.[44]

"For the first time in Canadian history," gushed one commentator, "Canada possesses a government so constituted as to personnel, and dowered with a mandate so weighty and insistent, that policies quite Utopian in normal times may not be merely practical, but obligatory." The Union government had a stellar array of talent, and a platform that promised state intervention in the economy, votes for women, national prohibition, collective bargaining for labour, fair wages, honest government, an end to patronage, and the assertion of Canadian nationhood within the Empire. But was it really a government of national unity? Or a patched-together coalition of English Canadians, opposed by French Canadians, excluding "foreigners," and seen as hostile to labour and farmers?[45]

"Canada was saved, yesterday" wrote the *Winnipeg Free Press* the day after the election — a sentiment echoed across English Canada. But it had been saved not from the Hun but from Laurier and Bourassa, from "foreigners," "slackers," and radicals. Borden hoped that men who had only been waiting for a fairly administered system of conscription would now step forward. But in Quebec, serious riots broke out during the Easter weekend of 1918 that left several dead, and young men were going into hiding. In March 1918, Borden broke his promise not to conscript farmers' sons and ignored their anguished protests. "I have been astounded," wrote

Queen's University political economist O.D. Skelton, "by the violence of anti-farmer sentiment among even educated city people, resenting the alleged profiteering, and selfish slackering [*sic*] of the farmers on the military issue. At the same time the gap between workmen and employers is growing rapidly, in spite of well-meaning endeavours to conciliate them."[46]

In the midst of all this turmoil, the sudden achievement of victory brought renewed hope that the bright new world promised by the war might at last be realized. A flood of books, pamphlets, and articles articulated divergent visions of the new Canada that would be born from the travail of war. Leacock advocated "work and pay for the unemployed, maintenance for the infirm and aged, education and opportunity for the children" as the solution to the "unsolved riddle of social justice." Mackenzie King saw a new era of peace and labour harmony. Agrarian activist W.C. Good envisioned a revived rural economy. Journalist C.W. Peterson told Canadian industry to "wake up" to the problems of economic reconstruction. Feminist Nellie McClung proclaimed a new era for women. The Methodist Church called for radical social reform to build the Kingdom of God on Earth.[47]

But hope was mixed with fear — fear of the future, fear of Bolshevism, fear of moral decline, fear of the stranger, fear of the loss of old ideals and values, fear that the new Europe for which the soldiers had died was already collapsing in violence and revolution. Canadians were "war weary, nervous, irritable," reported the Chief of the General Staff to the War Office in London. Newton Wesley Rowell, the Ontario Liberal leader who had joined the Union Cabinet, warned Borden that "people are not in a normal condition. There is less respect for law and authority than we probably have ever had in this country." Dafoe pitied the political leader faced with the problems of postwar reconstruction. "It is going to be demanded of him that he do things that cannot be done; things that are mutually contradictory and destructive; and whatever he does will have more critics than friends." There was a universal awareness that the war was a clear dividing line between an uncertain present and an old world that had passed away forever.[48]

What of those men who were so central to the hope for a new world, whose memory everyone pledged to keep sacred and whose welfare everyone promised to ensure? What would the veterans be like when they came back? After years of fighting for a noble cause, of testing their manhood and their courage, of enduring hardship and horror in the trenches, would they now lead their country in building a better world? Or would they return unruly, vengeful, enraged at a country unworthy of their sacrifice? Stephen Leacock poked fun at society's ambivalence to the returned soldier: "In fact, a widespread movement had sprung up, warmly supported by the business men of the cities, to put him on the land.... At the same time an agitation had been started among the farmers, with the slogan 'Back to the city,' the idea being that farm life was so rough that it was not fair to ask the retuned soldier to share it."[49]

The real soldiers, still overseas, in some measure justified this fear. They had time to brood, time to vent their frustrations in riots and brawls, but mostly, time to think about the past and their future. Will Bird, returning to Canada on a troop ship in February 1919, woke up suddenly one night:

> In my fine sheets I could not sleep and began to forget where I was. I seemed to be in an atmosphere rancid with stale sweat and breathing, the hot grease of candles, the dampness of the underground. I saw cheeks resting on tunics, mud-streaked, unshaven faces ... men shivering on chicken-wire bunks. Then, from overhead, the machine-gun's note, louder, higher, sharper as it swept bullets over the shell crater in which I hugged the earth ... the rumble of guttural voices and heavy steps in an unseen trench just the other side of the black mass of tangled wire beside which I lay ... the long-drawn whine of a coming shell ... its heart-shaking explosion ... the seconds of heavy silence after, then the first low wail of the man down with a blood-spurting wound.... It was too much. I got up and dressed, although it was only four o'clock in the morning.
>
> It was cold but I wore my greatcoat, and to my amazement there were other dark figures near the rail. We stood, hunched together, gazing ahead into the darkness. Presently another figure joined us, then another. In an hour there were fourteen of us, and no one had spoken, although we were touching shoulders. The way we stood

made me think of a simile. Ah — we were like prisoners.
I had seen them standing together, staring over the wire
to the field beyond, never speaking. And we were more or
less prisoners of our thoughts. Those at home would never understand us, because something inexplicable would
make us unable to put our feelings into words. We could
only talk with one another.

All at once the watchers stirred, tensed, craned forward.
It was the moment for which we had lived, which we had
envisioned a thousand times, that held us so full of feeling
we could not find utterance. Far ahead, faint, but growing
brighter, we had glimpsed the first lights of home![50]

Bird's journey was a metaphor for the Canada he was coming home to.
All Canadians, each in their own way, had undergone a four-year passage
through suffering and fear and were now peering into the darkness ahead
to catch a glimpse of "home." Home could not be the place they had left
in 1914. It would hopefully be a better place that would realize the dreams
and justify the ideals for which they had sacrificed so much. But each person
peering over the rail had a different vision of the future. Which of the many
crusades set in motion by the war would come to fruition? Who would see
their hopes realized? Who would see their dreams dashed? The only constant
among Canadians as they searched the darkness ahead was uncertainty.

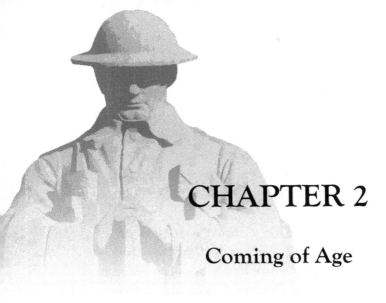

CHAPTER 2

Coming of Age

The ocean liner *Mauritania* ploughed its way through the cold swell of the North Atlantic, its lights extinguished and its passengers required to wear lifejackets at all times. Just after midnight on November 11, the ship's purser, "in tremendous excitement," came to Sir Robert Borden's cabin with "the startling announcement" that the war was over. Borden could rejoice that he was no longer the leader of a nation at war. But he well knew that even more serious challenges awaited those who must now make the peace. The world, he wrote in his diary, had "drifted far from its old anchorage and no man can with certainty prophesy what the outcome will be." What a change from those sunny days in August 1914 when news of war in Europe had not seemed urgent enough to cut short a Muskoka golfing holiday![1]

Borden had left Ottawa three days earlier in response to an urgent telegram from the British prime minister, David Lloyd George. Armistice negotiations had begun, wrote Lloyd George, and it was "very important that you should be here in order to participate in the deliberations which will determine the line to be taken" by the "British Delegates" at the peace conferences that would follow. "Also," added a later cable, "on many questions now coming under consideration I should value your advice greatly." Borden gave Lloyd George his first piece of advice right away. The British government had merely *informed* Canada of the talks, and Lloyd George had referred only to *preparations* for the peace conference. This was not good enough. Canadians, Borden wrote, "take it for granted that Canada will be represented at the Peace Conference." Otherwise, a "very

Imperial War Museum, London IWM ART 2856

Signing the Treaty of Versailles, Paris, June 29, 1919
This painting by Sir William Orpen imaginatively depicts the signing of the Treaty from a British point of view. The Germans in the foreground are cringing and subservient, the Italians and some other allies have been crowded to the side, British officials are under the central mirror. Canada, in the person of Sir George Foster (second row, fourth from left — Borden had gone home) is taking its place for the first time on the international stage. Hughes of Australia is at the right in the back row; to his right is Botha of South Africa — Smuts, who was a more important player, is not shown. In fact Foster was not there — he had gone home because his wife was ill. C.J. Doherty and Arthur Sifton signed for Canada.

unfortunate impression would be created and possibly a dangerous feeling might be aroused." Borden was a pussycat compared to Australia's dyspeptic premier, "Billy" Hughes, who spluttered his outrage that "conditions [for] peace should have been decided without Australia and presumably other Dominions being consulted."[2]

Canada was, in the end, invited to the Paris Peace Conference. Its tiny delegation consisted of Trade and Commerce Minister Sir George Foster, Customs Minister Arthur Sifton, and Justice Minister Charles J. Doherty, supported by External Affairs Legal Advisor Loring Christie and a few staff and occasional expert visitors. It had no independent intelligence or research and was chosen more to represent the different factions of the Union coalition than for any knowledge of international affairs. Only Christie, a Nova Scotian with a Harvard law degree, who had been recruited at age twenty-eight from a promising career in the U.S. Department of Justice, could move easily among the rising stars in the British and American delegations.[3]

Nonetheless, for six months in 1919 this delegation found itself "in the midst of things," as Foster put it, "representing Canada, which takes a place on perfect equality of expression and direction with all the other nations." As part of the British Empire Delegation, the Canadians, said Christie, were "at the heart of the machine" with access to all the papers, committees, and leaders at a conference deciding the future of the world. They enjoyed fine restaurants and somewhat risqué performances in theatres, though the teetotalling Foster was careful to assure his wife that "nothing outré or unusual took place." In the same way, Canada was cautiously leaving the confines of a comfortable childhood, asserting its status as a nation, anxiously entering a new world redolent with ancient hatreds, strewn with pitfalls, and rife with threats of war.[4]

I

There had never been any question of consulting Canada in August 1914 when the British government declared that the Empire was at war. Nonetheless, as a self-governing Dominion, Canada would decide for itself how it would contribute to the war effort. The Boer War had set the precedent that Canadian troops would form a separate contingent within the Imperial army. Canadians would fight, not with the blind obedience of colonials, but in defence of their country, the Empire, and the values on which both were based.

Canadians were British North Americans. Many were English, including more than a million recent immigrants. But many others were of Celtic origin, or spoke French, or had recently arrived from Europe, or had migrated back and forth across the American border. Canadians had invented responsible government, which allowed self-governing colonies to become Dominions within the Empire. They had blended federalism with parliamentary institutions to create a "political nationality," an empire within an Empire, that now spanned half a continent. Laurier saw no paradox in referring to his "Canadian British citizenship," and Bourassa insisted that French Canadians were "as British as any other race in Canada," not "by blood or language" but "by reason and tradition." "Britishness" and "Canadianness" were more instincts than thought-out ideas. But it was these instincts, as much as the work of its statesmen, its poets, or its railway-builders, that underlay the growing feeling of nationhood in a vast, diverse, and newly prosperous country.[5]

By the turn of the century, this liberal concept of "Britishness" was being modified by the prevalent theories of race. The term *race* referred not only to such attributes as skin colour, with which it is most often associated today, but also to the concept that each nation had a distinct national character, which was the product of heredity and long cultural evolution. These ideas were usually benign. But at their most extreme they could be used to support the Social Darwinist belief that the "fittest" races were destined to prevail in a global competition for survival. The superiority of the Anglo-Saxon "race" was amply demonstrated, according to proponents of this theory, by the rising power of the United States and the global reach of the British Empire. Other "Nordic" races were in the same league — perhaps including French Canadians. "Foreign" immigrants, "coloured" races, and aboriginal Canadians certainly were not. If Canada were to prosper it would need to remain, racially as well as politically and culturally, British.[6]

It was taken for granted that Canada was destined to be a great nation in its own right. But what did that mean? Some considered it enough to remain a colony in the mightiest empire that had ever been. Others believed Canada would ultimately be an independent country. But for many English-speaking Canadians, who called themselves "Imperialists," the best expression of Canada's national maturity would be to participate as an equal partner in a united and reformed British Empire.

Imperialists differed in their views on what such an Empire should look like. To Sir George Parkin, secretary of the Rhodes Trust, it would combine all members of the British "race" — including the French Canadians — into a "Greater Britain," one that was divinely ordained to govern "less-civilized" races and bring order and progress to the world. Others looked to the military strength of a united Empire to defend British civilization against global rivals. Liberal Imperialists like Wrong saw the Empire as "a great school of political life," which would evolve into a free association of peoples united by a common loyalty. Canadians were almost always looking at the Empire through the prism of their own nationalism. Thus, businessmen "loyal" to the Empire might still demand tariff protection against British goods; farmers might see no incompatibility with free trade with the United States; and few journalists hesitated to tout the superiority of young, virile Canada over the effete and class-ridden "old" country.[7]

In Britain, a growing number of leaders were looking outward to the Empire for the energy, innovation, and strength needed to offset the declining power of the mother country. Lord Milner, who had been high commissioner in South Africa after the Boer War, established the Round Table, which linked his own disciples, who were rising members of the British establishment, with an influential network of businessmen, politicians, intellectuals, and bright young men in the Dominions. A conflict quickly developed within the Round Table between those, mostly in Britain, who wanted a centralized Empire, and those (including almost all the Canadian members) who believed the Empire could only survive as a permanent alliance of autonomous Dominions — and it foundered in 1916 over this issue. But while it lasted, the Round Table provided an opportunity for many Canadians, including the students Wrong and his colleagues sent to Oxford, to become acquainted with leaders in Britain, and to have the heady feeling of knowing the "right people" and participating in a great global enterprise.[8]

Many Canadians, especially French Canadians, were deeply hostile to Imperialism. To Henri Bourassa, it stood for Anglo-Saxon dominance, colonial oppression, and permanent involvement in Imperial wars, and it prevented the development of a distinct Canadian nationality based on equal partnership between its founding peoples. English-speaking nationalists like J.W. Dafoe and O.D. Skelton saw the Round Table as a plot to seduce naïve colonials into schemes of Imperial centralization.

Imperialists never really came to grips with how a united Empire would reconcile the national interests of all the Dominions, what role the non-white components of the Empire (especially India) would play, or why any British government would subordinate itself to domination by colonials. All they really had in common was an almost mystical belief that taking part in the glorious mission of the British Empire would create what Leacock called a "Greater Canada" — in all the meanings of that phrase.[9]

As prime minister between 1896 and 1911, Sir Wilfrid Laurier had been preoccupied with preserving Canadian unity in the face of all these conflicting loyalties and ambitions. Canada, he promised, would come unhesitatingly to the defence of the Empire if it were ever seriously threatened. But he steadfastly resisted all proposals for Imperial centralization. Canada's contribution to the Empire would be to settle its West, develop its resources, and build a strong Canadian nation.

Laurier's balancing act became increasingly difficult as German naval expansion challenged British global supremacy. English-Canadian Imperialists demanded that Canada make an immediate contribution to the British navy. Bourassa was adamantly opposed. In 1910, Laurier tried to find a middle way by creating the Royal Canadian Navy, which could join the British fleet in time of war *if Parliament approved*. This backfired when an unlikely alliance of English-speaking Imperialists and

Sir Wilfrid Laurier

Library and Archives Canada C008103

Bourassa nationalists ganged up to defeat him in the election of 1911. When the new Borden government passed a bill to contribute $35 million to buy battleships for the Imperial navy, the Liberal-dominated Senate blocked the measure. When war broke out, Canada's navy consisted of two obsolete cruisers.

Borden was an Imperialist, but he was also an ardent Canadian nationalist. A stolid, phlegmatic figure with a square jaw and white hair parted in the middle, he had been a wealthy corporate lawyer who became prime minister almost by accident. Like the country he led, there was nothing in his experience that would have prepared him for the titanic struggle in which he was now engaged. He readily accepted that Imperial statesmen would make the big decisions and Canada would play its part with men, food, and resources. But be bristled when the British too often took Canada for granted and brushed aside its concerns. In 1915, when Borden diffidently requested more information about the conduct of the war, Colonial Secretary Bonar Law (himself a Canadian by birth) sniffed that his government was "not able to see any way in which this could practically be done," and that unless Borden had anything specific to propose, "it is very undesirable that the question should be raised." As he visited the front, Borden began to doubt British military and political leadership. On January 4, 1916, he told his high commissioner in London, Sir George Perley, that he could no longer tolerate "having no more voice and receiving no more consideration than if we were toy automata." But he still had nothing concrete to propose and he instructed Perley not to deliver the message.[10]

Then, in late 1916, British munitions minister David Lloyd George ousted Herbert Asquith as prime minister and formed a new government with a small War Cabinet in which Lord Milner played a prominent role. Drawing on some of Milner's young men, Lloyd George set about revolutionizing the British government and the British Empire. He needed allies against the military and industrial establishment and he needed more men from the Dominions. In the spring of 1917, he took the bold step of inviting the Dominion prime ministers to an Imperial War Cabinet. Bonar Law sneered that once the colonials got their teeth into policy the British would never get rid of them.

He was right. During IWC meetings in 1917 and 1918, Borden and his fellow premiers learned a great deal about the conduct of the war, much of which they did not like. He also, with the advice of Loring Christie (who was an active Round Tabler), began to articulate a more concrete vision of the Empire. Resolution IX of the Imperial War Conference, drafted by Borden and Jan Smuts of South Africa, provided that within a year after the end of the war an Imperial Conference would draw up an Imperial constitution "based upon a full recognition of the Dominions as autonomous nations of an Imperial Commonwealth" with an "adequate voice in foreign policy" and "continuous consultation in all important matters of common Imperial concern."[11]

Borden hailed this as the dawn of a "new and greater [I]mperial commonwealth." But the Imperial War Cabinet was not a cabinet in any real sense. Borden called it "a Cabinet of Governments," but that only meant that the Dominion premiers, each responsible to his own parliament, met periodically to discuss common policies. There was, to the chagrin of some British Round Tablers, no permanent bureaucracy. Nor was Borden entirely correct in suggesting that the Dominions and Britain met "on terms of perfect equality." The IWC was only one of many committees created by Lloyd George, and the Dominions were only a few of the pieces on his chess board. Major decisions continued to be made by the British War Cabinet, the Admiralty, and the Imperial General Staff without consulting the Dominions. The Empire had changed, and forever, but working out what that meant would have to wait for calmer times.[12]

II

The war also decisively changed Canada's other major relationship, that with the United States. Canadians had always been ambivalent toward their southern neighbour. Some, like Wrong, believed that the American Revolution had been a terrible mistake, and looked to the day when the Empire and its daughter republic would work in harmony. Other intellectuals deplored America's capitalist excesses, its democratic vulgarity, and the presence there of so many "southern" races — French-speaking Catholics added godless materialism to the indictment. When Laurier negotiated Reciprocity, or free trade, in agricultural and natural products with the United States in 1911, Canadian businessmen fearing the loss of tariff protection shouted "no truck or trade with the Yankees" and helped defeat him.

But few objected to Andrew Carnegie's grants for public libraries, teachers' pensions, and education and research. Canadian capitalists welcomed over $700 million in American investments, Canadian farmers looked to America for markets, and over 90 percent of Canadian labour unions were affiliated with the American Federation of Labor. A million Canadians were American-born — 14 percent of the population of Saskatchewan and 22 percent of Alberta's. Sports like baseball, popular music like ragtime, comics, magazines, and customs like Santa Claus and Thanksgiving, united English Canadians and Americans, as did their common British heritage and Protestant religion.

Americans and English Canadians had not, as American scholar Samuel Moffett claimed in 1907, "been welded into one people." Canadians still looked to Britain as the epitome of civilization and to the British tie as an offset to American dominance. But they also knew that Britain would never engage in serious conflict with the United States simply to protect Canadian interests. With British encouragement, Canada took increasing responsibility for cross-border relations and established a small Department of External Affairs. When the Great War broke out, Canadians and Americans were preparing to celebrate one hundred years of peace.[13]

Canadians were bitter that America remained neutral: "America counted her profits while Canada buried her dead," wrote a young historian after the war. But, as Borden told the Lawyers' Club of New York in 1916, Canadians increasingly realized the need to "become more and more of a bond of goodwill and friendship between this Great Republic and our Empire." Canadian politicians, journalists, academics, and businessmen used their networks to explain British war aims and the common ideals that bound the British Empire and the United States together, and these efforts did much to win Americans to the British cause. Thousands of Americans crossed the border to join the Canadian military.[14]

When the United States entered the war in April 1917, the two countries became allies, co-operating closely to harmonize regulatory controls on railways and shipping, ensure the flow of raw materials in both directions, and coordinate military activities. Canada had borrowed heavily in

New York to finance the purchase of American raw materials for munitions production, and Britain was having difficulty financing war purchases in Canada. Now the Canadians negotiated a three-cornered bargain in which Canada was exempted from borrowing restrictions in the United States, got a share of an American war loan to Britain for purchases in Canada, and had the Imperial Munitions Board designated as the Canadian procurement arm of the U.S. Bureau of Ordnance. When the British balked at naming a Canadian high commissioner in Washington, Borden appointed Lloyd Harris, the IMB's representative in Washington, as chairman of a Canadian War Mission reporting to the Canadian Cabinet.[15]

Canadians were for the first time being recognized and admired by their southern neighbour. Finance Minister Sir Thomas White, a Toronto businessman who had been one of the key opponents of Reciprocity, was now telling the U.S. treasury secretary that in "our attitude towards constitutional liberty and all social problems, our people are very much alike and understand each other better I think than any other two peoples in the world today." Canada served the Empire by becoming its bridge to the United States. But at a price. American trade and investment would increasingly drive the Canadian economy. And, after three years when censorship kept out American media, Canadians were once again exposed to an overwhelming flood from south of the border.[16]

III

Canadians had given very little thought to war aims, other than the defeat of Germany and all it stood for. But Borden was now well aware that building a new world order that would guarantee Canada's security and justify its sacrifice would be even more important than winning the war. He thus remained in Europe from November 1918 until May 1919, first at the Imperial preparatory conference in London and then at the Paris Peace Conference — an unprecedented absence for a Canadian prime minister. Mindful of the need to ensure that Canadians understood the important work being done in Paris, the government appointed J.W. Dafoe and a French-speaking counterpart to write dispatches for newspapers back home.

For Borden, the bedrock of any stable postwar world order would be a permanent alliance between the British Empire and the United States, "the two great English[-]speaking commonwealths ... sufficiently powerful to dictate the peace of the world." To make this happen, America would have to share in the responsibility "for securing the welfare, the advancement, and the safety of backward races." The Empire would have to "keep clear, as far as possible, of European complications and alliances." And it would have to be restructured, as provided for in Resolution IX of the Imperial War Conference, into a Commonwealth of autonomous Dominions. Borden agreed with Lord Milner that this would be "one of the most complicated tasks which statesmanship has ever had to face." Just how difficult became immediately apparent when the Dominions gathered in London in November 1918 to prepare for the peace conference.[17]

That conference was clearly going to be controlled by Britain and the other Great Powers. They had already agreed that they should each have five plenipotentiary delegates, with smaller countries to be given one or two. The Dominions, it was assumed, would be represented by the British delegation. That, Borden told the preparatory conference, was simply not on. Canada had lost more men than the Americans. It would not accept a status below Portugal, Siam, or the Hedjaz. The Dominions should have their own seats, and the British Empire Delegation should "represent not only the British Isles, but the whole Empire." If the other Powers did not understand this, "it would be not only proper, but necessary, for the British Government to set it forth fully." Borden would repeat this mantra throughout the peace conference, whenever the question of Canadian status arose — sometimes coupled with a threat to "pack his trunks, return to Canada, summon Parliament, and put the whole thing before them."[18]

Perhaps, suggested Lloyd George, Borden could represent the Dominions as one of the five British plenipotentiaries. No bloody way, said Hughes of Australia. Finally, the British agreed to propose separate representation for the Dominions, and President Wilson agreed they should get two seats each (except New Zealand, which got one, and Newfoundland, which got none). But *in addition*, the Dominions would be part of the British Empire Delegation and would occupy one of its five seats, in turn, as their interests required. In January 1919, the Imperial preparatory conference moved to

Paris and morphed into the British Empire Delegation. The Dominions had got the best of both worlds.[19]

The circumstances in which the Paris Peace Conference was convened were far from auspicious. The war had set loose idealism, fear, ambition, and greed in equal measure. President Wilson and his vision of a League of Nations had raised hopes everywhere for a new era of peace. But international financial systems, trading patterns, agricultural trade, and industrial production, were in shambles. Three European empires had collapsed, and the squabbling successor states indulged their mutual hatreds. Germany's fledgling democracy hung by a thread as ex-soldiers fought in the streets and starvation stalked the cities. The Allied armies were melting away, returning soldiers faced mass unemployment, and war-weary countries were sinking into political unrest and industrial upheaval. An unstable Italy alternated between truculent demands for territory and petulant displays of wounded national pride whenever they did not get their way. France, Japan, and Britain (and several Dominions) had seized German colonies and Turkish provinces, and they now had to reconcile the promises made to their new subjects with the secret treaties they had signed with each other. Britain had lost its American investments, the American navy now challenged British supremacy, and Irish- and German-Americans hated the British Empire. "'Tis surely a sad mess," wrote Foster in his diary, "out of which to evolve a new Europe."[20]

Hovering over all this was the spectre of Bolshevism. Even as Canadians won glory on Vimy Ridge, Russia had been plunged into turmoil with the abdication of the czar. Lenin's Bolsheviks had seized power in November 1917, made a separate peace with Germany in March 1918, and executed the royal family in July. As the Allies had retreated before the German spring offensive, they had sent whatever troops they could spare (including some Canadians) to help White Russian forces fighting the Bolsheviks. Information from Russia reached Paris in dribs and drabs — a brutal civil war, starving people, bodies in the street, unshaven commissars in ruined palaces with their muddy feet on the mahogany.

Bolshevism sent a galvanic shock through victors and vanquished alike. A communist (Spartacist) revolution was bloodily suppressed in Berlin and there was a short-lived communist coup in Bavaria. A communist government in Hungary so alarmed the peacemakers that they sent Smuts to investigate. Militant unions and socialists in all countries uttered Bolshevist slogans, and radicals like the American Lincoln Steffens proclaimed they had "seen the future and it works." But to others, Bolshevism was a mortal threat to civilization itself. In 1918, Joe Boyle, the Klondike gold magnate who had spent the last years of the war in Russia, told Borden (and through Borden the Imperial War Cabinet) that if left unchecked Bolshevism would overrun Germany and a million men would be needed to defeat it. In February 1919, Winston Churchill descended on Paris to plead that "Bolshevism must be strangled in its cradle." Instead, Lloyd George and Wilson decided to invite the Russian adversaries to a peace conference on the Turkish Island of Prinkipo, with Borden to chair the British delegation. But the White Russians expressed outrage, Lenin made unacceptable demands, and the initiative collapsed.[21]

Borden was now playing in the big leagues, interacting daily with the people and issues that were reshaping the world, learning the rules of the game — sometimes the hard way. When he spoke up in a plenary session to support the complaint by smaller countries that the conference was being dominated by the Great Powers, French president Georges Clemenceau waited until everyone had finished and then replied in English:

> Sir Robert Borden has reproached us, though in a very friendly way, for coming to a decision.... With your permission I will remind you that it was we who decided there should be a conference at Paris, and that the representatives of the countries interested should be summoned to attend it. I make no mystery of it — there is a Conference of the Great Powers going on in the next room. Sir Robert Borden has the less reason to be unaware of it since he yesterday did us the signal honour of making a statement before us on questions concerning the British Colonies.

Borden got the message. Canadians were privileged to be in that next room. As a prime minister recognized by Milner as "capable of taking the wider view," even while advancing Canadian interests, Borden could serve the Empire as vice-president of the Committee on the Boundaries of Greece. Sifton could negotiate treaties on waterways and aviation and the International Labour Organization. Foster could play an important role on the Supreme Economic Council.[22]

Borden was probably more in tune with Clemenceau in his approach to the proposed League of Nations. The League, he told Lloyd George in November 1918, was a great dream, "so commanding that no right thinking man could withhold his sympathy and support to any proposal which gave the faintest promise of success." But it was the Anglo-American alliance that would make the League work, not the idealism of British and American League of Nations societies or the eloquence of Jan Smuts, for whom the League was "the embodiment and living expression of the moral and spiritual unity of the human race."[23]

Regardless of what the League was to become, it was essential that the Dominions be full members of it. There was ready agreement that they should have seats in the Assembly. But even their friends found it difficult to swallow the Dominions' demand to be also eligible for election to the League Council. After all, the British Empire would hold one of the permanent seats on the Council, and by their own admission it was unlikely any Dominion would ever seek separate election. But if they were not *eligible,* they were not fully sovereign. So, once again, the British were demanding that the evolving quasi-constitution of the Empire be permanently enshrined in international practice. And, once again, the Dominions got the best of both worlds. Borden persuaded Wilson, Lloyd George, and Clemenceau to sign a memorandum declaring that they interpreted the League Charter to mean that the Dominions could be elected to the Council. Wilson had come to see Canada as a useful ally and the growing Anglo-American friendship as vital. His advisor, Colonel House, hoped that once the Dominions enjoyed the protection of the League the British Empire would break up. Either way, the issue would come back to haunt Wilson.[24]

The Canadians also won a more difficult fight for full membership in the International Labour Organization. By the time the ILO was being debated, American delegates were feeling a backlash from Washington, and the British Labour Party was unwilling to fight Canadian battles. The initial draft of the ILO charter explicitly precluded the Dominions from being members of the governing body. With serious labour unrest in Canada, and given that most unions in the Canadian Trades and Labour Congress (whose secretary had come to Paris) were affiliated with the American Federation of Labor, this was unacceptable. Canadian workers, said Arthur Sifton, would "see the Japanese and Italian delegates and their respective governments individually and collectively sizzling in the lowest depths of Hell before they will agree to accept a standing inferior to the negroes [sic] of Liberia." When Canada threatened to sign the treaty and then withdraw from the ILO, Wilson once again intervened to have the offending clause struck from the charter.[25]

There remained two concluding acts in the drama of Canadian status. Borden wanted each Dominion to sign the Treaty of Versailles with Germany in its own right. They did, but with their names indented under the signatory for the British Empire, which left their status ambiguous. Then the British insisted that the king must sign the treaty at once, in order to give the Germans no chance to back away. Borden was determined that the Canadian Parliament should ratify the treaty, and the king could not sign for Canada until it had done so (Borden rejected Milner's absurd argument that Canada's presence at Paris implied its approval). In the end, the British decided that the king did not have to sign immediately after all, and he did so only after all the Dominion parliaments had ratified.[26]

IV

Beyond securing recognition of Canada's new status, building the Anglo-American alliance, and playing a helpful role in the Empire delegation, the Canadians showed little desire to become embroiled in the complex and dangerous affairs of Europe. They took no part in negotiating the treaties with Austria, Hungary, Bulgaria, and Turkey, which the British signed for the Empire. Sifton carefully ensured the exclusion of North America from treaties on navigation and aviation. Lloyd Harris, promoted to the head of the Canadian commercial delegation in London, played an important role in Allied commissions to relieve famine in Germany and restore industry and commerce — always with a view to ensuring that Canada got its share of contracts, as well as future trade.[27]

The delegation was particularly opposed to Article X of the draft League of Nations Covenant, which provided for all members to come to the defence of any member state that was attacked. Canadians, wrote Justice Minister Doherty, "their hearts still wrung by the grief that a terrible war has brought them," would "look with critical eye indeed on a clause so easily susceptible of being read as making everybody's wars their wars." This viewpoint got little traction with the other Allies. After all, with no standing League army, what other guarantee of security would France and the new countries of Central Europe have? What was the League all about, if not uniting to resist aggression? Borden and Christie got nowhere when they argued in the Empire Delegation that Article X should be struck out or amended. But they did succeed a few weeks later in having a clause added to an Anglo-American treaty that guaranteed aid to France against any German attack, which exempted the Dominions from any such obligation "unless and until it is approved by the Parliament of the Dominion concerned."[28]

Nor was Canada willing to let the interests of any other Dominion get in the way of its own. When "Billy" Hughes declared that Australia and New Zealand intended to take over German colonies in the South Pacific, Borden told the Imperial preparatory conference that American public opinion would be outraged "if the British Empire came out of this war with a very great acquisition of territory." Canada, he added piously, "did not go into the war in order to add territory to the British Empire," and its primary interest, and that of the Empire, was in good relations with the United States. Smuts saved the day with an ingenious proposal that conquered territories would be assigned by the League to "developed" countries (including Australia, New Zealand, and South Africa, as well as Britain, Japan, Belgium, and France) as "mandates" with the responsibility to prepare them (eventually) for self-government. This idea appealed to Wilson, but there was a "pretty warm scene" in the British delegation before Hughes backed down. Borden then worked to smooth relations within the delegation and with the Americans.[29]

Everyone agreed that Germany must be rendered incapable of starting another war. But Borden, together with the younger members of the

British and American delegations, became increasingly concerned that any demand for reparations that would cripple German economic recovery would actually make future wars more likely. Thus he rejected his Cabinet's proposal to claim as reparations Canada's war pensions or the costs of the Halifax explosion. In June, the ever-changeable Lloyd George, who had promised his voters that he would squeeze Germany "until the pips squeak," now convened a special meeting of the British Empire Delegation at Fontainebleau to reconsider its position on reparations and other punitive provisions of the treaty. Foster, who had repeatedly fought "Billy" Hughes's extravagant demands within the delegation, once again expressed Canadian concerns (Borden had gone home). But the French were not in the mood for such second thoughts, and Wilson was appalled by the *volte-face.* The reparations provisions of the Treaty of Versailles stood — and would fuel a growing belief in the English-speaking world, expressed in the fall of 1919 by J.M. Keynes in his book *The Economic Consequences of the Peace,* that the Allies had imposed a "Carthaginian Peace" on Germany.[30]

Beyond the world of the North Atlantic, Canada's global interests mostly focused on trade, immigration, and investments in the Caribbean and Brazil, which it was quite content to manage within the framework of the Empire. The government did for a time consider the possibility of taking over administration of the British West Indies. Canada would gain an "increased sense of responsibility due to administration of a territory largely inhabited by backward races," thought Borden, but the "coloured population" would likely be "more restless under Canadian than under British control" and would want representation in Parliament. In any case, Milner was not about to give Canada the privilege of governing colonies unless it was prepared to play a more active role in the Empire as a whole. Once it became clear the Americans wanted no new colonies, the idea of Canada taking any was a non-starter.[31]

Canada did take on one important task, at the request of the British and Americans, when Borden agreed in July 1918 to send four thousand troops to Vladivostok, in eastern Siberia, as the main British contribution to an international force that would secure the flow of arms and supplies to the White Russians fighting the Bolsheviks, support Czech troops controlling the trans-Siberian railway, and offset Japanese influence in the region.

Canada also dispatched a trade mission, hoping to supplant a German company which had controlled Siberian trade. At Borden's insistence, a Canadian, General Elmsley, was given command of all British forces.

This contingent was still being assembled when the war ended. Suddenly, it became deeply unpopular, especially as many of the men being sent were conscripts. But Borden, already en route to London, was not ready to renege on his commitment and directed that the deployment go ahead. Labour meetings in Victoria — attended by soldiers in spite of attempts by the authorities to break them up — heard speakers shouting "Hands off Russia" and calling on them to desert. Dockworkers tried to prevent supplies from being loaded. On December 21, 1918, some French-Canadian conscripts mutinied and were marched onto their ships between lines of soldiers with fixed bayonets.[32]

The government then learned how much easier it was to get into an expedition than to get out of it. The mutually suspicious Allies had no agreed objectives. The Japanese pursued their own interests in eastern Siberia; the Americans and British wavered between active intervention and withdrawal; the Czechs feared betrayal; the White Russians squabbled. The Canadians in Vladivostok languished through a bitter winter in a city swollen with refugees and rife with crime, murder, and typhus. A few officers and men joined a British force up-country. A detachment of Mounties charged into a blizzard to protect people they thought were in danger. A contingent of troops marched to relieve a threatened Japanese force, luckily not encountering any Bolsheviks, and were lavishly rewarded with sake. Lieutenant Raymond Massey found himself challenged to a duel when he accidentally spilled beer on a Czech major-general. The trade commission, a collection of oddball characters, had little success in the surreal environment of eastern Siberia. General Elmsley quarrelled with the senior British officer but acquitted himself well in a difficult situation.

By February, Borden had decided that fighting the Bolsheviks was, as he told Churchill, "a course whose consequence it was impossible to foresee," and he resisted all of Churchill's attempts to change his mind. In April, the troops began to leave, and by June, all were home, except nineteen who had died and at least four Russian-speaking Canadians who had deserted.[33]

V

The Canadian delegates who returned from the Peace Conference in mid-1919 had learned much about the world. Borden confessed that the "fierce antagonisms, the ancient hatreds, and the bitter jealousies of European nationals there assembled were not inspiring." Christie had learned that the new Empire could only work if its members "really make up their minds that they will play together, that they have in fact some important common objects, that there is actual business that they can transact better together than apart." Dafoe returned with renewed conviction that "the North American continent is a good place to live." But his tour of Canadian battlefields, which he described in a series of articles, had also demonstrated that unless the peace satisfied "the aspiration which turned millions of peace-loving men into militant crusaders ... much of the sacrifice will have been in vain." "For good or ill," he concluded, "we are in the world and must bear our part in the solution of its troubles."[34]

But Canada had changed much in their absence. Pride in Canada's new status within the Empire and hopeful support for the League were being eroded by a growing mood of skepticism about what the war had in fact achieved. Nationalists like O.D. Skelton feared that Borden's new Empire would really be "a body sitting in London" deciding "whether or not we will make a reciprocity treaty with the United States, or upon what terms we will secure coal or let our paper go." Lawyer John S. Ewart of Ottawa argued that a united Empire of autonomous states was a "dangerous fallacy" — the only options were independence or colonial status. Bourassa charged that emphasis on the Empire impeded Canada's unity and independence and made it more vulnerable to American domination. W.F.

Manitoba Archives N19450

John Wesley Dafoe

Nickle, an independent Conservative MP, secured parliamentary approval for a request that the king not confer any more titles on his Canadian subjects; Canada, he said repeatedly, would have no "cheap, tinselled aristocracy."[35]

These divergent views surfaced during the special session of Parliament convened in September 1919 to ratify the peace treaty. The government (Borden, Rowell, Doherty, Sifton, and Foster) declared that Canada had asserted its national status at Paris and that the Empire was evolving into what Doherty called "the greatest experiment in democratic government that the world has ever seen" — with room for English and French Canadians. The Liberals, with no leader in the House (Laurier had died in February and their new leader, Mackenzie King, had not yet taken a seat), attacked from different directions. Nova Scotia warhorse W.S. Fielding asserted that Canada was a colony, nothing more, and it was "a colossal humbug" to pretend that "our statesmen who went to Paris did some Canadian business." French-speaking Liberals like Lucien Cannon argued that, on the contrary, the seats Canadians occupied at Paris "were not big enough for the country they represented." The so-called new Empire, said Henri Béland, was "a fever of [I]mperialism, the main symptom of which is a blind desire to centralize in London the administration of Canadian affairs." Canada, said Ernest Lapointe, should "go forward and occupy among the nations of the world the place she deserves. But the mere assertion of an illusion or a dream as being a fact does not make it so."[36]

Even more revealing was the debate on the League. Borden expressed the hope that "not force but right and justice shall be the arbiter of international disputes," and that with status came responsibilities. Humbug, said Fielding — our war dead did not "give us a claim to make ourselves ridiculous by undertaking to deal with things of which we know nothing." What, asked others, would Canada do if the League ordered us into a war, perhaps against another member of the Empire? Major C.G. Power, a decorated Irish-Canadian from Quebec, expressed a growing mood of isolationism: "Our policy for the next hundred years should be that laid down by George Washington in the United States … absolute renunciation of interference in European affairs — and that laid down by the other great father of his country in Canada, Sir Wilfrid Laurier — 'freedom from the vortex of European militarism.'" Relations between French and English Canadians, said

Rodolphe Lemieux, were more important than the boundaries of Poland. But Lapointe cautioned that for Canada the only alternative to the League would be the old diplomacy, a new arms race among European empires, and more wars into which Canada would be dragged.[37]

While this debate was going on, Edward, Prince of Wales, whose movie-star looks and personal charm masked a deep inner turmoil, was making a ten-week tour of Canada. Lloyd George and Lord Milner hoped his vis-it would solidify Canadian support for the Empire, and one of Milner's Round Tablers was sent along as a political advisor. The prince was im-mensely popular. So many people shook his right hand that he had to use his left. In Winnipeg, crowds broke through police lines. In Ottawa, he laid the cornerstone of the new tower in the rebuilt Parliament Buildings. (Opposition Leader Mackenzie King called him the "Sir Galahad of the Royal Household, the young knight, our future king, whose joy is in the service of others.") He bought a ranch in Alberta because "I want to feel I have a home in the West." In Toronto, where he was passed hand over hand to escape the crowd, he told his mistress "they've done their very best to kill your poor little boy to-day." He delivered his message countless times in a manner that blended Imperial dignity with youthful, democratic *joie de vivre.* "I want you to look at me as a Canadian, as one of yourselves, as one deeply interested in the welfare of Canada," he told a Toronto audience. "Besides being Canadians we are all Britishers which, for lack of a better expression, means loyalty to the British flag and to British institutions — in other words, citizens of the British Empire."[38]

The prince was less politically successful in his subsequent tour of the United States. America was imploding in the aftermath of war. Anyone or anything deemed "un-American" was subject to attack. "The Americans," wrote Loring Christie, "are in a very unlovely mood.... Towards the rest of the world the attitude just now is one of impatience; they do not care very much what happens to us and they do not mind whether we know it or not." Liberal intellectuals believed that President Wilson had betrayed his ideals at Paris. Isolationists attacked membership in the League of Nations as a violation of the time-honoured principle of avoiding foreign entangle-ments. Irish- and German-Americans accused Wilson of tricking America into fighting a British war. Republicans simply hated him and resolved to destroy his handiwork. Senator Henry Cabot Lodge of Massachusetts convened a sub-committee on the Treaty of Versailles, which, after lengthy hearings, demanded that America not sign the treaty unless fourteen reservations were accepted by all other signatories. In September 1919, Wilson embarked on a cross-country tour in a futile attempt to salvage his work, but suffered a debilitating stroke. For the next year, the White House would be run by his wife and a small coterie.[39]

Canada was caught in the crossfire of this nasty debate. It was one thing for Americans to borrow Canadian arguments to attack Article X. It was quite another for senators to repeatedly allege that making the Dominions full members of the League had been a scheme to get "six British votes." The "Borden letter" that recognized Canada's eligibility for election to the Council was "revealed" as evidence, in the words of one senator, that Wilson had gone to "the edge of treason." One of the fourteen reservations put forward by the Senate sub-committee demanded that either the Dominions be disqualified from membership in the League Council or that the United States get six votes. Ex-President Taft, now a senator who supported the treaty but detested Wilson, wrote his friend George Wrong that Canada's "vanity" in demanding a right it would never exercise would lead to American rejection of the treaty. In vain Rowell argued in a letter to the *New York Times* that Canada was an independent country with the right to belong to both the League of Nations and to the smaller league of nations that was the British Empire.[40]

With the Senate deadlocked, the British sent former foreign minister Lord Grey to Washington to try to salvage the treaty. Grey's proposal, that Canada declare that the Dominions would not vote on any dispute that might lead to war between a foreign power and a country of the British Empire, was dismissed out-of-hand by the Canadian Cabinet. Borden, in the United States to recover from illness, overruled his ministers. But no other Dominion would agree to any such reservation, nor would the Canadian public have tolerated such a humiliation. On March 19, 1920, the Senate finally rejected the treaty. A year later, a Republican non-entity, Warren G. Harding of Ohio, was elected president by a landslide, promising "not heroism but healing, not nostrums but normalcy." Canada was now the only North American member of the League.[41]

Canada could ill afford to hold a grudge. Trade with the United States had grown to $1.3 billion a year, with the balance in America's favour, and American investment in Canada had grown by leaps and bounds. Some form of direct Canadian representation in Washington was urgent. But the government insisted that it be "upon lines which will maintain and even emphasize the solidarity of the Empire." How could that be achieved? One possible solution was the proposal Lloyd George had made in February 1919, to appoint Borden as the British ambassador in Washington — which was quickly abandoned when a leaked report rattled the Canadian Cabinet and shook the stock market. Another was Lord Milner's proposal for parallel embassies, one representing Canadian interests and the other British, under a single ambassador — which upset the Foreign Office. The Canadian government suggested a Canadian minister within the British Embassy — but the Americans would not accredit an official at this level to the president. Finally, in May 1920, a compromise was announced: a Canadian minister would be the second-in-command of the British Embassy and would act as *chargé d'affaires* in the ambassador's absence.

Christie hailed this as the beginning of a Canadian diplomatic service woven "into the fabric of the present diplomatic service of the Empire." Mackenzie King was less impressed. Why, he asked, should a Canadian minister have charge of a British embassy? "In matters between Canada and other countries, Canada should manage her own affairs," as should Britain, "always when necessary with co-operation and conference between the two." In the end, no suitable candidate could be found and a crucial element of Canada's relations with the United States and the Empire continued unresolved.[42]

VI

Borden's dream that a united Empire composed of autonomous Dominions, acting in concert with the United States, could be a decisive force for international peace, was now in shambles. By 1920, the United States was lapsing into isolationism. Imperial diplomatic unity, which had worked well in the hothouse environment of Paris, was proving a far more difficult proposition in the real world. The British Foreign Office had never accepted the Colonial Office demand that the Dominions be consulted on matters of foreign policy in which they were not directly concerned. Now, harassed by crises everywhere and unrest at home, increasingly disillusioned with Europe and the League, they were even less inclined to do so. For his part, Colonial Secretary Lord Milner complained that the Dominions were cherry-picking the issues on which they wanted to engage and leaving the British to handle all the rest on their behalf. How were people to know when Britain spoke for the Empire, and when only for itself? In the spring of 1920, the Foreign Office did not bother to inform the Dominions when the foreign secretary attended the first Council of the League.[43]

When the first League Assembly met in November 1920, there was no British Empire Delegation and attempts to coordinate positions were only partly successful. Canada and South Africa voted to admit Austria and Bulgaria, which the British opposed, while Canada voted against admitting the Baltic States because it could not undertake to defend them against Russia under Article X. Canada's delegation (Rowell, who had resigned from the Cabinet in June, Doherty, and Foster) was without instructions and its members were not the best of friends. Rowell spoke eloquently on the admission of enemy states, an international court of justice, and humanitarian issues. Doherty moved that Article X be struck from the Covenant, a motion that was buried in a committee. Rowell "hurt and stung" Europeans when he told the Assembly that "it was European policy, European statesmanship, European ambition, that drenched this world with blood and from which we are still suffering and will suffer for generations. Fifty thousand Canadians under the soil of France and Flanders is what Canada has paid for European statesmanship trying to settle European problems."[44]

Not until June 1921 did the Imperial constitutional conference which Resolution IX had called for within one year of the end of the war take place. No one knew what to call it — they settled on "Meeting of Representatives of the United Kingdom, the Dominions, and India." The meeting agreed to the proposal of the new Canadian prime minister, Arthur Meighen (who replaced Borden in July 1920), to renew the commitment to continuous consultation embodied in Resolution IX — and little else.

Instead, it was hijacked by yet another Canada-Australia battle, this time over the Anglo-Japanese Treaty, which was due for renewal in 1922.[45]

This treaty had been signed in 1902 to safeguard British interests in the Far East. To many Canadians, Japan was a fascinating culture, a magnet for missionaries, and a potentially rich market for wheat and lumber. The Japanese navy had protected Canada's west coast during the war. But in British Columbia there was strong resentment of Japanese immigration and fear of Japan's rising power. At Paris, Borden had once again had to face down "Billy" Hughes and negotiate a compromise when Japan proposed language in the League Covenant recognizing the equality of all races, which challenged not only the "white Australia" policy but also discriminatory laws in the United States and Canada. Now Japan had taken over the German sphere of influence in China, occupied Korea, acquired mandates over German colonies in the North Pacific, and had designs on Manchuria. Australia and New Zealand believed that renewing the treaty would restrain Japan and stabilize the Pacific, and the British agreed with them. But the Canadians knew that the United States would see renewal as giving a free hand to Japan, their only plausible rival in the Pacific. Christie hoped to resolve the dilemma by persuading the United States to convene a conference of the Pacific powers, but the British rejected the idea.[46]

Meighen, a staunch champion of Imperial unity, now found himself confronting the elder statesmen of the British Empire. He insisted that Canada would refuse to ratify any renewal of the treaty, that American friendship was a *sine qua non* for Canada, and that the Empire should not condone, much less encourage, Japanese aggression in China. Hughes was equally insistent that the vital interests of Australia and New Zealand were at stake and the Empire must support them. The debate raged for days until the British Embassy in Washington confirmed that, sure enough, renewal of the treaty *would* upset the Americans and touch off a naval arms race in the Pacific. Lloyd George then got the lord chancellor to declare that the treaty did not need to be renewed after all, and the meeting agreed that a Pacific Conference was now a good idea.[47]

In the fall of 1921, the United States convened a naval disarmament conference and a conference of the Pacific Powers in Washington. The Washington Treaty capped the battle fleets of Britain, the United States, Japan, France, and Italy in a ratio of 5 to 5 to 3 to 1.5 to 1.5. It thus limited the Japanese fleet and allowed the Anglo-Japanese Treaty to slide into limbo. It also ended the supremacy of the British navy and established the United States as a dominant naval power. To a limted degree, it nudged the United States out of isolation and improved Anglo-American relations. For the last time, the British Empire fielded a united delegation, with Borden representing Canada, and the Dominions signed the Washington Treaty in the same way as they had at Paris.[48]

In December 1921, in the middle of the Washington Conference, the Meighen government was defeated in a general election and a minority government led by Mackenzie King took power. King well understood that being part of the British Empire gave Canada a stronger international position — and the privilege of not always having to take a stance. But he believed that the Empire should be a Commonwealth of independent states, working together but not meddling in each other's affairs, with each having its own representation abroad. This approach could appeal to Western agrarians and French Canadians, isolationists and internationalists alike — all but the most die-hard Colonialists or Imperialists.[49]

In September 1922, a British force was being threatened by a Turkish army at Chanak, and the British appealed to the Dominions for help — and, unforgivably, they made the appeal public before the Dominions had time to react. Meighen, reverting to an older Tory loyalism, shouted that Canada's response should be "ready, aye, ready." King's reply (which echoed Borden's reservation on the Anglo-French Treaty) was that Canada's Parliament would, alone, determine what action, if any, it would take.

The following year his government negotiated and signed the Halibut Treaty with the United States, which set the precedent that a Dominion could make its own treaties where only its own interests and not those of the Empire were involved. At the 1923 Imperial Conference, King insisted that the final communiqué describe the Conference as "representatives of the several Governments of the Empire" whose "views and conclusions on Foreign Policy … are necessarily subject to the action of the Governments and Parliaments of the various portions of the Empire."[50]

From there it was a short step to the Balfour Declaration of 1926 that Britain and the Dominions were autonomous and not subordinate in any way one to another, and to the Statute of Westminster of 1931 that embodied this concept in law. In 1927 and 1928, Canada established full diplomatic relations with the United States, Japan, and France, exchanged high commissioners with Britain and later with other Dominions, and established a diplomatic mission in Geneva. In 1923, King eased Christie out of External Affairs and brought in professor O.D. Skelton of Queen's, who had just completed a biography of Laurier, as his principal advisor. Appointed under-secretary in 1925, Skelton began to build a distinctively Canadian foreign service.

Yet now that, in the words of Jan Smuts, "Canada has had her way in everything," King drew back. In the later 1920s he actually resisted efforts to further decentralize what was now called the British Commonwealth, and he refused to establish a Canadian citizenship, secure the right to amend Canada's constitution, or end appeals of Canadian judicial decisions to the Judicial Committee of the Privy Council in London. Like most English Canadians, he valued the British connection when it did not impinge on Canadian sovereignty. Like Laurier, he also knew that maintaining the vestiges of the Imperial tie would minimize commitments abroad, avoid domination by the Americans, and deflect divisive issues at home.[51]

So what, after all, had been achieved? Was Paris what Margaret MacMillan calls a "false dawn" for Canada and the other Dominions? Imperial diplomatic unity was a wonderful dream, but it was too difficult for the British to manage a global foreign policy and a huge, dependent Empire and still cater to the Dominions — and impossible if the interests of Dominions clashed. Canadians, by the 1920s, were increasingly convinced that there was little in perfidious Europe or the wider world that merited their attention. However they might occasionally resent their neighbour to the south, they rejoiced in the peace and freedom of North America, symbolized by the Peace Arch, Peace Bridge, and Peace Park. They did accept some

Oscar D. Skelton

global responsibilities as the only North American member of the League — Borden, Rowell, Dafoe, and Foster all served as presidents of the League of Nations Society, which by 1929 had twenty thousand members. But most would have agreed with Senator Raoul Dandurand when he told the League Assembly in 1925 that Canada lived in a "fireproof house," far from the combustible materials of Europe. Peace and security would be guaranteed if Britain was strong, the Commonwealth was united, the Americans were well-disposed, and Canada kept out of harm's way.[52]

Trying to be an independent nation within a united Empire was neither consistent nor logical. An exasperated Round Tabler, A.J. Glazebrook, described George Wrong to Lord Milner in 1922 as "a woolly bah lamb whose convictions are moved about by every little storm in a teacup. At present he is very nationalistic, but anon he will meet somebody who will set him on the other line, and he will be a prophet of the Empire; but nothing for very long." But when Wrong told Dafoe in 1916 that Canada's place in the Empire was "one of those questions which will not be determined by reason but by feelings," he was offering a far more perceptive assessment of the Canadian reality — and of what would make a Commonwealth of independent nations work effectively in war and in peace, once it had become clear that a unified Empire was a chimera.[53]

Though they began with very different concepts of what they wanted Canada and the Empire to be, Borden, Rowell, Christie, Meighen, Skelton, King, and others who managed Canada's transition to nationhood in the aftermath of the global cataclysm that was the First World War showed a remarkable consistency. Under the pressure of events and with the world rapidly changing around them, they followed a pragmatic, incremental course. In the end, there emerged a Commonwealth of sovereign states that derived its strength from common loyalty and concerted action in pursuit of shared ideals and mutual interests. This framework could encompass Canada's independence, express its complex identity, reduce the stress on its fragile unity, offset the influence of the United States, and shield it from those affairs of a troubled world with which it was not yet prepared to engage. Canada could begin to heal its wounds, develop its identity as an independent nation in North America, and take its place, however tentatively, in the councils of the world.

CHAPTER 3

Returning Heroes

Sergeant Major Brooke Claxton and his artillery battery arrived in Montreal on May 11, 1919. "Like the June day we left," he recalled, "the sun was shining brilliantly as we marched proudly between crowds of cheering Montrealers. Before too long we were at Peel Street barracks." The men lined up for one last parade. "The senior artillery officer present made a one-sentence speech, saying that we would always remember that we had done our job, the friends we had made and lost, the units we had been with, the country we had served. There were no heroics, no glamour and no glory, which was just as it should be. Our relatives and friends were waiting. We stepped into civvy street." In Toronto, Gordon Sinclair's regiment was less eager to parade up University Avenue. Some of the men had broken ranks to join wives and children they had not seen in years when their colonel rallied them to make one last good show. "You've given parades for people all over France," he told them. "You've given parades in Germany. You've given parades for the King of England. You've given parades down in Halifax.... Tomorrow I won't have a job, so this parade is for me."[1]

This was an army of citizen soldiers. By 1918, it was also a Canadian army, with as many soldiers born in Canada as in Britain, and its ranks filled with soldiers who mostly came from cities, were mostly unmarried, who had only a grade-school education — and half of whom had never held a permanent job. Of the six hundred thousand men, and a few thousand women, who had put on Canadian and Imperial uniforms, 345,000 had served in France and Belgium, and more than one in six of those were dead. Most of the two hundred thousand wounded had been saved by modern

Canada, Patent and Copyright Office/ Library and Archives Canada PA-135768

Wounded Soldiers returning to Halifax aboard the HMT *Olympic*, 1919
Men whose disabilities range from mild to severe are happy to be coming home after a long ordeal, but they face an uncertain future.

medical science. But seventy thousand had injuries ranging from ghastly burns or mutilated faces to blown-off limbs, or, if they were lucky, a piece or two of shrapnel they would carry for the rest of their lives. And 10 percent of the wounded had been treated for "shell-shock" or neurasthenia.

Young men barely out of adolescence had learned to kill. They had endured cold, damp, trench foot, bronchial infections, lice, bad food, boredom, constant fatigue, and terror that defied every instinct of self-preservation and challenged all concepts of manliness. They had grown accustomed to their comrades talking to them one moment, then being obliterated by a shell the next; to masses of men being mowed down by machine guns; to men coughing up their lungs or ripping off their skin after a gas attack; to cowering helplessly in a dugout under earth-shaking, body-pounding shelling, unable to fight back or flee. They had developed a cold fatalism: Death would come if "your number was up," but hopefully to someone else. The sacred mission of the war had resolved into an intense camaraderie, their world compressed to their line of trench, the men of their company, the omnipresent mud and stench, the small pleasures to be savoured, the next battle to be fought.

Country lads had learned to drink, to swear, and to avail themselves of willing ladies in France and England. An astonishing sixty-six thousand soldiers contracted a venereal disease, including over eighteen thousand who had syphilis — unmentionable before the war but now requiring tests, treatments, and distribution of condoms. Day after day, their courage had been tested; and if it failed, the punishment was harsh, ranging from being labelled a malingerer to, in extreme cases, being one of the twenty-two soldiers shot for cowardice or desertion. They hated officers who sought glory by risking the lives of their men. But they respected those who had mastered the skills of war, shared their danger, and exercised wise discipline. Officers had their own demons — a gentleman's code, an appalling casualty rate, a fear of failure, the temptation of alcohol.[2]

They had been automatons in a war beyond their control or comprehension, fighting bravely and with increasing efficiency. They had "got the job done," but at a terrible price. "We were ... robbed of our boyhood," recalled one veteran, "plundered of our youth, and flung deliberately into a hellish testing furnace before we were old enough, many of us, to know the ordinary ways and pitfalls of a peacetime world."[3]

I

After November 11, there was one thing on which almost all these citizen soldiers agreed — they had no further business with the army. They wanted to go home, and at once. Families in Canada and dependents in Britain conveyed the same message in hundreds of letters and petitions. There was, wrote Acting Prime Minister White to Borden two weeks after the Armistice, "an extraordinary sentiment in Canada in favour of getting all our men home and at work as soon as possible."[4]

But the Armistice was only a truce. Who knew whether the Germans might regroup and fight again? The Allied leaders meeting in Paris were well aware that their power over events — including their ability to control Bolshevism and impose harsh terms on the Germans — would vanish when their armies went home. So the Canadian 1st and 2nd divisions were assigned to be part of a British army of occupation in the Rhineland.[5]

Many of these soldiers had bitter memories of what they had endured in the trenches and what they had seen in the villages they had liberated. But, as one observer reported, any desire they had to punish the Germans "died away into a sort of exasperated bewilderment" as they encountered a "mild and docile" civilian population. They were threatened with severe punishment for any looting or abuse of civilians — indeed, said Currie, they were under more restrictions than the Germans. "I am not going to try to make you believe," he wrote his minister, "that all our troops are Sunday-school lads. We have the foolish officer, who so far forgets himself as to get drunk, but those are very, very few indeed. We have too, the bad character, who meets the lone German in the dark and relieves him of his watch, but these cases are also negligible." The lads did get a bit rowdy at Christmas, and Cologne was declared off limits to Canadians; but Canadian officers saw this only as further evidence of British heavy-handedness.[6]

Currie established his headquarters in a palace belonging to the kaiser's family and delighted in sleeping in the emperor's bed. Soldiers billeted with German families played with the children, distributed food, and began to learn the language. "You can't lie very cold and distant," wrote James Endicott, "when some jolly old frau about five feet high and six feet broad, insists on going through your kit to see if your socks, etc., need mending and wants to know if you get lots to eat and that if you don't you must eat with her" — especially when two sons in the home, his own age, had been killed. Germany had committed crimes for which it would not soon be forgiven, he added, "but these people here have never heard of 'world power.'" "In a few weeks," wrote "Staff Officer" in the *University Magazine*, "a million English soldiers will have looked upon the Germans, and will be governed by what they see; and what they see is, — grave men, placid women who move in the streets as solemnly as a governess going to church, and little children with the pallid unwholesome face of hunger."[7]

For most Canadian soldiers, none of this was enough to overcome the boredom, rain, and endless hours of guard duty and drills. By late 1919, the Canadians were moving out of Germany. But the 3rd and 4th divisions quartered in Belgium and France had even less to do. Will Bird recalled that at least a third of his company were "out having fun, being entertained at little parties and dances," and NCOs reported them all present when officers called the roll. "To prevent us from thinking too much," wrote a soldier, "lectures on re-establishment, anti-bolshevism, agriculture, and other topics were delivered to the troops. Near the end of January the 'Dumbells'* put on their good entertainment.... The moving picture shows were open each evening."[8]

There was a fine balance between keeping men busy and imposing strict discipline — especially when this was done by inexperienced officers who had not shared the hardships of the Hundred Days. "The war was over," recalled Bird. "The men were not going to be treated like dogs while the officers had a gay old time." Bird was disgusted at being assigned to guard a prisoner who had been absent without leave — "he is no criminal but a Forty-Twa [Black Watch], the same as you and me, and a far better soldier than either of us. Because some pigeon brain has hysterics when a man doesn't come back on the due date, these men are used like dirt. I'll be proud to know them after we are demobilized, but I'll never have a thing to do with those who are responsible for them being called prisoners."[9]

Only experienced officers could keep order in such a situation. When it appeared his men would mutiny after headquarters ordered four hours of daily machine-gun drills, Claxton advised them to make "no catcalls; not a sound" when the colonel reviewed them, in the hope that he would give a "patriotic oration referring to 'Bolshevik influence,'" issue the order for drill, and then be persuaded to leave. Then, after each level of officers had left, the sergeant majors could march the men off to a "drill" that would never happen. "This was all very improper," he remembered, "but if it had not been handled someway [sic], there would have been a stubborn refusal, the calling in of other troops from neighbouring units and even possibly bloodshed and condign punishment for everyone." More perceptive than Claxton's superiors was General Elmsley, commander of the Canadian force in Vladivostok, who took Lieutenant Raymond Massey off other duties to stage music-hall shows for the men. "We're up against a situation that is

---

* A group of soldiers who entertained Canadian soldiers in the trenches in 1917 and 1918 with songs and sketches, who continued after the war as a vaudeville troupe until 1932.

tougher to handle than a fighting war," he told Massey. "That's five thousand men with nothing to do ... in this cesspool of a place."[10]

But few generals had Elmsley's resourcefulness or authority. There were frequent incidents of rowdiness, followed by court-martials, when Canadians were given orders they considered unreasonable, like wearing greatcoats in the pouring rain. At Nivelles in Belgium on December 17, men of the 7th Brigade protested Currie's order that soldiers march in steel helmets and full equipment, and the following day hundreds refused to march and interfered with soldiers who did. Currie downplayed the event and officials dismissed the unrest as the work of a few "socialistic" agitators; but over sixty soldiers were court-martialled and given sentences of up to five years.[11]

It was not that the authorities did not understand or sympathize. Planners had been considering demobilization since the middle of the war. Those in Ottawa wanted the most skilled men to come back first, to get the economy running so that there would be work for other returning soldiers. The Canadian General Staff had developed an elaborate plan to return the men to twenty-two dispersal areas in Canada. Thirteen documents had been prepared for each man to fill out before embarking — documents that in total contained 363 questions and required eighteen signatures. All of this was supposed to help the men fit smoothly into the many programs for rehabilitation, training, and employment that would be waiting for them on their return. Planners in London wanted the army broken up into drafts so they could be efficiently assembled and quickly transported. But General Currie wanted his men to return home in regiments, under their officers, to parade in triumph through their home towns — and if units were broken up and mixed together, he warned, "I would not care to answer for the discipline." Any soldier in the camps not wearing a brass hat had a much simpler answer — send the men who had been at the front the longest, and those with families, home first. In the end a compromise was reached — the major units of the Canadian Corps would return under their own officers; the balance would be dissolved into drafts based on locality and length of service. Married men would have priority.

But moving three hundred thousand people across the Atlantic, in winter, with dock strikes, influenza, and competition for shipping from the Americans and other Dominions, presented incredible logistical problems.

Halifax, devastated by the 1917 explosion, could not handle the largest ocean liners and the railways claimed they could only move twenty thousand men a month. To further complicate things, Currie insisted that instead of embarking from France, the Canadian Corps should go first to England to say goodbye to friends and relatives — so 125,000 Canadian troops had to be transported across the Channel and housed in England. To make things worse, the first, hastily organized transports to Canada in December 1918 proved disastrous. Returning soldiers on the liner *Northland* told reporters in Halifax of seasickness, bad meals, poor sanitation, decks reserved for officers and civilians while the men were held below, and a cold, hungry Christmas Day in quarantine — and three days later dependents on the *Scandinavian* had even worse tales to tell. The government responded to public outrage by imposing better living conditions on ships for Canadian soldiers than what the Australians and Americans required.[12]

So most of the men would have to stay, at least for a time, in England. Nine camps were established — two for men being brought from France and Belgium; one for soldiers with dependents; and the remainder for mixed drafts, convalescents, and others. Chaplains, physical education instructors, the Khaki University, the YMCA, and the Salvation Army did their best to keep the men occupied. Officials from Ottawa informed them of the programs that would be available to them on discharge and helped them fill out the paperwork. They would be grouped according to their dispersal point in Canada, have medical exams, and then be given two weeks' leave. That was the plan. But of course things quickly got snarled and men wound up waiting longer than they should have, in deteriorating and overcrowded camps, with increasingly mixed units, with rumours abounding, and the lure of "Tin Towns" where soldiers spent their pay on drink and were cheated at dice.

Currie's prediction proved accurate. Disturbances in November and December were sparked by mundane incidents like soldiers being insulted, cheated, or turned away from a dance. Graham Spry recalled that men at Buxton were paraded in full gear at four in the morning to prepare for boarding, stood in the rain for two hours, were lectured by a pompous colonel about how to behave when they got back to Canada, and were then dismissed when the colonel was handed a note saying the ship had engine trouble. That afternoon a newspaper reported that the ship had sailed with nine thousand Americans. "The lads just went mad.... They went … around roaring and whooping and drinking too much and the poor MPs had an awful time." In January, a gun battle (fortunately without injury) broke out among railway troops; soldiers beat up military police at another camp; at a third, soldiers raided a canteen and one man was killed.[13]

The worst flashpoint was at the large camp at Kinmel, near Rhyl in north Wales, the final assembly point for Canadian drafts awaiting transport from nearby Liverpool. By February, there were seventeen thousand men with forty-eight men sleeping in huts designed for thirty. It rained incessantly. Men were on half rations, with no coal for stoves, they had not been paid, and the officers were often absent in Rhyl. On March 4, a riot broke out after a rumour spread that other troops were embarking before their turn. Tin Town was looted, then the officers' quarters, then canteens and stores. After a night of rioting, the camp commander tried to quell the violence by cutting off the liquor supply. But soldiers continued to riot, settling scores with each other, attacking stores, firing shots. Eventually, other soldiers fired on the rioters. When it was all over, five were dead and twenty-five wounded.[14]

The gallant Canadians, once the darlings of the British establishment and warmly welcomed by the local population, were now a rowdy mob in the eyes of the British press. Military investigations, hampered by the fact that witnesses and some participants began to disappear as units were shipped out, meted out punishment. In April and May there were riots in other camps, and in June a fight at Epsom resulted in the death of a British police sergeant, a protest from the king, increasingly stern responses from the military command, and more arrests, court-martials, and prison sentences. British and Canadian authorities decided that it would be good to get rid of these men as quickly as possible, and shipping suddenly became available.[15]

Sailings increased from about fifteen thousand men in February to over forty-one thousand in March. After a lull in April, almost fifty thousand left in May and the camps began to close. By the end of the summer, most were home, except for the prisoners in British jails, almost all of whom were released by 1920. About twenty-two thousand Canadians elected to stay in England and slightly more Imperials went to Canada, along with British war brides and new dependents. "In all," according to Desmond Morton and Glenn Wright, "267,813 Canadian soldiers and 37,748 dependents crossed the Atlantic in the year after the Armistice."[16]

Life on a transport ship was hardly a bed of roses. Men were jammed below decks in hammocks; the air was foul with the odours of sweat and seasickness; reveille was still at 0600, and there were sick parades, inspections, and compulsory drills. But the food was usually good, the YMCA supplied amusements, paycheques were handed out, and soldiers could now begin to think about their new life. One soldier recalled that as the ship approached the harbour, a "great tear, the size of a pea, gathered in one of my eyes, rolled down to the end of my nose and splashed off onto the deck. My tough-fibred little corporal was standing beside me and saw it. He looked at me in surprise and then smiled. It was not a derisive smile."[17]

Most soldiers were landed at Pier 2 in Halifax, where they were given food and other gifts by YMCA volunteers. They were then loaded onto special trains, usually in units under their officers, for a journey of several days in colonist cars to their point of demobilization. By May, a thousand men an hour were being loaded, and as quickly as one train moved out another was brought in. For tens of thousands of British brides and children, long days on a crowded train rolling through an empty landscape in winter was their first experience of the country they had heard so glowingly described from so far away.[18]

The Princess Patricia's Canadian Light Infantry held its last parade in Ottawa on a March morning before a huge crowd with a speech by the governor general. Ethel Chadwick, an Ottawa diarist, noted the contrast between the returning soldiers and those who had so bravely left in 1914. The founder of the regiment now had one leg, only thirty-nine of the originals were left, and the flag made by Princess Patricia was "a shabby-looking rag now, but O how glorious." By ten in the morning every man had his railway ticket, papers, and a civilian suit of clothes. Lieutenant Colonel Agar Adamson, one of the few original officers, regretted the end of a long adventure and enjoyed several days of camaraderie with fellow officers. But by ten in the evening his men were all gone.[19]

The scene described by Claxton in Montreal was repeated all over Canada. The day after discharge, the men turned in their equipment (or not), got their back pay and service badge, the first instalment of their War Service Gratuity, the clothing allowance, and a transportation warrant if they had still farther to go. Officials of the Department of Soldiers' Civil Re-establishment provided information on pensions, soldier settlement, and employment offices, and a host of federal, provincial, and municipal agencies fell over each other to provide canteens and services to returning heroes. Discharges at Toronto were eight a minute by June.[20]

Thus, in the first months of 1919, Currie's grand army simply melted away.

II

What to do with them once they were home? Canada had never before raised a mass army of citizen soldiers. After previous wars, veterans and their families had generally been left to shift for themselves. That could not be allowed to happen his time.

At the outset of war, Patriotic Funds headed by prominent citizens and their wives had been established in every city and town. By 1916, they were brought together into a national organization, run by professionals and staffed by trained volunteers, with payments standardized by a government board. Class and rank still mattered — in 1917 the wife of an overseas private received a separation allowance of $20 a month while the wife of a lieutenant colonel got $60. The Patriotic Funds also exercised what they called the "Third Responsibility" of guardianship, which often meant in practice that middle-class volunteers monitored the welfare of wives and widows, checked up on their behaviour, and provided advice and instruction on how to manage their households, spend their income, and raise their children.[21]

Also in 1916, the treatment of wounded and disabled soldiers was wrested from the medical establishment (half the nation's doctors had joined the military), and folded into the new Department of Soldiers' Civil Re-establishment (DSCR), whose exceptional public servants combined administrative and technical expertise with willingness to experiment and co-operate with others. At Imperial army hospitals in England, doctors were breaking new ground in the creation of artificial limbs, the treatment of shell-shock, and the use of plastic surgery and prosthetics to give a semblance of normality to shattered faces. Canadian doctors contributed to this work and brought its lessons back home. Canada became a pioneer in orthopaedic research and surgery, plastic surgery, and the clinical treatment of gas burns, tuberculosis, and venereal disease. In Canada, the DSCR established hundreds of hospitals and convalescent facilities to provide specialized long-term treatment for wounded and disabled soldiers.

Not only was the treatment of disabled veterans a major issue, there was the question of how to return these men to society. The DSCR official in charge, Dr. J.L. Todd, firmly believed that getting them back into the labour force as quickly as possible would not only save money but speed their recovery. The DSCR worked with universities and schools, and with public and private agencies, to develop educational programs, train men, and find them work. Pearson House in Toronto, patterned after a British institution, was established for training of the blind. Some military hospitals were fitted up as sanatoriums for pneumonia and TB patients. A government factory manufactured state-of-the-art artificial limbs. Needless to say, there were many disputes and not a few hiccups. But the program largely achieved its objective of making disabled soldiers see themselves — and making Canadians see them — as productive members of society. By the end of 1919, only about eight thousand disabled veterans were still in hospital; by 1922, those who remained were only the relatively few sad cases who would need lifelong care.[22]

Governments, breaking new ground in taking responsibility for disabled soldiers and their families, knew that patronage, political interference, and favouritism — formerly taken for granted in any program run by the state — must now be avoided at all costs. Equally to be avoided was what a veterans' association called "the destruction or the weakening of the spirit of independence in our returned comrades." The Pensions and Claims Commission, established in 1916, hoped to apply "objective" criteria to determine why a soldier was disabled, how great the disability was, and whether he could provide for his family. It is hardly surprising that human beings were not always capable of "scientific objectivity." Was a person really injured or was he trying to sponge off the system? Were the increasing

Archives of Ontario C224-0-0-10-7 (C224-8)

Wounded soldiers en route to hospitals in England.
These men have some of the more terrible wounds, including burns and disfigurement, that doctors treated after the war — but they are alive.

number of men reporting that they could not focus, concentrate, or control their behaviour casualties of war or victims of their own lack of moral fibre? And why was a brigadier's eye worth six times as much as a private's? The families of disabled soldiers who depended on a pension — up to $300 a year, plus allowances for children — found themselves under constant bureaucratic scrutiny and "visitation." Most men did not get the full pension, and many proud veterans did not make a claim — at least not at first.[23]

Widows usually had no option but to accept the guardianship of the commission. They lost their pensions if an inspector found they were cohabiting, bootlegging, or had become prostitutes, or if they remarried (though they got one year's payment as a dowry). It took time for commissioners to recognize that widows inherited their husbands' responsibility to look after aging parents. Children's entitlements ended at age sixteen for boys and seventeen for girls unless they were physically or mentally infirm or making "satisfactory progress in a course of instruction approved by the [c]ommission" — usually technical or domestic education. In 1919, a parliamentary committee under N.W. Rowell recommended that the widows of all ranks up to lieutenant receive $720 a year, which was increased to $900 the following year (plus allowances for children and a cost-of-living bonus) — and it debated for two days whether pensions should be paid to "unmarried wives." By the end of 1920, 177,035 men, women, and children were receiving pension cheques.[24]

Even more daunting was the challenge of reintegrating hundreds of thousands of returned men into the world of work. As late as 1917 a special committee of Parliament had complacently reported that "a new country like Canada, with vast unexplored natural resources, which we all believe will be developed after the termination of this Great War, contains countless opportunities for ambitious men to win their way." But in the fall of 1918, with two hundred thousand people suddenly thrown out of work as munitions factories closed, and another three hundred thousand men due to return within weeks, the government recognized the need for urgent action. A Repatriation Committee was established under Minister of Immigration J.A. Calder, directed by Ottawa businessman Herbert J. Daly and his assistant Lieutenant Colonel Vincent Massey, with Cabinet ministers and government officials advised by representatives of business, labour, women's groups, veterans groups, and municipalities. "It can hardly be expected," the committee warned,

> that the natural processes of industry, guided only by the somewhat wayward compass of public demand, will secure the immediate reabsorption of the thousands of men and women whom the war caught up out of their former trades and scattered into new and temporary occupations. But Canadian industry is extremely adaptable, and with careful planning on the part of Governmental agencies and sympathetic co-operation from all classes of the public, it is hoped that the extent of unemployment and the length of the period of dislocation will be reduced to a minimum.

A federal-provincial conference in November 1918 discussed housing, technical education, highways, resettlement, employment, training, and a range of other issues which would require co-operation between both levels of government, and during the following year legislation was passed providing federal funding in all these areas.[25]

On December 18, 1918, the government announced a War Service Gratuity of six months' pay at $70 a month for a private who had served overseas for three or more years ($100 if he was married), with lesser amounts for shorter service or service in Canada. Besides back pay, soldiers would also get a range of other allowances and services, including a year's free medical care. Twenty-five million dollars was loaned to the provinces for housing, and the provinces were assisted to develop employment bureaus. The DSCR established an information bureau and an employment bureau, with offices in eighty-nine towns and cities, to encourage businesses to hire veterans and to match men with jobs. The DSCR later claimed that they had placed over twenty-two thousand men twice, and that some two hundred had found ten or more positions! The training program for disabled soldiers had by 1922 provided courses to over fifty thousand veterans. For those who could not find work, the government voted $40 million for emergency relief in the winter of 1919–20. Since there was no unemployment insurance system, the Patriotic Fund, whose life had been extended in June 1919 by Parliament, was remobilized at Christmas 1919 to identify recipients and distribute funds — up to $50 for a single man and $100 for a large family.[26]

The great hope, and an enduring myth among veterans and politicians alike, was that returning soldiers could be settled on the land. The aim, Minister of the Interior Arthur Meighen told the House in April, was "to make settlers of those who have proven themselves the backbone and stay of the nation in its trouble," to "fortify the country against the waves of unrest and discontent that now assail us," and to strengthen "the basic class — the agricultural class … the best blood and bones of our nation." Ontario set aside lands cleared by internees in the clay belt near Kapuskasing, with experimental farms, roads, and infrastructure. British Columbia drained marshes in the lower Fraser Valley and assembled land around Osoyoos. In January 1919, Meighen established a Soldier Settlement Board and in April his department identified 144,000 acres of "unused" lands on the

Prairies, including First Nations and Doukhobor land, for allocation by the board. Soldiers would pay a down payment of 19 percent with the balance payable in twenty-five annual instalments at 5 percent interest. Loans of up to $1,000 for improvements were available as well as free building plans, training, and advice. For soldiers buying an existing farm, there were loans for land, stock, equipment, and buildings. By the end of 1919, the board had provided $51.6 million in credit to 17,218 soldiers.[27]

If experience and not myth had guided public policy, the dangers of this plan would have been obvious. Local committees established by the board did ensure that the land was good value and that the farmer was fit to work it, and they often suggested that soldiers get experience as a hired hand or at an agricultural college. They turned down most war widows, nursing sisters, and older or disabled men. Nonetheless, thousands of soldiers bought land and quickly fell into debt — as indeed did all other farmers — buying expensive equipment and still trying to learn farming when prices collapsed in 1921. "Nobody could ever make a living on them," recalled one farm wife of small holdings in the B.C. interior, "but in their ignorance they thought they could." The Ontario government had to resettle all but one of the vets in Kapuskasing. Many soldiers who had farming experience made a go of it, but one-fifth of the almost twenty-five thousand soldier-settlers had abandoned their land by 1923, and almost half by 1930. Most of the $100 million spent on the program went down the drain.[28]

The services available to the soldiers when they got off the troop trains, and the mechanisms created to care for disabled soldiers, widows, and families, were remarkable for a country with no experience in running a welfare state and with a history of political patronage and federal-provincial squabbling. The pensions were generous compared with other countries. But their enormous cost ballooned the already massive war debt. This was a cost that had to be paid, wrote journalist Sir John Willison in November 1919, "with grace and gratitude." Canadians would simply have to "work harder, spend less, submit to taxation with equanimity," if the soldiers were "not to go through life handicapped and penalized for heroic services to the State which they defended." "We are told very often," Willison concluded, "that we must have patience with the soldiers. Sometimes perhaps the soldiers feel that they must have patience with us."[29]

III

"We had come back with the idea of starting in where we had left off, and carrying on from there," recalled veteran Norman James. "Unfortunately, the place we had left off wasn't there anymore. We were in a new Canada, and we didn't know our way around, and we didn't know whether we liked it or not."[30]

Men who for long months had dreamed of romantic reunions ("I will take you in my arms and you will put your arms around my neck and I will hold you very tight and look into your eyes ... and I will put my lips to yours and close my eyes and I will stay like that") now faced the traumatic reality of meeting a partial stranger. Gordon Robertson, returning after two painful years in hospital, spent a horrible first night on a troop train as his squalling son, born after his departure, competed for his wife's attention. Wives had become independent, some had endured poverty, some had been unfaithful. Others learned with shock that their man had strayed from the straight and narrow — perhaps even picked up a "packet" — over there. The problem of trying to fit this new reality into the conventions of courtship and marital behaviour accepted in those innocent days before the war was one many faced.[31]

Families were unsettled when their young lad returned as a man who was sometimes loud, sometimes withdrawn, who sometimes drank too much, and often seemed to prefer the profane company of other veterans. Nellie McClung found her beloved son "silent, with a strange tension in his young face.... I knew there was a wound in his heart — a sore place. That hurt look in his clear blue eyes tore at my heart strings and I did not know what to do." Frank Pegahmagabow, the most-decorated First Nations soldier, would flee into the bush during thunderstorms. Veterans woke up screaming, were startled at loud noises or whistles, found themselves trembling, unable to concentrate, suffered flashbacks and bouts of violence and depression. "I never unfroze fully," recalled a soldier who went back to university. "The horror of the war was in the background of my mind, although it was suppressed.... At the time I wasn't so clearly aware that I was suppressing these things."[32]

Canadians — and pension boards — had no idea what post-traumatic stress disorder was. Most could accept "shell-shock" as a legitimate condition resulting from concussion or traumatic injury. But for the vast majority of men who could not prove such a causal relationship, authorities often wondered if their inability to settle down, to hold a job, to keep out of trouble, was simply a sign that they had always been predisposed to unmanly behaviour, or that they wanted a pension because they could not find work. "Shell-shock" spurred advances in psychiatric understanding and care, and some prominent psychiatrists stepped in to rescue men who were being mistreated in ordinary hospitals. But for the vast majority of men having to submit claims to pension boards as they got older and symptoms recurred, there was often little understanding or sympathy.[33]

Some soldiers had jobs to go back to, or at least some idea what they wanted to do. But for many, recalled a vet, "the army experience was no good for them. They had no job, no experience, so they had to start at the bottom." Raymond Massey had served five years in the artillery, had been treated for shell-shock, had pulled strings to go to Vladivostok, and had then spent two years at Oxford. On his return, he found that the best he could hope for in his family's company was $30 a week after five years — less than his pay as a lieutenant. "While you were in the army and fiddling away at Oxford," said his crusty boss, "other men have been learning this business and they are going to have the responsible jobs and the pay raises. Before you!"[34]

"I could not at once make up my mind what to do," recalled Pierre Van Passen. "As a matter of fact, I cared very little as to what was going to happen.... Faces and voices of old acquaintances looked and sounded familiar, and yet we did not understand each other. Something had come between us. Friends wanted to hear stories of the battlefield, experiences, heroism, and you felt like vomiting when the subject was mentioned." French Canadians and members of minority groups who had made friends among English-speaking soldiers overseas, women who had faced danger and experienced responsibility, boys now grown into men, returned to a narrow and stultifying life. "I hated to leave the army, the crowd," recalled a vet. "I was just as lonesome as could be, because for so long you had always been with the gang, day and night. Come what may, bad or good, you always had your gang around you." Some came back "burned-out wrecks, pos-sessed only of tragic disillusioned minds and broken bodies;" others "just became what you call old soldiers, old bums. They never did settle down. They hung around, spent all their war gratuities, and they bartered." By late 1919, many employers were reluctant to hire returned soldiers, believing they were likely to quit soon after, or, if they stayed on, that they would drink too much or would have to be fired for some other reason when they could not accept the discipline of a job. Veterans in turn believed employers were prejudiced against them.[35]

Restlessness sometimes manifested itself in more violent ways. In Win-nipeg on January 26, 1919, a mob of soldiers attacked an outdoor socialist meeting, wrecked the Socialist Party of Canada headquarters, and trashed nearby restaurants owned by "foreigners." In Winnipeg, Hamilton, Toron-to, Vancouver, Calgary, and Edmonton, veterans rioted that spring, beating up "foreigners" or "slackers," breaking windows, attacking anything that symbolized their frustrations and fears, threatening reprisals if their de-mands were not met. Most tragic of all was Filip Konowal, a Ukrainian-Canadian Victoria Cross winner, who was arrested after leading Ottawa's Peace Day parade in July 1919 for murdering a man in Hull. He was found not guilty by reason of insanity and was institutionalized for seven years.[36]

There were more constructive ways for returned soldiers to make their voices heard and their power felt. In April 1917, delegates (who called each other "comrade") had assembled in Winnipeg to form the Great War Vet-erans' Association (GWVA). Led by twenty-six-year-old wounded machine gunner Grant MacNeil, they had demanded a pension of $1,200 a year (to be equal for officers and men), better treatment by the Pensions Board, a better discharge gratuity, a burial fund, land for veterans, conscription (of men and of wealth), more government control of vital industries, and action against "foreigners." They were careful to portray themselves not as "a collection of disgruntled, dissatisfied, unhappy men," but as an "orderly gathering of returned soldiers, seeking again to become civilians, hoping that we may yet be allowed to serve our country in a civilian capacity as truly as we tried to do when we proudly wore our khaki." Such a relatively moderate veterans' organization had its uses, and some police forces gave the names of rowdy ex-soldiers to the GWVA rather than turning them over for prosecution. But the GWVA limited its membership to soldiers who had crossed the Atlantic, and rival organizations thus sprang up.[37]

By the end of the war, soldiers were, like the rest of the population, becoming increasingly militant in demanding that the promises they believed had been made to them be kept. In February 1919, a veterans' assembly adopted the Calgary Resolution, which demanded a bonus of up to $2,000 for each man who had served at the front, with lesser amounts for those who had served in England or at home. MacNeil and the GWVA leadership knew that such a bonus would cost at least a billion dollars and would only exacerbate the problems of veterans. But when the GWVA met in convention in July, it was clear, as one member put it, that if they did not support the bonus, "I might as well go out to the bughouse here. It would not be safe for me to go back." The Association therefore demanded a graduated bonus based on the needs of soldiers and the country's ability to pay, coupled with resolutions attacking Bolshevism and pledging to uphold the constitutional order. Over the next two months, its leaders tried to convince senior cabinet ministers that accepting this moderate position would head off more radical demands. On August 27, Borden delivered the government's final answer: "No."[38]

Predictably, the bonus campaign then passed to more radical hands. "Let us put a peaceful demand, and if it is not answered, I say let us take it by force," cried J. Harry Flynn at a Toronto rally on September 7. Rallies in Hamilton, Winnipeg, Montreal, and elsewhere dispatched telegrams to Ottawa. During the special session of Parliament in September 1919, a parliamentary committee under J.A. Calder, which included several ex-soldier MPs, heard testimony for almost two months from pensioners, soldiers' wives, veterans groups, and officials. The GWVA tried to recapture the initiative by revealing Flynn's questionable background and offering its own proposal for a bonus that would be delivered through a partnership between the GWVA and government. Debates were heated and the committee was sympathetic, but it could not evade the reality that such a bonus would cost two-thirds as much as the war itself. Finance Minister White said the government would resign rather than agree. Most MPs then backed off. Bonus agitation continued into 1920, with some support from populist politicians like Toronto mayor Tommy Church. The Liberal Party made vague promises of a bonus in its 1919 platform, but once in office made no effort fulfil them.[39]

Somehow, most returned soldiers settled into something like a normal life in 1919 and 1920. For the majority, the period of restlessness proved temporary. Most men simply wanted to "throw it off and get back to their way of life and get married and get a good job — that's the main thing — and forget about it." "We are home among familiar faces and amid our own people," said another, "and we thank God for that, and we want to forget as soon as possible the beastliness of war." Others, especially farm boys, had reported on their questionnaires that they did not want to return to their old jobs, and they now had the opportunity to start a new life. Raymond Massey left for London to start an acting career that would make him a star of stage, cinema, and television; Bird, a Nova Scotia lad with little education, failed at running a general store before he became a successful journalist and novelist. Van Passen became an internationally renowned war correspondent and peace activist. Young McClung, Spry, and many others sought further education and went on to distinguished professional careers. Claxton became a leading member of the "nationalist network" in the 1920s,* and as a cabinet minister between 1944 and 1954 was an architect of the modern social welfare system and the Canadian military in the nuclear age.[40]

No one can ever really know the anguish of the families whose men would never return, for whom the language of heroism and sacrifice was increasingly inadequate to compensate for their loss or suppress their growing doubts about what the war had achieved. Or measure the stress of living, day in and day out, with a young man damaged by the war. Or share the struggle of the twenty thousand widows who in 1925 were supporting themselves, children, and aged parents on pension cheques. But families coped, as they always had. "Romance," says historian Dan Azoulay, "may have been a casualty of the Great War, but the patient seems to have recovered quite quickly." Long-deferred weddings were celebrated, fiancés resumed their courtship, single men found wives, settled down, raised children and grandchildren, and saw their legacy live on. In the end, what Cynthia Comacchio has called the "infinite bonds of family," more than

---

* See Chapter 11.

any government policy or program, allowed the heroes to return, to find stable lives, to begin to heal.[41]

IV

Newspapers, magazines, lecture halls, and theatres were full of stories about the war in the early months of 1919. Men in uniform were everywhere. Andrew Macphail's collection of John McCrae's poems, *In Flanders Fields*, topped the bestseller lists, as did two war novels by Ralph Connor. There were regimental histories and records of the contributions of provinces, cities, and companies. There were dedications of war memorials, German artillery pieces in public parks, lists of the fallen illuminated by leading artists, and commemorative windows in churches. Monuments portrayed romantic images of sacrifice, like the statue in the CPR's Windsor Station in Montreal that shows a winged angel carrying a dying soldier to glory.[42]

July 19, 1919, was designated Peace Day, to mark the signing of the Treaty of Versailles three weeks earlier. Three-quarters of Vancouver's population turned out and there was a two-mile-long parade in Saskatoon. In August, Toronto's Canadian National Exhibition featured the Prince of Wales, war heroes like Billy Bishop, simulated aerial dogfights and sanitized depictions of trench warfare, and displays showing the treatment of wounded soldiers and the opportunities for returning vets. The Canadian War Artists exhibition, which had won rave reviews in London and New York, opened in Toronto that summer.[43]

At eleven o'clock on November 11, 1919, at the request of the king, all British subjects observed two minutes' silence. In Toronto, traffic came to a halt; and there was a deep silence, followed by the noise of sirens, whistles, and bells, a parade of tanks, a flypast of planes, and a celebration with military bands and fireworks. Two years later, Remembrance Day became an annual event and the poppy was introduced world-wide as a symbol of remembrance, which also provided revenue for disabled veterans.[44]

But the mood was already beginning to change. Soldiers who returned late in 1919 found no welcoming parades and few men in uniform. The war art collection was packed up after showings in Toronto and Montreal and would remain in storage for decades. By 1921, when sales of L.M. Montgomery's *Rilla of Ingleside* fell below expectations, it was clear that romantic stories about the war were becoming passé.

Sir Arthur Currie came home in August 1919. He was met by a few junior dignitaries in Halifax and given a low-key reception at city hall. There was a bigger crowd when he arrived in Ottawa, but the response to his address to Parliament was restrained. He was promoted to full general and made inspector-general of the Canadian army, but Cabinet, faced with the veterans' demand for a bonus, made no special award like the £100,000 given by the British government to General Haig. Currie had never been popular with his men. Though he cared for them deeply, his aloof manner and his pudgy appearance had attracted their ridicule when they did not excite their hostility.[45]

Worse, he had a bitter enemy in an aging Sam Hughes, who had vowed to get even when Currie had refused to appoint his son to command a division. On March 4, 1919, Hughes ranted to an embarrassed House of Commons that if he had been in charge, "the officer who, four hours before the Armistice was signed ... ordered the attack on Mons thus needlessly sacrificing the lives of Canadian soldiers, would be tried summarily by court martial and punished so far as the law would allow." An exhausted Currie could not publicly fight back, and although a few generals and MPs did, no one from the government defended him. An old charge of embezzlement hung over Currie, and who knew what Hughes might know, or say? In 1920, Currie was appointed principal of McGill University. But the Hughes allegations, which quickly ran through the army, convalescent hospitals, and veterans' organizations, fuelled a growing suspicion that there would have been fewer fallen heroes if there had been fewer incompetent officers and vainglorious generals.[46]

Currie had wanted to establish a permanent army of twenty thousand men, backed by a militia of three hundred thousand. There were also calls for a Canadian navy and air force. Admiral Lord Jellicoe, the British naval hero, toured Canada in November 1919 to encourage support for a new Canadian navy within an Imperial fleet. Britain made a $5 million gift of surplus aircraft, and an Air Board was established in June 1919, which became the Canadian Air Force the following year (the designation "Royal" was added in 1924). Canada would now have three full armed services. But what war were they preparing for? "The people of this country do not propose to submit to the god of militarism," wrote the *Farmers' Sun*, the voice of the United Farmers of Ontario. "We have just fought a five years' war to make wars to cease." The government had no answer to the firm conviction among war-weary Canadians, including the veterans, that their sacrifice had bought, if nothing else, the gift of lasting peace.[47]

Any remaining enthusiasm for military spending quickly vanished in the face of the staggering cost of the war and the escalating costs of veterans' resettlement and pensions. In the midst of labour unrest in 1919, the government briefly tried to increase the permanent militia to ten thousand, but it was soon slashing militia estimates, and it continued to do so for the next several years. The naval estimates were also attacked in Parliament. When cabinet rejected even his scaled-down naval plan in 1920, the responsible minister threatened to abolish the navy altogether. The air force was almost eliminated in the budget cutting of the 1920s. During the next two decades, only a few thousand weekend warriors and a small group of professional officers (some with staff training at British military colleges) kept alive the Canadian military tradition.[48]

Enthusiasm for veterans' associations also faded as returned soldiers enjoyed a brief period of prosperity, fuelled by pent-up demand and the assistance provided them by all levels of government. The GWVA had been seriously weakened by the "bonus" campaign. Rivalries between different veterans' groups and infighting among their leaders prevented efforts to unite them. Then it was discovered that there was $2 million left in Canada's share of the Imperial army's Canteen Fund. British General Haig and Canadian senior officers began to press for one organization for all veterans, all services, all ranks, which could take charge of this money as well as the revenue from the sale of poppies, provide halls for fellowship, and represent their interests. In 1925, the Canadian Legion was born, with Currie as one of the honorary presidents, with an executive heavy with officers, and with none of the militant democracy of postwar veterans' organizations.[49]

As it turned out, veterans would need these champions. The postwar economic boom collapsed in late 1920. By Thanksgiving of 1921 vets in Toronto were parading with signs asking what they had to be thankful for. Physical and mental disabilities flared up and became chronic as men aged — the forty-three thousand men receiving disability pensions in 1919 became almost seventy-eight thousand by 1933. In 1924, the King government established the Ralston Commission, which took a humane look at the pension system and recommended remedies for obvious grievances. But it was abundantly clear that not only did there have to be some control on the cost of pensions, but they could never really compensate men for what they had lost, or their families for what they had suffered.[50]

Most veterans never abandoned their belief that the war had been just. The disillusionment they felt by the late 1920s was less with the war than with a peace that had not fulfilled its promise. "The Mayor has told us that the people of Canada are looking to us to straighten things out and start the 'New Order' in Canada," Norman James told a crowd that had gathered to welcome him home. "Candidly, friends, we wish you wouldn't do that. To begin with, we're a bit tired, and perhaps a bit disillusioned, and don't feel quite up to the job. And then, to be frank with you, we were hoping that YOU would do something about that while we were away." As Currie wrote just before his death in 1933: "Has the great sacrifice really turned to glory, the glory of a better time? Has the world done anything more in these fifteen years than give lip-service to the ideals for which our fallen comrades gave their lives?"[51]

By the mid-1920s, the public imagery and symbolism of sacrifice was becoming less religious and romantic and more national and secular. Glory and heroism were replaced by ineffable sorrow. The Vimy Memorial, planned in the mid 1920s but not completed until 1936, is awesome in its solemn simplicity, with its allegorical figure of Canada mourning her lost sons. The Commonwealth Cemeteries on the battlefields of Europe were beautifully designed and landscaped with simple headstones symmetrically arranged, identical for officers and men. The only religious symbol was the inverted sword embedded in a cross that dominates each cemetery, with an inscription suggested by Rudyard Kipling, "Their Name Liveth for Evermore." They were conceived as places of profound peace and reflection, "silent cities" in the words of British poet Edmund Blunden, where "the dead speak yet through the achievement of beauty."[52]

Photograph by Carolyn Bowler

Commonwealth War Graves at Tyne Cot, Belgium, near Passchendaele.
The wall around the outside of the cemetery lists the thousands of names of soldiers in Imperial forces who died in the Ypres Salient in 1917 and 1918. More than half have no known graves.

War memoirs in the 1920s portrayed the reality of war in spare prose that was the opposite of the "high diction" of earlier accounts — but they still reaffirmed the ideals for which the war had been fought and the heroism of the men. In *The Great War as I Saw It* (1922), Canon F.G. Scott does not shrink from describing horror and death, and his search for his son's body is deeply moving. His faith is severely shaken when he has to act as chaplain to a soldier who is shot for desertion, but he insists that it was the shirker at home and not this brave volunteer who should have been in front of the firing squad. James Pedley and W.B. Kerr, writing in 1930, were less restrained in portraying the seamier side of army life, in questioning the wisdom of officers, and documenting the waste and suffering of war. But though Kerr describes Passchendaele in stark detail, he points out that unlike some British troops, "we were as resolved as ever to carry the war to a victorious conclusion, as confident as before in what we considered our own strength, our initiative and tenacity, as unshaken in our determination to continue the task which we had assumed for the sake of the world until that task should be accomplished."[53]

The appearance during the late 1920s of memoirs of generals and politicians, the publication of the German diplomatic documents, and a well-publicized libel suit brought by Currie in 1928 against a newspaper that revived the Hughes accusations, revealed more details about why the war had happened and how it was fought. A wave of novels in 1929 — notably Erich Maria Remarque's *All Quiet on the Western Front*, Robert Graves's *Goodbye to All That*, and Ernest Hemingway's *A Farewell to Arms*, along with more nihilistic works like Jaroslav Hašek's *The Good Soldier Schweik* (translated in 1930) — portrayed the horror of the war with none of its glory, and depicted its ideals as hollow, its sacrifice as butchery, its soldiers as helpless victims.

A few Canadian authors copied this "realistic" style and embraced this theme. Most notable was Charles Yale Harrison's *Generals Die in Bed* (1930), whose hammer-blow prose was the antithesis of high diction. His narrative depicting Canadian soldiers as brutal, emotionally atrophied, destroyed by the war, who sack Amiens, murder prisoners, and commit atrocities, was a conscious attack on everything previous writers had held to be of value. An American by birth who had served with the Canadian forces, Harrison claimed to have seen what he portrayed. He was lauded by American critics but drew a storm of criticism from Canadian veterans and the public. To Currie he was a cheap sensationalist and his book "a mass of filth and lies" that "appeals to everything base and mean and nasty."[54]

Only those who were there, veterans argued, could fully comprehend what had really happened. Will Bird had indeed been there. His 1930 memoir, *And We Go On*, recounts in unpolished, riveting prose, the killing and dying, the snipers and trench raids, the terrible battles such as Passchendaele, the blessed moments behind the lines, the comradeship with often doomed friends, the sudden acts of violence and equally unforeseen acts of mercy, and the miracle of survival almost by accident. The men do their duty, however much they might complain. There is a moral code — you respect courage and the endurance of those who have shared your ordeal — and there is a rough sense of justice. The men look after their comrades and remember the good times, the soft bunks and good meals, the outsmarting of the system.[55]

In the 1930s, Bird wrote regular magazine columns that chronicled the experience of veterans, advocated their causes, and acted as a sounding board for their views. In a 1933 column, he reprinted an item from the *London Evening News* that he believed also expressed the feelings of Canadian veterans. Veterans, it read, "cannot, even among themselves, tell the whole truth" about the war. They had been, against every decent instinct, "forced to take part in a monstrous crime against their own humanity." Now they were "the lonely ghosts of a vanished generation." They would "believe no promises, accept no excuses, listen to no arguments. They have seen war, and seen through it. For that reason, if for no other, they are worth cherishing." Bird added that if leaders had "one-half the fellowship of the trenches in their souls there would be no more wars, no preparing for them, and a prosperity beyond our dreams. The 'spirit of the trenches' was a priceless potion."[56]

Bird spoke for his comrades and for his country as the Great Depression, renewed conflict in Europe and around the world, and disillusionment with the peace, took their toll. The title of his memoir said it all: *And We Go On.* That is what the thousands of soldiers caught in the maelstrom had done during the war. That is what they and their families did as they adjusted to peace. They went on.

CHAPTER 4

A Visit from the Spanish Lady

Arthur Lapointe, a soldier in the 22nd Regiment near Arras, France, felt very strange on the morning of June 30, 1918. As he recalled in his memoirs, "my head swims with sudden nausea, everything around me whirls, I totter, then fainting, fall headlong to the ground ... my head feels as though a vice were squeezing it and my heart is pounding painfully." Lapointe went to bed for two days. On the third, he drank two bowls of milk scrounged by a friend. On the fifth day, he received the welcome news that he was being sent to England for officer training. Then, on November 2, in London, he was stricken with headaches, joint pain, and severe indigestion, which the medical officer attributed to the effects of rheumatism and poison gas. As crowds celebrated the Armistice, Lapointe wrote he was "too sick to get out of bed. A nurse brings me a sedative and I drink it, hoping it will ease the racking pain."[1]

Recovery took longer this time. At the end of November, he received news that a brother back home was ill. His sister appeared to him in a dream. Dressed in mourning, she led him to the graves of his brothers and sisters. She, too, was dead, "but God in his mercy has allowed me to spend this day with you." When he arrived home in February 1919, he learned that three brothers and two sisters had died of the flu. He had planned to return in triumph as an officer in the only French-Canadian regiment in the Canadian Corps. Now, God had punished his pride and his life would be "an empty mockery." "Dear God, if it was only for this I came home, why did I not fall in action out there? Many are sleeping to-day in France, who would have been so happy to come home."[2]

Glenbow Archives NA-3452.2

Telephone workers in High River, Alberta wearing masks during the influenza epidemic
Pictures like these illustrate the fear influenza generated, as well as some faith that science could stop its spread, and a sense of camaraderie and dedication as each person did their bit to fight it.

"During the past year," said a Saskatoon clergyman in October 1918, "large demands have been made on our courage.... We have had war, partial crop failure and today we are in the middle of pestilence." This was "the Spanish Lady," the killer flu. In the fall of 1918, it killed at least fifty thousand Canadians, many of them men and women in the prime of life, and it brought suffering and tragedy to many thousands more.[3]

I

Lapointe had fallen victim to a new type of influenza that broke out among the Allied armies in the spring of 1918. It brought a high fever, severe ache, and prostration for three to five days. It temporarily incapacitated over two hundred thousand soldiers in the British Expeditionary Force. It jumped the trenches to the German side and may have contributed to the failure of their spring offensive. There was also an outbreak in Canada among soldiers and the civilian population. It was taken seriously by medical specialists, but, because few people died and most cases were never reported, it got lost among the many other crises competing for the attention of the authorities and the public.[4]

Sometime during the summer of 1918, this new flu turned into a killer. In mid-August, American troops were struck down in huge numbers in Brest, France, and there were simultaneous outbreaks in Sierra Leone and in Boston. Within days, it had made rapid advances into the American army in France, into West Africa, and into the eastern United States. Camp Devens near Boston, filled to bursting with forty-five thousand men awaiting transport to France, was a perfect incubator for what was becoming known as the Spanish influenza, and the military transport system was an ideal transmission belt into other military camps and surrounding cities. By October, influenza raged in every American city, and in that month alone it claimed 195,000 lives.

After ravaging American camps in France, it crossed to the German army, but fortunately it did not strike the British armies until just before the Armistice. When it did, thousands of young men waiting to go home were added to the long lists of war dead. A Canadian officer wrote in his diary: "I was detailed for burial duty as three of our men had died from the flu in hospital. It was very distressing. The hospital people told me ten men had died that morning and were buried quickly as infection spread rapidly. 'Last Post' was sounded almost all day long." Will Bird was enjoying his final leave in London when his best friend Tommy, who had shared his long ordeal in the trenches, suddenly became ill and went to the hospital. By the next day Tommy was dead. "The world crashed around me. It was dark when I found myself back at the quarters we had shared, and midnight before I stopped pacing the room. But there was simply nothing I could do."[5]

Within the next three months, an estimated one-third of the world's population was infected and as many as fifty to one hundred million may have died. In Africa, whole villages were wiped out and bodies went unburied. Aboriginal peoples in the Americas were decimated as were parts of India and China. Only isolated islands and remote populations escaped.

Most of those who contracted the flu in the fall of 1918 suffered no worse symptoms than those of the spring. But for 10 to 20 percent of people, the experience was far worse. Flu epidemics have always claimed small children and old people, but in 1918 this statistical U-curve became a "W" as the death rate was highest for those between fifteen and forty-five, peaking at thirty-two. Healthy, fit people died within hours, some literally dropping dead on the street. Blood pressure dropped, the pulse slowed, circulation failed. Victims coughed up pints of green and yellow pus and spat blood as they drowned from within. Their skin turned blue-black and they emitted a foul odour. In some cases, they suffered hallucinations or went psychotic. Many who survived the initial infection fell victim to pneumonia and other secondary infections — a death more lingering but no less horrible, usually coming on about the tenth day.

In major cities, the epidemic lasted four to six weeks. By the third week, isolation wards overflowed, hospitals were swamped, and makeshift hospitals were treating desperately ill people in scenes from Dante's *Inferno*. Then it tailed off gradually, and in most cities it was over by December. Another wave struck in the winter and spring of 1919, with death tolls that would have been serious by any standard other than the one that had preceded it. But, though people like Lapointe who had caught flu in the spring of 1918 could become ill again in the fall epidemic, those who had been ill in the fall escaped further illness. After a minor recurrence in 1920, the killer flu simply went away.[6]

Influenza is caused by a virus, variants of which attack humans, birds, pigs, and other animals. The flu virus consists of five or six strands of RNA — a primitive form of genetic coding — encased in an armour of protein and fat, and its sole purpose is to replicate itself. Two proteins, hemagglutinin (H) and neuraminidase (N), protrude in large numbers from the surface of each virus. There are fourteen H subtypes and nine N subtypes, which are "keys" that allow entry to specific cells. Whether it will attack a pig or a person is determined by its variant (A, B, or C), and which subtype of each protein it has (H1N1, H2N1, et cetera). In humans, the H proteins bind to sialic acid receptors in the cells of the nose and throat, then the viral RNA enters the cells and hijacks the cells' genetic material to force them to produce copies of the virus. Within about ten hours, an infected cell explodes and spews millions of new viruses into the bloodstream. The N protein keeps the virus from being trapped like flies on flypaper on the sialic acids released from the doomed cells. The virus is now free to invade thousands, then millions, of healthy cells in the lungs. The victim begins to feel ill and the body begins to fight back.

Dying cells send chemical cries for help, called cytokines, which trigger responses such as fever, fluid secretion, and elevated heart rate. Specialist cells in the bloodstream identify the foreign invaders, chop them up, and send information to the spleen, which begins to manufacture proteins called antibodies, which bind to the virus and destroy it. The H and N proteins now become the signature, or "antigen," which the antibodies recognize and attack. A struggle begins within each human body as desperate as any battle on the Western Front. If the antibodies get the upper hand, the patient will recover. If the virus overwhelms the body's defences, the patient will die. In any case, the victim spreads the virus in breath and bodily fluids, which can then infect others.

If the host recovers, the virus will not get a second chance to reinfect them. Specialized cells will "remember" its antigen signature and will quickly stimulate production of antibodies if there is any similar invasion in the future. This "immune reaction" means that most viruses, after an initial pandemic, either die out or become "enzootic," living relatively harmlessly within a host population whose "herd immunity" can be inherited. That is the secret of vaccines — they are created from cultures of a killed, weakened, or similar but harmless virus, and cause the body to develop an immune reaction in advance of any actual infection.

But influenza is a tricky virus. It attacks quickly, spreads easily, does not kill its hosts *en masse*, and combats "herd immunity" through regular subtle changes in its HN "signature." As the virus replicates itself billions of times, errors creep in — usually fatal to the virus, but occasionally just different enough to produce a new "signature" that is not recognized by the immune system. This process is called "antigen drift" and is responsible for regular, seasonal outbreaks of flu. But a few times in a century, something more serious, what is known as an "antigen shift," occurs, and produces a wholly new strain. This is usually the result of mixing flu viruses from different animals. A human infected with a pig or bird virus may get sick but will likely not spread it; but if the foreign virus's RNA fragments combine or "re-assort" with fragments of a human virus, a new, virulent human influenza is born. If this virus can then incubate in enough people and spread quickly beyond its epicentre, the way is open for a worldwide pandemic. There were pandemics in 1800, 1830, 1843, 1857, 1874, and, most seriously, in 1889–90 — the latter outbreak affected 40 percent of the population. After 1919, there were pandemics in 1957–8, 1968, 1976, and 2009.[7]

We now know that the 1918 flu was an H1N1 strain, which supplanted the H2N2 strain that had caused the 1874 and 1889 outbreaks and was endemic in the population. Historian Mark Humphries has produced evidence that the original virus was brought from China to Europe by labourers in 1917, and that the much more lethal fall virus probably evolved in Plymouth, England, from which ships transported it to Boston, Sierra Leone, and Brest. What is not yet clear is why the fall version was such a killer, but not for everyone. Living conditions, genetics and herd immunities, the virulence of infection, medical and nursing care, secondary pneumonia, and the pre-existence of other respiratory issues including TB, can explain much. It is possible that the large number of sudden deaths among the fifteen to forty-five age group may be explained by "cytokine explosion," the massive overreaction of a healthy immune system.[8]

II

All that Canadians knew in the fall of 1918 was that a terrible new disease was spreading across the country just as their attention was focused on the final struggle on the Western Front. In early September, two students at Victoriaville College in Quebec got sick after attending a Eucharistic Congress in Boston. Within days, over four hundred students and teachers were ill. Sick men were taken off American ships at Quebec City, at Sydney, Nova Scotia, and at St. John's, Newfoundland in September. Flu broke out in mid-September at an infantry camp at Niagara where Polish troops from the United States were training. Authorities assured the public that quarantines would limit the outbreaks, but people slipped through. Every time medical workers went home to their families, or people who did not yet know they were sick got on a train, influenza jumped over the futile attempts to contain it.[9]

Military camps were an ideal place for disease to breed. Given that they were staffed by Canada's most able doctors and nurses, they should also have been the best places to contain it. But nothing in their experience had prepared them for this plague. In late September and early October, a terrible drama played out in camp after camp — a slight increase in respiratory cases for a few days followed by a huge spike lasting a week or so, then a slow tailing off for two or three weeks. At the St-Jean military hospital there were twenty-one deaths. An army doctor in New Brunswick recalled that twenty or thirty people could get sick in the morning and half of them would die by nightfall. "There wasn't enough staff left alive to administer treatment to anyone. It was a case of 'survive yourself, or die.'" Troop ships also incubated and spread disease — when the *City of Cairo* with 1,057 troops reached England on October 11, nearly all the men had caught the disease, thirty-two had died at sea, and 244 were taken to hospital on arrival. "We could hardly move between the cots. And oh, they were so sick," recalled an English volunteer nurse. Between September 9 and December 12, there were 10,506 cases of influenza among the 61,063 troops in Canada and 45,960 cases among servicemen overseas, of whom 776 died — and that is very likely an underestimate.[10]

In those desperate days of September 1918, when the war hung in the balance, military authorities were under overwhelming pressure to get more men to the front — and to Vladivostok. In Winnipeg, soldiers from a camp under quarantine were allowed to attend a public patriotic lecture and others were allowed to go on recruiting drives. In Quebec, soldiers from infected barracks rounded up fugitive conscripts, then assembled them in camps where men were already sick. Rather than quarantine a train, ship, or camp, military authorities removed the sick and sent the "healthy" men on their way. By early October, soldiers bound for Siberia were being taken off troop trains and put in local hospitals all across Western Canada. The death rate among those admitted to hospital when the trains arrived in Victoria was 2.5 percent and the soldiers awaiting transport had to be quarantined. The comment by an Edmonton newspaper that "every sort of outrage had been justified by military urgency" was not wide of the mark.[11]

Wherever sick soldiers entered hospitals, there were sick civilians within days. The Eastern Townships, Montreal, and Quebec were hit in September — Montreal peaked on October 21 with 201 deaths and 1,088 new cases — one death every nine minutes. Halifax was reporting 125 new cases each day by October 14 and was desperately calling back nurses it had sent to help in Boston. In October, Ottawa and Hamilton had death rates twice the national average. By mid-October, ten thousand of Toronto's staff and students were sick out of a total school population of about sixty-seven thousand, and fifty people were dying each day. Winnipeg's epidemic did not peak until November 21 — in all, twelve hundred people died. Vancouver peaked at twenty-four deaths on October 27, followed by further waves in December and March as sick people from the B.C. interior and coastal villages, soldiers, and native people, flooded into town. By early November, the disease was ravaging the northern Prairies, Haida Gwaii, Newfoundland and Labrador, and the rural districts of Ontario, Quebec, and the Atlantic provinces.[12]

Each city lived a similar nightmare for the four to six weeks it was under siege. Streetcars had their windows open and ferries and train stations limited the number of people in their waiting rooms. In some cities, people wore gauze masks in the streets. Isolation wards were quickly overwhelmed and makeshift facilities were established in schools and warehouses. There were sick people everywhere, in hospitals, in homes, on the street, in houses with quarantine placards. The flu, wrote Mackenzie King in Ottawa, "is like a plague & prevalent everywhere. The city hall is surrounded by Red Cross cars & young girl VAD* workers are doing splendid service in all parts of the city. The number of families without anyone to help them, persons dying & others ill & unfed beside them — is frightful, right & left men &women are being carried off suddenly to their graves." Some people stayed in their houses, avoided crowds, prayed; others plunged into nursing family members, volunteering to help others, bringing comfort where they could.[13]

And everywhere there was death. In Montreal, priests gave last rites on the streets. There was a constant procession of funerals toward Mount Royal Cemetery and a special funeral streetcar, painted black and lettered in gold, carried nine or ten coffins a day. The eight coffin makers in Hamilton worked almost round the clock. At The Pas, Manitoba, when the undertaker became ill, a friend was called on to build caskets in his kitchen (covered with cloth for white victims, painted black for First Nations), while his nine-year-old daughter made little satin pillows and the parish priest brought in the measurements of dying people. In Saskatchewan, some bodies were buried so quickly that families lost track of their loved ones forever. A Toronto resident who was seven at the time recalled: "It was as if a black,

* Voluntary Aid Detachment: see page 103

sombre cloud fell over all. People closed their doors and stayed within to keep their lives. When we did go out we saw black crepe sashes on front doors, and when we heard the church bells ring at St. Alban's we knew another one had died." Stores advertised mourning clothes: "A charming veil for a small or medium hat shows small chenille dot on a fine mesh, with border of inch-wide ribbon: 36" long by 16" wide, $1.75."[14]

In the cities there was infrastructure and information, and many Prairie farmers fled to the towns if they could. In rural communities, mining towns, logging camps, and on farms, often in the grip of winter when the flu struck, people had to cope, with the help of friends, family, and local doctors. "When sickness enters the home, only those living on an isolated Prairie homestead far removed from medical aid, with limited transportation and communication facilities, realize their helplessness," said the Saskatchewan Bureau of Public Health. In the East, farmers went to the edge of their properties every morning to see whether there was smoke rising from neighbours' chimneys. Country doctors travelled by horse and sleigh and slept between calls. Neighbours, afraid to enter a house, fed cattle, drew water, left food at the door, and took away laundry for washing. More often, women, even with children at home, pitched in with care, cleaning, washing, and feeding. "There were no Christmas gifts that year, and no tree, but we were too sick to care," recalled one survivor from a family of sixteen children.[15]

Across Prince Edward Island there were 101 deaths, often lonely farmers, staying in isolated houses, makeshift hospitals in schoolrooms, or hotel rooms. When help reached a village near Battleford, Saskatchewan, they found in the general store the bodies of the storekeeper and his wife, with three more bodies inside a nearby tent. The only sound was a young boy digging graves for his father, mother, brother, and sister. In Corbin, a coal mining town of fifteen hundred in the East Kootenays of British Columbia, half the town fell ill, and those who remained visited homes and dug graves in the frozen soil. At Drumheller, Alberta, Gertrude Murphy, a teacher turned volunteer nurse, cared for twenty desperately ill men. "Immigrants from Rumania [sic], Poland, Austria, Italy, Hungary, far from home and frightened, in their delirium raved in their native tongues. Some thought the disease they had was the Black Death."[16]

Lucy Maud Montgomery in Leaskdale, Ontario, observed the panic sweeping Toronto but believed the flu would not touch her. Then she began to feel ill, and after two days the doctor "found me with a ridiculous temperature and a heart that was almost out of business. I would not — probably — have lived till morning." The doctor gave her strychnine for her heart and medicine to induce sweating, then left to tend to other patients. That night, she sweated so profusely that she had to call the maid to light oil stoves to dry out blankets and night-dresses — a task that was both risky and desperate, for she well knew the danger of pneumonia (which carried off her best friend and a relative). "I was in bed for ten days. I never felt so sick or weak in my life. The first time I went downstairs I collapsed and Ewan had to carry me up. I am still taking strychnine for my heart, my nerves are bad yet — for a month after I got up I would cry if a door slammed or if I couldn't find a hairpin when I was doing my hair! — and I have not yet been able wholly to shake off the depression and languor that is the worst legacy of the plague."[17]

These experiences paled beside those of the native peoples of the Canadian North. From Labrador through the Western provinces to the High Arctic, the flu struck with devastating force. Many native people were undernourished, had chronic diseases like TB, were living in unheated homes, and as winter set in were concentrated in crowded conditions. As the flu hit them they had to tend trap lines, keep fires burning, feed dogs, find food, and tend to relatives. Many contracted pneumonia when they went out too soon after recovering.

In the communities on the Labrador Coast served by the Grenfell and Moravian missions, the flu killed more than 30 percent of the Inuit and Innu populations in a matter of weeks. At Cartwright, on October 30, Grenfell missionary Henry Gordon recorded: "Not a soul to be

Lucy Maud Montgomery

seen anywhere, and a strange, unusual silence," with "whole households ... inanimate all over their kitchen floors, unable to even feed themselves or look after the fire." As Gordon, himself ill, travelled up the coast through forming ice and howling winds, he found similar stories in settlement after settlement: twenty-one people dead, ten still in their beds with no one strong enough to bury them; 150 people dead out of 220 in another settlement, where the bodies had to be consigned to the sea since they could not be buried in the frozen earth; at another place, a seventy-two-year-old woman had lived without fire and almost no food for days, chopping ice for water while starving dogs tore at the door.[18]

At Cumberland House in northern Saskatchewan, a survivor recalled: "There were no doctors there but there was a nurse, the wife of an RNWMP* man. She tried to get the people something to eat. She pulled dead bodies to the church on a hand-sleigh because with everyone sick there was nobody to bury them until spring." One-fifth of the population of Norway House in Manitoba died in six weeks. As one Cree elder recalled, "Somebody was walking over there and somebody dropped, just like a shot. Even the children, about 10-year[s] old, they just fell down and died. Like that. They don't, you don't bother anybody, just fall right down." First Nations in British Columbia experienced a death rate eight times that of the white community and memories of the epidemic were preserved in their oral traditions. Mounties ordered to enforce quarantines became involved in relief work and expressed shock at the cavalier attitudes of some Indian agents.[19]

In every city and town, calls went out as the flu set in for retired doctors, part-time nurses, and anyone else with experience. With so many doctors and nurses away, some sixty thousand Canadians had taken courses in first aid and home nursing, including a Voluntary Aid Detachment (VAD) of young women with rudimentary nursing training. In Toronto, "Sisters of Service" were recruited to man food stations, visit homes, deliver food, wash bedding and clothing, and fumigate houses. Teachers were pressed into service as schools closed, along with schoolgirls, church women, and housewives. In Ottawa, senior officials in the federal government were asked to assess how many female clerks could be released for volunteer nursing work. "I want to make it absolutely clear," said Mayor Harold Fisher of

---

* Royal North-West Mounted Police, soon to become the RCMP.

Ottawa, "that people are dying in our midst because they are not provided with proper care. They are dying because we do not know about them. We know where they are, but we have nobody to send. Knitting socks for soldiers is very useful work but we are now asking the women of Ottawa to get into the trenches themselves."[20]

For their part, men kept roads ploughed, delivered mail, soup and hot food, dispensed drugs and remedies, drove people to clinics and volunteers to homes, and kept transportation and businesses running. Policemen, firemen, and volunteers delivered meals, reported sickness, and carried food and fuel into homes. Two brothers from Gananoque were called home to help their physician father, who, together with a retired doctor, was seeing eighty to ninety patients a day; on October 12 alone they made house calls on seventy-five patients. "We would start off in the morning with twenty or more calls to make, both in town and in the country, and everywhere we would overtake or meet a funeral." Over lunch the doctor would dictate prescriptions to his sons. His wife dispensed medicines to people lined up on the walk leading to the office door at the side of the house and took temperatures and pulse rates of patients waiting to see the doctor.[21]

Volunteers worked punishing hours and in some cases paid with their lives. More than a hundred doctors died in Ontario and the Prairies alone. A Saskatchewan village was renamed in 1927 in honour of its heroic nurse. A teenager serving in a mining community in British Columbia recalled: "We really weren't under any medical supervision at all. It was all just guesswork. We tried to be as nice to them as we could and just be with them when they died."[22]

III

Canadians faced this terrifying plague poised between their traditional healing practices, faith, and fatalism, and the growing modernist conviction that through science they could control their destiny. In the end, both beliefs played a role.

Like their ancestors for millennia, Canadians accepted disease and death as the inevitable lot of humanity. Mortality rates in 1914 were three times those of today. The leading causes of death for those between fifteen and fifty were tuberculosis, typhoid fever, respiratory disease, puerperal complications, and peritonitis. Children died of diarrhoea, diphtheria, tuberculosis, scarlet fever, whooping cough, and measles — one in six did not see their first birthday. Several major cities in the first two decades of the century saw outbreaks of smallpox, cholera, and rabies. During the war, tuberculosis killed some forty to fifty thousand Canadians. Medical examinations of recruits revealed for the first time just how unhealthy Canadians were.[23]

At the same time, they believed, or hoped, that after half a century of progress in science and medicine, disease could be contained and doctors could fight it. By the time of the Great War, a revolution in medical teaching, with Canadian Sir William Osler in the lead, had replaced the art of medicine practised by the old country doctor with the science of medicine practised by hospital-trained physicians. Medical societies and colleges strengthened professionalization, and medical journals allowed ordinary doctors to contribute their clinical experience and to have access to the latest research. Nursing had also become a profession, with accreditation, schools, and hospital training. Modern, well-equipped hospitals had been built in the major cities and, by the 1920s, in every middle-sized town; they were efficiently run, well-equipped, and well-staffed places that could serve as community health centres, centres of research and education, and headquarters for specialists like surgeons, paediatricians, and pathologists.[24]

The biggest breakthroughs were in public health. Vaccines against twenty infectious diseases were being manufactured at labs such as the Connaught in Toronto, and antitoxin production was given a boost by the Great War. By 1914, all Canadian provinces had health boards and major cities had public health departments headed by medical officers of health, with departments responsible for statistics, communicable diseases, laboratories, public health nurses, food inspection, child welfare, sanitation, and health education. Full-time inspectors, nurses, social workers, and physicians were joined by voluntary organizations such as the St. John Ambulance, the Canadian Red Cross, the Canadian TB Association. Ontario towns cut the death rate from diphtheria by almost two-thirds. Winnipeg drastically reduced deaths from typhoid fever, scarlet fever, diphtheria, and tuberculosis. Vancouver and other newer cities could build wider streets, better housing, and water and sewage systems. Toronto was the first to chlorinate its water in 1910, and its schoolchildren were regularly inspected for cleanliness, taught hygiene and nutrition, and treated and inoculated for infectious disease.[25]

There was still far to go. City slums were unhealthy places to live and raise children, and factories were dangerous places to work. Ignorance often delayed reform. There was resistance to pasteurization of milk in Montreal. Many French Canadians resisted inoculation, as did a few working-class leaders in Toronto and Winnipeg. Middle-class reformers were frustrated by this obduracy, but they were often insensitive to the culture, customs, and beliefs of the people they blithely sought to remould — too often ready to believe the poor were immoral, ignorant, and to blame for their poverty and sickness. Hospitals too often favoured those who could afford to pay and treated poorer outpatients as indigent. But the reformers were also right. Education and altered lifestyles, combined when necessary with state enforcement, *were* a big part of the answer for many common diseases.[26]

The public health practitioners who would direct the response to the epidemic in the major cities — men like Underhill in Vancouver, Mahood in Calgary, Douglas in Winnipeg, and Hastings in Toronto — were trained in the best practices of the day and trusted by their communities. They had access to a network of public health and medical experts across North America. They had legal authority conferred by public health acts, moral authority as experts, and the temporary authority bestowed by a society facing an emergency. But the tools and techniques that had proved successful against diseases like cholera and typhus were quite inadequate against a fast-moving enemy whose cause remained a mystery. The confusion between provincial and local officials, and between cities, and differences of opinion among practitioners, often limited their effectiveness.[27]

They did what they could to get ready, learning all they could (if they got the chance), about the experience of other cities, assembling people, supplies, and equipment. Medical officers of health in all cities and towns issued guidelines that followed the advice of the American Public Health Association. Influenza, they knew, was an infectious disease, likely airborne, and they hoped that better hygiene, reducing transmission, and isolating cases could reduce its spread. "Don't play the fool," said Dr. Underhill, get fresh air, eat well but do not overeat, avoid liquor, keep the bowels clear, exercise, keep houses clean, avoid public places and sick people, sleep and work in clean fresh air, don't spit, and in the case of ladies, dress appropriately to avoid chills. If you do get sick, go to bed, hang a sheet between sick people in a room, wear gauze masks, and get lots of fresh air, good food, and rest. And children, warned Underhill, don't share hankies, don't lick anyone else's sucker or marbles, and do stay away from crowded motion picture halls.[28]

Above all, they advised, *don't worry.* Public health officers were concerned that fear would be at least as potent a cause of disease as germs. "It's fear that's killing a lot of them," said a doctor about the immigrants Gertrude Murphy was treating in Drumheller. "They won't fight it. They just give in — and die." This advice had no scientific basis. But only an orderly, disciplined, hopeful society could fight the flu and keep the war machine running. The press at first dutifully trumpeted the "no cause for concern" line, until it began to report the extent of the epidemic, the daily funerals, and the personal stories of illness, tragedy, home remedies, and miraculous cures.[29]

Public health officers followed standard practice for tracking and containing an epidemic. They sent out police, firefighters, and volunteers to collect information, and plotted fresh outbreaks with pins on huge maps. They mandated reporting of disease and placarding of infected houses. They prescribed penalties for spitting and other unhealthy practices. They commandeered schools, warehouses, drill halls, and disused hospital buildings for emergency hospitals. They sought staff and scrounged beds, linens, and essential supplies from hotels and private houses. They issued regulations for the collection, transport, and burial of bodies.

But once it became clear the epidemic could not be contained, they faced decisions that were political and psychological as much as medical. They had to weigh what measures would be effective and enforceable against what was justified by science. They had to respond to public pressure and rapidly changing circumstances. They changed their minds and their tactics, and increasingly they improvised. Medical officers like Underhill pleaded with sick people to get out of slum districts and into hospitals where they could at least be given palliative care and avoid secondary infection. But when these facilities were overwhelmed, Mahood and Douglas told people to care for patients at home. Some cities and many doctors argued that schools should be closed. But Underhill and some others argued that children were not the most vulnerable and would be better protected and monitored in school than on the streets.[30]

Some cities, like Halifax (whose authorities had seen the devastation in Boston), quickly shut down all places where the public might gather, including funerals, and placed restrictions on hours of business. Underhill stoutly resisted such measures because he believed they would not work and would produce social divisions, though he eventually bowed to pressure. People were asked to curtail their use of public transport and the telephone because so many drivers and operators were sick. In Montreal, people using the phone were advised to talk through a handkerchief or sterilize the mouthpiece with cotton soaked in antiseptic. Munitions plants remained open and Victory Bond rallies were usually permitted. Middle-class people were happy to see pool halls and saloons closed anyway, but department store and factory owners protested that they fumigated their premises regularly and that closure would work hardship on their employees. Labour leaders saw the closure of businesses

Men wearing masks in Alberta during 1918 epidemic

as an attack on workers, the closure of places of entertainment as an attack on their lifestyle and morale, and the banning of public assemblies as an attempt to stifle protest.[31]

Also problematic was quarantine. Some Prairie towns declared themselves "closed," by forbidding trains to stop or cars to enter, and encouraging non-residents to leave. But putting quarantine placards on houses effectively imprisoned the occupants, kept men and women from working, prevented deliveries of food and medicine, and may well have encouraged people not to report disease — especially in places like Vancouver and Winnipeg with large transient populations. In the end, enforcement was almost impossible. Many police were sick and there were too many doctors unwilling to quarantine a family. Even when they were enforced, quarantine measures did little good once the flu was widespread in the population. The University of Saskatchewan escaped contagion by virtually incarcerating its staff and students, but when it reopened in January 1919, 150 people became ill and six died.[32]

Some public health officers, like Mahood of Calgary, required everyone to wear gauze masks in public to reduce airborne transmission. Magazines and newspapers featured instructions on how to make and wear these masks. Others considered this requirement unenforceable, and anyway, wet cotton was an ideal breeding ground for germs. Most places required only people who met the public to wear masks, if they imposed any requirement at all. Masks did at least show that people were doing their bit, and they may have blocked some aerial transmission (they certainly discouraged spitting). But most people wore them only when they were being watched or having their picture taken.[33]

One debate that took place everywhere was whether to close the churches. Scientifically speaking, churches were just another gathering place, of course, but there was a strong feeling among the faithful that ordering their closure would rob people of the comfort they needed in this terrible time. Perhaps, thought a Saskatoon cleric, the flu was a divine message "detaching us from the apparent pleasures of this world and making us think of the life to come." Most churches did close. Some printed sermons in the newspapers and encouraged families to hold prayer meetings at home. Others held outdoor services. In Montreal, Archibshop Bruchési instructed the *curé* of every parish to celebrate mass at Notre Dame on behalf of his parishioners who were told to stay home. Then an army of priests with attendants in full regalia set out from the church to parade the Sacred Host through the city, before crowds that knelt on the pavements, many with candles in their hands, and with bugles blowing and bells ringing.[34]

As public health officers tried to contain the disease, the best scientists in North America were gathering information, taking samples from sick patients, trying to chart the nature and course of the disease, looking desperately for a treatment or a cure. In 1918, medical science lacked the necessary information to understand how viruses worked or what actually caused people to get sick. Labs began to produce vaccines against a bacterium that had been discovered in studies of the 1889 outbreak, but most scientists doubted it was the cause of the disease. Others tried to make vaccines from the serum of infected patients. Still others used a combination of both and added known influenza strains. Ten thousand doses of one type were distributed in Ontario. Winnipeg vaccinated people using a flu serum developed in the Mayo Clinic and manufactured by the provincial laboratory. Some soldiers in Calgary got vaccines, railway workers were offered free inoculation, and later on there was a campaign to vaccinate Native people in the north. But most cities could not get enough, most medical officials were skeptical, and there is no evidence that any of them made any real difference.[35]

Doctors could do little more than ease the symptoms of their patients (aspirin did seem to lower fever and reduce pain), offer advice about keeping the house and patient clean, and try to head off pneumonia. Mostly, they dispensed comfort and reassurance, in the time-honoured way of doctors since long before the age of scientific medicine. The son of one country doctor recalled that his father "found people curled up in bed, highly feverish and without hope. He propped them up on pillows so their lungs could clear. I attribute his remarkable success with this dreadful illness, for which there was no specific cure, to his appearance of confidence and the hope he inspired."[36]

Many people relied on folk medicine when science failed them — if they had ever trusted science at all. There was a remarkable array of remedies used in different places — Native remedies like wild ginseng, skunk oil, and musk; Chinese remedies, including a form of acupuncture; traditional remedies like cotton bags with camphor, mothballs, garlic, vinegar, salt herring worn around the neck, sulphur placed in the shoes, handkerchiefs soaked in eucalyptus, chewing cinnamon or herbs, leaving sliced onions around the house for four days. Who was to say that that they, or the doctor in Corbin who prescribed "Stay in bed, take Epsom salts, and more Epsom salts," were wrong if they avoided the flu or recovered from it?[37]

Advertisements appeared daily in newspapers for carbolic sweeping compound and other cleaning products. Other ads screamed the effectiveness of patent medicines ("discovered in the laboratory of M. Pasteur of Paris that the microbe of the disease of influenza was rendered inert by this essence"). Pharmacies sold medicines whose active ingredients included alcohol, chloral hydrate, cocaine, and opium. Quacks peddled advice such as eating three cakes of yeast a day (which, the Saskatchewan Bureau of Public Health pointed out, would stop the disease by killing the patient). Ads for bicycles, which boasted that the healthy exercise of riding them would prevent the flu, appeared alongside ads for life insurance.[38]

Alcohol was recommended by doctors and quacks alike. Many doctors prescribed a few drops on the tongue of a sick child, or brandy or Scotch to be administered orally to adults. Perhaps Missouri Bill of Corbin was a little extreme in advising that "the only sure way to cope with the flu was to hang your hat on the bedpost, go to bed, and drink moonshine until you could see two hats." The sale of liquor was banned as a war measure. But many, including teetotallers, now gathered at government dispensaries waiting for their "prescription," and in many places supplies ran out. Taken in moderation, liquor may have raised the morale of the sufferer, and probably helped the caregiver even more.[39]

As the disease finally began to abate, there was pressure in each city to lift restrictions as soon as possible. There was a widespread public expectation that the epidemic would end with the war, as if they were somehow linked, and on November 11 nothing could keep people in their homes. Underhill, who had resisted closing businesses, was now attacked when he did not immediately reopen them. As fear abated, a backlash set in against public health officers whose advice and edicts had failed to stop the plague. When the closures were lifted, people flocked to the movies, dance halls, taverns, theatres, and sports venues in an orgy of celebration. During the weeks after reopening, there was an uptick in flu deaths in several cities.[40]

In the end, it was the common sense and caring of ordinary people, coupled with a rudimentary knowledge of germ theory and sanitation — keeping sick people rested, fed, and hydrated, and keeping rooms clean, boiling the bedding of patients, airing out bedrooms — that probably saved the most lives. Communities in rural areas, ethnic enclaves, and middle-class suburbs, came together in mutual assistance. Tried and tested remedies like mustard plasters, castor oil, and cinnamon oil may at least have provided some relief while patients recovered.

But as for medical science, the reports of the conferences conducted in 1919 by the Canadian and American Medical Associations to analyze the lessons learned by the epidemic make sombre reading. Public health and medical science had been, in the words of the B.C. medical officer of health, "ill-prepared to meet the overwhelming calamity." In the words of historian Margaret Andrews, "the influenza pandemic reduced the medical community to a state of helplessness not unlike that which prevailed during the epidemics of the pre-bacteriological era." To underscore their humiliation, the secular saint of modern medicine, Sir William Osler, died of the flu in Oxford.[41]

IV

The flu touched the lives all people, city or rural, aboriginal or immigrant, man or woman. The urban poor died in higher numbers by a factor of three or four, but the flu reached into the homes of the wealthy and the notable and carried off people in the prime of life. Some people got it, some didn't, some recovered quickly, some died. Some responded heroically, others lived in panic and fear. A young girl whose father brought home a new Victrola to celebrate her mother's thirty-fourth birthday found herself motherless, fatherless, and sisterless within two weeks.[42]

The flu added to the stresses on a society already near the breaking point. Crops went unharvested, mines and resource industries lost production and markets. With thousands of their workers ill as the disease swept across their national networks, railways struggled to move troops, material, and goods — on October 1, 1918, fourteen thousand railway workers were ill in Eastern Canada alone. The Metropolitan Life Insurance Company paid out eighty-three thousand influenza death claims in North America in 1918 compared with only twenty-five thousand war death claims. Life expectancy in the United States dropped from fifty-four years to forty.[43]

Gender roles were altered by the flu as they had been by the war. It was the nurses and volunteer women who provided what was most needed — care and nurture. They organized kitchens, prepared food and relief kits, responded to calls, requisitioned supplies, entered the homes of sick people and helped them recover. For many middle-class women, going "into the trenches" against influenza may have been their first venture onto the other side of the tracks, their first close encounter with poor and immigrant families.[44]

These families had to keep going to work, to work when they were sick, to ensure that their homes were not quarantined. They could go to hospital as outpatients, with thousands of others, for often perfunctory treatment. They would call a doctor only *in extremis*. Doctors had to make a living too, and believed that people who could pay should, so unless the doctor treated a person as a charity case, his fees were a crippling burden. If the patient died, a funeral could cost at least $100 — families, especially those with multiple deaths, might have to choose between spending the widow's nest-egg or accepting a "pauper's burial."

Surely, said many social reformers, a government that could mobilize its people for war had a responsibility to ensure their health in peace. There were calls for government medical insurance as a reconstruction measure and the federal Liberals included it in their 1919 platform. Saskatchewan took steps in 1919 to increase the number of rural doctors by raising their annual salary from $1,500 to $5,000, to increase the number of "union" hospitals serving more than one town, and to increase the free medical care provided in cities. But even labour and agrarian reformers were not yet ready to abandon the idea of self-help and personal responsibility, or to take on the cost of health insurance on top of a staggering war debt.[45]

The military had been appallingly cavalier in ignoring the impact of their actions on the public welfare. In Quebec, after bishops and the legislature demanded they stop rounding up recruits until the contagion was over, the military appeared to comply, but in most cases, they went right on. Their stubborn insensitivity — it may well have reflected their resentment of

French Canadians — stoked the already blazing outrage over conscription. In Toronto, assembling men at a base camp where influenza was raging was denounced by populist mayor Tommy Church as nothing short of murder. The *Globe*'s expression of concern at the "tragic toll of soldier lives" due to "official carelessness, mismanagement, and neglect" reflected a growing resentment at the high-handedness of a government that had become too fond of ruling by Orders-in-Council. Why, asked Calgary social gospeller William Irvine, had it not used these wartime powers to regulate unnecessary travel or enforce sanitary measures — was it to protect profits and dividends? If the government had acted as it should have, he said, there would have been much less flu in the West and hundreds of lives have been saved.[46]

Many people, like Mayor Fisher of Ottawa, pointed out that during the crisis there had been "no organization competent to handle the problem on a national scale. The control of the disease was necessarily left to local bodies, many of them ill-informed and all of them inevitably lacking a coordinated effort." Women's groups, medical associations, even labour and manufacturers, had long been demanding the creation of a national department of health. Borden, preoccupied with many other problems and fearing provincial opposition, was reluctant at first. But influenza, and the criticism of the government's handling of it, changed his mind. On June 6, 1919, the Department of Health Act received royal assent.

One of the first decisions of the new department, with the Dominion Council of Health (composed of leading provincial health officers), was that its role in a future epidemic would be to disseminate information about the disease and its treatment, ensure that there were adequate hospitals, trained doctors, nurses, and volunteers, and coordinate the work of the provinces. By 1920, the department was staffed by some of the most progressive public health officials in the country. It created a vital statistics service for Canada and a public health laboratory, and established programs in public health research, investigations of health services, national TB and VD control, mental health, national hygiene, maternal and child health, food and drugs.[47]

At the provincial level, ministries of health were also formed or expanded, which financed schools, health units, local programs, research, and VD and TB education, detection, monitoring, and treatment. As the 1920s progressed, communities throughout the country voted funds for hospitals as eagerly as for war memorials. Schools of hygiene and public health were established in large universities, and provincial labs became more sophisticated. In Montreal, programs of public health, infant care, and TB treatment were expanded, and pasteurized milk finally overcame resistance. If health insurance was still far in the future, public health measures to create a strong nation and a fit "race" were very much in the present. And they brought results. By 1941, the death rate in Canada had been cut in half from what it had been in 1919, and life expectancy for men had risen from 55 to 66.7 years and for women from 58.4 to 70.4.[48]

But doctors still did not know what caused influenza or how they would treat it if it came back again. Medical research in the 1920s brought stunning breakthroughs, including the discovery of insulin in Toronto, the virtual conquest of TB, and the first antibiotics. Then, in the 1930s, scientists in Britain and the United States discovered viruses. In 1933, they isolated the influenza virus and began to establish its connection with animals. By the 1940s, the World Health Organization could track and predict flu outbreaks, though reliable vaccines were still years in the future.[49]

The most lasting impact of the flu was on the many families suddenly faced with the loss of a child, a breadwinner, or a mother. "This was a terrible time for Mother to be left alone with seven children under 16 and the new baby only a few days over one month old," recalled one Saskatchewan survivor. Six-year-old Charlie Leonard of Winnipeg, whose father was recovering from war wounds, was discovered with his mother's body, with which he had been alone for a day and a half. In Moose Jaw, the Children's Aid Society had to construct a new building to house the many new children being admitted, and in Quebec, Catholic orphanages expanded to meet the demand. It is probably fortunate that the majority of flu orphans, like Charlie, were raised by extended families, friends, and neighbours.[50]

Looking back on this epidemic, one is most surprised by what did *not* happen. For all the tensions such a terrible visitation caused or accentuated, society in general responded with remarkable composure. "I was never aware of any panic," recalled Dorothy Macphail, who as a young volunteer nurse in Montreal saw people die daily and her fellow workers get sick. "Somehow people stayed steady." People could confront horror with humour, giving the flu nicknames like "The Spanish Lady" or composing ditties such as:

A flea and a fly had the flu
They neither were sure what to do
"Let us fly," said the flea
"Let us flee," said the fly
So they flew through a flaw in the flue.[51]

At a time when people still died young and most did not expect to live until retirement, people were more accepting of tragedy, more likely to seek comfort in religious faith, and less inclined to trust — or blame — science or government. "Mamma died on Wednesday morning, October 30," wrote a little girl in Saskatchewan who also lost her sister. "Father Benoit came to give her the Last Sacraments. Mamma said to him: 'You will help Martin to bring up the children?' Father promised he would, although it was not Martin whom he would help. Mother must have been surprised when she met Daddy and Beth already in heaven before her." Only acceptance of the inevitability of disease can explain why the flu did not cause more serious social strains, and why it was so quickly forgotten. The *Canadian Annual Review* for 1918 devoted only one of its more than six hundred pages to the influenza epidemic. People wanted to forget the war, but couldn't. They wanted to forget the flu, and once it was over, they could.[52]

The victims of the 1918–19 flu are not buried in well-tended cities of the dead, or commemorated in cenotaphs in public squares, or listed on illuminated rolls, or honoured in stained-glass windows in churches. If you want to find them, you will have to walk through dozens of old cemeteries and seek out moss-covered tombstones from the first half of the twentieth century. If you look closely, you will be struck by how many names on these stones have a death date of 1918 or 1919 and a birth date in the 1880s or 1890s. These graves were new once and were often visited by families keeping alive the memory of a loved one, until, with the passage of years, their own names were added on the stones. Families moved away, people forgot. The stones remain, the only memorials to the thousands who perished in those terrible months when the Spanish Lady came, passed like the black wing of the Angel of Death, and was gone.

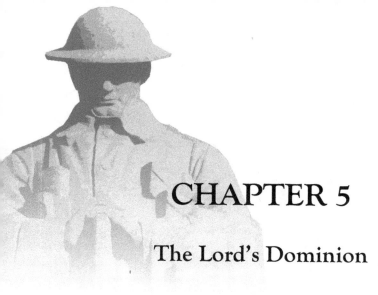

CHAPTER 5

The Lord's Dominion

Five days after the Armistice, Lieutenant Colonel George Kilpatrick, a Presbyterian chaplain, rose to address Canadian soldiers in the cathedral at Mons, at a service of thanksgiving for the men who had fallen in the last days of the Great War. The dim November light washed through ancient stained-glass windows onto grey pillars and golden reliquaries. The names of the generations whose remains rested beneath the stone floor had long since been worn away. Only days before, these weary soldiers had lived in constant fear that they, too, would be among the dead. Now Kilpatrick offered them a message of reassurance and hope. The terrible ordeal they had endured had not been in vain. Their suffering and sacrifice had been part of God's plan. They had saved civilization and redeemed themselves. And now God was calling them to an even greater challenge — nothing less than the creation of that "Ideal State which Christians call the Kingdom of God."[1]

Back home a month earlier, the Methodist Church, meeting in General Conference with influenza raging all around it, had adopted a startlingly radical report from one of its committees. "The war is a sterner teacher than Jesus and uses far other methods," read a conference document, "but it teaches the same lesson. The social development which it has so unexpectedly accelerated has the same goal as Christianity, that common goal is a nation of comrade workers, as now in the trenches fights so gloriously — a nation of comrade fighters." The Methodist Programme, as it came to be known, declared it "un-Christian" for capital to make huge profits while labour sought a living wage, and demanded a voice for labour in the management of business as well as a share of its profits and risks. It denounced privilege,

Timothy Eaton Memorial Church

The Timothy Eaton Memorial Church

Timothy Eaton Memorial Church Toronto
An example of the power and confidence of the Protestant Churches in Canada and the philanthropy of a leading Methodist family. The church, in what were then the suburbs of Toronto, served a rising, affluent middle class. This picture is taken from the program for its opening in December 1914, as Canadian soldiers go to fight in the Great War.

profiteering, company towns, speculation in land, grain, foodstuffs, and natural resources, and the watering of stock. It called for co-operatives, old age pensions, unemployment insurance, and state ownership of mines, water power, fisheries, forests, communications, transportation, and public utilities. No other church went quite that far. But all major denominations were now, each in its own way, giving a clear answer to the millions of Canadians who had struggled to understand how so much suffering could be part of God's plan. God was calling them, as he had called the soldiers, to renew their spirit, to rebuild their nation, to seek social justice, to usher in the Kingdom of God on earth.[2]

Churches were at the heart of Canadian life in 1919. The Christian heritage of beliefs, stories, and symbols underpinned Canadians' moral codes, defined their concepts of home life, gender roles, character, and conduct, informed their political discourse, and impelled the young to striving and idealism. Big city churches and cathedrals reflected the optimism of a growing country. Small towns in Ontario and the Maritimes were "a profusion of spires" — each church surrounded by its graveyard and bordered by its manse, its activities engaging all aspects of community life. In the West, small wooden churches were symbols of new identity and common faith. All over Quebec were convents and monasteries, and every town was dominated by its Catholic church with its silver spire and its priests' house, a world of faith that reached into every home.[3]

Most English-speaking Canadians were Protestants. Anglicans, Presbyterians, and Methodists predominated across the country, with Baptists most numerous in the Maritimes. Virtually all French Canadians were Catholics, but except in Gaelic, Irish, Métis, and immigrant communities, Catholicism was a minority religion in the rest of the country. There were pockets of Lutherans, Salvation Army, Greek, Russian and Ukrainian Orthodox, Jews, Doukhobors, Mennonites, Hutterites, Mormons, and Asian religions. What is most striking is that there were almost no declared atheists and very few fundamentalist denominations.[4]

Of course, some took their religion more seriously than others. Businessmen might be pious on Sunday, and then ruthless during the week — or, like Flavelle, Rowell, or the Masseys, they might regard philanthropy as a moral imperative for wealthy men. The working man might go to mass, and then spend his leisure hours in the saloon. A few might openly express doubts; others might embrace spiritualism, theosophy, and other beliefs; most kept their views to themselves. The majority who did attend church probably limited their theology to believing that if you lived a moral life you would get to heaven.[5]

But it was an accepted truth that Canada was a Christian country. "The policies of States," explained President Falconer in 1920, "are determined largely by the moral quality of their citizens. There is national character according to which a nation acts, and in which sudden changes are not to be expected." Canada's very title, "Dominion," embodied the Protestant belief that Canada could become "The Lord's Dominion," under His protection: a nation that could expect to enjoy peace, progress, and prosperity as long as it remained true to God's plan and followed the commandments of Christ. Outside "Christendom" lay uncivilized souls needing salvation — many of the Native Peoples and "foreign" immigrants at home, people living in the slums and on the frontiers, and, of course, the "natives" in Africa and Asia.[6]

I

For all their appearance of power and confidence, the Protestant churches in Canada had been in flux for a generation. Beliefs that had been the bedrock of Christianity for centuries — that the Bible (including the story of Creation) was the infallible Word of God; that a fallen humanity deserved eternal punishment for its Original Sin of disobedience; that God had sent His Son to atone for this sin by His sacrifice on the Cross; and that with the aid of Divine Grace those who followed Christ's teachings would be resurrected into eternal bliss, and that those who did not would be condemned to eternal punishment — all these had been undermined by science, material progress, and Darwin's theory of evolution. Matthew Arnold expressed in poetry the fear of troubled Victorians that the "sea of faith," once at the flood, was now in full retreat, with "melancholy, long, withdrawing roar."[7]

Protestant theology had been able to respond to this challenge with the emergence of philosophical Idealism as the dominant element in late nineteenth-century thought. Idealism was based on the belief that behind all creation was a universal truth, the Will of God, which could be discovered by human reason. All branches of human inquiry — science, theology, philosophy, law, liberal arts, social sciences — were portals into this truth. History was the record of God's plan as it evolved through time, revealed in the steady human progress from primitive savagery to the advanced civilization of modern times. To British Idealists, Victorian civilization and Imperial rule were irrefutable evidence of their exalted place in the divine plan.

To Protestant Idealist theologians, religion itself was a story of evolution. God had revealed Himself to each stage of civilization in a way the people of the time could understand. Christianity had also evolved, and Protestantism, which rejected priests, popes, and rituals in favour of discovering God through the Bible, was the highest stage of that evolution. Because it was a record of progressive revelation, expressed in stories, metaphor, and poetry, the Bible was not to be read literally but interpreted using the tools of historical research, linguistics, and textual analysis — an approach that became known as the Higher Criticism. This new theology centred on the person and teachings of Christ, who was the embodiment of God's Love and the clearest revelation yet of God's plan for humanity. Idealist theology inevitably downplayed some elements of traditional Christian doctrine. But by removing mystery on the one hand and the possibility that Creation might be only the product of chance on the other, it reconciled science, evolution, and religion, it provided an emotional basis for faith in the example of Christ and His immanence in the world, and it allowed the Protestant churches to maintain their moral and social authority and power.[8]

God was now understood, as Charles Gordon wrote in 1914, by "the word that Jesus used — Father. God as the Infinite, Eternal, Holy, Righteous Father of mankind: that is the picture which it is the Church's function to hold up to men. The word 'Father' and all that is tender, compassionate, sympathetic, protective in it, must be found in any true witness to God. He is the Father of mankind, because vitally united with them. They are the same kindred." The Kingdom of God was not an otherworldly abstraction but something that must also be built on Earth. As the American Walter Rauschenbusch put it in 1907: "There are two great entities in human life, the human soul and the human race — and religion is to save both." This belief, in the immanence of God, the example of Christ, and the need to create the Kingdom of God on earth through social and moral reform, came to be known as the "Social Gospel."[9]

In the hands of Social Gospellers, traditional religious causes such as temperance and observance of the Sabbath acquired a new impetus and meaning. John G. Shearer, a Presbyterian minister who founded the Lord's Day Alliance, and T. Albert Moore, secretary of the General Conference of the Methodist Church, campaigned for the right of the workingman to a day of leisure, and it is the measure of their success that by 1919

John G. Shearer

United Church Archives 76.001/P5913

all provinces and municipalities had enacted Lord's Day regulations. In Toronto, it was forbidden to buy ice cream, a newspaper, or a cigar on Sunday, to play sports, to fish, or take a steamboat excursion — and streetcars were permitted only because people needed them to go to church. What today seems like grim Puritanism was in large part an effort by Social Gospellers to use the power of the state to reform society by reforming men and women.[10]

But by the Great War many Social Gospellers had come to believe that it was the other way around — that souls would only be saved when society was reformed. In 1914, the Methodist Department of Temperance and Moral Reform became the Department of Social Service and Evangelism. The formidable alliance of Shearer and Moore transformed the Lord's Day Alliance into the Moral and Social Reform Council, and then in 1913 into the interdenominational Social Service Council of Canada, with a mandate to study social conditions and to advocate for social reform. Some Social Gospellers became Christian socialists, and some labour leaders, like Toronto city councillor Jimmy Simpson, were devout Christians.

Churches and allied agencies established settlement houses in the inner cities to provide food, shelter, and education to immigrants and poor families. In 1907, Methodist J.S. Woodsworth made the All Peoples' Mission in Winnipeg into a model centre for working with the immigrant poor, and his books *My Neighbour* (1908) and *Strangers Within Our Gates* (1911) were clarion calls to address the social conditions that gave rise to poverty. The line between churches, governments, and private charity became blurred as children's aid societies, YMCAs, and other volunteer societies sprang up to pursue charity and social reform. Schools of social work were created at Toronto and McGill, and "scientific" social surveys were undertaken by churches on issues affecting inner cities, industries, immigrants, women and children, and farms. In 1913, Woodsworth left All Peoples' to head up the Bureau of Social Research, which undertook social studies in the West.[11]

The culmination of this movement was the National Congress on Social Problems, convened in March 1914 by the Social Service Council. For three days, over two hundred delegates debated a wide range of problems — industrial life, urban reform, labour, child welfare, rural decline, immigration, temperance, prisons — and heard radical proposals for state and church engagement in social issues. Charles Gordon wrote in his introduction to the congress report that "there is in our nation so deep a sense of righteousness and brotherhood that it needs only that the light fall clear and white on evil to have it finally removed."[12]

Gordon was a central figure in the Social Gospel movement. After study at the University of Toronto, he travelled to Scotland where he fell under the influence of Idealist theology and then spent four years as a missionary in frontier Alberta. In 1894, he began forty years as minister of St. Stephen's Presbyterian Church in Winnipeg. During the war, Gordon enlisted as a chaplain with the rank of major, was mentioned in dispatches, and toured Canada and the United States preaching support for the war. In 1921, he became moderator of the Presbyterian Church and was a key figure in creating the United Church of Canada.

But it was under the pen name of Ralph Connor, whose Christian adventure novels were international bestsellers for two decades, that Gordon achieved his most lasting impact. In person gentle and thoughtful, Gordon's speaking and writing were forceful to the point of pugnacity. He is the hero of his own autobiography, engaging in manly sports, revelling in the outdoors, embracing his role as a "sky pilot." In his novels, red-blooded young men go through a religious odyssey of doubt, unbelief, and final commitment to Christ, usually winning the love of the high-minded but very feminine heroine. Set-piece debates alternate with swift, sometimes violent action to advance the plot. His heroes learn to subordinate themselves to the will of God, fight for morality and justice, and build a nation and an Empire for which some willingly sacrifice their lives. Connor's novels expressed his belief that God was goodness raised to the ultimate power, that all sinners could be redeemed, that to follow Christ's example was the most beautiful thing a man or woman could do,

Charles W. Gordon (Ralph Connor)

United Church Archives 76.001/2212 N

and that real faith could only be expressed in action. "The type of Christianity your heroes present," wrote an admiring reader, "is so simple direct and practical, almost devoid of doctrine, but leaving no section of life unsanctified, that I believe it must influence many lives for good."[13]

Under the influence of the Social Gospel, the Protestant churches became important civic institutions, with an array of clubs and activities, publications and campaigns, and large central bureaucracies. But tensions inevitably arose between the new approaches and the traditional role of the churches. The new theology required educated ministers who could understand and expound it, and they tended to settle in the larger churches, increasingly distant from the slums whose people they aimed to uplift. Wealthy men like Flavelle were uncomfortable with doctrines that attacked their wealth rather than validating their piety and philanthropy. The Higher Criticism had triumphed over strong opposition, including heresy trials in some churches. But many ordinary believers continued to prefer the clarity, certitude, and emotional appeal of the "old-time religion," with its promise of personal salvation after earthly suffering.[14]

II

Catholicism faced many of the same challenges in responding to rationalism and science and adjusting its message and its methods to an urban industrial society.

After a generation of steadfast opposition to modernism, Pope Leo XIII's 1891 encyclical *Rerum Novarum* committed the Church to engaging with the new order, by responding to greed, materialism, and secularism with measures that would restore social justice and harmony — but always under its aegis and in accordance with its beliefs. The state, said the encyclical, "ought to concern itself in a special way with the weak and indigent," but the "law must not undertake any more, or go further, than is required for the remedy of the evil or the removal of the danger," and it must not intrude on the family or the private lives and property of individuals. In the end, said one French-Canadian cleric in 1920, "every social question is at bottom a moral question, and every moral question is a religious question."

This could be a very conservative message (as it increasingly was when the Vatican moved to the right under Pope Pius X after 1903) or a call to social action — and it proved in time to be both.[15]

In English Canada, the work of Catholic churches often resembled that of the Social Gospellers. In Toronto, St. Michael's Hospital, St. Vincent De Paul Catholic Children's Aid Society, and St. John's Industrial School paralleled similar institutions run by the state or Protestant non-denominational bodies, and often worked closely with them. The Catholic Church mobilized the Gaelic communities of Nova Scotia and launched what would become a proud tradition of supporting co-operatives and social reform. Some of the finest Catholic educational institutions in the world trained priests and educated the laity. In immigrant parishes and the new West, Catholic churches worked to alleviate poverty and integrate newcomers into Canadian life and the Canadian Catholic Church.[16]

In French Canada, where the Catholic Church was supreme, the number of clergy in relation to the population was truly astonishing (one to about five hundred in 1891), as was the variety of monastic and teaching orders, hospitals, charities, and social organizations. In the cities, Catholic orders and institutions operated nursery schools, men's and women's clubs, *gouttes de lait* (centres for providing milk to poor children), hospitals, raffles and sports, and the Association Catholique de la Jeunesse Canadienne-française. Church schools combined secular teaching with a curriculum that reflected Catholic values and French-Canadian identity. There were Catholic commercial travellers' associations, mutual societies, *caisses populaires*, insurance companies, craft guilds, and newspapers (only in the case of *Le Devoir* did the Church refrain from setting up a competitive journal).[17]

The École Sociale Populaire in Montreal, founded in 1911 (with a similar organization in Quebec City), trained Catholic activists, published pamphlets, organized retreats, and initiated in 1920 the *semaines sociales du Canada*, which brought together several hundred people each year for colloquia on social issues. One of its founders, Arthur Saint-Pierre, outlined the "Catholic" approach to a wide range of social problems. State intervention, he wrote, would be needed to regulate female and child labour; hours of work; preserve the Lord's Day; ensure healthy conditions in factories, workshops, and homes; protect workers against foreign labour; maintain rural stability and home life; protect the public against financial disasters, speculation, and trusts. But it would be the Church, as the guardian and preserver of society, as opposed to materialist individualism, that would determine the nature of state intervention and define its boundaries, ensure the moral and spiritual well-being of the people, and protect society from unwholesome influences.[18]

The Church hierarchy was not obeyed all the time, in all things, by all people. Montreal and Quebec City bishops and scholars, with conflicting approaches to ultramontanism and nationalism, struggled for supremacy in the Quebec Church, while the archbishop of St. Boniface, who served the French-speaking residents of the West, fought to remain independent — all bolstering their positions with periodic appeals to Rome. A small minority of reformers fought for the rights of women and labour and for a more liberal approach to education, social reform, and theology. Lay Catholics like Bourassa obeyed the Church but challenged the right of the hierarchy to interfere in politics. And the Church in Quebec always had to deal with a large Protestant minority, including businessmen and social reformers, as it sought to assert control over the social and moral policies of the provincial and local governments.[19]

The French-Canadian Catholic Church had always been subject to attacks from English-speaking Protestants. But it also faced a growing challenge from English-speaking (especially Irish) Catholics. English-speaking Catholics wanted to fit into a North American urban environment. French-Canadian Catholics saw their Church as a bulwark of their national identity. They fought over missions to aboriginals and immigrants in the West; they fought over Catholic schools and universities; they fought over who would control the institutions of the Church. The Twelfth Eucharistic Congress of the North American Church, held in Montreal in 1910, was a proud opportunity for French-Canadian Catholics to proclaim their providential mission to spread Catholic ideals in a materialistic North America. But it was also the scene of an impassioned impromptu speech by Henri Bourassa against a proposal that English be adopted as the working language of the Church in North America. The first of the regulations limiting French instruction in Ontario was adopted in 1912, not at the behest of the Orange Order, but of the Irish Catholic Bishop of London who had been ousted from the University of Ottawa by French-speaking Catholics.[20]

III

Today we might well wonder why, when war broke out in Europe, Social Gospellers would not have agreed with James A. Macdonald — the Presbyterian minister who was editor of the *Globe* — that preachers had only to "drive home the idea of war's barbarity and paganism and sin, and international war, like duelling between individuals, will collapse like a thing uncivilized and intolerable." Instead, almost all of them agreed with Charles Gordon that Prussian militarism, thrown "in the teeth of Christian civilization," made "peace impossible" and the "war worthwhile."[21]

The concept of history as the unfolding of a divine plan, the rhetoric of redemption through emulation of the sacrifice of Christ, and the reforming zeal of the Social Gospel, flowed easily into the belief that the war was a holy crusade for Christian civilization. English-speaking Catholics joined the crusade as eagerly as their Protestant counterparts, and even most Catholic bishops in Quebec initially portrayed the struggle as just. Social Gospeller W.B. Creighton, editor of the Methodist *Christian Guardian,* denounced pacifism as a "vice revealing the terrible fact that the conscience has lost its sensitiveness and the soul has lost its courage." By 1915, only a handful of radical Social Gospellers, socialists, Quakers, and Mennonites opposed the war. Macdonald had to resign from the *Globe* and left for Japan to recover his health.[22]

The clergymen who took the most direct action to support the crusade were the several hundred ministers, priests, and divinity students who went overseas as military chaplains. In an environment totally alien to their colleges and pulpits, they quickly realized, like the young padre in Ralph Connor's novel *The Sky Pilot in No Man's Land,* that they could only reach their men by humbly meeting them on their own ground. In doing so, they became uncomfortably aware that for all their engagement in society, their churches had done a poor job of reaching ordinary people. "Even the Christian soldier," wrote Lieutenant Colonel E.H. Oliver, principal of the theological college at the University of Saskatchewan, "can scarcely tell you what it means to be a Christian beyond 'trusting' in Christ and saying your prayers."[23]

They also soon learned that the experience of war had alienated many soldiers from even these rudimentary beliefs. Soldiers "felt the need of power greater than their own and fell back on God," reported Kilpatrick; they prayed silently before a battle, but they had little time for long prayers, complex messages, or the abstract teachings of divinity schools. They wanted a message of salvation that reached them personally and rituals that spoke to their present experience.

Will Bird's friend Tommy, a Methodist who still believed in God but now wanted nothing to do with churches, expressed a common view:

> I'm going to have my own belief in my own way. It's all going to be between Him and me, and no preacher is going to have anything to do with it. They tell you it's wrong to hate another man, wrong to kill a man, and that's a commandment, and yet they get up in pulpits and out on church parades and tell you that we're fighting for the Lord and talk as if the Germans were devils, and that it's all right to kill them.

E.A. Corbett of the YMCA wrote in 1918 that he had seen

> no evidence of a revival of religion here. The Church Parade with its formalism and its compulsion is an abomination to the [soldier], and in his illogical way he blames the church for it. He sees no reason why he should have to stand 'at attention' in a hurricane of wind and rain to listen to what for the most part is a very platitudinous and prosy presentation of religious truth. Frankly, it does not interest him, and of course does not touch his heart.[24]

"Our experiences over here are epochal," wrote one Methodist chaplain, "and have done for us what no Conference, no College, no Congregation could do." Padres were embarrassed by criticism from home that their men, who were showing incredible valour in the face of unspeakable terror, were being corrupted by drinking or card-playing. Some came increasingly to question the official vision of the war, like the padre who told Tommy that he intended to preach that war is a crime. "'Don't do that,' cried Tommy, 'You'll lose the few you've got if you turn hypocrite. The war hasn't changed. If it's wrong now it was wrong in '14, and what did you shout then?' The padre's eyes flooded full. He could not talk." Of 426 Methodist ministers and probationers who went overseas, thirty-nine resigned on their return, and another 113 theology students did not complete their degrees, apply for a station, or formally resign.[25]

Most of the chaplains retained the conviction Kilpatrick expressed at Mons, that the war had fulfilled God's plan. They had seen Christian virtue embodied in their men and the Atonement demonstrated on the battle-field. But many came to believe that their churches needed drastic reform. "The Church must remain a Church and dare not develop into a Social Club," wrote one. "The dignity, orderliness, and spirituality of Christian worship must be maintained. It must have a clear evangel for war-worn and sin-stricken mankind." The churches needed to stress the divinity of Christ and the importance of the Cross, and revive traditional teachings about re-pentance, individual salvation, and unconditional loyalty to Christ — even while renewing their commitment to the cause of labour and social reform. They needed to work together in Canada, as the different denominations had done at the front, to build the Kingdom of God.[26]

At home, the crusading spirit of the war radicalized the Social Gospel. By 1918, the Social Service Council of Canada had grown to encompass all the major Protestant churches and a wide range of educational, philanthropic, and volunteer organizations — Shearer as its full-time secretary supervised fourteen full-time provincial secretaries. It published a "Lord's Prayer," which called on believers to "'Hallow Our Father's Name' and to pray and work for the new social order in which His will is done 'as in heaven'; in which his children have 'bread' ... in which each shall prayerfully seek to shield all from temptation and evil; in which there shall be 'universal righteousness and social justice through the evangel of Christ.'" It was in this atmosphere that the Methodist General Conference of October 1918 that adopted the Methodist Programme also removed the references to "witness of the Spirit" in its examination questions for students seeking ordination.[27]

Salem Bland, a leading Methodist advocate of the Higher Criticism and of the Social Gospel, pushed these ideas to their furthest extent in his book *The New Christianity*, drawn from sermons and speeches delivered

in the months after the war. As a
teacher at Wesley College in Winnipeg, Bland had trained and influenced a generation of labour and
agrarian reformers as well as Social
Gospel ministers, and was a well-
known public figure. In 1917, he
was dismissed, apparently for bud-
getary reasons, but he believed he
had been targeted for his views.
Eventually, he settled at the massive
Broadway Methodist Tabernacle in
a working-class district of Toronto,
where his radical ideas made him a
figure of controversy, and he was
the main author of the Methodist
Programme.[28]

Salem Bland

United Church Archives 76.001/485N

The New Christianity argued that the war, and the rise of organized
labour, were ushering in a new phase of religious evolution. The war had
spelled the death knell of capitalism and of Protestantism (which was inex-
tricably linked with it). The new world would come about not by violent
revolution but by the universal recognition that the ideals of Labour and
those of Christ, "who was Himself a working man and whose friends and
apostles were among the poor" were identical. The new Christianity would
have no priests and no "other question to candidates for membership than
the Apostolic Church put, Dost thou believe in the Lord Jesus Christ?" "It
will live to establish the Kingdom of God on the earth. Its helpful, healing,
redeeming, Christ-like activities will be infinite in the Christian and in the
heathen lands." While Bland acknowledged the labour strife and international upheaval of 1919–20, he asserted that it was the "prophetic mission"
of churches to "interpret labour to itself" so that it would move the world in
the right direction at that historic moment. Some violence was inevitable, as
in Russia; but under divine providence history would unfold for the best.[29]

Bland was going too far, even in the charged atmosphere of the postwar
world. So was William Ivens, a Methodist minister who organized a "La-

bour Church" in Winnipeg, as did A.E. Smith in Brandon, and William Irvine, a Presbyterian turned Unitarian in Calgary. By early 1919, the eight Labour churches across the West were popular non-denominational meeting places attracting speakers on socialism as well as a wide range of religious and humanist subjects, and they considered the Methodist Programme too moderate. *The New Christianity* sold well when it was published in 1920, but it received only lukewarm reviews in Methodist publications (much to Bland's surprise) and there was no second edition. This may have been due in part to a warning given to T. Albert Moore by Lieutenant Colonel Hamilton of the RCMP security service, that the book would be "acclaimed from every revolutionary platform" and "lend to the revolutionary movement an air of religious sanction." [30]

Indeed, by late 1919 many church leaders were becoming frightened by some of the results of their radical rhetoric. Support for the rights of labour was supposed to mean Christian compromise between enlightened businessmen and reasonable labour, not class struggle and bitter strikes. The new world was supposed to be a godly community of brotherhood, not a radical socialist utopia. In June, the Presbyterian General Assembly cautioned labour against abusing its power and called for a co-operative approach to industrial relations. Businessmen like Flavelle and S.R. Parsons of British American Oil (an important figure in the Canadian Manufacturers' Association) fought back against the Methodist Programme. After a debate between Bland and Parsons, a Methodist conference in Toronto agreed to a compromise that called for a greater role for labour in the operation of industry, but asserted that the Church was committed to no economic theory except what would conform to the teachings of Jesus Christ.

United Church Archives 76.001/4118N

T. Albert Moore

The Social Gospel was at a parting of the ways. Bland remained within his church and for three more decades was a mentor to younger Social Gospellers. But Woodsworth had resigned from the ministry when he declared his opposition to conscription and the war. He then worked as a longshoreman in Vancouver, and by 1919 was giving lectures across the West, developing his socialist ideas, and heading to Winnipeg to participate in the last days of the General Strike. The Labour churches were all but dead by 1921. Ivens and Irvine left the ministry to enter labour and agrarian political movements. A.E. Smith became one of the leading members of the Canadian Communist Party.[31]

IV

By the end of 1919, the Protestant churches were beginning to appear vulnerable and uncertain as they faced three major dilemmas. First, the tension between social service and evangelism, a source of strength before the war, was now a cause of discord. The war had radicalized the Social Gospel, but it had also convinced a growing number of church leaders (including the chaplains) that they needed to return to an evangelical faith based on the Atonement, the Cross, and the Resurrection. "Any other Gospel is no Gospel," said leading Presbyterian scholar Thomas Kilpatrick (father of George), but is, rather, "a mere imagination of man, vapid, flaccid, useless." Second, the war had caused many people to doubt their faith, to "have done with the church," to seek new alternatives to traditional religion. Finally, and related to the other two, the war had shaken the Idealist belief in a divine plan working through history, of which the war had been a part — and in the process robbed the churches of much of their confidence and authority. The struggle of churches to address this new reality was to go on for the next several decades.[32]

"We need a creative period in the church's thought," wrote Presbyterian George Pidgeon. "All upward movements of the past have sprung from a rediscovery of God ... in His relation to human life." But there seemed little evidence that the war would bring this about. "We look around today," said Dyson Hague, an influential Anglican professor at Wycliffe College in Toronto. "In Canada at least, and the Canadian Church, we do not see these glorious evidences of a revivified Church, and an awakened nation.... There is a revival. But it is a revival of selfishness, worldliness, disobedience, irreverence, Sunday non-observance, and a defiance of authority and order, such as never has been known." What message could the churches now give the returned soldiers, especially those who wanted nothing more to do with their churches?[33]

This was the question that preoccupied the returning chaplains. Fired with zeal to get home and share their experience, they had instead to wait overseas with their soldiers, educating them for civilian life, ministering to their spiritual needs, and trying to keep calm in the camps. In the spring of 1919, a committee of Methodist, Presbyterian, and Anglican chaplains, which included Kilpatrick and Oliver, sent to Protestant clergy across Canada a "Chaplains' Message to the Churches of Canada," which they were asked to read to their congregations on the second Sunday in June. The message called for Christian truth to be presented in accordance with the "newer conceptions of God, Man, and the Universe" and for "Providence and Prayer, Salvation, Heaven and Hell" to be given "a fresh presentation in the Church's teaching." But the churches must also "become passionate prophets in the new City of God" by being concerned with all aspects of life and social reform. The message called for a better trained clergy, better education of the laity in the fundamentals of Christian faith, removal of archaic language from the hymn and prayer books, and making Holy Communion a more joyful celebration of fellowship, church union, and outreach to veterans.[34]

The Chaplain's Message seemed gratuitous, inconsistent, and even contradictory to many at home and its reception was at best a lukewarm one. The Anglican Church refused to order it read and its newspaper advised the padres to get over the war and get on with life. The Presbyterians at least devoted a special sitting of their 1919 General Assembly to returned chaplains and circulated their message without comment to every congregation. The Methodists published a condensed version in the *Christian Guardian* with special emphasis on the call to balance social reform and evangelism. That was all.

As they adjusted to civilian life and the challenges of a changed society, and comforted bereaved families and wounded soldiers, many chaplains began to share this uncertainty and doubt. Many had trouble finding work, since most of the calls and missions had been given out, and for some a small-town pulpit no longer seemed attractive after the excitement of war-time. As labour and agrarian unrest deepened, many shared the unease of their churches about the consequences of social upheaval. And, like other returned soldiers, they now wanted to leave the war behind. "I am fed up on the whole subject and the whole experience," wrote Oliver. "I want to escape that utter depression of soul that overwhelms me when I think of Ypres and Passchendaele, the hell of Lens, the mad ruin that stretches from Vimy and Arras to Cambrai and Valenciennes. The sheer havoc and appalling desolation of it all haunts me."[35]

Instead, the Protestant churches united in an ambitious program of renewal called the Inter-Church Forward Movement, patterned after the Victory Loan campaign. There was a central committee, known as the Committee of Forty, representing all the major Protestant denominations, a national director, directors in each denomination, provincial executives and organizers, and local community organizers. Prime Minister Borden was its honorary chairman, the governor general was its patron, politicians like Rowell and Foster made speeches and appeared on platforms. It, at least, fulfilled the chaplains' hope that the Protestant churches could unite and build on the idealism of war.

Between November 1919 and March 1920, similar messages were preached each Sunday from all pulpits, and a plethora of discussion groups, minister exchanges, evangelical crusades, clubs, meetings, and outreach activities tried to stimulate spiritual awakening, attract new members, promote ecumenicalism, and find a middle ground between evangelism and social service. Social surveys were taken of the state of the churches. The Methodists set a target of half a million current members playing a more active role and a quarter of a million new members. Then, a week-long campaign in February 1920 raised a "Thank-offering" to be divided among the churches. The principal of Knox College set the tone: "If on the eve of our great Thank-offering, our noble dead whose bodies sleep in Flanders Fields, could speak to us, would they not say, 'Give as we gave to you!' 'Give as Christ gave to the world!'? What a challenge to sacrificial giving."

The campaign was in many ways a huge success and revived the enthusiasm and commitment of the faithful. The financial campaign exceeded its objective of $11 million by 25 percent. This was a tribute to the organizational work done by business leaders, but it also showed how an emotional appeal, a blending of the social and evangelical, could still get results — a large proportion of donations came from workihg people and the poor.

But on the spiritual side, many church leaders shared the assessment of the Methodist Ministerial Association that "none of those discussing the subject could see any real spiritual gain that had come out of the campaign." The Methodists achieved less than 50 percent of their enrolment goals. Where, asked the Presbyterian *Witness*, was the evangelism that was supposed to have been a main feature of the movement? Chown himself admitted responsibility for "a failure on the part of some preachers to discriminate clearly between social service and evangelism." Social service was "a great thing" but "it fails to impart the greater gift of divine life." Canon H.J. Cody, a key figure in the Anglican Church, said that 1919 "might well be described as a year of disillusionment." [36]

Radical Social Gospellers attacked the Forward Movement for selling religion like soap, overemphasizing fund-raising and then using most of the funds for church work and not social service. But to others, the Social Gospel itself was the problem. A columnist in the Anglican *Canadian Churchman* attacked Salem Bland for proclaiming that "the one big thing the Church of God is interested in and existed for, is the settlement of labour questions in a manner satisfactory to its present leaders.... There is no use pretending to have fellowship in that sort of thing, and it is better to say so in plain English." Others thought there was too much emphasis on theology, "an interminable wrangling," said a writer to the same paper, "over homoiousion and homoousion, interesting no doubt to those who take delight in such hairsplitting, but infinitely wearying to those who do not." People were looking for answers, not questions, for normalcy, not quests.[37]

V

"In many minds," recalled Methodist S.D. Chown, "the war shook with the violence of a moral and intellectual earthquake the foundations of Christian faith. It shattered many structures of belief in which devout people found refuge from the storms of life."[38]

This was especially true of young people, who were wrestling with these issues as young people always do; but in this case, they were doing so in the aftermath of a terrible war. As twenty-four-year-old veteran Harry Cassidy wrote to his fiancée, Beatrice Pearce, in 1924:

> Being unsettled in mind is inevitable, Sweetheart, when we are subjecting all of our ideas and beliefs to searching criticism — when we see religion, orthodox morality, patriotism, criterions of success, orthodox ideas on everything and anything — when we see these things, which have had something of divine right about them during the greater part of our lives, pricked full of holes…. We have lost absolute standards of right and wrong, of judgement, of evaluation, and we have not yet set up other standards in their place.[39]

"There are so many people who are afraid to say they don't believe but continue pretending to believe as they have been taught," Beatrice wrote Cassidy in 1921. Going further, she confessed:

> Personally I don't mind admitting that I don't know what is what. I thought perhaps that I might get things somewhat settled in my own mind, but I haven't…. I don't think I have ever felt the presence of God, and that seems to be one of the characteristics of a true religious belief. But I am not going to worry and fume about it…. I am going to have a friend, to whom I can tell everything. The kind of friend who will understand and whom I look on as perfect. I am going to call that person, Jesus.

Many university students, especially returning veterans, who refused to abandon all religious belief, turned to organizations like the Student Christian Movement, founded at Guelph in 1920.[40]

Many people found refuge in what Maurice Hutton called "artificial substitutes for Christianity" — fads and fantasies that seemed to proliferate in the 1920s. One of the more serious of these was spiritualism. Lectures on the occult by Sir Arthur Conan Doyle and scientist Sir Oliver Lodge were well-attended, and articles on the subject appeared regularly in the press. For some, like Mackenzie King, séances and table-rapping showed the immanence of God and the reality of a world beyond. To others, it was a "science" that might revive Christian belief — Dr. Hamilton of Winnipeg, who lost a son to influenza, conducted hundreds of experiments with séances, trying to photograph the spirits of the dead summoned by the medium. To many bereaved families, spiritualism offered the comfort that their sons or husbands were still alive in another world and could communicate with them. Serious spiritualists like Lodge and his friend Professor James Mavor denounced the attempts of fake spiritualists to reap "an unwholesome harvest out of the war." Leacock was depressed by the thought that spirits had nothing better to do than worry about our affairs. "They seem to me to make but mournful and pathetic figures flitting about us in the dark, murmuring their trite inanities. We would sooner see them asleep in the churchyard and at peace."[41]

For those who retained their faith, the war produced what Dyson Hague called a yearning for a "revival of spiritual life and power which will deliver us from the miasma of a mere churchy materialism, and the vagueness of a mere humanized new era, and give us a time of refreshing from the Lord Himself, a refreshing and recreating breath from the heights above, to cool our fevered brows and give us life once more." Hague was a contributor, with several other Canadian theologians, to a set of essays called *The Fundamentals*, written between 1910 and 1915 by conservative evangelicals in Britain, the United States, and Canada, which attacked the Higher Criticism for undermining the essentials of Christian faith and sought a renewed emphasis on the more traditional doctrines of the church. The name caught on and the World Christian Fundamentals Association, founded in the United States in 1919, proved a point of contact and direction for "fundamentalists" within the mainline churches.

But as time went on, some fundamentalists increasingly emphasized biblical literalism and the atonement of Christ, His bodily resurrection and return to earth, the conversion experience, the wrath of God, the coming end of the world, and the punishment of sinners. Rejecting reason, science, and progress, they turned the language of Idealism on its head to portray the war as divine punishment for departing from the path of God. Their radicalism, militancy, and uncompromising rhetoric widened divisions within mainstream churches, especially among the Baptists.[42]

Thomas Todhunter Shields, the pastor of Jarvis Street Baptist Church from 1910 to 1955, would "have no compromise with the enemy. I have declared again and again that I have resigned from the diplomatic corps; I am a soldier in the field, and as God gives me strength, everywhere, as long as I live, in the name of the Lord, I will smite [modernism], and I will make it as hard as I possibly can for any liberal professor to hold his position." In 1923, he forced McMaster University to revoke an honorary degree offered to the president of Brown University. When, in 1926, his congregation censured his abusive allegations against a McMaster professor, he founded his own denomination and school. Baptist factions fought for control of churches and church colleges throughout the 1920s and left the church weakened and divided.[43]

Many fundamentalists left mainstream churches and founded a variety of new ones, especially in the West. These were usually governed by their congregations and built around a charismatic preacher. These churches developed networks of Sunday schools, Bible classes, Bible colleges, and retreats. Many came from the United States, such as the Seventh Day Adventists, Brethren of Christ, and Jehovah's Witnesses, which often preached "end times" eschatology and the prophecies of a "rapture" in which the righteous would be transported to heaven and the world dissolved in a lake of fire. By the early 1920s, Pentecostalism was the fastest growing religious denomination — a movement rather than a church, known for its emphasis on "baptism in the Holy Spirit" as evidenced by speaking in tongues, faith healing, and the gift of prophecy.

Canada made a strong contribution to this North American movement. Robert E. McAlister of Cobden, Ontario, became national secretary of the Pentecostal Assemblies of Canada and founded the *Pentecostal Testimony* in 1919. Aimee Semple Macpherson from Woodstock, Ontario, established a continent-wide ministry out of Los Angeles using all the techniques of advertising, media, and "star power." William Aberhart of Alberta began leading Bible study groups in Calgary just after the war; by 1923 he needed a theatre to hold them; and in the late 1920s he brought radio evangelism to Canada with his *Back to the Bible Hour.* Oswald Smith began revivalist crusades in Toronto in the late 1920s using the tools of radio, theatre, and mass publicity. In Quebec, construction began on St. Joseph's Oratory, inspired by the saintly Brother André. But in most parts of Canada, fundamentalism in the 1920s remained less prominent and less extreme than in parts of the United States, and there was no Canadian equivalent of the Scopes Monkey Trial.[44]

By the 1920s the Catholic Church in Quebec, like the Catholic Church as a whole, was turning in a more conservative direction as a result of the war. Bourassa and other religious conservatives became increasingly concerned about the war's impact on the family, the social order, and the Church. Catholic labour leader J.P. Archambault called for unions led by "workers motivated by the Catholic spirit" rather than "workers imbued with revolutionary ideas." The Church asserted increasing control over the agrarian and labour movements, over education and social agencies, and over morals and customs within the province. Ironically, this made possible a greater degree of progressive social action. Hospitals, the *gouttes de lait,* and public health and education initiatives flourished in the 1920s. In many ways, the Catholic Church succeeded in doing in Quebec what the Protestant churches had hoped to do in the country as a whole — establish itself as central to the moulding of social welfare and national character.[45]

One element of the Social Gospel that had survived postwar disillusionment — and, indeed, came to be seen as an effective response to it — was the movement to unify the Protestant churches. As early as 1902, the Methodists, Presbyterians, and Congregationalists had agreed on a Basis of Union, and all three churches had formally approved it in 1910. Church unity would be an essential step in making Canada "The Lord's Dominion" — not to mention counteracting the power of the Catholic Church — and some churches in the West were already forming united congregations.

But the unity movement revealed increasing resistance to such grandiose visions from those who wanted a more personal, evangelical religion and objected to the dilution of basic creeds and the submersion of older identities. In 1910, twenty out of seventy presbyteries of the

Presbyterian Church had voted against unity, and although the Basis of Union was amended to meet their objections, opposition grew to 40 percent in 1915. In 1916, and again in 1921, the Presbyterian General Assembly voted to press ahead, but a Presbyterian Church Association was formed to fight the union at all costs. When a bill was brought before Parliament, which provided that the Presbyterian Church as a whole would enter the new United Church, with individual churches then free to vote themselves out, Presbyterian dissenters fought back. A vicious and increasingly personal propaganda war erupted, with churches and families divided, and small-town clergy, like Lucy Maud Montgomery's husband, fighting to protect their livings. In the end, Presbyterian congregations were allowed to vote on whether or not to join, and one-third, mostly in Ontario and Quebec, stayed outside. The Presbyterians retained some church properties, but only after a prolonged battle did they gain the right, in 1939, to call themselves the "Presbyterian Church in Canada." What had been intended to promote Protestant unity had instead seriously weakened it.

The United Church of Canada, inaugurated on June 10, 1925, was a great achievement, the culmination of the life's work of a remarkable generation of Social Gospel ministers that included Shearer, Moore, Gordon, Creighton, Bland, Chown, Oliver, Kilpatrick (father and son), Pidgeon, and many others. As the largest single Protestant church, it could now pursue its objectives of evangelism, social service, and nation-building, with an open-minded, tolerant theology. "Canada is our parish. It is ... the vision of the Dominion[-]wide service that inspires the new union," said E.H. Oliver. "There will not be a hamlet or rural community in the whole land where the United Church will not serve."[46]

But it comprised fewer than a quarter of Canadians — not even a majority of Protestants. The United Church went forward in hope as a powerful institution and an important force in the religious and moral life of Canada. It would adapt to depression and war and achieve its "golden age" in the 1950s. But it was under constant attack from fundamentalists, Presbyterians, and new theologies. It had less influence, and less confidence, than it would have had if unity had been achieved a generation earlier.

VI

It would be simplistic to say that the war destroyed belief in God. Many people did become atheists or agnostics, though they may not have trumpeted these beliefs. But even for those who retained their faith, the war undermined the Idealist belief in the working of God through history, the coming of the Kingdom of God on Earth, and the need to express devotion to Christ through social and moral reform. These beliefs had given the churches power and confidence, and had placed them at the vanguard of social reform. But they had also led them to send thousands of men into the horror of war, convinced they were doing God's will and that by their stripes the world would be healed. Many people like Chown (who had visited military hospitals at the front) now had to admit that it was difficult to see where the hand of God had been in all this. When W.B. Creighton confessed in 1924 that the war had been a "hideous, utterly unchristian, unforgivable crime," for which many were now ready to "seek pardon for our ignorance and our lack of the Spirit of our Master," he was relinquishing much of the authority his church had exercised before the war.[47]

Creighton and Chown were part of a minority. The vast majority of churchgoers continued to find inspiration and comfort in traditional beliefs and practices, to follow the guidance of priests and ministers, and to believe in the justice of the war. The mainstream Protestant churches largely resisted the external challenges of fundamentalism and secularism and remained powerful institutions with millions of devoted followers. An increasingly conservative and anti-modernist Catholicism would remain dominant in Quebec until the Quiet Revolution. The Catholic Church in Quebec and the Social Welfare Council in most other provinces would shape social welfare and public morality for a generation.[48]

But the energy and confidence that Idealist theology and the Social Gospel had given the Protestant churches before the war would not return. James G. Endicott, son of a senior official of the Methodist Church (and second moderator of the United Church), found that expressing skeptical opinions on Church doctrine — something considered normal and welcome before the war — now put him in a tenuous position. Theology professors were abandoning Higher Criticism in favour of regarding the Bible as the word of God, the only truth open to Man, and not susceptible to criticism by humans corrupted by original sin. In some ways, the United Church Statement of Faith, adopted in 1940, is a less liberal document than the twenty Articles of Faith in the 1925 Basis of Union (which was largely drafted in 1910).[49]

The unity of knowledge, with theology the queen of all, that had been the hallmark of Idealist philosophy, was shattered. Protestant theological colleges found their enrolment declining and their roles increasingly marginal in major universities. Philosophy and religion were parting company. The social sciences and religion were also separating, as "expert" social scientists discovered that religion no longer underpinned their work — that, indeed, it got in the way. Schools and universities, the public and foreign service, and the new network of nationalist institutions were full of young men and women putting the ideas of the Social Gospel into practice, but in a purely secular setting. Science and religion were also drawing apart. Relativity and quantum mechanics could not easily be contained within philosophical Idealism. Freudian psychology, popularized in 1924 by Clarence Darrow's defence of child murderers Leopold and Loeb, completed the work of Darwin by showing that within each of us lurks the primal savagery of our animal ancestors, for which the remedy was not repentance or Divine Grace, but therapy. By 1940, many educated people would have agreed with Stephen Leacock that belief was harder to maintain in "this present shrunken [E]arth, its every corner known, its old-time mystery gone with the magic of the sea, to make place for this new demonic confine, loud with voices out of emptiness and tense with the universal threat of death."[50]

In the minds of many thoughtful observers, society's need for religion was no longer matched by a theology that could appeal intellectually and emotionally to all. As Maurice Hutton put it,

> we are living in an interregnum, waiting for a revival of a Christianity more passionate and more comprehensible, more scientific, more Platonic than we have found it; for the voice of a Master who shall again speak with authority and justify the way of God to men: the ship as yet is still in

the doldrums, swaying and sagging on the lazy water: the wind of revival, the wind of a true dawn is not yet come to fill the drooping sails and strain the languid spars.[51]

The great vision of a world made new by sacrifice and devotion that Kilpatrick had preached to his soldiers at Mons, the clarion call of the Methodist Programme for social reform that would create the Kingdom of God on Earth, the overarching dream of "The Lord's Dominion," were all passing into history.

CHAPTER 6

Intoxicating Liquors

"The whole of North America ... is passing under a new tyranny. It is new, at least, in the sense that the particular form of it, under the name of Prohibition, is a thing hitherto unknown in the world. It is old in the sense that the evil that inspires it is that against which for ages the spirit of liberty has been in conflict." Many readers would have been astonished that such angry words came from Stepheh Leacock, then at the height of his fame as a humorist. There was nothing funny in his warning that the ratification on January 16, 1919, of the Eighteenth Amendment to the U.S. Constitution, which prohibited "the manufacture, sale, or transportation of intoxicating liquors," and the passage in October (over President Wilson's veto) of the Volstead Act establishing the legal and enforcement framework for Prohibition, was a "social catastrophe." Where temperance had been a subject of "good-natured ridicule rather than fear," Prohibition, with a "vast continental propaganda, backed by unlimited money, engineered by organized hypocrisy," was a "social tyranny, backed by the full force of the law."[1]

Needless to say, the advocates of Prohibition did not see it that way. To N.W. Rowell, Prohibition was "the glad sound of liberty, liberty ... the Tyrant is slain and we are free." "Where the liquor traffic holds sway, there the children do not laugh and the people do not sing," American evangelist Billy Sunday told a Toronto audience in September 1919. "If the whisky people could, they would make the old world a puking, spewing, vomiting, maudlin, staggering, bleary-eyed tottery wreck.... I am fighting in the interests of decency and virtue, and Jesus Christ and His Cross are at stake. God has planned it so that the saloon crowd shall not damn the world."

A float in an Ontario parade advocating Prohibition in 1916
Similar campaigns, building on wartime sacrifice and desire for social and moral reform, resulted in Canada going "dry" between April 1918 and December 1919. Referendums in most provinces in the early 1920s approved Prohibition.

Prohibitionists were, in the words of Winnipeg journalist J.A. Stevenson, "determined to abolish the last beer glass from the [E]arth as sternly as General Gorgas drove the last mosquito from the Panama zone."[2]

To still others, Prohibition was a business opportunity. On Christmas Day, 1919, and for several days thereafter, Harry and Sam Bronfman worked around the clock unloading freight cars at the railroad siding at Yorkton, Saskatchewan, filling their warehouses with imported Scotch to quench the thirst of drinkers in the "dry" Prairie provinces. Moving nimbly to keep ahead of changing laws and regulations, they would graduate to the far more lucrative business of selling liquor to American bootleggers. From 1922 to 1924, Sam and his new wife Saidye would travel across North America, lining up buyers and contacts and purchasing a Kentucky distillery, which was dismantled and shipped to Montreal. As the decade progressed, the Bronfmans would partner with the British Distillers' Corporation Limited to market the leading brands of Scotch, buy the venerable Seagram's distillery, and build the Seagram brand into a byword for quality in Canadian whisky. They would found the first great Jewish-Canadian family dynasty in Montreal, cultivating politicians and business leaders, giving liberally to charity, and working to advance the position of Jews in Canada. Like so many others who made their fortunes in the Prohibition era, Mr. Sam, as he became known, would spend the rest of his life seeking respectability.[3]

Most popular accounts of Prohibition have echoed Stevenson's 1919 depiction of it as "an austere and melancholy Puritanism which will expel all traces of sweetness and light from our civilization." It was bound to fail, they concluded. You can't legislate morality and you can't keep people from getting what they want. But this does not explain why temperance was so passionately pursued for over a century, why far more plebiscites were held on the liquor issue than on any other in Canadian history, why the people of eight Canadian provinces voted to make themselves "dry," sometimes several times, or why the Americans went through the difficult process of amending their Constitution to abolish the liquor trade. J.W. Dafoe, Sir John Willison, George Wrong, N.W. Rowell, Sir George Foster, Sir Joseph Flavelle, Sam Hughes, and several of his generals, all supported it. So did Nellie McClung and most feminist leaders. So did all the farmers' organizations. So did J.S. Woodsworth, Jimmy Simpson, and others who believed, like Elmo Roper of Alberta, that "Labour stands opposed to economic waste and for the betterment and progress of humanity."[4]

The tide of Prohibition was at its flood in 1919. Since 1916 there had been continuous campaigns, with monster parades, rallies, petitions, plays, songs, pageants, pamphlets, cartoons, and posters. Leaflets dropped from airplanes in 1919 urged voters not to "allow Ontario to become the SLUM of this continent," nor to "expose your own CHILD to the temptation and misery of booze," but to act "for HOME and COUNTRY!" All provinces except Quebec had voted themselves "dry" — that is, they had banned the public sale and consumption of alcohol — and Quebec was slated to join them on May 1, 1919, according to a bill forced through the Quebec legislature by Premier Gouin the previous year. In April 1918, the federal government had prohibited the importation, manufacture, and interprovincial sale of alcoholic beverages, and passed the Canada Temperance Act in early 1919 which made these prohibitions permanent.[5]

But total victory still eluded the Prohibitionists. Quebec brewers published full-page ads praising beer as a healthy alternative to hard liquor and asking whether "the Oldest Manufacturing business in Canada" was to be "legislated out of existence." Premier Gouin was forced to call a plebiscite, and in April 1919 an overwhelming majority approved the sale of 5 percent beer and 13 percent wines. In British Columbia, a growing "Moderate Party" was demanding the sale of spirits in government-controlled stores and the regulated private sale of beer and light wines. Then, in the summer of 1919, the Canadian Senate rejected the Canada Temperance Act. A new act passed by the House of Commons in November extended the wartime measures only to the end of the year, then each province would hold a referendum in the fall of 1920 or the spring of 1921, to determine whether to invoke the Canada Temperance Act in its jurisdiction. Prohibition was becoming a "never-endum."[6]

What people today find most perplexing is why so many Canadians a century ago were so concerned about someone else taking a drink. "The drinking of alcoholic liquor is not a moral or political crime," wrote Stevenson. "It may be a serious human error and lead to evil consequences for the race. But in any event the case should come before the bar under fair rules of evidence and not in an atmosphere of prejudice and emotion." Why not concentrate instead on "wise economic organization and the exercise of the true temper of statesmanship" to build "a social and economic system which would make poverty and misery practically unknown and eliminate with them the main incentives to alcoholism"? The Prohibitionists' answer in the overheated atmosphere of 1919 was obvious — drink *was* the issue. Social reform, wise and honest government, and industrial progress and prosperity, would only happen once John Barleycorn was dead. Otherwise, all the sacrifice of war, and all the hopes for a better world, would be in vain.[7]

I

All through human history, alcohol has been, in the words of Mac Marshall, the "best known and most widely used means of altering human consciousness." In pioneer Canada, whisky was a by-product of frontier grain farming. Country taverns were meeting places, and "bees," social gatherings, or sporting events — all generously lubricated — were a respite from toil and hardship. In the Maritimes, trade with the Caribbean made rum the drink of choice. Beer drinking increased with British immigration and the growth of towns. The astonishing quantity of drink, including champagne, sherry, and port, consumed by the Fathers of Confederation at the Charlottetown Conference of 1864 makes one wonder how they ever wrote a constitution — or perhaps it explains their work. Among the rising middle classes, wines at dinner were *de rigueur* — "Lady Gay" in 1914 told her readers to provide "a white wine, sherry, claret, Burgundy and champagne" for a dinner of eight, and "one wine, preferably claret, for a small dinner" (with another beverage provided in order to respect the wishes of abstainers). Women often had on hand a "cordial," or medicines for "women's complaints" that they might not even realize contained alcohol. But women who frequented bars or drank too much in public were irreparably branded as "fallen."[8]

Alcohol was big business. Wines and Scotch whisky were imported, but all other forms of drink were made in Canada. In 1902, Gooderham and Worts of Toronto produced two million gallons of whisky per year — 40 percent of the Canadian total — with the most efficient production methods and quality control. One hundred breweries, led by Molson's of Montreal, whose advertising showed wholesome young women proclaiming the purity and healthfulness of India Pale Ale, produced more than fifty-six million gallons of beer — including bottled beer for home consumption. Duties on alcohol comprised 10 to 13 percent of federal customs revenue and half to two-thirds of excise taxes. Licences on bars and hotels were a gold mine, and all levels of government fought bitterly over the right to issue them and collect the fees. Appointments to regulatory bodies were sought-after patronage plums.[9]

The bar, or "saloon" — the "fecund mother of all the vices" in the words of Charles Gordon — was the arch-Satan for temperance forces in the early twentieth century. Saloons were drinking places pure and simple with a stand-up bar where men gathered to "treat" each other and enjoy male company. The bars could be dirty, smelling of tobacco, booze, men, and the farms or factories where they worked. They could be bright and cheerful, with a polished mahogany bar, brass rail, silver spittoons, a huge mirror over the bar, a wall-full of bottles, and an array of beer pumps. They could be meeting places for sailors, lumbermen, construction workers, farm labourers, and immigrants — the latter often had their own bars, where they could speak their own languages and sing their traditional songs. They could be the country hotels described by Stephen Leacock, where the bar "constitutes the hotel proper" with "bedrooms on the floor above, many of which contain beds," where a beer-pump floods the bar with beer, some of which "spills into glasses and has to be sold," and where all drinks cost five cents. Leacock made hotel-keeper Josh Smith the central character in his 1912 masterpiece *Sunshine Sketches of a Little Town.* His hotel is the place where all the leading men of the town meet for a drink. When he faces charges because he has closed the bar while the judge was still outside, he wins over the licensing board by setting up a fancy restaurant (which is closed when the license is renewed), and the townspeople by paying for a children's amusement park and solving a number of problems including the church debt. He then runs for Parliament on a platform of total Prohibition.[10]

Evangelical Protestants denounced alcohol as profaning the temple of the body and leading innocent young men into drunkenness, crime, wasted lives, and early death. They saw saloons as places where low-lifes gathered, where men gambled and engaged prostitutes, where crime and social unrest festered, and where the surrounding streets were unsafe for respectable women. And they were not wrong — convictions for drunkenness rose from ten thousand a year at the turn of the century to sixty-one thousand by 1913. In Ralph Connor's novels, the saloon owner is often the villain, and cleaning (or smashing) the saloon up is the task of the righteous hero.[11]

Barroom in Corona Hotel, Edmonton, 1914

Glenbow Archives NA.1328.2977

For men, it was a matter of choice whether to patronize a saloon; wives and children were totally dependent on them and the choices they made, however, and they often paid the biggest price for money spent in a bar. Drinks costing five cents could quickly drain the paycheque of a man earning a dollar a day. Henry Clay Work's song "Father, Dear Father" was widely sung and had even appeared in some hymnbooks. The cover of its sheet music showed "Little Mary" watching the "shameful midnight revel" from the barroom door as she pleads with her father to come home to mother and her sick brother Benny. The song concludes:

> Father, dear father, come home with me now,
> The clock in the steeple strikes three;
> The house is so lonely, the hours are so long,
> For poor weeping mother and me;
> Yes, we are alone, poor Benny is dead,
> And gone with the angels of light;
> And these were the very last words that he said
> "I want to kiss papa good-night."

This song was fifty years old by the end of the war, but its message was fresh and vivid enough to women like Nellie McClung's friend Jennie Gills, who was "'expecting' again, and her husband had celebrated the last occasion by getting roaring drunk and coming home with the avowed intention of killing Jennie and the new baby." Or young James Gray, whose childhood innocence eroded each time he brought his father home from the bar and witnessed his mother's stoic endurance and his father's tearful repentance. In 1922, Gray's father had to tell his family that the booze that had already cost him his right arm had lost him yet another job, as well as any possibility of further education for James. "It seemed to take forever for the enormity of the news to break through to my mother. She just sat and stared and stared and stared at him. Then she got up, took off her apron, and fled out the front door and down the street."[12]

The Women's Christian Temperance Union (WCTU), founded in the United States in 1874, was the response of Protestant women to the scourge

Glenbow Archives NA 1399-1

The executive of the Regina chapter of the WCTU in 1908
Those present include Louise McKinney who became the first woman member of the Alberta legislature.

of liquor — and to their own social powerlessness. By 1914, it had sixteen thousand members, who included liberal and evangelical Christians, rural and urban women, moral reformers, and women with a wider feminist vision. A few might be militant, like Bertha Wright of Ottawa who led groups of women to protest saloons in Hull and were roughed up by mobs of angry men. But most relied on education and persuasion, at which they were skilled, imaginative, persistent, and effective.

They fought local battles for restrictions on saloons and liquor sales and lobbied provincial education ministers to place temperance on school curricula. They sponsored essay contests and gave out medals for speeches and slogans. They distributed thousands of pamphlets, poems, songs, plays, and stories for use in schools and Sunday schools. Children were pledged to purity as "Little White Ribboners," and when they became teenagers they joined "Better Hope Groups." Expectant mothers promised to enrol their babies at birth, or after weaning if they had taken alcohol during pregnancy. Millions signed cards pledging "by the help of God, to abstain from the use of all intoxicating liquors, including wine, beer, and cider, as a beverage, from the use of tobacco in any form, and from all profanity."[13]

Alongside the WCTU, the Dominion Alliance for the Total Suppression of the Liquor Traffic emerged as an umbrella organization led by F.S. Spence, the son of an Irish Methodist minister and a tireless journalist and pamphleteer. Spence persuaded Protestant clergymen to surrender their pulpits to Alliance speakers once per year and the collections from these "Field Days" funded a head office with ten organizers and thirty clerical workers by 1911. Spence crusaded for women's suffrage and urban causes such as parks and playgrounds, planning, and public ownership of hydro — he was for many years a Toronto alderman but lost his two attempts at the mayoralty because of his opposition to Sunday streetcars. He was president of the Alliance's Dominion Council from 1912 until his sudden death in 1917, when his even more militant brother, Ben Spence, became the leading spokesperson for the Alliance.[14]

Temperance forces got laws passed in most provinces restricting and regulating bars. Until 1890, the North-West* was "dry," and liquor could never be sold to Indians. At the local level, under the federal Scott Act (1878), which allowed municipalities to decide by a 60 percent vote to ban the sale or public consumption of liquor, a substantial proportion of municipalities voted themselves "dry," even in Quebec. In 1906, Prince Edward Island went totally "dry" and Nova Scotia in 1910 was nearly so.[15]

But many who advocated temperance were not willing to go as far as total prohibition. The Catholic, Anglican, Lutheran, and Orthodox churches denounced the evils of drunkenness as vehemently as their evangelical counterparts. In Quebec, where archbishop Bruchési denounced alcohol as "a real national curse," the Church founded the Ligue anti-alcoolique in 1907, and by 1910 a variety of Catholic temperance societies had recruited over three hundred thousand members. But these churches firmly believed that temperance meant moderation and self-control, not state compulsion. "Wine, gentlemen," Monsignor Tauchet told a Quebec Temperance Congress in 1910 "is like gold, good or bad. The reasonable quest for gold is useful; the frenzy for gold nefarious. The moderate use of

---

* The North-West Territories was divided in 1905, with portions of the land given to the new provinces of Saskatchewan and Alberta.

wine is licit; the immoderate use of wine is forbidden." When the temperance forces cornered Laurier into holding a national referendum in 1898, they were outraged when he disregarded the majority for Prohibition in English Canada on the grounds that the turnout was low and there was a strong majority against it in Quebec.[16]

Social Gospellers placed the moral and religious arguments for temperance within the broader agenda of social reform. Their propaganda depicted the "liquor interests" as capitalist beasts of prey feeding off the misery of the masses. Real social progress could not be made unless the state, which after all licensed the bars, intervened to protect ordinary people. "What a ghastly and incongruous folly," wrote Gordon in his introduction to the 1914 Social Service Congress report. "How woefully has the State failed to protect the poor, the worker, the child, the weakling, the intemperate, the defective from the foes that prey and fatten upon them." "Prohibition," Nellie McClung admitted, was "a hard sounding word, worthless as a rallying cry, hard as a locked door or going to bed without your supper." But the liquor traffic "was corporeal and always present; it walked our streets; it threw its challenge in our faces!" Doctors were now describing alcohol as a poison for which there was no safe dose, which destroyed health and produced stunted children, and alcoholism as a disease and not merely a weakness of the will. "Banning the bar" went hand in hand with clearing slums, building schools and playgrounds, providing social clubs for men, and treating alcohol addiction. "We can only have full civil rights, full social justice, full personal liberty, by restraining the vicious and selfish from doing wrong to others," declared Spence.[17]

By 1914, Prohibition had become a complex social issue blending science, morality, gender and class relations, and fears of social upheaval, physical degeneracy, and the decline of the "race." In 1913, the Presbyterian General Assembly was told that "scientific investigations" had shown "that more than any other factor alcohol is responsible for race deterioration. Evidence regarding the relation of alcohol and poverty, idiocy, insanity, vice, inefficiency, and physical degeneracy has convinced rulers, statesmen and governments that their greatest enemy is not without but within their borders." Social Gospeller J.G. Shearer pushed this paranoia to its limits in 1910 when he claimed that Winnipeg's (admittedly notorious) bars were places where innocent young women were kidnapped (often by "Chinese and Japanese") and sold into "white slavery."[18]

One response to these fears was the "social purity" movement, which preached "pure" food, air, sunshine, thoughts and habits, self-discipline and efficiency — and no alcohol. Purity was symbolized by the colour white, as in milk, light, dresses, and skin, and expressed in a poem entitled "The White Ribbon" (1912):

> Pure and unsullied as new driven snow,
> Fair with the whiteness of the lily, gleams
> O'er all the earth like sunshine's rarest beams,
> The spotless honour of our little bow.
>
> ...
>
> Go, ribbon white! entwine the world around,
> Carry thy message over land and sea.
> Save from the drink all those within its snares,
> Guide each aright who now the emblem bears.

Social purity was aimed at both sexes — a "white life for two" — and marriages producing healthy children, free from any hint of corruption or taint of drink.[19]

By the Great War, it seemed that the temperance movement had gone about as far as it could. Its militancy was generating equally staunch opposition, and politicians, like Rowell in Ontario, who ran on Prohibition platforms were usually defeated.

But the war, as the Saskatoon *Phoenix* pointed out, brought "public opinion *to a focus* on the matter of temperance reform." "Liquor in-

Newton Wesley Rowell

Canada, Department of National Defence/ Library and Archives Canada PA005109

terests" were now attacked for wasting precious grain as well as corrupting the young men on whom the country depended. "Anyone who will vote in favour of liquor might as well enlist under the Kaiser as far as patriotism goes," said a Manitoba newspaper. "Some of the bars," charged a Saskatchewan temperance pamphlet, "are meeting places for our Empire's enemies and breeding-centres of sedition." The Anglican Church for the first time joined the Prohibition movement, as did business leaders, who saw it as a means to increase efficiency. Even most ethnic groups in the West came on board as did notorious tipplers like Bob Edwards, the eccentric editor of the Calgary *Eye Opener.* King George V declared his intention to abstain for the duration and the Russian czar banned the sale of vodka. The liquor industry kept a low profile and breweries vainly attempted to promote beer as a "temperance" beverage. The only place the crusade fell short was the attempt to declare military camps and regiments "dry" — drinking (and smoking) were too important to the morale of soldiers.[20]

II

Between April 1918 and the end of 1919, Canada was as "dry" as it would ever be. You could not buy booze in stores or drink it anywhere in public. There were no saloons or hotel bars. Half the breweries closed, and the rest made soft drinks, ice cream, a drink called Malta, or "near-beer" like Labatt's "Old London Brew" ale and "Comet" lager. You could drink this stuff in "standard hotels," poolrooms, and cafes, but at 1.5 percent alcohol it was more likely to drown you than get you drunk. In Ontario, you could purchase locally made sherry and port. You could make your own wine and beer (or moonshine) but not sell it or serve it outside your home. You could get liquor by prescription — the Bronfmans paid doctors a fee for every "prescription" written for one of their products. "Towards Christmas especially," a B.C. civil servant later recalled, "it looked as if an epidemic of colds and colic had struck the country like a plague." Or you could try an over-the-counter remedy containing alcohol, like Liver and Kidney Cure, Dandy Bracer, Zig Zag, Rock-a-bye Cough Cure, or a "blood purifier" known as Ayers Sarsaparilla. If you had had the foresight to stock up when liquor was still legal, you were all right for a while. But as your wine cellar and liquor cabinet started to draw down, you might begin to wonder how long you could still drink and remain on the right side of the law.[21]

For many people that was not very long. Seizures of illegal stills rose from 191 in 1917 to over eleven hundred in 1923, in places as unlikely as an abandoned Methodist church in Saskatchewan and the organ loft of a Baptist church in Calgary. Some breweries continued to produce the "real stuff" for sale to hotels and bars in disguised barrels. "Blind pigs" (illegal bars) and bootleggers appeared everywhere. "Prohibition certainly seems to promote ingenuity and cunning and the variety of devices used to defeat temperance legislation is amazing," wrote Stevenson.

> Hardened smugglers would hire an officer of the law as cheerfully as they would hire a taxi and the enormous profits which they secured, enabled them to offer attractive pay.... Government officials seem to think that a Temperance Act is not a law to be enforced, but a source of profit for themselves and the public seem to regard such an attitude as eminently natural and almost worthy of encouragement.

"Oh, yes, it was open enough," recalled a Nova Scotian. "The law didn't want to stop it no more than we did. They come up and every now and then you'd pay a fine ... and that was it. They never cleaned you out." "Yes I voted for Prohibition," said one convicted Alberta moonshiner, "and I'd vote for it again. I went broke farming."[22]

Once it became legal once again to manufacture liquor and transport it between provinces (on January 1, 1920), a person could have liquor shipped via the mail, even in "dry" provinces, by mail-order houses including the Hudson's Bay Company. The Bronfmans, who had come from Romania in 1891 to seek their fortune in Saskatchewan and made a modest fortune with a small chain of hotels, reopened the mail-order business they had established before 1918. In 1920, Harry Bronfman established the Canada Pure Drug Company in Saskatchewan, bought the contract to sell Dewar's from The Bay, and, with a big loan from the Bank of Montreal and solid political connections in Regina and Ottawa, got his Yorkton hotel designated a bonded warehouse. Unloading boxcars full of Bronfman liquor at Yorkton frequently delayed the CPR's Winnipeg-to-Edmonton train by up to thirty minutes. The federal government had no wish to interfere as long as fees and taxes were paid, and sometimes ordered local officials to look the other way when liquor was shipped onward without clearance because a bonded warehouse overflowed.[23]

This bonanza ended in October 1920 when the three Prairie provinces voted in referendums to invoke the Canada Temperance Act, which prohibited shipment of liquor into, as well as manufacture and sale within, their jurisdictions. But a far more lucrative commercial prospect lay close to hand for the Bronfmans, and for hundreds of others. On January 16, 1920, it became illegal in the United States to manufacture, sell, or consume alcoholic beverages. But Congress refused to fund enough police and inspectors to enforce Prohibition adequately. Almost immediately, a huge illegal liquor trade, including manufacturing, bootlegging, and "speakeasies" (not-so-secret bars) sprang up. Good quality — and not so good quality — Canadian booze was in demand and soon began to cross the border. "You cannot keep liquor from dripping through a dotted line," said the feckless American official in charge of enforcement.[24]

Cadillacs or Packards with their back seats removed, and equipped with oil injectors to emit black smoke or chains to stir up dust to elude pursuers, travelled back and forth across the border on the Prairies. Elsewhere, boxcars could be fitted with hidden compartments and boats with submerged containers. A "mosquito" fleet of small craft plied the Detroit River and the waters of Lake Erie. In the Atlantic, schooners from Canada — which by 1925 included half the Lunenburg fishing fleet — brought booze to ships anchored in "Rum row" just outside the U.S. territorial limit, and smaller American boats then took the precious cargo to U.S. ports at night. Airplanes carrying mail and freight added liquid cargo. Or people could just carry it across, in small or large quantities, in cars, bicycles, boats, or on foot. In 1924, it was estimated that five million gallons of liquor were smuggled into the United States, the vast majority through Canada.[25]

"It's easy money," said a Saint John taxi driver in 1923. "I've run many a load over. I've bought it here for sixty dollars a dozen, all duty paid and all done up in burlap sacks. An ordinary touring car will carry forty dozen and I've sold it for a hundred dollars a dozen across the line, a profit of sixteen hundred dollars on a load. Even if you get knocked off every fourth load and lose your car, you're ahead of the game." Bootleggers were a fraternity — ex-soldiers, ex-cops, people at loose ends, young men and women looking for money and adventure — on both sides of the border. Their shipping and receiving points were well-known and their networks reached back into Canada and out into the American criminal organizations that controlled the illegal trade in booze.[26]

Canadian authorities took the position described by Harry Hatch of Hiram Walker: "[T]he Volstead Act does not prevent us from exporting at all. It prevents somebody over there from importing. There's a difference." Legally manufactured liquor could be shipped to destinations such as "Cuba," "Mexico," or "Peru." Canada Customs would sign off as long as the export paperwork was in order, the excise tax was paid (if applicable), and stamped documents certified that the shipment had arrived at its "destination." What happened on the other side was not their business. Small boats from Windsor could make the round trip to Cuba two or three times a day. The Bronfmans set up "boozoriums" along the Saskatchewan-U.S. border, bonded warehouses where American bootleggers could pick up cargo, cash-and-carry. Their cars, during their time in Canada, were registered as common carriers for the Bronfman-owned Trans-Canada Transportation Limited. The Bronfmans were not smugglers — all transactions took place legally in Canada, the warehouses were inspected, and daily returns were made to the Saskatchewan government.[27]

By 1924, the Bronfmans had moved to Montreal and were producing high quality products, including their flagship brand, Crown Royal. Their main competitor — and bitter rival — was Harry C. Hatch, whose career was similar to the Bronfmans'. He had operated liquor stores in Whitby and Toronto, run a Toronto mail-order business, and controlled the Corby distillery near Belleville. In 1923, he and some partners bought Gooderham and Worts, and in 1927 they merged it with Hiram Walker and developed their Canadian Club brand for the American market. In 1925, they shipped 125,000 cases across the Detroit River in small boats dubbed "Hatch's navy." Of the major breweries, Molson's limited its sales to Quebec where beer could legally be sold; but Labatt's, located in western Ontario, relied on the U.S. market and developed a lager beer to suit American taste. By the mid-twenties, 80 percent of Canadian beer going to the United States was crossing from southwest Ontario. "Rum running has provided a tidy bit toward Canada's favourable balance of trade," said the *Financial Post*.[28]

"Rum-running" was not all fun and games, despite the romantic legends that have grown up around it. Big money meant gangs, hijacking, and fights between rivals. Albenie J. Violette, (who called himself Joe Walnut) built a bootlegging and distilling empire in New Brunswick enforced by gun-toting gangs. In 1922, Paul Matoff, a Bronfman brother-in-law, was murdered at Bienfait, Saskatchewan (the case was never solved). In 1930, a Hamilton gangster and his wife were murdered, reputedly by Al Capone's mob. An Alberta bootlegger was hanged for murdering a policeman. The Prohibition era in Canada was peaceful in comparison with the United States, where ruthless criminal empires bought politicians and police and defended their turf with Tommy guns. But Canadian booze exporters were contributing to this crime and violence. In 1923, when Sam Bronfman got prized tickets to the Dempsey-Firpo championship fight in New York, his benefactor was a business connection by the name of Meyer Lansky.[29]

It also became an irritant in relations with our biggest trading partner. The Americans were in a terrible position, reduced to plaintively urging Canada, Britain, and other countries to please prevent the export of liquor to the United States. The British *chargé d'affaires* airily responded that "no useful purpose was likely to be served by such legislation so long as the American authorities along the border, and particularly in the town of Detroit, were apparently working hand-in-glove with the liquor smugglers." "Canada would show itself to be the simpleton in the family of nations," huffed the Toronto *Mail and Empire*, "if it entered into any engagement to help make the United States dry and thus made itself answerable to that country for a failure." Rum-runners arrested outside the three-mile limit demanded that the British and Canadian governments protect them. The United States retaliated by refusing to permit the transit of liquor to Yukon Territory through the Alaska panhandle.[30]

Some concessions were made, such as a treaty quietly signed in 1924 that, in effect, extended the U.S. right of search to twelve miles offshore. Further agreements provided for exchange of information between border officials on cargoes destined for the other country, and for transit to Yukon through Alaska. After the new Canadian legation in Washington took over the file, the King government in 1929 passed legislation outlawing clearances of liquor shipments to the United States. The smuggling trade simply moved to the French islands of St. Pierre and Miquelon. That same year, the Canadian-registered rum-runner *I'm Alone* was sunk by the U.S. Coast Guard in the Gulf of Mexico with the loss of one life. Both sides agreed to submit the case to arbitration. The owners of the vessel were compensated for the vessel (but not the cargo), the family of the deceased was also paid compensation, and what could have been a nasty blow-up instead became an example how friendly neighbours managed disputes.[31]

The real casualty of Prohibition in Canada was public respect for the law. If liquor could be legally manufactured, it would be sold, and not just into the United States. Bootlegging and blind pigs undoubtedly rescued dozens of poor families from destitution, but at the cost of routine tolerance by police and officials of illegal activity, with occasional fines (not to mention bribes or in-kind services) as a kind of licence fee. Rum-runners and bootleggers were powerful local figures who had a lot of friends and contributed to political coffers. Police were enforcing a law that often neither they nor the community agreed with, and which they frequently violated themselves. When did you search, whom did you arrest, and what did you do when you found something? Best to leave well-enough alone. The B.C. Prohibition Commissioner was convicted for importing seven hundred cases of whisky. "The law, what is the law?" said a Windsor rum-runner in 1924. "They don't want it in the cities. They voted against it. It is forced upon them. I have a right to violate it if I can get away with it.... Am I a criminal because I violate a law which the people do not want?"[32]

The federal government was inviting corruption when it abetted the lucrative export of a good that was illegal in the United States, on the grounds that Canada was only profiting from American stupidity. Alcohol exported legally could be imported back into Canada illegally, along with other American goods. In 1927, the Canadian government had seized so much illegal liquor that it could not find warehouses to hold it all. Corruption in the Customs Department nearly ended Mackenzie King's career in 1926, when an inquiry into textile smuggling revealed that not only was his minister of national revenue (now safely in the Senate) thoroughly bent, but the chief Customs officer in Montreal was *inter alia* selling confiscated liquor through a dummy company, sailing a seized boat at his cottage, running a farm along the Quebec-Vermont border through which textiles and other goods passed, and supporting drug dealing and car theft.[33]

But enforcing a law that is held in contempt could be even worse. In October 1919, Ontario voters elected a United Farmers of Ontario government on the same day they voted the province "dry." The new premier, E.C. Drury — a staunch Prohibitionist — appointed as his attorney general W.E. Raney, a lifelong opponent of liquor, gambling, and horse-racing. Impeccably dressed, full of pugnacious energy, and utterly humourless, Raney relentlessly enforced the Prohibition laws and attributed all opposition to a sinister clique of "Toronto mouthpieces of the bootlegging and gambling fraternities." In 1920, he created a special liquor squad and established a network of informers, several of whom were found to be criminals themselves. In Essex-Windsor, the officer was a Methodist minister, J.O.L. Spracklin, whose extra-legal methods included killing a leading club owner (for which he was acquitted). Each year, as support for Prohibition began to wane, Raney, pressed by zealots like Ben Spence, introduced new laws and regulations to tighten enforcement. Three hundred physicians lost their licences for "prescribing" liquor. In 1922, the Dominion Alliance requested a law that would restrict people from serving liquor at home to more than three to five people, and would require people to report to police how much liquor they had in their homes — they could then be charged if subsequent reports showed "abnormal shrinkage." Even for Drury, this was going too far and the project was shelved.[34]

Prohibition was supposed to bring about a more moral, productive, and just society. It was never supposed to mean violations of civil liberties and invasions of private homes by fanatical Prohibitionists and their informers. It was never supposed to bring corruption and disrespect for law and civil authorities. It was never supposed to lead to murder and crime, as Westerners began to fear after the Matoff murder was followed by a wave of bank robberies. As war-time idealism and hyper-patriotism began to subside, second thoughts began to set in. "Did somebody slip something over on us while the casualty lists blinded our eyes with tears?" wrote H.F. Gadsby:

Did the cold water people get by while we were looking
the other way? Was Prohibition a mood — all blue — or
was it a conviction? Did we give up drink because giving
up things was the fashion — horse races, baseball, ban-
quets, time, money — all as nothing compared with the
lives our boys gave up on the battle field? Did we give it
up because it was the easiest, safest, long-distance way of
martyrizing ourselves — of suffering something for the
war which implied personal discomfort? Why did we give
it up[?] And when we gave it up did we mean it?[35]

III

For three years after the war, the tide flowed strongly in most places in favour of Prohibition. Plebiscites in the Prairie provinces and Nova Scotia in
October 1920 invoked the Canada Temperance Act. Ontario followed suit
in the spring of 1921 and New Brunswick a little later. Quebec in 1921 forbade the export of liquor to provinces that had invoked the Canada Temperance Act and the federal government increased taxes and restrictions.
But the Quebec referendum of 1919 was followed by a breakthrough in
British Columbia when voters in 1920 approved government sale of liquor.
As referendum followed referendum, the margins in favour of Prohibition
got narrower and the cities voted "wetter."

What had once brought together a diverse array of causes, interests,
and people, was now becoming a wedge issue dividing them. As Stevenson had predicted, it was widening the fault lines in "a country of such
diversity of racial elements and human types," including immigrants
with different drinking habits where it was "impossible to prescribe a
uniform regime for all of them." It was yet again putting Quebec at
odds with the rest of the country, though Ben Spence was careful to tone
down his habitual anti-French rhetoric. It was dividing city people from
country people — Stevenson warned that by voting the cities dry out of
jealousy, farmers were losing their own opportunity to replace the dreary

country hotel with a more attractive "focus and rallying point for its common activities."[36]

Prohibition was also alienating labour, whose radical leaders had once supported it. In March 1918, some five thousand workers and war veterans from all parts of Ontario marched on Queen's Park demanding stronger beer: "[I]f you are going to make it, make it fit to drink." The Trades and Labour Congress repeatedly presented similar demands in Ottawa, which were endorsed at the TLC congress in Hamilton in September 1919 — and Tom Moore, president of the TLC (no relation to the Methodist leader T. Albert Moore), appeared frequently on platforms supporting moderation. By 1923, even William Ivens, founder of a Labour Church and a hero of the Winnipeg General Strike,* was shouted down when he tried to defend Prohibition at a meeting of workers. Business leaders who feared radicalism now realized it was better to sacrifice some efficiency and let workers have their beer.[37]

It was alienating the veterans. Returned soldiers were probably fortunate not to have the old saloons replace their wet canteens as they made the transition to civilian life. But they resented restrictions on the clubs where they gathered to share a beer with old comrades — even if the law was seldom enforced. In 1919, Toronto vets marched to protest efforts by the WCTU to ban rum and tobacco from their canteens. "Drinking is a social custom of man, just as tea drinking is a social custom of women," said a B.C. veteran. "We don't interfere with their custom, so don't let them interfere with ours." Another veteran in 1920 expressed disgust at being "supervised" like "the inferior races … a nice standing for a race who proved their fighting value on the Fields of France."[38]

The middle and upper classes had welcomed the demise of the saloon, but had probably not fully realized that their own wine cellars and liquor cabinets, or their ability to serve a drink in private, would be at risk. Prime Minister King (who drank very seldom) recorded in his diary in April 1921 that two cases of whisky he had asked a minister to purchase in Montreal arrived on the same day that he voted in the Ontario referendum. A.J. Andrews, who played a crucial role in breaking the Winnipeg General Strike and was legal counsel and family friend to the Bronfmans,

---

* See Chapter 8.

made sure he had ample stock on hand — on one occasion he placed an order for seven cases of wine, six of brandy, five of Scotch, ten of gin, two of liqueurs, and one of rum.[39]

Even some middle-class women began to regret their decision. "We don't believe in totally abstaining from a glass of beer or wine, yet eating up a pound of sweets in an hour or so and regarding that sort as temperance," declared the newly formed Women's League on Temperance and Government in 1921. Many of the girls who had played such an important role in WCTU campaigns had now grown up to regard the institution as old-fashioned and its propaganda as repressive. Many "new women" of the 1920s saw taking a drink as a symbolic act of rebellion against the old mores. One member of the Montreal elite recalled dances where men would carry hip flasks and "there would be private rooms hired and some people would just stay there and drink all evening."[40]

If the old saloon had "destroyed the man with the dinner pail," declared a pamphlet for the Manitoba Moderation League, "the drinking habit under Prohibition is destroying the man with the dinner jacket as well." Leacock complained that the old masculine saloon had been replaced by a "palm room" supplied by bootleggers, and that women no longer had any inhibitions about coming there to drink. "Now, no child is going to stand outside of it and sing, 'Father, dear Father, come home with me now.' She doesn't have to. Mother is in there too, and so is little Benny, who was sick. Mother brought him over with her because she thought that a couple of shots of gin might brighten him up." A Saskatchewan moderate charged that Prohibition had put country hotels out of business, "making millionaires of those who evade the law and taxing the law abiding citizens to pay for our mistake," benefitting only "the mail order houses and the Chinamen."[41]

Perhaps most seriously of all, Prohibition widened conflicts within and among the churches. The Anglican Church rejoined the Catholic, Lutheran, and Orthodox churches in opposing Prohibition as a violation of individual conscience and free will. The United Church, at its first General Council in 1925, felt compelled to defend Prohibition, but its advocates increasingly based their case on the older moral arguments rather than the progressive doctrines of the Social Gospel. When an aging Social Gospeller, Ernest Thomas, tried to find moderate ground for dialogue in the late 1920s, he provoked a storm of opposition. Prohibition had become an albatross for liberal Protestantism.[42]

IV

It would be wrong to believe that a society that had wholeheartedly approved Prohibition in 1918 had become implacably hostile to it by 1922. The bedrock support for Prohibition, especially in rural areas and the evangelical churches, remained firm. Some former supporters were now willing to admit that it had been a mistake, and those who had never supported Prohibition were now free to voice their opposition. But the crucial shift was in the middle group who had approved Prohibition in wartime but were now ready to countenance what Stevenson and others had advocated as early as 1919 — government control of the sale of liquor. By 1922, Moderation Leagues, patterned after those that had won the 1920 victory in British Columbia, were operating in most provinces. One by one. they forced new provincial referendums on the government sale of liquor, and on whether or not to allow alcohol to be sold by the glass in public places. They kept their distance from the "liquor interests," pointed to the fact that government sale of liquor in British Columbia and Quebec was bringing millions into the public coffers, and attracted moderates by stressing that government sale need not mean the return of the saloon.

Manitoba, Alberta, and Saskatchewan all approved government sale in 1923. That same year, in Ontario, the United Farmers government was defeated by Conservative Howard Ferguson, but the Prohibitionists gathered their forces one last time to vote down government sale in a referendum the following year. Ferguson did allow the sale of stronger beer (called "Fergie's foam") in "standard hotels." Then, in 1926, wanting to end once and for all what had become a tiresome and divisive political issue, he called an election, ran on a platform of government control, and after winning a majority, inaugurated government liquor stores the following year. In Nova Scotia and New Brunswick, government control was instituted by the late 1920s, but Prince Edward Island remained dry. Nova Scotia voters were persuaded to approve government liquor stores in 1927 in order to pay the provincial share of Old Age Pensions.[43]

Government liquor stores provided a revenue bonanza for provinces, but the emphasis was always on ensuring that drinking was treated as something people did behind closed doors. The Liquor Control Board of Ontario was typical of government stores across the country: drab, utilitarian places where holders of a liquor permit (which could be revoked for any violation of liquor laws or for driving offences) had their purchases duly recorded. Liquor was stored in a back room and handed to the customer in a brown paper bag. "Respectable" people like teachers, clergy, women, politicians, and bank managers darted in furtively when no one was looking — if they dared go at all.

But in most provinces there was continuing resistance to public sale of liquor by the glass. "The people of Manitoba know what they want and what they do not want," said a Winnipeg newspaper that had previously supported Prohibition. "They want government control of the liquor business....They do not want anything approaching the old system of public drinking.... On one point they are just as emphatic as they are on the other." Quebec approved sale by the glass in 1921 and Alberta in 1923, but British Columbia voters in 1920 rejected it, as did Manitoba and Saskatchewan in 1923. Sale by the glass was approved only in 1927 in Manitoba, 1935 in Saskatchewan, 1934 in Ontario, and not until 1948 in Nova Scotia and 1964 in Prince Edward Island.[44]

Great care was taken to ensure that places where liquor and beer could be sold by the glass should not become saloons. Ontario, when it finally allowed them, set the standard in creating cheerless "beverage rooms," where men — ladies could only come in through a separate door if escorted — sat four to a table. Patrons could not pick up a glass or carry it to another table or drink walking around. They could only get small snacks. They could not have games or entertainment. Beverage rooms were closed during dinner. No more fancy mirrors or polished bars, much less spittoons. They might as well have been designed to encourage drinking rather than limit it. Liquor licenses for restaurants were expensive, and minors were not allowed to eat where liquor was served, so most restaurants stayed dry until the 1970s. Only with a new wave of feminism, immigration, and a more sophisticated generation of baby boomers, did civilized drinking become once more a fully respectable social activity.[45]

Prohibition did not die so much as slowly fade away. We might well argue, from our vantage point in history, that drinking habits would have changed anyway as society evolved. Other changes, like the decline in public smoking for example, have come about because laws and regulations tracked a gradual change in public attitudes. Indeed, perhaps Prohibition set social reform back, by becoming in its final years a weapon in the hands of moral zealots against urban sophistication, social progress, and the enjoyment of life. Perhaps it actually led to a decline in respect for legal and religious authority. Perhaps Prohibition provides irrefutable evidence that only persuasion and social evolution, rather than the heavy hand of the law, can control practices that are harmful to vulnerable people.

Most of those who supported Prohibition, even if they later turned against it, would have disputed any such contention. The saloon was a real social evil, especially when compounded with slums, poverty, and the powerlessness of women. There was no doubt in their minds that legislation against these evils had been needed to "remove their cause, rather than to warn or win men away from them."[46]

And it worked. If Premier Drury had been too optimistic in hoping that "liquor will be out of business as affecting the new generation," social reformers could note with satisfaction that liquor for domestic consumption dropped from 4.6 million gallons in 1918 to 750,000 gallons in 1923, and recovered only to one million by 1926. Beer increased from thirty-five million gallons in 1917 to over fifty-two million gallons in 1926, but per capita consumption of alcohol dropped from .703 gallons per person in 1917 to .225 in 1925. James Gray believes that Prohibition brought change "greater than in any other ten-year period in Western Canadian history. With the pauperizing effect of unrestrained boozing removed, a new tranquillity came to family life in the cities and towns. As drunkenness disappeared from the streets, crime of all kinds declined sharply." It is probable that social upheavals like the Winnipeg General Strike owed much of their relative peacefulness and discipline to the absence of liquor. Employers across the country reported that men worked more efficiently and safely, that Monday morning absenteeism was down, and that workers now had more money to spend on furniture and food — could it be that at least some of the middle-class prosperity of the later 1920s was due to money being available for consumer goods that was not spent in saloons? Hospitals reported fewer cases of alcohol-related disease, insurance companies reported people living longer, using smaller amounts of other drugs and stimulants, turning to more wholesome pursuits, staying in school longer — and, in Toronto people were consuming more water![47]

And it should be recalled that it took two generations after total Prohibition ended before we learned to drink in a "normal" way, an epidemic of lung cancer before most people realized that smoking was a bad idea, and thousands of needless traffic deaths before designated drivers became widely accepted. The balance between respecting the right of individuals to do what may be bad for them, the obligation of the state to protect vulnerable people (even from themselves), and the interests and well-being of society as a whole, will always be difficult to find and harder to maintain. As we wrestle with a host of social problems, from a "war on drugs," to control of tobacco and marijuana, to the regulation of salt, trans fats, and sugar in our food, to government-run casinos and lotteries, we may well feel a degree of sympathy, and more than a little humility, as we look back on the struggle of our ancestors with the problem of "intoxicating liquors."

CHAPTER 7

Family Matters

Little noticed among the spate of books that appeared in 1919 prophesying the new Canada that would emerge from the war was one entitled *The Girl of the New Day*. Its author was Ellen Mary Knox, the much-admired principal of Havergal College, an Anglican girls' school in Toronto. Knox had a first-class degree from Oxford — extraordinary for a woman — as well as a strong religious faith and an equally firm belief in science and progress. In her book she painted an exciting picture of her adopted country after the war — a nation that could build houses in the suburbs, provide labour-saving devices and telephones to farmers' wives, "turn saloons into tea houses," restore the Bible "to its proper place" and "deepen the spiritual life of our Churches." She wanted her graduates, the "young girls of the new day" to know that they would play an important role in building this new world.

Cover of *Maclean's* Magazine September 1919
This is an example of young women, culture, and consumer goods replacing war stories and symbols in the media by late 1919. This image shows the new hair and dress styles, and an image of youth, wholesomeness, confidence, and unabashed, if innocent, sexuality.

To do so, they would need physical, mental, and moral strength. They would need to emulate their pioneer ancestors "who toiled, hemmed in by the ever-lasting trees, who wearied in the loneliness by day, and shuddered at the howling of the wolves by night." Like their soldier brothers, they would need to "enlist whole-heartedly in the struggle" and place themselves "at the strategical point where you can serve your country best." They would need to cultivate a sound mind, focus their physical and nervous energy, train their bodies, and wear sensible clothing — no more corseted delicacy. They would need to avoid temptation and not lead men into temptation, for the war had changed men. Many would have jobs, though their choice of professions might be limited, and they should never marry solely for financial security or to avoid being an old maid. But most *would* marry, and motherhood would "undoubtedly prove itself a stairway of light" if they chose to do it well. Unlike their own mothers, they would be able to call on medical science and receive expert knowledge on pregnancy, childbirth, nutrition, and child care; and their children would have nurseries and kindergartens.

"I wonder," she told her young graduates, "how many of you realize how lucky you are in having these calls. How harshly, as it were, the doors creaked upon the hinges of their houses before they were set open." She had no illusions about the challenges that would face them. It was no fun for a farm wife to slop the pigs on an isolated homestead on an early winter morning. Nor was it easy for a city stenographer to be competent, tactful, and respectful of demanding men, for a sales clerk to be always courteous, for a nurse to perform her thankless drudgery, for a librarian to be always punctual and disciplined. Professional women would face prejudice and barriers, and most would envy their sisters who reigned as queen in a home of

Courtesy Havergal College Dr. Catherine Steele 1928 Archives

Ellen Mary Knox

their own. But with enough discipline, preparation, and nerve, the girls of the new day would push back boundaries and play their vital role in shaping the nation's character and building its future.[1]

Principal Knox's book was aimed at a fairly narrow audience. Many more people were reading magazines like *Maclean's*, on whose covers, by the summer of 1919, photographs of generals were being replaced by pretty young women. Inside, war reminiscences were giving way to women's columns, romantic fiction, and articles on hair, cosmetics, fashion, popular culture, sport, films, beauty contests, and children. Advertisements for consumer goods, beauty products, and child-care items showed the increasing influence and freedom of women, and balanced an image of youthful femininity with that of wholesome motherhood.

And no one could fail to notice the women now casting their ballots in federal and provincial elections and referendums on Prohibition. Journalist Marjorie MacMurchy predicted that "enfranchised Canadian women will apply themselves intelligently and with energy to the basic economic problems of national existence. It is only through the help of women that the future can be made secure." Her friend Lucy Maud Montgomery was more inclined to believe that "matters will jog on in pretty much the same old way for a good while yet — or if they do not, it will be owing to the war and conditions arising from it and not to the franchise." But the war had changed the issues on which women were voting. It had brought the state into matters once considered the preserve of families or private philanthropy. Women were now citizens in a society that no longer placed them on a pedestal, no longer regarded them as dependents, no longer saw the home and the agora as separate spheres.[2]

I

To fully comprehend the extent of the change that had occurred, we must understand how severely restricted the legal position and social role of women had been before the war. The Victorian concept of women as frail creatures with delicate psyches and fragile reproductive systems — sexually passive, homebound angels who nonetheless bore hardship, embodied moral virtue, brought comfort, and nurtured children — dominated pop-ular literature, medical opinion, and public discourse. Protecting and cher-ishing women, placing them on a pedestal, was regarded as another sign of the superiority of Western civilization over ancient or primitive cultures that degraded, enslaved, or brutalized them.[3]

Despite some reforms won by organizations like the National Council of Women, a wife in 1914 still derived her identity, and her nationality, from her husband, who had the sole right to determine where the family would live and the sole ownership of all family property. He could disavow his wife's debts, but she could not disavow his; she could make a will but could not sue or give evidence against him. He could desert his family (though not commit bigamy), but he could be forced to make support pay-ments — if he could be found. He was the guardian of the children, though Ontario women could apply to the courts for guardianship. To get a di-vorce, she had to prove adultery, incest, or extreme cruelty — often at great damage to her own reputation. If she accused a man of seduction or rape, she had to prove it in an open trial where his word would be worth more than hers and her sexual conduct would be thoroughly scrutinized. She could not vote or hold public office. Her position was even more restricted in Quebec, except that in some municipalities property-owning women could vote in local elections. As leading feminist Sarah Rowell Wright told the Social Service Congress in 1914, the legal status of Canadian women was about the same as that of "Indians, and criminals, and idiots."[4]

The reality for most women was nothing like being on a pedestal. Even more than boys, girls usually had a fleeting childhood and little education before they had to take on the adult responsibilities of work or marriage. Adult women formed one-seventh of the paid work force — 44 percent in the Quebec textile industry. For those who worked as domestics, life was narrow and confined, with long hours and the possibility of abuse against which they had little protection, until or unless they were "rescued" by mar-riage. Marriage for all but the better-off meant further long hours of unpaid labour at home, managing family finances and raising children, and often some form of work outside the home or on the farm. For urban woman at the lowest levels, it meant crowded, unhealthy slums, and for their children the possibility of becoming a "neglected" street kid. As homesteaders in the

West, wrote Nellie McClung, women "suffer the hardships — cold, hunger, loneliness — against which there is no law; and, when the homestead is 'proved,' all the scrub cleared, and the land broken, the husband may sell the whole thing without his wife's knowledge, and he can take the money and depart without a word. Against this there is no law either!" [5]

By the early twentieth century, there was a strong movement among middle-class women to improve their legal status. Most proposed reforms met resistance, but male opposition was particularly visceral to any suggestion that women be given the right to vote. Many men simply resented this challenge to traditional definitions of masculinity and their dominant place in the world and the family. Some intellectuals, however, were genuinely concerned about the wider threat such a drastic change in gender relations would pose to the social and moral order and the future of the "race." God, Henri Bourassa thought, had created men and women differently — men as logical but rather brutal, and therefore suited to being businessmen, warriors, workers, and citizens; women as emotional and nurturing, and better fitted to be wives and mothers. Upsetting these roles would leave women uprooted and helpless in a materialistic, relentlessly changing world. Women would be corrupted by the sordid business of politics. The home and family, the bedrock of the national character, would be destroyed. "No man," Leacock wrote, "ever said his prayers at the knees of a vacuum cleaner, or drew his first lessons in manliness and worth from the sweet old-fashioned stories that a vacuum cleaner told." "Feminization" of society, thundered Andrew Macphail, would produce social unrest, a less fit race, and national decline. [6]

Even as they refuted these arguments, many middle-class women reformers nonetheless shared at least some of the assumptions that underlay them. Sarah Rowell Wright assured the 1914 Social Service Congress that women did not want the vote merely to grub around in politics, but to effect social and moral reforms that would make society a more decent place. Like the Social Gospellers they often were, middle-class reformers — "maternal feminists" as later historians have called them — placed their main emphasis on applying feminine values to change society as a whole and to "uplift" the underprivileged. "Women are naturally the guardians of the race, and every normal woman desires children," wrote Nellie McClung.

"The woman who really loves her own children, wants to bring them up to manhood and womanhood in purity and goodness, and wants to see them have a good chance in life — is the woman that wants to see other people's children get their chance too."[7]

They wove temperance, health and hygiene, moral reform, sexual virtue, medical and social science, and theories of "race," into a tapestry of ideas and symbols. They used organizations like the WCTU to empower themselves and force change. Adelaide Hoodless, wife of a wealthy furniture manufacture, helped found the YWCA, persuaded a tobacco millionaire to endow institutes of domestic science at McGill and Guelph, and founded the Women's Institute to allow farm women to exchange ideas and teach young girls handicrafts and homemaking. By 1915, there were 892 Women's Institutes across the country, with thirty thousand members, which united in 1919 to form the Federated Women's Institutes of Canada. Lillian Massey endowed a Faculty of Household Science at the University of Toronto, which was soon imitated by other universities.[8]

Dr. Helen MacMurchy — a graduate of Woman's Medical College and the University of Toronto, the first woman to intern at John's Hopkins under Sir William Osler, the first female resident at the Toronto General Hospital in obstetrics and gynaecology, a pioneer public health officer — wrote searing reports on the shockingly high rate of infant mortality in Toronto. Slum conditions were, of course, to blame, but she concluded that the major problems were ignorance and the necessity for mothers to work. "Where the mother works, the baby dies," was her harsh conclusion: "Nothing can replace maternal care." The solution was not only slum clearance, but mother's allowances, education, public health, and inspection of homes.

By 1914, governments at all levels had passed laws regarding school attendance, parental care, and juvenile delinquency; established public playgrounds, social settlements, social workers, and youth centres; and created enforcement mechanisms such as juvenile and family courts, reform schools, and morality and truant officers. Many of the agencies administering these measures were private organizations, which worked in close collaboration with the state. The Children's Aid Society, which under J.J. Kelso mobilized political and economic elites, churches, and provincial and local governments, was given the power to visit homes, enforce regulations, place "neglected children" in selected foster homes, and care for children committed by the courts.[9]

Keeping young women from poverty and vice also meant protecting them from their own innocence and ignorance. Travellers' Aid societies met young girls at train stations to ensure they were not being lured into a brothel instead of the domestic service jobs they had been promised. Surveys, anti-brothel campaigns, and "clean-up" operations had by 1920 reduced prostitution in most large cities — or at least taken it off the main streets. Young men also needed rescuing. A.W. Beall (who was first hired by the WCTU of Ontario as a "purity agent" and in 1911 transferred to the Ontario Department of Education) gave lectures to schoolboys about the evils of masturbation and other bad habits that would defile their bodies and dissipate their vital energies. "It is up to you," he told generations of Ontario boys, "to each of you, to become an A.1 father of A.1 children," and he made them repeat: "JESUS CHRIST AND CANADA EXPECT ME TO BE AN A.1 BOY." This campaign was taken up in schools and by a wide variety of church groups who also sent lecturers across the country preaching moral purity and healthy habits.[10]

Moral purity was important not only for individuals but for society and the future of the "race." "Every child," said Sarah Rowell Wright, "has the right to be well born." People who were healthy, intelligent, and pure would produce the best children. Education and uplift would ensure that more people developed these qualities and passed them on. But the opposite was also true: as a botany professor wrote in 1919, immorality, prostitution, and alcoholism would produce "defects such as feeble-mindedness, epilepsy, deaf-mutism, and disposition to tuberculosis and other diseases," which could also be passed on to their children. "To put no hindrance to the breeding of unfit and degenerate persons exposes our country to the gravest risk of regression," the professor warned, adding that this danger was compounded by recruiting immigrants from "inferior stocks." This was an extreme view, but if society had a responsibility to uplift people and improve "the race," it also needed to protect itself from physical and moral degeneracy. Those who were irremediably "feeble-minded," thought Dr. MacMurchy, should be isolated, protected from abuse and exploitation, and as a last resort sterilized. "We must make a happy and permanent home for them during their lives," she wrote in 1920. "Their only Permanent Parent is the State."[11]

In Quebec, Marie Gérin-Lajoie, Caroline Béique, and Josephine Dandurand founded the Fédération nationale Saint-Jean-Baptiste in 1907, which brought together twenty-two women's organizations, including anglophone ones, and quickly grew to twelve thousand members. The Fédération campaigned for pasteurization of milk and pure milk depots, reducing infant mortality, training mothers in hygiene and nutrition, pensions for teachers, better working conditions in factories and stores, improved marriage rights for women, Prohibition, elimination of prostitution, and censorship of "immoral" films.

Gérin-Lajoie, who acquired a legal education by studying her father's law books and only accepted marriage when her suitor agreed to grant her equal rights, dominated the movement for two decades. Though she met strong clerical opposition, she was deeply committed to working within the Church and was careful to portray her work as reinforcing rather than challenging traditional feminine values. She encouraged women to vote in municipal elections to save their sons from saloons, their daughters "whose virtue is gradually being eroded by immoral theatre," and their children "contaminated by the filth in the streets." When Archbishop Bruchési agreed to appoint a chaplain to the Fédération, he told them that though he reluctantly accepted the term *féminisme*, he demanded that it be given a "Christian meaning," namely, "the zealous pursuit by woman of all the noble causes in the sphere that Providence has assigned to her." "There will be no talk in your meetings," he admonished them, "of the emancipation of woman, of the neglect of her rights, of her having been relegated to the shadows, of the responsibilities, public offices and professions to which she should be admitted on an equal basis with man."[12]

Outside the mainstream of middle-class reformers were socialists, proponents of free love, and radical suffragists like Flora Macdonald Denison, Dr. Emily Stowe Gullen, and others who demanded fundamental change in the status of women and the relations between the sexes. Labour leaders like Helena Guttridge of Vancouver fought for suffrage as well as the rights of women as workers. In 1912, the International Ladies' Garment Workers

Union sent two international organizers to work with the three hundred women involved in an unsuccessful strike of clothing workers against Eaton's. But most labour unions were slow to espouse the cause of women, whom they saw as cheap workers who could be used to lower wages, "de-skill" the workplace, and break strikes. Even in towns such as Paris, Ontario, where the Penman factory employed a large female workforce, traditional ideas of gender roles and the family prevailed.[13]

Still, there remained the vote, without which most of the reforms maternal or radical feminists wanted could not be enacted except with the consent of male voters and politicians. Nellie McClung was the maternal feminist leader who saw most clearly that persuading men to enact reforms, and making arguments to them about why women should have the vote, was a trap. Women should not *ask* for citizenship, she argued, they should *demand* it. As she told Premier Roblin of Manitoba in 1914, "we are not here to ask for a reform, or a gift, or a favour, but for a right — not for mercy, but for justice." Born in Ontario in 1873 and raised on a pioneer farm in Manitoba, McClung was already well-known as a writer and speaker when she moved to Winnipeg in 1911 with her pharmacist husband and

their five children, and she quickly became a leading voice there for suffrage as well as other social causes. In a widely publicized mock parliament staged by women's groups, McClung played the role of a woman premier receiving a delegation of men asking for the vote. Imitating Roblin's voice and mannerisms, she first complimented the men on their appearance, then condescendingly refused their request: "politics unsettles men, and unsettled men mean unsettled bills — broken furniture, broken vows and divorce." Her opponents knew how to get even — she was constantly subject to vicious personal

Nellie McClung

attacks, epithets like "hysterical," and "battle-axe," and insinuations that her children were "neglected."[14]

By 1914, there was significant support for women's suffrage. A few labour unions in Vancouver and Winnipeg had given their strong endorsement. Frances Beynon's woman's page in the *Grain Growers' Guide* (the voice of Prairie farmers) had become a forum for reform ideas, and referendums on women's suffrage conducted by the newspaper in 1912 and 1913 were overwhelmingly favourable. Religious reformers, politicians like Rowell in Ontario and Norris in Manitoba, and educators like James L. Hughes, as well as Quebec nationalist Olivar Asselin, had declared in favour. Even Leacock conceded that there was really no good reason not to allow women to vote. Yet, like Prohibition, women's suffrage appeared stalled. Premiers Roblin of Manitoba, Hearst of Ontario, and Gouin of Quebec remained vehement in their opposition. Most middle-class women were not prepared to put up the determined fight — and certainly not to stage demonstrations, violence, and hunger strikes like the British suffragettes — to force a reluctant, male-dominated society to grant them the vote. When militant British suffragist Emmeline Pankhurst visited Canada in 1913, Borden declared that any violent actions by Canadian suffragists would ensure his opposition, then ducked the issue by declaring it a provincial matter.[15]

II

As with Prohibition, the war changed everything. Borden recognized immediately that while the "manhood" would defend the nation, the family and the state would now play a greater role. Over four hundred women joined the military as nurses; many others signed up as nursing assistants, ambulance attendants, drivers, cooks, and clerks; and forty-three were killed. Besides the hundreds of thousands at home who did volunteer work, sold war bonds, served as nurses, or assisted with patriotic fund programs, thirty-five thousand women were employed in the munitions industry, and others worked in the steel and cement industries and on the railways as firemen, freight handlers, and trackmen. A survey of eight munitions plants in Quebec showed that women made up over one-third of the workforce, of whom 22 percent were married, about 6 percent had come from domestic service, and 15 percent were employed for the first time. The Royal Bank employed seven hundred women by 1916 as opposed to 250 before the war, and almost all the elementary school teachers in Ontario and over half the secondary teachers were women. In 1918, women were required, like men, to register as potential workers.[16]

At the same time the war sanctified motherhood. In McClung's *Next of Kin* (1917), a departing soldier, "just a sort of bo-hunk from the North Country," encounters a woman seeking a surrogate son. "I'll be your war-mother," she says. "I am your Next of Kin. Give in my name and I'll get the cable when you get the DSO, and I'll write to you every week and send you things." When the boy remarks that all this is rather sudden, the mother replies, "I lost my boys just as suddenly as this." McClung wrote even more movingly about "losing" her own son:

> It should not be so hard for mothers to give up their children. We should grow accustomed to it, for we are always losing them. I once had a curly-haired baby with eyes like blue forget-me-nots, who had a sweet way of saying his words.... Soon I lost the blue-eyed baby, and there came in his place a sturdy little freckle-faced chap.... Then I lost him too. There came in his place a tall youth with a distinct fondness for fine clothes, stiff collars, tan boots, and bright ties.... Then came the call! And again I lost him! But there is a private in the "Princess Pats" who carries my picture in his cap and who reads my letter over again just before "going in."

On December 1, 1919, the first Silver Crosses were awarded to the mothers of fallen soldiers.[17]

The causes for which maternal feminists had fought were now essential to national efficiency. Prohibition came to fruition. The state became a surrogate husband to soldiers' wives and widows. Mother's allowances were instituted in all provinces west of the Ottawa River between 1916 and 1920. Western provinces began to enact minimum wage laws for women. Divorce laws in several provinces gave the wife the right to veto transactions involving the common home and property, as well as a share of her husband's estate if there were children. Other laws made women the legal guardians of their children. A Women's War Conference in 1918, in which key ministers of the federal government met with handpicked delegations to discuss how women could help win the war, spent most of its time on suffrage, health, the welfare of children, female unemployment, and Prohibition. No one could ever again convincingly argue that women were delicate creatures who should not be involved in public life. Public life had come to them.[18]

Opposition to women's suffrage simply collapsed in English Canada. In May 1915, the Manitoba Liberals under T.C. Norris defeated Roblin; the following January, Norris's government granted suffrage to women, and later extended this to include the right to hold public office. Less than a year later, Saskatchewan followed suit; Alberta gave women "absolute equality" with men, and in 1917 British Columbia gave women the right to vote and to hold office. In Ontario, Premier Hearst reversed his bitter opposition to granting women the vote, though he resisted giving them the right to hold office until faced with imminent defeat in 1919. Nova Scotia gave women the vote in 1918, New Brunswick in 1919, and Prince Edward Island in 1922. Federally, after using some women's votes to win the 1917 election, Borden introduced a bill in March 1918 that granted all women the vote on an equal basis with men — not, he said, because of their sacrifice, but because they were entitled to it and because public life would benefit from their participation. The Dominion By-Elections Act of July 1919 established that a woman derived her citizenship on her own, not from her husband, and that she could hold public office. The Dominion Elections Act of 1920 consolidated these measures within a wholesale reform of the electoral system.[19]

Only in Quebec did the walls hold. Feminism was sideswiped by the clerical and nationalist reaction to attacks on the language and the patriotism of French Canadians. Bourassa's opposition became implacable when Borden used women's votes to impose conscription (in vain the Fédération nationale Saint-Jean-Baptiste argued that the votes of Quebec women would strengthen the opposition to conscription). After the war, Premier Taschereau told delegation after delegation "with disconcerting frankness that though women might some day get the vote, it would never come from him." When in 1922 the Church applied pressure on Gérin-Lajoie to withdraw from the movement, she first tried to secure support among the Quebec bishops, then in May took her case to the congress of the International Union of Catholic Women's Leagues in Rome. The congress decided that women's suffrage was not contrary to the teachings of the Church, but that specific initiatives would need the approval of Quebec bishops. This decision, which Gérin-Lajoie always believed was due to Bourassa's influence, demoralized francophone feminists and widened the gulf with frustrated English-speaking reformers. Quebec women only got the vote in 1940 and had to wait even longer for many of the other rights women had won in English Canada.[20]

III

By the end of the war "the new woman" was a familiar catch-phrase. Wartime employment, the increasing rejection by young people of older taboos and moralities, and a new longing for life, youth, and fun, had loosened previous social constraints. At the same time, the war had exalted the ideas of motherhood, family, a virile "race," and "homes fit for heroes." The "new woman," like Principal Knox's "girl of the new day," would be a sometimes uneasy blend of older feminine virtues and newer ideas of freedom, equality and national efficiency.

The "new woman" was better educated. By 1920, girls were staying longer in school; many got training in private domestic science or business "colleges," and some even got a year or two of high school. There were, however, still far more teenage girls in the workforce than teenage boys, and only fifty thousand women in post-secondary education. No longer regarded as delicate creatures, girls could now exercise and compete in sports, even if their athletic uniforms were silly by today's standards. Nineteen eighteen saw the first organized inter-school competition in basketball, track and field, and softball for girls. Canadian female athletes became household names in track and field, swimming, skating, basketball, softball, and golf. More girls could now enjoy not only childhood but a period of adolescence, with greater freedom, more leisure, and some education.[21]

Dance halls, cinemas, and other public entertainments allowed young people to escape the watchful eyes of parents. The "sheiks" and "vamps" of the cinema portrayed romantic longings and sexual fantasies once kept hidden. The abrupt change in fashion (shorter, looser, one-piece dresses with low waists and fringed hems, stockings, bandeau bras that created the "flat look,"); the increased use of beauty aids like lipstick, mascara, and makeup; and dances like the Charleston — all epitomized the sexual freedom, zest for life, and rejection of traditional ideas of femininity. "Dating" became the norm, with groups of young people going out together, and serial pairing before "going steady" and engagement.[22]

The mores of the early 1920s were a blend of prolonged adolescence, rebellion against norms and expectations, and a serious desire by women to declare their independence and play a full role in society. This was often expressed through women engaging in such symbolic acts as smoking, drinking, or getting their hair cut short, or "bobbed." James Gray describes what happened in his Winnipeg office in 1922 when a "vivacious younger woman in her early twenties" had her hair bobbed during lunch. "The news of her decision was carried through the building … it did something for her personality; made her almost schoolgirlish in demeanour." Some days later, a "rather homely older woman" took the same step and also changed personality. "She seemed much more inclined to smile than before, though that might have been a self-conscious reaction, indicating she was not quite comfortable with what she had done." Within a few more weeks, half the women in the building had bobbed their hair in what was seen as "an historic, if not a giant, step for womankind away from her subservient role in human society."[23]

But greater sexual freedom brought danger and responsibility. Girls were lectured that they must not tease or "egg on" young men, for they would bear the consequences if they did. It was as hard as ever for a woman to prove rape or abuse. Principal Knox was typical in warning her "girls of the new day" of the fate that awaited them if they fell from virtue. Unmarried pregnant girls were usually exiled to relatives and the unwanted child might be sent to an orphanage.[24]

The majority of young working women still lived at home. For those in the city on their own, church homes and "respectable" boarding houses, recreational centres, and YWCAs provided curfews and supervision. Large companies furnished recreational facilities and canteens for their female employees. Government publications and magazine articles offered women advice on how to dress and behave at work, how to use their time and money efficiently, how not to provoke improper advances, and how to combine ambition with self-effacement. By the end of the 1920s, young women going to work with their hair bobbed, wearing short dresses and cloche hats, and attending dances and parties, were no longer considered unusual, much less a threat to the moral or social order.[25]

In Quebec, the Church hierarchy was less enamoured of the "new woman." Clerical attacks on modern fads and fashions as "unnatural" to the "hereditary instincts" of French Canadian women were probably laughed at; but less funny was the conclusion of the Dorion Commission of 1933 that women "have not really evolved" and were created "to be the companion of a man ... above all, a wife and a mother." The bishop of Valleyfield denounced the "ridiculous" vanity of women who purported to be educated and declared that there was "absolutely no comparison to be made with, and no similarities to be found in, boys' education." Nonetheless, Quebec urban women who might once have joked of "going to heaven with a broom in my hand" were now buying cosmetics, wearing the new fashions, seeking education and training, and holding jobs in much greater numbers.[26]

But what work would the "new woman" do? At the end of the war those who had worked in munitions plants found themselves unemployed and most were not rehired when their plants reverted to normal production. Those who had replaced the "bank boys" who were at the front were now told by a woman banker that "the most successful banking woman amongst us will cheerfully retire to her own hearthstone, preferring the love of a husband and little children to thousands a year and a seat in the council of the mighty!" Governments kept their promise to hire returning soldiers by laying off women, and, in spite of official policies to the contrary, they limited female advancement and reserved the best jobs for men. "You took a job during the war to help meet the shortage of labour," said a pamphlet issued by the Ontario Ministry of Labour. "You have 'made good' and you want to go on working. But the war is over and conditions have changed. There is no longer a shortage of labour.... Do you feel justified in holding a job which could be filled by a man who has not only himself to support, but a wife and family as well?" It was undoubtedly with reluctance and resentment that many women gave up their wartime jobs. But give them up they did.[27]

Marjorie MacMurchy, an erstwhile apostle of women's ability to do "male" jobs, wrote a booklet for the Canadian Reconstruction Association listing "suitable" occupations for women, including stenographer, nurse, teacher, beekeeper (!), milliner, retailer, clerk, and telephone operator. In 1919, the Ontario Technical Education Act provided for domestic science courses for girls and manual training for boys. All provinces began to teach typing, stenography, and business practice in public schools, and private business colleges sprang up everywhere. In Quebec, after 1923, girls could be given training in Catholic schools in homemaking, and by the end of the decade they could be trained as telephone operators, teachers, nurses, and secretaries.[28]

There was plenty of work for women in these fields with the postwar expansion of corporate offices, schools, hospitals, service and retail industries, restaurants, and hotels. From 1921 to 1941, the percentage of all clerical and sales positions occupied by women rose from 32.8 to 40.5, while in light manufacturing, the proportion declined from about one third to less than one-quarter of the work force in the largest cities. In smaller centres, women worked in industries such as furniture making, ore sorting, fruit and vegetable packing, cigar making, fish processing, jam production, textile and clothing manufacturing, shoemaking, and food processing. At the bottom of the scale, domestic service occupied a declining proportion of the female work force, and these jobs were increasingly filled by immigrants, as were other "personal service" jobs such as hotel maid, laundress, waitress, and hairdresser.[29]

Women remained barred from some professions and faced discrimination and quotas in most others. Women teachers were paid less than men. The boss in the school, hospital, office, store, hotel, or factory was almost always a man, and women could be disciplined for any lapses in "lady-like" behaviour. Better education meant a chronic oversupply of women seeking work in business and offices. Minimum wage and other labour laws for women were almost impossible to enforce. Manitoba required that women and children in retail could "only" work fourteen hours a day and sixty hours a week, and had to be able to sit down when not busy. Even for the good jobs, like telephone operator, clerk, and stenographer, pay was much lower than for comparable male occupations, and a waitress in Winnipeg might make $15 a month. The Powell Match Block Factory in Nelson, B.C., like many small manufacturing industries, employed women (including unemployed teachers or nurses) on an assembly line, without coffee breaks, standing for eight hours a day, for twenty-five cents an hour, while men operated machinery and did "skilled" work at much better pay.[30]

The biggest career limitation for the "girl of the new day" was the knowledge that everything — freedom, job, dancing, and dating — was only temporary. "The life of the average woman," wrote Marjorie MacMurchy in 1919, "is divided, generally, into two periods of work, that of paid employment and that of home-making." Probably most women looked forward to marriage and motherhood, and for many it may well have offered an escape from shabby living conditions, low pay, lack of opportunity for advancement, and vulnerability to abuse. Even single career women opposed married women competing for their jobs — the Calgary Business Girls' Club in 1922 petitioned for a law "compelling married women to stay in their homes where they belonged." Most did — in 1921, 40 percent of women aged twenty to twenty-four were working, only 20 percent of those aged twenty-five to thirty-four were, and there were many fewer involved in paid work in the higher age groups.[31]

IV

"Nations are built of babies," said Dr. Helen MacMurchy. Total war had made motherhood a "sacred national duty" and reconstruction of the nation (and replenishment of its population) would require, said the National Council of Women, "a realization of the power of consecrated motherhood." The tragic waste of life in the war also drew attention to the equally tragic loss of infants and children through childhood mortality and poor health. The Women's War Conference had called for a national Department of Health, not only to deal with infectious diseases, but to address the treatment of alcoholism, venereal disease, "feeble-mindedness," maternal and child health, pensions for mothers, safe food and drugs, health and sex education, child poverty, hygiene, and drug use. "If we are to be a great nation,"

Helen Reid, a key administrator of the Patriotic Fund, told the conference, "we must begin at the bases, the health of the nation, and see that we have healthy boys and girls born to be our future citizens."[32]

By 1921, the average age of first marriage for women (below twenty-five) and men (twenty-seven) was much lower than in 1901. Three-quarters of Canadian women were married by age thirty-four and almost 90 percent of women and 91 percent of men eventually married. Birth rates had been falling for two generations and would continue to do so, but they remained high by today's standards. More than half of families with children reported three or more and 12 percent reported six or more. Immigrant families had more children in the first generation, and the Quebec birth rate of 37.6 births per thousand was described as "the highest rate of natural increase of any civilized country." But by 1940 the average family in Quebec had only three children, and only one woman in five had more than six children.[33]

Marriage was now being described in a Department of Health publication as "a partnership ... sacred, lasting, and enabling, giving beauty, dignity, and glory to you and to your home and country." Couples spent more time in courtship — he making sure she would be a good mother, housewife, and cook; she satisfying herself that he would be a faithful and dependable provider. Premarital sex was still taboo, though "petting" was permitted, as well as more frank discussion of sexuality. Still, when they became man and wife, most couples knew far less of each other, and of what they could expect in the bedroom and in daily living than we would consider normal today.[34]

The main purpose of marriage, and the primary role of women, was still to produce children. There was little to choose between what Helen MacMurchy told women in 1923 — "The greatest happiness you will

Dr. Helen MacMurchy

University of Toronto Archives A1973-0026/293P (67)

ever experience comes each time it is your lot to bring into being the flesh of your flesh" — and what Quebec cleric Athanase David said in 1922 — "The mother, who never stands so tall as when she is kneeling beside the cradle, in this role deserves a greater solicitude and a greater degree of sympathy from one and all."

But as Principal Knox had pointed out, the mothers of the "new day" would have the advantages of education and expert advice. By the early 1920s, most doctors had some training in obstetrics and gynaecology, and pregnant women and new mothers were now treated as "patients." Expectant mothers were constantly urged to get rest, good food, stay healthy, and keep calm, to *see their doctors*, and *not* to rely on outmoded advice from their mothers and relatives. Medical authorities insisted that having children in hospitals was safer. Unfortunately, the evidence was to the contrary — the death rate in hospital childbirth rose in the 1920s before falling sharply with the development of antibiotics in the late 1930s. Even so, by 1928 about 30 percent of Canadian women were having their babies in hospitals, which at the very least allowed the mother rest, recovery, and instruction.[35]

Expert advice was also needed in the home, which was, according to one, "the poorest run, most mismanaged and bungled of all human industries." Helen MacMurchy believed that education of women, more than anything else, would produce healthy children, alleviate the worst aspects of poverty, and build a stronger "race." "We teach reading," she wrote, "and we leave parenthood to come by chance. It does not so come." In 1920, MacMurchy was appointed director of the Maternal and Child Welfare Division of the new Department of Health, and the following year it published the *Canadian Mother's Book*. "The Government of Canada," it declared, "knowing that the nation is made of homes, and that the homes are made by the Father and Mother, recognizes you as one of the Makers of Canada. No National Service is greater or better than the role of the Mother in her own home. The mother is the First Servant of the State."[36]

This book was accompanied by fourteen "Little Blue Books," of which some eight hundred thousand were circulated in the 1920s, on subjects as diverse as nutrition, childhood diseases, pre- and post-natal care, child-rearing, looking after old people, and housekeeping. They provided, in detailed, readable, but no-nonsense language, a blend of practical advice, admonitions, encouragement, and science, with a strong element of religious moralizing and nationalism. "You will be able to nurse the baby," nervous young mothers were instructed, "for you know it is better for the baby, better for you, and better for Canada. It saves the baby's life." "Youth," the books informed young parents, "has faith, teachableness, imagination and other gifts of greatness which are only given once and which if not cherished and used, wither away without bringing forth the flower and fruit of good character and citizenship in Home and Church and Country." Parents must therefore be "kind, quiet, polite, serene, self-controlled, sympathetic … not the angry parent." This was "The Canadian Way."[37]

This pioneering use of government resources to provide expert advice was part of a torrent of information that descended upon mothers — from schools, social workers, and regular "mother and baby" columns in popular newspapers and magazines (which were also full of advertising for condensed milks, baby foods, medicine, clothes, and toys for children). Dr. Alan Brown, a pioneer pediatrician at the Sick Children's Hospital in Toronto, inventor of Pablum, and mentor to a generation of doctors, was a prolific author whose most widely read book was *The Normal Child: Its Care and Feeding* (1923). Most of this expert advice blended older ideas of health, hygiene, maternal care, and the importance of play and character development with newer concerns such as medical care and mental health. By the later 1920s, the emphasis was on a Freudian, behaviourist approach to discipline and training to produce well-adjusted children. "It was formerly believed," wrote two leading experts in 1928, "that mother instinct or mother love was the simple and the safe basis for the problems of training[;] it is now known that a much more reliable guide is the kitchen timepiece." Children should be put on a schedule and left to "cry it out" until they learned to conform.[38]

Most women probably took such "scientific" advice with a grain of salt. Many, though, with more education and a desire that their children be "well born," were more receptive to what science had to offer in the area of birth control. Though some feminist reformers demanded greater dissemination of information and advice on family planning, there were no prominent Canadian birth control advocates like Marie Stopes in England or Margaret Sanger in the United States (though their books and lectures did reach many Canadian women). MacMurchy and most doctors were as adamant as any Catholic bishop that birth control and abortion were moral abominations and "race suicide." Doctors were forbidden to prescribe, advise, or practise either, and there were criminal penalties for providing contraceptive devices. Undoubtedly, many sympathetic doctors quietly ignored the law regarding contraception. For those women without advice or assistance in family planning, however, the use of folk medicine to induce abortion, primitive self-abortions, or "back-alley" jobs certainly cost many women their lives or health.

Besides giving advice, all levels of government were ready to assist, regulate, and protect, even as the state receded from other aspects of its ambitious wartime role. Mother's allowances, like war widows' pensions, provided modest support for single women with children, although this support was accompanied by means and morals tests and intrusive inspections. Public programs and private agencies, including the Canadian Council on Child Welfare (founded in 1921 by Charlotte Whitton, a disciple of Shearer), reflected the belief, strengthened by the war, that society had a duty to "reinforce and strengthen the endangered family, by drawing on the community's resources, not only in material relief, but in character and spiritual strength as well." Neonatal, infant, and child mortality were cut almost in half between 1921 and 1939 — though diseases like polio remained killers and death rates in outlying areas, in urban slums, and among aboriginal people, remained shockingly high.[40]

V

The homes in which families raised their children were as varied as the cities, farms, regions, occupations, and cultures of Canada. As a reconstruction measure, the federal government made money available to the provinces to provide the "homes fit for heroes" that wartime rhetoric had promised. A Little Blue Book outlined plans for building and financing a home. Ellen Knox's hope that more single family homes would be built in the suburbs began to be realized, not only for the middle class but for many in the working class as well. Even smaller houses and flats were being built away from the worst urban slums. These new homes were designed around a kitchen, had indoor plumbing, porcelain sinks and flush toilets, central heating, perhaps an icebox, a telephone, and electric light, and were compact, functional, and easy to clean. By the late 1920s, a family of five in Montreal with an income of $2,000 a year could furnish a five-room flat with plain but serviceable furniture and enjoy a basic diet. Prosperity after 1924 made it possible for most male workers to achieve the ideal of being the sole breadwinner.[41]

Although the husband usually controlled the family income, women were now well-established as consumers. By 1922, washing machines had become more practical, though they were still, at $115–130, prohibitively expensive. In 1924, says James Gray, Winnipeg Hydro included an electric water heater with each washing machine, and it allowed for purchase on credit, with a down payment of $15 and the balance payable over two years. This was so successful that the utility began selling stoves the same way, extended the payment to three years, and added it to the electricity bill. Thus "washday lost its terror for the housewives of [W]estern Canada, and the washerwoman's occupation became the first redundancy of the electrical age." In every large city and many smaller towns, hydro authorities marketed electric stoves, water heaters, irons, and other appliances using the new tool of consumer credit. Newspaper advertising depicted household appliances, lighting, and labour-saving devices being enjoyed by happy homemakers and families. Department stores displayed goods in sections that would attract women, and many women came to see the store, and the catalogue, as a special place for them. A Little Blue Book outlined a notional urban budget of $1,850 as follows: heat, $120; food, $240; clothes, $201; church and charity, $118; life insurance, $177; rent, $300; savings, $350; medical, $83. Better-off people might budget 20 percent for "better life" expenses; the worse-off would have to trim back where they could.[42]

The middle-class lifestyle embraced increasing numbers of people, but it remained a mirage for families in the poorer neighbourhoods of cities, in smaller towns, on the farm, and in the mining, fishing, and frontier communities. Even though children stayed in school longer, almost half of boys and nearly two-thirds of girls left school at sixteen. Most women still had their babies at home, with the assistance of midwives, family members, or country doctors. Electricity had still reached only 69 percent of occupied dwellings by 1939. In 1929, only about 5 percent of Canadians earned the $2,500 necessary to pay income tax, and the average annual wage was only $1,200.[43]

Women were still considered responsible for the success or failure of a marriage. A woman was judged on whether she kept a clean house, whether her children were well-behaved, whether her husband was well cared-for, whether they observed customs and codes, whether, in short, they were "respectable." Many had to tolerate occasional infidelities, and perhaps more than occasional assaults, and somehow cope when their husband fell short as a breadwinner. Despite a small uptick during the war, Canada's divorce rate in 1921 was the lowest in the Western world. Manitoba recorded its first absolute decree of divorce in 1919. In 1930, only six provinces had divorce courts. Until the 1960s, divorce could only be granted in Quebec by an act of the federal Parliament. Adultery was the only sure ground for divorce, and most women could not afford the legal costs, much less the social stigma — and judgments about child support, custody, and division of property seldom favoured the woman.[44]

Even an unhappy marriage might be better than no marriage at all. Of the 10 percent of women who never married, some were professional women; some, especially in Quebec, were nuns, who made immense contributions to education, social welfare, and health care; but the majority did not choose their fate. Some had lost fiancés in the war or by industrial or other accidents, influenza, TB, or other diseases. Like widows and abandoned wives, they might live in households as maiden aunts or as part of blended families, they might find jobs, or they might maintain a precarious independence with work, pensions, and welfare. Besides pensions for war widows, Ontario dispensed mother's allowances to twenty-six hundred women in 1920; by the end of the decade it was helping fifty-six hundred women and seventeen thousand children.[45]

It was even worse to be old. Most young families continued to accept responsibility for aging relatives, who could usually find a home, and a place, within an extended family. But few people had a pension. Government old-age pensions were not instituted until 1927, and because they required provinces to pay their share, they did not become effective in most of the country until the 1930s. If they had no pensions or savings, family, or the ability to work, old men survived at subsistence level, and older women faced an even bleaker prospect. The good news, if it can be called that, was that most people did not live to normal retirement age or much beyond.[46]

What about dad? The war had been a dehumanizing experience that called into question the prewar idea of "manliness" but put nothing in its place beyond a stoic devotion to duty, and, for younger men, the role model of the silent movie star. The patriarchal father with absolute power over his family was in some measure a casualty of the war. Men had to cede authority to women in the management of the home and the raising of children, and they increasingly shared parental responsibilities in a marriage that was now more of a partnership than separate spheres. They, too, were now lectured by "experts" on their role. They, too, were now exposed to the judgment of neighbours, doctors, church, and peers. The identification of masculine worth with employment and success was for many men a heavy responsibility and unemployment a crushing blow.[47]

VI

In the federal election of 1921, women voters swelled the electorate to an unprecedented size. One woman, Agnes Macphail, was elected to the House of Commons. Louise McKinney and Roberta MacAdams had been members of the Alberta legislature since 1917; women had been elected to the legislatures in British Columbia (1918) and Manitoba (1920); and Ellen Smith in British Columbia had become the first woman cabinet minister. In 1921, Nellie McClung was elected to the Alberta legislature as a Liberal and Irene Parlby was appointed to the Cabinet when the United Farmers of Alberta formed the government. These feminist leaders championed the causes for which women had demanded the vote — old age pensions, mother's allowances, minimum wages, Prohibition, more liberal divorce legislation, as well as other social issues.

But Macphail was isolated and miserable in her first session, sitting as the only woman in the masculine world of the House of Commons. As an Opposition member, McClung found that her collegial style did not fit in the partisan world of politics. In the 1921 federal election, women divided their votes among Liberal, Conservative, Progressive, and Labour candidates in roughly the same ratio as men did — as Lucy Maud Montgomery had predicted. They may have had more of an electoral impact at the provincial level, particularly within the farmers' parties that made women an integral part of their political organization, and on issues like Prohibition. But most women, like most men, still saw politics as a man's world, and most women seemed happy to be citizens but not active participants. The maternal feminists were aging and their movement had won most of its battles.[48]

But not all. Following a decision by the Federal Court of Canada in 1927 that women were not "persons" eligible to be appointed to the Senate, Emily Murphy, Irene Parlby, Nellie McClung, Henrietta Muir Edwards, and Louise McKinney appealed the case to the Judicial Committee of the Privy Council. In 1929 it ruled that women were indeed "persons," and that "the exclusion of women from all public offices is a relic of days more barbarous than ours." While these "Famous Five" are rightly considered heroes, it was disturbing that they had to fight this battle at all, that they had so few male champions, and that this sweeping judgment came from a British, not a Canadian court.[49]

It is hardly surprising that the vision of the first generation of feminists was more limited than that of later women building on their achievements. Yet the change that had come about by the 1920s would have been unimaginable at the turn of the century. By the time Ellen Knox died in 1924, her "girls of the new day" had more education, more economic power, more legal rights, more political involvement, more freedom, and better work than their mothers had ever dreamed of. As mothers themselves, they could draw on scientific and medical advice in performing a role that was seen as central to the strength and wellbeing of the nation. There was still a long way to go. But they were now citizens. They could never again be taken for granted or ignored.

CHAPTER 8

Class War

Any veteran of Mons walking down Main Street, Winnipeg, at eleven o'clock on the morning of May 15, 1919, would have felt a sense of *déjà vu*. An eerie stillness suddenly descended upon the city. Workers walked away from offices, factories, railway shops, construction sites. Streetcars headed for their barns. Telephone and telegraph operators quietly left their posts. Within hours, it was impossible to get a haircut, mail a letter, buy a meal, take a taxi, get a newspaper, go to a show, gas up a car, have milk or bread delivered, purchase meat at the butcher, or buy groceries at the store. Within days, food began to spoil and garbage piled up. Winnipeg was all but cut off from the outside world. Thirty thousand workers and their families — half the people of Canada's third-largest city — were challenging the political and social order of the day and demanding it be fundamentally changed.

No one in Canada had seen a general strike like this before. The city was in the hands of a strike committee. Moderate labour leaders and social-ist firebrands who had never before agreed on very much moved quick-ly to ensure that police stayed on the job, that water and electricity were provided, and that milk, bread, and ice were delivered. Thousands of men gathered daily in parks for orderly strike meetings, veterans' assemblies, or Labour Church services led by former Methodist minister William Ivens. "Take everything to the Central Strike Committee," they were told. "If you are hungry go to them. We will share our last crust together."[1]

"It is worth a strike to see this marvellous spirit of comradeship and unselfishness," said the strike newspaper. "Offers are tumbling in for homes for girls who are in need of room rent. We have a spare room. Send us up

Manitoba Archives, Winnipeg Strike 28 collection N12316

Bloody Saturday, June 21, 1919
Mounted Police confront crowds on Main Street, Winnipeg. In the ensuing riot, two people were killed, many more were injured, and the Winnipeg General Strike came to an end.

a couple. Tell the committee we can help them out if they are stuck. Tell the girls that they are welcome at our place to such as we have." The Women's Labour League, led by socialist Helen Armstrong, served twelve hundred meals daily and organized child care, food distribution, dance centres, and self-help networks, especially in immigrant areas. "The women will do without milk," one wife told her husband, "and we will make some shift for the kiddies, but you must win." This solidarity would in later years be the most cherished memory for those who took part in the strike.[2]

But to many other Winnipeggers, the strike meant that Bolshevism had come to their city. Nellie McClung was appalled that the leaders had "hypnotized themselves into the thought that nothing short of social revolution and the overthrow of constitutional authority will save the world." J.W. Dafoe of the *Free Press* equated the strikers to Germans denying milk to children. Middle-class Winnipeggers mobilized to restore essential services and defend the constitutional order. That two halves of a major city could so profoundly misunderstand each other was a stark reminder that conflicting dreams of a better world could instead lead to confrontation and tragedy.[3]

I

Winnipeg was but one chapter in a countrywide labour revolt in 1919. Rapid industrialization had produced jobs, but little job security, and there was no insurance against unemployment or injury on the job, no protection against the harsh conditions of mining, construction, or forestry camps, or against the threat of cheap immigrant labour. Employers had behind them the full weight of the legal system, police, company goons, and, when necessary, the militia.[4]

Workers had formed labour unions, which at times had become powerful — in the 1880s, the Knights of Labour had attracted as many as fifty thousand workers. After 1900, the international unions of the American Federation of Labor (AFL), which were big enough to confront the large corporations, had all but taken over the Canadian labour movement. The AFL unions were organized by craft, or skill (except for the United Mineworkers), and practised the "business unionism" preached by their founder, Samuel Gompers — bargain for wages, honour contracts, do not engage directly in politics.[5]

But organization by craft left out the growing number of unskilled workers in factories, resource industries, construction, and railways. New industrial unions, which organized all the workers in a factory or an industry into a single union, potentially presented a much more direct challenge to capitalism. The International Workers of the World (IWW) in the American West — popularly known as the "Wobblies" — openly advocated using the weapon of the strike to establish workers' control and ultimately a socialist state. British Columbia saw bloody labour battles in 1912 as militant unions confronted two-fisted mine-owners and hard-nosed railway bosses.[6]

In the early twentieth century, the "labour question" was in the air everywhere. Labour politicians won office at the civic, provincial, and federal levels, often in association with the Liberal Party. Anyone in a town of any size might attend or read about lectures by American Socialist Party leader Eugene Debs, British Labour leader Kier Hardie, anarchist Emma Goldman, or a legion of Christian socialists, Single Taxers, and labour messiahs. They could borrow books like Edward Bellamy's *Looking Backward,*

Henry George's *Progress and Poverty,* Charles Booth's *In Darkest England,* or even *The Communist Manifesto.* They could educate themselves in study groups and hone their speaking skills in church basement meetings and Chautauqua debates.[7]

At the extreme end of the socialist spectrum was Marxism. Marxist socialism had come to Canada by different routes — directly from the United States, with immigrants from Eastern Europe, and, most importantly, with the large influx of skilled British workers in the years before the war. Essentially, Marxism was Idealism without the Will of God. It saw history as the record of a succession of socio-economic systems, each of which arose in response to human need, flourished for a time until its contradictions made it obsolete, and was then overthrown by a more advanced system. Thus feudalism had been replaced by capitalism, which had brought unparalleled industrial development and scientific progress. But capitalism had also created an alienated "proletariat," the "surplus value" of whose labour was appropriated by the owners of the means of production. It was therefore historically inevitable that, once workers became aware of their oppression, capitalism would be overthrown by a "dictatorship of the proletariat," which in turn would give rise to a stateless commonwealth where all would contribute according to their abilities and receive according to their needs. This was "scientific socialism" — it could, in the words of one socialist paper, "diagnose the malady of our social ills, expound the course the disease will run and foretell the final outcome of the fitful capitalist fevers from which society suffers."[8]

But there was a contradiction. Did one simply wait for history to take its course? Yes, said "impossibilists," who believed their task was to "educate and then *educate* the workers" to their oppression, and who reserved their bitterest venom for "labour fakirs" and social reformers whose efforts would only delay the inevitable crisis of capitalism. No, said a much larger group of "revisionists," who argued that the workers should use their political and industrial power to advance the progress of history. Marxist movements were constantly riven by ideological conflicts, expulsions, and secessions.[9]

The first successful socialist party in Canada was the "impossibilist" Socialist Party of Canada (SPC) based in British Columbia, which elected members to city councils and the provincial legislature. In 1911, "revisionist" defectors formed the more moderate and pragmatic Social Democratic Party (SDP), whose leading figures were people like Jimmy Simpson in Toronto, John Queen and Abe Heaps in Winnipeg, and Ernie Winch in British Columbia, with affiliated autonomous branches in the large East European immigrant communities. Then a new generation of British immigrants, including Bill Pritchard and Bob Russell, revitalized the SPC, so that by 1914 the two parties each had about five thousand members across the country. But there were probably never more than fifty thousand people in the organized left in Canada, and as historian Ian McKay says, "you could count the socialist legislators in Canada on your fingers, and still have enough left over to play 'Chopsticks.'" O.D. Skelton wrote in 1911 that socialism was "likely to remain sporadic and exotic," because Canada was a heterogeneous society that was not fully developed industrially, because it saw itself as a land of opportunity; and because the Catholic Church in Quebec was implacably hostile.[10]

II

The Great War revived a labour movement weakened by bitter strikes and becalmed by the 1913 recession. Men had jobs again and joined unions — membership more than doubled during the war. The AFL-dominated Trades and Labour Congress (TLC) supported the war, but the government showed little willingness to take labour into its counsel. As prices rose faster than wages, unions resorted to strikes — there were over 120,000 strike-days in Ontario alone in 1918.[11]

Conscription enraged labour. Pressure from AFL headquarters and the Borden government persuaded the 1917 TLC convention to support conscription, but its newly elected president also demanded the nationalization of mines, railways, munitions works, and other key industries, including banking, "even if a general strike is necessary to bring it about." The convention also decided, for the first time, to give direct support to the labour parties that were springing up to contest the upcoming federal election. In 1918, labour editor Joseph Marks called for a "new democracy," in which "the workers of the Dominion will take their rightful place and make their influence felt in shaping the destinies of the Dominion, in conjunction with the other progressive forces of the state, so that the sacrifices of those who have died to make the bounds of democracy greater yet shall not have been in vain." Certainly labour's vision of a new world did not include enriching "the Coal, the Milk, the Bacon, the Milling or Munition Barons."[12]

The Bolshevik Revolution of November 1917 radicalized the Canadian labour movement. An Alberta miner reported that "the sole topic of conversation both going in and coming out, is socialism or Bolshevikism [sic]." Jimmy Simpson, who wanted a Canadian version of the British Labour Party, was moved (to his later regret) to declare that he would rather be a member of the Bolshevik government than of the British House of Commons. Socialists of Finnish, Ukrainian, Russian, and Baltic origin hailed the liberation of their former homelands from the hated czars. A University of Toronto student signed a letter to the student newspaper "yours for revolt and in revolt, Karl Marx."[13]

To Marxists like Bob Russell, this was the beginning of "the most important stage of Capitalistic development, namely the period of Revolution, wherein we witness in some of the European countries the passing of the Capitalist system of production and the introduction of the Co-operative Commonwealth." Russell and other SPC leaders like Pritchard, Jack Kavanagh, Victor Midgley, and Dick Johns, were young, self-educated organizers shaped by the bitter British labour battles of the early twentieth century. They had been a tiny minority on the margins of the labour movement; now they had real power and were riding the tide of history. "We are going to use our political power," said an SPC member to a royal commission in June 1919, "to get hold of the reins of government and introduce what measures we think fit; and we shall not show the master class the slightest consideration whatever." But revolution did not mean taking up arms or throwing bombs. Their job was to organize workers to ensure that history took its proper course.[14]

To the Canadian security services, this was a serious threat to the war effort. The security apparatus was comprised of the Dominion Police (a small force that relied in part on private detectives), the Royal North-West Mounted Police (a federal force with jurisdiction west of the Lakehead), military intelligence, the Press Censor's Office, the Department of Immigration and Colonization, and private railway police. They recruited informers to track socialists' activities, and in some cases used more direct methods. In July 1918, a Dominion Policeman killed Ginger Goodwin, a socialist who had fled to the mountains of Vancouver Island when he was conscripted after leading a strike. Enraged unions shut down Vancouver until a mob of returned soldiers wrecked the Labour Temple, tried to push labour organizer Victor Midgley out a window, then forced him to kiss the Union Jack.[15]

C.H. Cahan, a Conservative corporate lawyer, reported to Borden in the summer of 1918 that there was "widespread unrest and discontent" in the land, especially among the Russians, Ukrainians, and Finns, who were "being thoroughly saturated with the Socialistic doctrines which have been proclaimed by the Bolsheviki faction of Russia." Socialists, he claimed, were circulating propaganda advocating the "destruction of all state authority, the subversion of religion, and the obliteration of all property rights." In October, Justice Minister Doherty established a Public Safety Branch with wide powers under the War Measures Act, with Cahan as its first director. Orders-in-Council banned publications in an "enemy language" (including Finnish and Russian); made it illegal to distribute, sell, own, or read a large swath of literature; and outlawed the IWW, the Social Democratic Party (including its ethnic wings), and several minor revolutionary and socialist parties. Raids were conducted on offices and homes across Canada, publications were seized, up to a thousand people were arrested, and some were sentenced to three to five years in prison.[16]

But within the Union government, and in the business world, there were cooler heads and saner minds. The Cabinet began to consult unions and include labour representatives on committees on reconstruction and war production. N.W. Rowell and Agriculture Minister Thomas Crerar, supported by business "progressives" like Sir John Willison, advocated labour reform, especially the introduction of the "Whitley Councils" then being tried in Britain — permanent joint councils of management and labour for each company, which it was hoped would ensure industrial peace in wartime. Borden replaced his incompetent labour minister with Senator Gideon Robertson, a burly telegrapher well connected with the AFL/TLC leadership. Robertson spent the summer of 1918 heading off railway strikes, a Nova Scotia steel strike, and other potential disturbances. In their fall convention, the TLC retreated from the radicalism of the year before and elected as its president Tom Moore, a carpenter who was prepared to work with the government. Shortly after the war ended, the government lifted the ban on the SDP. In April 1919, it established the Mathers Royal Commission, which held hearings across the country to explore the causes of labour unrest. Samuel Gompers gave an unprecedented address to the Canadian Parliament. Meanwhile, Cahan had resigned in disgust and was issuing dire public warnings about the Bolshevik menace.[17]

The man who emerged as the leading champion of reconciling capitalism with the rights of labour was Mackenzie King. As Laurier's minister of labour, King had won a reputation for settling strikes, and was the author of the 1907 Industrial Disputes Investigation Act, which forbade strike action until a conciliation board representing the employer, the workers, and the public had investigated the situation and recommended a settlement. During the war, he resolved a serious labour dispute for the Rockefeller interests in the United States through what became known as the "Colorado Plan" — unions formed by the company and meeting with management in joint councils. In his book *Industry and Humanity*, and in a series of speeches in early 1919, he proclaimed the need for the "four parties to industry" — not only labour and capital, but also "management," and the state as representative of society — to "unite under the inspiration of a common ideal." "No longer," he wrote, would "Industry be the battleground of rival and contending factions; it will become the foundation of a new civilization in which life and happiness abound."[18]

But a business-dominated government in the desperate days of 1918 was too easily tempted to use its sweeping powers against labour, or any other "disloyal" element that stood in its way. An October Order-in-Council banned all work stoppages. Strike leaders were arrested at the CPR yards in Calgary; an SDP leader in Vancouver was sentenced to nine months for distributing a pacifist publication; in Winnipeg, the editor of a Ukrainian-language socialist newspaper was arrested. There were widespread protests. "Whither are we being shoved?" cried Winnipeg social democrat Fred Dixon. Why was the government bent on a course that would "very likely lead to labour troubles that will make what strikes we have endured pale into insignificance?"[19]

Boiling with resentment and fired with hope, labour was in turmoil in early 1919. Previously unorganized civic, office, domestic, and hotel workers were joining unions all across the country. Even police were forming unions. There were mass strikes in Quebec munitions, railway, and shipyard industries. In Toronto, eight thousand workers were off the job. Clifford Dane — who told the Mathers Commission that he was a Bolshevik — and J.B. McLachlan succeeded in establishing the United Mine Workers in the coal mines of Cape Breton. There were unprecedented strikes in the Halifax building trades and shipyards, the gypsum mines of Hants County, and a general strike in the industrial town of Amherst. At the other end of the country, the IWW was organizing mines and lumber camps in British Columbia. "A revolution by force of arms [is] conceivable under existing conditions," wrote a Western police informant in April 1919. Sir Thomas White telegraphed Borden in Paris to request that a British cruiser be sent to Vancouver to "steady" the situation. Borden responded that Canada could handle its own problems and things were much worse in Europe. But when he returned in May he found "a distinctive lack of the usual balance; the agitator, sometimes sincere, sometimes merely malevolent, self-seeking, and designing, found quick response to insidious propaganda."[20]

In the mainstream press, the imbalance was mostly in the other direction. The *Canadian Annual Review* for 1918 devoted dozens of pages to an apocalyptic description of Bolshevik "hate and violence" in Canada, which

> appeared under the guise of Social Democracy, or Labour rights, or continuous denunciation of Capitalists and moneyed classes; it had a basis wherever Russians and Jews and other foreigners gathered together with special centres in Montreal, Toronto, Winnipeg, Calgary, Edmonton and Vancouver; it was engineered also by IWW agitators from the States and operated in the Mines of Ontario, Alberta, and British Columbia.

Maclean's, Saturday Night, and the Montreal *Star,* using information provided by Cahan, the security services, and the chief press censor, published story after story of Bolshevik plots and foreign agents. Cartoons portrayed the Bolshevik as a dirty, hairy, red-eyed, misogynist, bomb-throwing monster.[21]

Some of this hysteria was spillover from a far more serious "Red Scare" that was sweeping the United States, where a reign of terror, with literally hundreds of bombings, violent strikes in the steel, coal, and Western mining industries, and a Boston police strike, was being met by an irrational fear of Bolshevism. Chicago evangelist Billy Sunday described a Bolshevik as "a guy with a face like a porcupine and a breath that would scare a pole cat." "If I had my way," he continued in his best Christian manner, "I'd fill the jails so full of them that their feet would stick out the windows." The American Socialist Party, which had captured over nine hundred thousand votes in the presidential election of 1912, was smashed. Troops were called in to quell a general strike in Seattle in February 1919. The Lusk Commission of New York State in June disseminated stories of socialist plots, Soviet agents subverting returned soldiers, and fomenting strikes. When his home was bombed that same month, Attorney General Mitchell Palmer set up a special force headed by a young J. Edgar Hoover to root out subversion. By December 1919, "Red Special" trains were arriving at eastern ports carrying radicals detained without trial (including anarchist Emma Goldman), en route to be deported to Russia; and in January 1920, the "Palmer Raids" arrested hundreds of labour and socialist leaders and seized a mass of "evidence."[22]

Bolshevism aroused the worst phobias of most Canadians — "foreigners," violent social upheaval, attacks on property and freedom, threats to religion, morality, and the purity of women (or the threat of immoral, radical women), even "feeble-mindedness." On the other side, it reinforced the conviction of radicals that history was on their side and that only strikes, including general strikes, got results. In March 1919, Mounted Police Commissioner Bowen Perry secretly met with Midgley, Kavanagh, and Pritchard. He found them "intelligent, well-read men" with "all the fervour of fanatics." They were not plotting revolution "in the ordinary sense of that word, but I do say that they are influencing a section of labour in the West and unchaining forces which, if they so desire, someday they will be unable to control."[23]

The socialists responded to their defeat at the September 1918 TLC convention by convening a Western Labour Conference in March 1919 in Calgary. Dominated by SPC members, this conference advocated not only collective bargaining and the lifting of restrictions on strikes, but also workers' control of industry — and it sent fraternal greetings to the Soviet

Union. Most importantly, it called for the establishment of One Big Union at a convention to be held in June.[24]

The One Big Union (OBU) was the ultimate in industrial unionism. It would consolidate all workers in all industries into a single, highly centralized union which could, by threatening general strikes, impose its will on capital and government. To become a reality, the OBU would have to persuade existing union locals to secede from their internationals and join it. OBU leaders, who were also Socialist Party of Canada members, fanned out across the West and made forays into the East in a concerted campaign to gather unions and councils into the fold. They made inroads in the mining country of Quebec and Ontario. But they were met by polite skepticism in the industrial heartland. Even radical labour leaders argued that industrial unions should be built within existing structures. Moderates objected to using workers as cannon fodder in a battle against the capitalist system. Traditional leaders fought for the survival of their craft unions and their concept of unionism. Still, by the June founding convention of the OBU, 24,300 out of some 45,000 union members west of the Lakehead had voted for secession from their TLC unions (the ballots of ten thousand Winnipeg unionists were hung up in the mails). This was sensational, but it was not enough to implement the OBU strategy — and their plans were thrown into disarray by the outbreak of the Winnipeg General Strike on May 15.[25]

III

Winnipeg had grown within a generation from a frontier town into a modern city of two hundred thousand, with the shops and yards of three transcontinental railways, food processing plants, a splendid city hall and provincial legislature, a grain exchange, department stores, hotels, and office buildings. The rich had their mansions along the Assiniboine River; skilled workers lived in modest houses near their work; East European immigrants lived north of the CPR yards in crowded slums. Winnipeg had one of the highest enlistment rates in the country, but it was also a centre of pacifism and socialism, while its employers were among the most intransigent in resisting unions.

In April 1918, civic employees struck and other unions threatened sympathetic action. A compromise was overturned by anti-unionists on the city council, and a general strike was averted only when a citizens' committee called in Labour Minister Robertson to help negotiate a settlement.[26]

In December 1918, speaker after speaker at a public meeting co-sponsored by the Winnipeg Trades and Labour Council (WTLC) and the SPC denounced "government by Orders-in-Council," the Siberian intervention, and the detention of "political prisoners." The meeting ended with three cheers for the Russian Revolution. Following an even more radical meeting in January (sponsored by the SPC alone), soldiers attacked socialist offices and "foreign" businesses. The militia commander did nothing to stop them, and one newspaper declared that there were "worse things than violence," including toleration of "treason" and of "destructive propaganda by citizens of hostile alien race."[27]

The flashpoint came in May 1919. Unions in the metal-working industries had long demanded to have their Metal Trades Council bargain collectively with the association representing all the employers, and had been repeatedly refused. The Winnipeg Builders' Exchange, on the other hand, was willing to negotiate with all the construction unions in the Building Trades Council, but it could not meet their wage demands. The building trades struck on May 1; the metal trades on May 2; and both appealed to the Winnipeg Trades and Labour Council, which agreed on May 6 to ask its member unions to vote on a sympathy strike. Within a week, eleven thousand had voted in favour, with only five hundred opposed. Last-minute mediation by the mayor and the provincial government proved futile. The unions walked out and were joined by thousands more non-union workers.

The WTLC established a General Strike Committee, which elected a fifteen-man Central Strike Committee. The majority of the Central Strike Committee were traditional trade unionists like British immigrants James Winning and Ernie Robertson, who had recently fought radicals for control of the WTLC. Only Bob Russell was SPC/OBU, John Queen was an SDP city alderman, and Social Gospeller William Ivens edited the strikers' newspaper. "There was no arrogance in the bearing of these men," wrote one witness, "but there was about them a quiet determination and an air of conscious power that I can never forget. The reins were in their hands and they knew it." Essential services, said the strikers' newspaper, would continue to operate because "for the present the Strike Committee believes that it is better to let them run." Water pressure was kept low to serve only the bottom floors where the workers lived.[28]

The Strike Committee probably never realized how threatening these actions would appear to the rest of the city. Milk and bread delivery wagons carried placards reading "Permitted by Authority of Strike Committee" to prevent their being attacked as scabs. These were removed after a few days but their message lingered, and Russell gloated that it was "a fine spectacle to see employers coming to the Labour Temple asking permission to operate their various industries." Even Ernie Robertson got carried away. "If we can control industrial production now, at this time," he boasted, "we can control it for all time to come, and we can control the Government of this country, too." Their biggest mistake, described by Willison as an act of "malignant folly," was shutting down the daily newspapers — "a case," said Ivens, "of simple justice to muzzle for a few days the enemies of freedom and truth." The mayor had hoped for "calmness, patience, and British fair play." Now he was insisting that the British flag "still flies over City Hall."[29]

In response, a Citizens' Committee of One Thousand was formed, with headquarters in the Board of Industry building. The Citizens' Committee never revealed who their members were, but their key leaders were half a dozen lawyers and businessmen. They had no more legal authority than the strikers did, but they were the establishment, offering their support to the authorities, and successfully portraying themselves as defenders of the constitutional order.[30]

The man who came to dominate the Citizens' Committee was Alfred J. Andrews, a pioneer Winnipegger who had seen action in the North West Rebellion of 1885, become a prominent lawyer, served as mayor, and was well known as a *bon vivant*. Andrews saw clearly that only the complete and utter defeat of the general strike would prevent any future such actions. "We say you've done a wrong," Andrews lectured Bob Russell at a round table conference called by the mayor to try to establish a dialogue. "You now have a chance to retire gracefully. If you do not do this, we will line up against you … the Dominion, Provincial and Civic Governments." His strategy was to take the city back service by service, break the solidarity of the strikers, undermine confidence in their leaders, and allow no compromise settlement that could be portrayed as a victory for the strikers, or any acts of violence that would make them into martyrs.[31]

The federal government viewed the strike with alarm. Militia commander Brigadier Huntly Ketchen arranged for a squadron of Mounted Police returning from Russia to be sent to Winnipeg, together with a further detachment from Regina led by Superintendent Perry. He also began recruiting a special militia. The Citizens mobilized cars, horses, and food. Ketchen arranged for machine guns to be shipped to Winnipeg disguised as "regimental baggage." Through the CPR, he established a secure telegraph link to Ottawa. By early June, he had eight hundred men fully equipped with armoured cars, guns, and ammunition, with the rest of the militia available on a moment's notice.[32]

On May 21, Gideon Robertson and Arthur Meighen (the acting minister of justice and ranking Manitoba minister) were dispatched by the Cabinet to Winnipeg. Andrews and several of the Citizens boarded their train at Fort William and for several hours gave them a thorough briefing. Meighen "knew practically all of them personally and knew that they were not citizens who would be easily victims of fear"; he agreed that when "not a child could have milk to drink except by permission of the strike committee," the "regularly constituted authorities were no longer in control." On May 26, he appointed Andrews as his eyes and ears with authority to gather evidence "on the conduct of the principal instigators."[33]

Robertson was outraged that unions for which he had brokered settlements only months before were now breaking their contracts, and he had "no hesitation in stating that the One Big Union movement is the underlying cause of the whole trouble, and that the Winnipeg General Strike deserves no sympathy or support from labour organizations outside." He ordered postal workers to

A. J. ANDREWS

Alfred J. Andrews (1909)

From Memorable Manitobans: Manitobans as we See 'Em, 1908 and 1909. Courtesy Gordon Goldsborough, Manitoba Historical Society

return to work or be fired. When they refused — the strike leaders assured them they would get their jobs back — they were replaced by workers recruited by the Citizens' Committee. Postal railway clerks then decided not to walk out, and the provincial government forced telephone workers back to work. On May 29, the city council replaced the firemen with volunteers recruited by the Citizens. The two ministers returned to Ottawa without having met the Strike Committee.[34]

By early June, the strike had reached a standoff with the stakes rising for both sides. The socialists had considered the strike premature, but they now realized that it simply could not be lost, and they pulled in Pritchard and Johns from the OBU campaign to speak and organize. The labour moderates who had expected the authorities to cave in now found support beginning to erode as families — many not even members of unions — ended their third week without a paycheque. Some men were beginning to drift back to work. Newspapers and services like Eaton's delivery were beginning to operate again.[35]

The strikers prided themselves on their discipline and order. "No matter how great the provocation, do not quarrel," said their newspaper on May 26. "Do not say an angry word. Walk away from the fellow who tries to draw you." But as tensions rose, small acts of violence were inevitable. When the

Free Press resumed publication and James Gray revived his paper route to augment his family's income, a neighbour woman threw a pan of dishes in his face, and some men beat him up. Gray made money delivering ice to homes whose need outweighed their sympathy for the strike.[36]

Andrews's strategy was beginning to work. Essential services were being restored. He controlled the information flowing to Meighen. He could block any premature settlement. On June 6, he told Meighen that the strike would collapse within

Gideon Robertson

Topley Studio Fonds/ Library and Archives Canada PA-033996

days, and that the strikers would have "suffered so much that their natural impulse will be to blame the strike leaders."[37]

But neither side could control everything. The *Toronto Star*, which had the only outside reporter in Winnipeg, published perceptive and sympathetic reports, but most other papers printed second-hand, sensational stories portraying the strike as OBU/Bolshevik-inspired. Sympathetic strikes were breaking out across the country. In Toronto, a general strike was approved and seventeen thousand workers walked out; but street-railway workers stayed on the job and within a short time the strike was called off. In Vancouver, a general strike engineered by the radical leadership failed when volunteers kept essential services running and some unions drifted back to work. The TLC leadership was holding the line but, as Willison put it, at the cost of opposing strikers "with many of whose demands they were probably in sympathy," and they made it very clear that labour would react strongly to any harsh measures of repression in Winnipeg.[38]

The biggest wild card was the returning soldiers, who began arriving in large numbers in May. In the past, returned soldiers had sided with authority. But these men were veterans of the Hundred Days and the camps in France and Britain, often restless and resentful of brass hats and "profiteers." On May 31, Sergeant E.A. Moore organized a march of soldiers to the Manitoba legislature to demand that the government make collective bargaining compulsory. The parade then went to city hall, where they crowded into the galleries, roundly booed the mayor, and promised to march every day until they got results. Two days later, two thousand returned soldiers crammed into the legislative chamber, with ten thousand waiting outside. They were addressed by the socialist returned soldier Roger Bray, who denounced capitalism, newspapers, the bullying of telephone operators, and the plight of the soldiers who had sacrificed everything while the Citizens' Committee lined their pockets. A daily "Soldiers' Parliament" was addressed by radicals but also by the mayor, General Ketchen, and Canon Scott, who had rushed to Winnipeg to try to make peace until he was ordered back to Ottawa.[39]

On the other side, Captain F.G. Thompson, a lawyer, began to round up returned soldiers for a counter-parade. Ketchen openly supported these efforts and the Citizens supplied cars. In an effort to arouse hostility among the soldiers, the Citizens' newspaper, the reviving daily press, and organizers of the counter-marches repeatedly labelled the strikers as "foreigners." On June 4, rival parades narrowly avoided clashing in front of the Legislative Building and there were incidents of intimidation and damage. The Citizens inflated the number of "loyal" soldiers, as did Andrews when he told Meighen that the mayor and "several of the officers" had to dissuade over five thousand of them from attacking the Labour Temple. But the fear of violence was real and with Andrews holding the pen, the mayor issued a proclamation banning parades.[40]

When it was reported that streetcars would soon be running again, the strikers upped the ante. On June 3, they abruptly removed permission for the delivery of bread, ice, and milk, and, going further, they closed theatres and restaurants. On June 5, on Andrews's recommendation, the federal government passed amendments to the Immigration Act that allowed the deportation of any non-citizen who by word or deed threatened the overthrow of the government by force. The next day (knowing full well that "foreigners" were not the real issue), Andrews conveyed the Ctizens' "outrage" that British-born Canadians had not been included in the legislation. Meighen acted quickly, and after forty minutes' deliberation, Parliament broadened the wording of the amendment to cover "any person."[41]

Meanwhile, two thousand "special" police had been recruited with the help of Ketchen and the Citizens. On June 9, the Police Commission — having been prevented by Andrews from acting prematurely a few days earlier — dismissed all but a handful of the regular police, appointed a new acting chief, and in the words of historian David Bercuson, replaced "a sympathetic or neutral civil authority with one that was, without pretence, hostile" to the strike. At once there was trouble — "specials" on horseback and others wielding wagon spokes waded into a crowd that jeered them and refused to disperse. During a day-long melee, they were showered with rocks and bottles, and a report went across the country that a Victoria Cross winner had been savagely beaten (some said killed) — it turned out that he had received two broken ribs from thrown bottles. On June 11, the mayor issued a second proclamation banning public demonstrations.[42]

As tensions rose in the city, officials of the AFL, railway-running trades unions (who had come to Winnipeg to prevent any spread of the strike into the large railway shops) were working to mediate a settlement of its original cause — the dispute in the metal trades. By the second week of June, the employers were ready to give ground and Premier Norris had promised to make collective bargaining compulsory. Andrews, who had earlier discouraged any premature compromise, now judged the time ripe to ask Robertson to come to Winnipeg to apply the extra pressure needed to finalize a deal. On June 16, an agreement was concluded that would allow collective bargaining across the metal trades, with a committee to settle grievances. But the railway shops were not included, and there was a provision that if negotiations broke down, "duly accredited international officers of the metal trade associations" would be called in to effect a settlement. Russell, acting for the Strike Committee, rejected this proposal.[43]

This apparent obduracy of the Strike Committee, expressed by a Socialist strike leader, opened the way for the Citizens' Committee to claim that the strike had never been a labour dispute, but was, rather, a revolutionary plot by a small group of socialists, which could only be resolved if they were removed from the scene. A bizarre secret meeting of about a hundred Citizens drew up a "hit list" of socialists and radicals. Andrews secured agreement from the provincial government, Meighen, Robertson, and Perry, to arrest them.[44]

In the small hours of the hot night of June 16–17, Russell, Ivens, Queen, Bray, Alderman Abe Heaps, and MLA George Armstrong were roused from their beds by officers of the Mounted Police. Bray was arrested in front of his children, and his wife was not given time to dress before the police started ransacking their house. The redoubtable Helen Armstrong made the Mounties wait while she confirmed with the Winnipeg police that the warrants were genuine. Johns was arrested in Montreal, and Pritchard was taken off a westbound train in Calgary. Four "foreigners" from the Mounties' list of "alien agitators" were also arrested — Mike Verenchuk (a wounded war veteran and a case of mistaken identity), Max Charitonoff, Moses Almazoff, and Oscar Schoppelrei — as was Sam Blumenberg, a well-known socialist businessman. Even as the prisoners were being whisked away, five hundred police were ransacking the offices of the Strike Committee, its newspaper, and ethnic socialist organizations.[45]

Andrews now put on another hat: special prosecutor in an immigration case. He taunted the prisoners (who, he told Meighen, "whined and shivered like curs") that they should not worry about not having access to counsel since they would be on the Atlantic within seventy-two hours. The fact that he had no authority to arrest anyone under the Immigration Act was remedied by getting the minister of immigration to issue a retroactive order. In case the province allowed them bail, which "would be interpreted as weakness," he had an additional charge sworn and a Mountie waiting to rearrest them.[46]

Andrews was surprised when there was a strong negative public reaction to the arrests. The strike was almost over, wrote Dafoe, who had been vehement in his opposition to it; now the government had created martyrs and would have to account for its actions. National newspapers such as the *Globe* counselled restraint. The British Labour Party protested, and TLC president Moore warned that organized labour would not "stand for strong arm methods for the suppression of legitimate labour demonstrations." Andrews quickly changed tack. He wrong-footed Meighen on June 21 by having the British-Canadians charged with seditious conspiracy rather than using the Immigration Act. He then wrong-footed the Citizens, Ketchen, and Perry by arranging for the strikers to be let out on bail, on condition that they take no further part in the strike, that they give no interviews and make no speeches, and that the Strike Committee show "no jubilation" over their release.[47]

James Winning and the moderate leaders who had not been arrested were willing to talk terms. But before discussions could begin, a delegation of soldiers met on the morning of June 21 with Andrews, the mayor, Perry, and Robertson, to inform them that they planned to march from city hall to the hotel where Robertson was staying, then to the Industrial Bureau, where they would hold a meeting to protest the arrests and the resumption of streetcar service. Robertson agreed to address the men and Andrews was dispatched to arrange for space in the Industrial Bureau. But when large crowds gathered, the mayor banned the march and asked Perry to dispatch Mounties to patrol the streets.

What happened next has been described many times and was captured on film, yet accounts still differ dramatically. A crowd of several hundred people attacked a streetcar on Main Street, tried to tip it on its side, and set fire to it. The Mounties, half in scarlet and half in khaki, charged with batons, but were met with resistance and retreated to regroup. They then caught sight of a comrade who had fallen from his horse after it tripped over a fender that had fallen off the streetcar. Their comrade was being beaten by several men. The police drew revolvers and, while the mayor, probably unheard, read the Riot Act, moved north, fired a volley into the crowd, then slowed to a walk and fired a second volley into the crowd around the streetcar, killing one Mike Sokolowiski instantly and leaving others lying on the road. They then continued southward and fired a third volley when they encountered a shower of bricks and bottles. They paused to regroup again, and then galloped north with revolvers in holsters.

The crowd, now fleeing down side streets, was trapped between the police and the "specials" with clubs. Pitched battles erupted, one lasting ten minutes. Over eighty were arrested. At the mayor's request, General Ketchen sent in troops, and for the next three days, soldiers with fixed bayonets and trucks with machine guns drove up and down Main Street while other soldiers patrolled most of the downtown. On June 23, "specials," with the mayor present, broke up a crowd gathering in Victoria Park.[48]

The Mounties claimed they had been fired on. Besides Sokolowiski, who seems to have been a bystander, another man was shot in both legs and died later of gangrene, while twenty-four civilians and six Mounties were treated in hospital — the Mounties for injuries from projectiles, the civilians for bullet wounds and beatings — and it is likely that many more did not go to hospitals. Upset by the "biased" report in the strikers' paper, Andrews got a warrant for the arrest of J.S. Woodsworth, who had taken over from Ivens as editor. Fred Dixon then assumed the editorship and turned himself in when Ivens was released.[49]

On June 25, Winning told Premier Norris that the strike would end if he appointed a royal commission to investigate its causes. Norris, who had walked a fine line during the strike, agreed, over the protests of the Citizens. The strikers thus won a small victory, and at eleven o'clock, after forty-two days, Winnipeg went back to work.

IV

The strike had electrified the country and was reported around the world. Most people breathed a sigh of relief, but many also shared the *Globe's* view that "if employers are wise they will aid in suppressing the revolutionary elements by establishing closer relationships with the responsible Labour organizations, admitting them to a larger share in their councils and the rewards of industry." The report of the Mathers Commission, published on July 1, 1919, expressed the hope that "by a gradual process of evolution a system may be ushered in by which the workers will receive a more adequate share of what their labour produces." The Liberal Party at its August convention adopted proposals, largely written by Mackenzie King, for conciliation, a living wage, an eight-hour workday, a weekly day of rest, unemployment and disability insurance, old age pensions, widows' pensions, and maternity benefits, "in so far as the special circumstances of the country will permit." Later in the year, Leacock called for shorter hours, "work and pay for the unemployed, maintenance for the infirm and aged, and education and opportunity for the children," as his solution in his book the *Unsolved Riddle of Social Justice*. University of Toronto political economist R.M. MacIver published a book with more elaborate proposals along the same lines. Charles Gordon served on provincial labour boards and, as Ralph Connor, later published a fictional account, *To Him That Hath*, in which a Presbyterian minister helps settle a strike by getting the parties to agree to conciliation and joint councils.[50]

In Ontario, moderate labour leaders had fought off the radical challenge while accepting industrial unionism and direct involvement in politics. By 1919, the Independent Labour Party (ILP), under leaders like Jimmy Simpson and Joseph Marks (whose *Industrial Banner* advocated political action along the lines of the British Labour Party) had brought together a variety of pro-labour politicians and even some farmer-labour candidates. In the October 1919 election, under a broad platform of opposing government by "the interests," eleven members were elected under the ILP banner and joined in a coalition with the United Farmers of Ontario — the first time in Canadian history that a labour party had been part of a government.[51]

Meanwhile, in the West, the TLC unions began their assault on the OBU, in what Bercuson describes as "labour's civil war." With the key OBU leaders sidelined, AFL union organizers descended on Western locals, seizing charters, expelling radicals, and reasserting their role in bargaining with employers. In May, when OBU strikes in the B.C. and Alberta coal mines foundered, the United Mine Workers moved in to settle with the companies. The security services harassed the OBU and deported IWW organizers. In August, a socialist who had not been involved in the strike was elected president of the Winnipeg TLC. By the end of 1919, thousands of workers were rejoining AFL unions. "Rejected by most workers," says historian Irving Abella, "attacked by government, ignored by employers who refused to negotiate with it, and undermined by the TLC and its international affiliates, the OBU died a painfully long ... unlamented death."[52]

But a National Industrial Conference held in Ottawa in September 1919 to try to find ways to reconcile capital and labour, instead revealed the continuing intransigence of the majority of businessmen. The conference was organized by the federal government and the Canadian Reconstruction Association,* with representatives from "labour" (the TLC), "capital" (the Canadian Manufacturers' Association), and a third group, chosen to represent "the public" (such as members of the Mathers Commission, "progressives" like Sir John Willison, and Mackenzie King, now Leader of the Opposition). S.R. Parsons (who was also leading the attack on the Methodist Programme) set the tone for "capital" by declaring that if labour would abandon the belief that "competition and profit should be done away with in favour of co-operation and service," forget their "little differences," and "get down to good, hard work, this country would progress in the next few months or in the next year or two as it never progressed before." During several days of heated debate, his colleagues rejected all proposals for collective bargaining and Whitley Councils, and all calls for regulation of wages, hours, and conditions of employment.[53]

In Quebec, international unions came under attack from clerical nationalists like Bourassa who proclaimed that only Catholic unions could combat Bolshevism. The Church denounced a violent strike at Davie Shipyards in 1919. In 1921, the Confédération des travailleurs catholiques du Canada was founded, with Jews and Protestants specifically excluded. Its constitution proclaimed a mission to maintain social peace, order, and justice. During the 1920s, the Confédération proved very useful to many employers in providing a docile labour force. But though the Confédération was strong in Quebec City and some smaller centres, AFL/TLC railway, manufacturing, and garment unions continued to hold sway in Montreal.[54]

Back in Winnipeg, the Citizens were preparing to settle scores. In July 1919, the "foreign" defendants were brought before an Immigration Review

---

* See Chapter 10.

Tribunal. Andrews was hoping for a quick trial and deportation to show that the "alien conspiracy" was being dealt with, and to intimidate the "foreign" communities. But the public spotlight was now on the hearings, prominent lawyers had been engaged, and much of the prosecution's case was based on the testimony of a paid spy. After lengthy hearings, Verenchuk was released in spite of attempts to fabricate a charge against him; Charitonoff was acquitted with a "scolding"; Almazoff had his deportation order overturned on appeal; and only Schoppelrei was actually deported, because he had entered Canada illegally — to enlist! Blumenberg was ordered deported, but was allowed to leave voluntarily for the United States. Outside the spotlight, though, it is possible that as many as a hundred "foreigners" arrested during the strike were quietly deported, some to Soviet Russia.[55]

Andrews's real target was the British-Canadian socialists. Meighen wanted to drop the matter, fearing that a messy trial would embarrass the government and delay reconciliation. But Andrews could only justify what the Citizens had done by demonstrating that they had headed off a revolu-

Manitoba Archives Winnipeg Strike 35 (N12322)

Strike Leaders during trial c. 1920
Back row, left to right: R.E. Bray, George Armstrong, John Queen, R.B. Russell, R.J. Johns, W.A. Pritchard. Front row, left to right, W.A. Ivens, A.A. Heaps.

tion. He pressed forward with preliminary hearings and when Minister of Justice Doherty returned from Paris, Andrews had government support and virtually unlimited funding.[56]

The trial of the strike leaders was a marathon, with preliminary hearings in July and August, and trials in November and December, before a jury of rural people vetted by the Mounties. The trials generated thousands of pages of testimony and engaged important legal issues that can only be briefly summarized here. What was clear was that socialism, not the strike, was on trial. Only socialists had been arrested, and two defendants, OBU leaders Pritchard and Johns, had only been in Winnipeg for a few days during the strike. Of the SDP defendants, only Queen was on the Strike Committee. Ivens had been highly visible but was not a key strike leader. Heaps, Armstrong, and Bray had simply got under the Citizens' skins. Bob Russell was the only key strike leader who was also an SPC/OBU kingpin, and he was detached for a separate trial that would be a template for the others.[57]

The Crown based its charge of seditious conspiracy on the premise that "Bloody Saturday" was the culmination of events set in motion at the December and January mass meetings in Winnipeg, at the Western Labour Convention in Calgary, and in hundreds of speeches made by the defendants, whose "natural result" would be "to bring into hatred or contempt or ridicule the government, the administration of justice, or to incite discontent in order to promote ill will and hostility between different classes of His Majesty's subjects." Andrews also played to the galleries by denouncing the defendants for opposing the war, God, family, country, and all the ideals for which fallen soldiers had laid down their lives.[58]

The defence lawyers attacked this concept of seditious conspiracy, which required no proof of actual sedition. They criticized the jury selection and Andrews's role. They argued that the ideas of the accused were the same as those of the British Labour Party; that convicting them would call free speech itself into question; that the strike was a labour dispute not a revolution; and that if the strike leaders were on trial for using inflammatory language, the Citizens should be as well — and then there was the question of their usurping the power of the state. But the judge, who presided over both the preliminary hearings and all the trials, accepted the prosecution's logic and allowed a mountain of socialist publications and correspondence to be introduced as "evidence." His three-hour charge to the jury in the Russell trial was a virtual instruction to find him guilty.

Russell was convicted and sentenced to two years and his appeals were denied. The other strike leaders were tried together. Four of them decided that if this was to be a show trial they might as well make a show of it. By acting in their own defence, they had the opportunity to address the jury directly. In his address, Queen ridiculed the use of literature that could be bought at bookstores as "evidence" of seditious intent. Ivens described what the Labour Church really stood for. Pritchard gave an impassioned two-day oration which expounded in detail his Marxist view of the world, what the OBU was really about, what revolution really meant, and why free speech was so important to a free society.[59]

The jury found Ivens, Pritchard, Johns, Queen, and Armstrong guilty of seditious conspiracy. They acquitted Bray of this charge, but found him guilty of being a common nuisance. They acquitted Heaps altogether. They recommended mercy for all, which was not granted — the first five got eighteen months and Bray got six months of hard labour. Fred Dixon, on trial for seditious libel, was acquitted after an eloquent defence of press freedom "in the historic tradition of Joseph Howe and William Lyon Mackenzie." The charge against Woodsworth was not pursued.[60]

Though he had never believed that Bolshevism was rampant in Canada, Borden did conclude that Canada needed a proper security service. Following a series of detailed recommendations by Commissioner Perry, Parliament passed an act to create the Royal Canadian Mounted Police, which became operational in February 1920. The new service absorbed the Dominion Police into the North West Mounted Police to form a national police force of twenty-five hundred officers — the largest that had ever existed in Canada. The RCMP security service set up a central registry, with files on people, organizations, and events, and its voluminous reports show extensive surveillance. Immigration tribunals continued to deport "undesirables," such as one Italian immigrant in Calgary in July 1919. "Being a man of some education," read the police report, "he was writing letters for the public press, most of them of a very inflammatory nature, and these were heavy evidence against him." How many more there were like him is not known, but it does appear that the number of deportations declined after 1921.[61]

V

By 1921, the nation was returning to the older dispensation where bosses bossed and workers worked. The economy slumped in 1920, and when prosperity returned, workers were as vulnerable as they had ever been. Most of the ambitious proposals in the 1919 Liberal platform were quietly shelved. Some companies established workers' committees, insurance plans, savings banks, and profit-sharing. Others provided cafeterias, playgrounds, and Christmas parties. But most businessmen remained firmly opposed to unions, let alone Colorado Plans or Whitley Councils.[62]

The steam went out of the labour movement. The rise of resource, service, and assembly line manufacturing, the decline of craft unionism, and the employers' counterattack, left the TLC nearly bankrupt by 1930. In Ontario, the ILP ministers, especially union leader Walter Rollo who served as minister of labour and health, performed creditably, but ideological debates and personal rivalries splintered a party that had never really had cohesion or a platform, and farmers and labour fell out over issues like the tariff and a strike on the Chippawa Hydro project. By the time the UFO/Labour government fell in 1923, the Labour Party had all but ceased to exist. In Nova Scotia, bitter strikes in the coal and steel industries, in which one-quarter of the active militia were called out, had resulted by 1925 in what historians Ian MacKay and Suzanne Morton describe as "grinding despair, petty betrayals, and state violence that proclaimed the death of the new social order so many had glimpsed, with so much hope, in 1919 and 1920."[63]

The Marxist left also fragmented. Some left the movement altogether. Dick Johns became a respected industrial arts educator. Bray became a market gardener in British Columbia and later organized for the CCF. Russell devoted his life to the OBU, which was by 1921 only a local in Manitoba (though a sports pool in its magazine proved a cash cow for a few years), and to unsuccessful candidacies for various socialist parties. Other former SPC members, such as Kavanagh and McLachlan, and social gospeller A.E. Smith, joined the Canadian Communist Party, which was founded at a secret meeting in an Ontario barn in 1921. These "soldiers of the international" toiled in obscurity through the 1920s, trying without much success to infiltrate labour unions, with many falling victim to the twists and turns of Stalinist ideology.[64]

But viable social democratic parties did emerge from the wreckage, and Marxists seeking a "third way" drifted toward other socialist options. By 1921, socialist parties from Manitoba, Alberta, British Columbia, and Ontario were coalescing into a national Independent Labour Party. In 1920, Ivens, Queen, Armstrong, and Dixon were elected to the Manitoba legislature while still in prison, and the following year Woodsworth was elected to the federal Parliament, to be joined by Calgary labour MP William Irvine and, in 1925, by Abe Heaps. Ivens would have a long career in Manitoba politics and Queen would serve as mayor of Winnipeg in the troubled 1930s. In 1932, the CCF brought together socialists, social democrats, agrarian socialists, and co-operators under a single banner with Woodsworth as its national leader. Members included Midgley, Pritchard, and Winch.[65]

The Citizens celebrated with a banquet but then faded away. Andrews continued to be a prominent lawyer; he eventually died in 1950, leaving no papers. Other Citizens' leaders also remained closed-mouthed. By contrast, the strikers published voluminous documents. The Robson Commission that Norris had established as part of the agreement to end the strike concluded that it had not been a revolution but a response to pent-up tensions in Winnipeg and the

obduracy of employers in the metal shops. Telephone operators, postal workers, and civic employees had to reapply for their old jobs; several hundred were not re-hired, and those that were lost their seniority and had to promise never to participate in a sympathetic strike. Many families had to rebuild their lives, some with breadwinners unemployed, and Christmas coming.[66]

The nature and meaning of the labour revolt and the Winnipeg General Strike have been hotly debated in the years since these dramatic events. In their immediate aftermath, many

J.S. Woodsworth in Parliamentary Library, 1930s

Yousuf Karsh, Library and Archives Canada, Arch ref no R613-427, e010751658

conservatives saw them as a narrow escape from Bolsehvism. Later historians, mostly social democrats, saw Winnipeg as a fight for the rights of labour, which fell victim to an irrational fear of aliens and Bolsheviks, a victory-in-defeat that launched a tradition of democratic socialism. Marxists have asserted that 1919 really was a revolutionary moment, a crisis of capitalism precipitated by the Great War, which was crushed by the state with the help of labour stooges. More recent leftist historians, while recognizing that there was no revolutionary conspiracy, have also acknowledged that the strike did challenge constitutional authority, and they are critical of its leaders for starting something they could not hope to finish. Some others have been more sympathetic to the Citizens, who at least managed to break the strike without brutal repression. Scholars influenced by the ideas of Antonio Gramsci* have portrayed Winnipeg as a real-life drama in which the accepted concepts and symbols of citizenship, social order, power, and justice were inverted, and for a brief shining moment, people lived in the free and just society of which they had only been able to dream.[67]

Labour unrest was widespread in Canada in 1919, as was the fear (and hope) of revolution — whatever revolution meant — and there was a counter-attack by threatened international unions and repression by panicked authorities. But O.D. Skelton had been right. Canada was not Russia, Britain, or even the United States. It was a heterogeneous, regionally diverse society, the parts of which had reached varying stages of industrial development. Many workers were radicalized by the ferment of the time, but radical leaders were not ready to conduct a successful revolution and the rank and file never wanted anything so drastic. Some labour battles, such as in the mines and mills of Cape Breton, remained desperate struggles between dependent communities and ruthless capitalists. But for most workers, the goal was better wages and working conditions, a decent life for their families, dignity and respect, a fairer society. Labour unions would continue to wage that struggle. A democratic socialist tradition had been born that would be a permanent fixture in Canadian political life. There would never be another general strike.

---

* Gramsci (1891–1937) was an Italian Communist who refined traditional Marxism by stressing the importance of ideas and culture, and developing the concept of hegemony — the means by which ruling elites legitimize their authority by creating narratives and shaping the ideas and values that animate society.

CHAPTER 9

United Farmers

On October 20, 1919, a bright Monday morning blazing with autumn colour, Ernest C. Drury walked with his wife to the old Temperance Hall, half a mile down the road from his prosperous farm near Barrie, Ontario. They were going to vote in a provincial election — his wife for the very first time. On the way they met Old Jimmy, an African-Canadian who had worked for years on their farm and was walking four miles to cast his vote. Drury was a leader of the United Farmers of Ontario, but he was not a candidate in this election. That evening he was astonished, like most of the province, to learn that the UFO had won forty-four seats and Labour eleven. "I went to bed," he recalled, "but it was a long time before I got to sleep. With the largest group in the House, it seemed probable that we would be called on to form a Government and I felt that we were not ready."[1]

Farmers' movements had been gaining strength across the country. But with no leader and only the barest of platforms, the UFO was not really a political party. Now it was like the dog that caught the car. Should it stand aside and let another party form the government? Or should it invite all the other parties into a grand coalition? Or combine with Labour to form a government? After much deliberation, UFO leaders decided on the latter course. They offered the premiership to two elected members, then to Ontario Hydro chairman Sir Adam Beck, then to their general secretary, J.J. Morrison, and finally to Drury. Drury accepted, and for three weeks sat in a rented office interviewing candidates for Cabinet posts, most of whom had little or no experience of elected office.[2]

In 1919, half of Canadians still lived on farms, or in villages and small towns. "At least 90 percent of the population of Canada," wrote journalist

The Milch Cow by Arch Dale
This widely circulated cartoon, first published in the Grain Growers' Guide December 15, 1915, portrays the view of the west (and indeed all farmers) that producers were feeding a giant cow milked by the fat capitalists in the East.

C.W. Peterson, "be they engaged in trade, industry, transportation, or in any other line of human endeavour, depend absolutely on our agriculture for their daily bread and the prosperity of their undertakings." To many city people in Eastern Canada, an old farmstead was still "home," where Grandma and Grandpa warmly welcomed the extended family. But the reality in many parts of the countryside, wrote Drury's friend W.C. Good, was that "men and money have been drained to the cities, leaving a disheartened remnant to battle against weeds, isolation and despair." Farmers, like so many other Canadians, believed the war had promised them something better, and they, too, demanded that this promise be fulfilled.[3]

I

In our urban society of today, we need imagination to conjure up a world where there was a horse for every two people; when the odour of barnyard and bake-oven, the sight of calves being born and pigs being killed, the dazzling stars in the blackness of a country night, were the heritage of many city people as well as those who still lived on the farm.

Canadian agriculture in 1919 was like a series of geological strata whose different layers embodied the evolution of techniques, crops, and machines, from pioneers wrestling a meagre living from small farms hewn out of the bush, to modern agriculture, including specialized farms growing potatoes in New Brunswick and Prince Edward Island, apples in Nova Scotia, or mixed fruits in the Niagara peninsula. Drury's own farm was a model. Educated at Ontario Agricultural College, he had applied scientific farming techniques, developed prize-winning sheep and hogs, replaced all-purpose cattle with beef and dairy breeds, and was growing vegetables for the city market, and hay and oats for horses. His was one of the first farmhouses with electricity, a bathroom, septic tanks, and running water. But it was still a family farm, with a few hired hands.[4]

The Prairie provinces had made the transition from frontier farming to modern agriculture within a generation. Again, there was a continuum — from large wheat barons with thousands of acres (some like W.R. Motherwell or Seager Wheeler of Saskatchewan experimenting with new crops and techniques); to smaller farmers, building up their land and equipment with hard work and frightening debt; to East European immigrants replacing sod huts with frame houses; to hired men, dreaming of one day farming on their own. Only six in ten homesteaders succeeded in clearing the land or building a house within five years, as was required to gain a permanent title. How well they did then depended on when they came, how much land and capital they had, how far they were from a railway, whether they had a community or extended family to share the work, and how much privation they could endure.

The West was wheat. The crop of sixty-three million bushels in 1901 grew to three hundred million in 1915 and wheat was one-quarter of all Canadian exports. Farmers were always being advised to diversify, and there was mixed farming in the parklands of Manitoba and ranching in Alberta. But once new varieties of wheat were developed that would thrive in dry land and short growing seasons, resist rust, and yield hard, protein-rich kernels that could be stored and shipped in bulk, and once the mechanisms were in place to finance the crop and transport it to Europe, it was a foregone conclusion that farmers would grow wheat, wheat, and more wheat. Everyone dreamed of a year like 1915 when an immigrant farmer sold his crop for $15,000. "It was like finding a gold mine in the field," his descendant recalled, "... it lifted him and Grandma out of the poor class, out of the peasant class they had been in the Ukraine.... Not rich, but they had money and their own land and they could look anybody in the eye."[5]

By 1921, the Prairie provinces had two million people, and Saskatchewan, with 771,000, was the third largest province in Canada. They were a vast carpet of wheat farms, with isolated houses under the huge dome of the sky, criss-crossed by railways and dotted with elevators and the small towns that grew up around them — unpainted wooden false-front stores along an absurdly wide main street, with a general store, land office, post office, hotel, Chinese restaurant, bar, community hall, and skating rink. There were ethnic and social distinctions, but in these towns newcomers could be integrated and a community could develop. Small wooden Protestant churches, and Catholic and Orthodox churches serving ethnic communities, sprouted up at crossroads. So did one-room schools with pot-bellied stoves that cooked half the class while the other half froze, where a trip to the outhouse in winter required real need, where badly paid teachers with inadequate equipment taught students who attended when they could. "What took place in these small country schools," recalled John Charyk, "was instrumental in cementing our democratic way of life. It can be said that Canada's future was written on the blackboards of the little rural schoolhouses."[6]

Whatever kind of farm you lived on, farming was hard work and a monotonous life that got worse the further you were from settlement. Your day began at 4:30 in the morning and ended at bedtime — "you can rest while you feed the pigs" went a popular adage. There were cows to be milked, animals to be fed and watered, manure to be spread, stables to be mucked, vegetables to be tended, and, depending on the season, a field to be ploughed, seeded, or harvested, apples to be picked and packed, brush to be cut, wood to be gathered, wool to be sheared, animals to be slaughtered, produce to be taken to market.

Western wheat farming was a race against a short growing season. After a winter of preparing seed and equipment, the land was harrowed in the spring with a disc or rake machine, seeded with a mechanical drill and harrowed again. In July came haying, which required a cutter and baler and men to stack the hay. When the wheat was ripe, a horse-drawn combine cut it down and tied it into sheaves, which were then "stooked" — stuck upright into the ground to allow the kernels to dry. "For the rest of my life," recalled one farmhand, "the memory of all those bundles laying there in rows all the way to the horizon & waiting for me to come along & pick them up, well, words really can't describe the feeling." A threshing machine driven from a stationary steam engine cut the sheaves, separated the grain and sieved it on a moving screen, then threw the grain out one pipe and the chaff out another. These machines travelled from farm to farm, with an engineer, men to feed sheaves into the thresher, men to catch the grain and sew the sacks, men to sweep aside the chaff, for fourteen hours a day.[7]

You could be killed or maimed by a kicking cow, a falling tree, a mechanical thresher, a fall from a horse or a hay wagon. Your skin could be flayed raw by stubble or burned brown by the blazing sun. You could have chronic diarrhoea, muscle aches, wet feet and rashes from damp, dirty clothing — and you just had to keep working. You could be ruined by a hailstorm on a summer's day, by an early frost, by poor judgment about how much to pay the workers, when to plant, or how to sell, by locusts or poor weather or a low price. If you had a good year, did you invest in better equipment, more livestock, even the house you promised your wife and family? You did not want to miss the opportunity or lose out to a competitor. But if you went too far into debt, you might be gone the next year.[8]

If you were a woman, life was harder still. In planting or harvest time you prepared a breakfast of potatoes, meat, eggs, or fish for the men, at noon a monster lunch (often served in the fields), at night a light supper. You cleaned rooms, emptied chamber pots, milked cows, separated cream and churned butter, washed dishes and cleaned pots. Once a week, you washed huge piles of laundry in boiling water, scrubbed them with lye-soap on a washboard, ironed with a flat-iron heated on the stove. You baked dozens of loaves and pies, made or mended clothes, or preserved meat and vegetables, sauerkraut and pickles for the winter. You raised children. And you had babies, possibly with a midwife present, seldom with a doctor, and never in the hospital — that was, recalled a pioneer, "for serious cases like pneumonia and a heart attack and operations and the like. Women having babies, they're not sick or hurt. They're just having a baby." In the long nights of winter, you might find time for games or singing, or seeking advice from the women's pages of farm magazines about how to stretch a budget or brighten a dreary home. Only a lucky few had electric light, furnaces, a bath, a toilet, or indoor water.[9]

You and your husband found respite in visits to town for supplies and social activities; in church, WCTU and charitable work; and in sporting events and festivals. There would be hockey, baseball, or curling; recitations by a visiting poet or lecturer; or the "school concerts and flag drills and Indian club swinging; plays and cantatas by young peoples' societies; Christmas concerts with Santa Claus coming down from the loft on a rope, to the loud acclaim and gasping surprise of the believers," recalled by Nellie McClung. You might go to dances, where you could meet someone like the bachelor who regularly walked ten miles to Vulcan, Alberta, danced all evening, and returned at sunrise for another day of backbreaking work. You might attend a community meeting to discuss a co-operative, complain about tariffs, or listen to a political candidate.[10]

Farming could break the strongest spirit. "Country cemeteries bear grim witness to the high mortality rate in young women," wrote McClung bitterly. Martha Ostenso's character Caleb Gare in her novel *Wild Geese* is an unforgettable depiction of how isolation, greed, and obsession with the land could strangle human feeling and make the farm a prison. But most recognized "some power about the land" that bound them to their farms in spite of all adversity. For all the harshness of the Prairies, McClung recalled that those who grew up there "remember her purple twilights, her phantom breezes, the smell of burning leaves, the ripe tints of autumn, the slanting snow.... I think of the times I watched the snow falling gently in a criss-cross pattern between our house and the Methodist Church, as I stood at the den window, knowing that the children were all safely in, and doing their homework on the dining room table."[11]

The happy memories of some became an ideology for others. "Were it not for the influx of fresh and virile blood from the country," wrote W.C. Good in 1919, "city-life would disappear from inherent weakness, and that much of civilization which is dependent thereon would disappear also." Good, a graduate of the University of Toronto and the Ontario Agricultural College, whose farm near Brantford was, like Drury's, a model of progressive agriculture, regarded cities as "in many respects a blot upon our civilization." Drury told the Social Service Congress in 1914 that while most of their discussions were concerned with the "cleansing of the sewers of our civilization," agrarian reform was about "the preservation of the springs of our civilization, of the fountain-head on which the whole depends." John MacDougall, in a 1913 study for the Presbyterian Church, lamented rural decline as a threat to Protestant moral values, and to "the race."[12]

The man who gave the most effective expression to this agrarian myth was Peter McArthur, who had pursued a writing career in New York and London before returning to the family farm in southern Ontario. From 1907 to 1924, McArthur wrote hundreds of weekly columns for the *Farmer's Advocate* and the Toronto *Globe*. His 1919 collection, *The Red Cow and Her Friends*, was only one of many books that conveyed his homespun philosophy through deceptively simple stories of animals and farm life.

To McArthur, the farm was "a place of peace, a place of refuge, and a home.... To live on a farm and enjoy all that it has to offer is the greatest good that can be attained by a poet or a philosopher." His farm was "hewn out of the wilderness by pioneers who had no other aim than to make a home and build a country where their children might be free." It would remain "right where it is through depressions, panics, wars, and every other kind of human foolishness." Its values were not in dollars. McArthur could not remember the prices he got for produce, but he could remember "how beautiful the apples were the first year we pruned and sprayed the old orchard ... how fine the oats looked the year we had them in the field back of the root-house, ... calves I had fed to admired sleekness and hogs that I had stuffed to fatness."[13]

By 1919, even McArthur could see that this idyllic vision was losing touch with reality. Good's book *Production and Taxation in Canada* said that Eastern agriculture would make no economic sense if it were not for intangibles like food and shelter and love of the rural life. Good urged farmers to improve their education, efficiency, and business sense, and he implored society to pay more for produce and place a higher value on rural development. But as James Gray observed, when farm children visiting the city found flush toilets, water that "came hot and cold from taps and did not have to be lugged in pails from pumps in the yard," gas-burning stoves with "no kindling to split and a wood-box that can never be kept full," and porcelain bath-tubs with taps, they knew where their futures lay. Farming, Leacock observed, was a great preparation for success in life, provided you got off the farm.[14]

II

Agrarian protest had a long history in North America and, in the nineteenth century populist movements tracked the frontier as it moved west. The Grange and the Patrons of Industry, like the Knights of Labour, had been imported into Canada from the United States, become powerful forces, and then withered just as quickly. All that remained of them by 1914 was the Dominion Grange (a shadow of its former self), a newspaper, the *Weekly Sun*, and a tradition of activism that Ontario farmers took with them to the Prairies. Politicians paid lip service to agrarian values, but farmers weakened their influence with their rock-ribbed loyalty to traditional parties dominated by businessmen and professionals.[15]

Some specialized producers formed marketing organizations, and farmers' co-ops pooled their products for sale and combined their purchasing power to buy their basic necessities. In Quebec, Alphonse Desjardins organized the rural network of co-ops and savings banks that bears his name. A national organization was formed under the leadership of Good's friend George Keen, and people like Desjardins, Good, Keen, Mackenzie King, and leaders of the Catholic Church in Quebec, saw co-ops as an agent of moral reform, a means of developing character and community, and an alternative to industrial conflict.[16]

But in the decade before the war, the epicentre of agrarian protest had shifted to the West. The people who controlled the complex networks of banks, buyers, elevators, and transportation systems that made wheat farming possible were far away, and they were the types of people farmers didn't much like. "If you put a banker, a railwayman and an elevator agent in a barrel and roll them down a hill, there will always be a son-of-a-bitch on top," ran a Western joke.[17]

At the local elevator the farmer had to accept the grade the buyer gave his grain, and unless he had enough to fill a railway car he had to accept the "street price." Grain growers' associations under the leadership of men like Motherwell had secured federal and provincial regulations and reforms, more railways, sidings and elevators, more competition among buyers, and independent testing of grades. Nonetheless, Robert Stead's fictional character Gander Stake well expressed "the farmer's deep-rooted sense of injustice over the fact that whenever he bought he had to pay the seller's price, but whenever he sold, the buyer dictated the figure." But what could he do? "'Oh, take it!' said Gander helplessly. This was not his world. He was a producer, not a seller."[18]

Behind the buyer was the Winnipeg Grain Exchange, which had evolved into a sophisticated mechanism for buying and selling wheat. It allowed trading in "futures," which meant the buyer could pay the farmer in cash against the price he would receive when the grain was delivered months later at the Lakehead. To its members, the Exchange was "the most efficient and well organized commercial institution in the Dominion of Canada; indeed it is today the largest cash wheat market on the continent of America." But to the farmer, it was, in the words of E.A. Partridge, a "combine with a gambling hell thrown in." A Saskatchewan farmer who had lost a foot in a farming accident, a large man of flashing eye and acerbic speech, Partridge in 1906 persuaded several thousand farmers to put up $25 a share to found the Grain Growers' Grain Company (GGGC), which would buy their grain and hold a seat on the Exchange. It took two years of legal and political warfare before the GGGC was allowed to occupy that seat, and it had to sacrifice its policy of paying credits on the basis of grain sold rather than shares held (which violated the Exchange policy against kickbacks). It also had to sacrifice Partridge, whose rhetoric had alienated both the Exchange and business-minded farmers like Motherwell.[19]

It was left to his chosen successor, Thomas Crerar, to build up the GGGC. He turned it into a behemoth, which by 1914 had fourteen thousand stockholders and a thousand branches, and handled thirty million bushels of wheat a year. A Scots Ontarian who had come west as a boy, Crerar believed in individualism and voluntary co-operation, with government intervening to level the playing field but otherwise staying out of the way. The GGGC bought a mill and distributed flour in carload lots. It bought a stockyard. It bought apples from Ontario growers' co-ops, lumber from its own timber limits in British Columbia, fence-posts, binder twine, and other supplies in bulk. It leased terminal elevators at the Lakehead and in Vancouver. Crerar was in the process of establishing an export company when wartime controls intervened in 1915.[20]

Partridge's next big idea was that provincial governments should take over local grain elevators and the federal government should own terminal elevators. In 1912, the Borden government bought the elevators at the Lakehead, but an attempt by Manitoba to establish a provincial system proved disastrous. So, the GGGC took over the Manitoba elevator chain, and in 1917 it merged with the Alberta Grain Growers to form the United Grain Growers, which by 1925 had 450 elevators handling 48.5 million bushels a year. By 1917, the Saskatchewan Co-operative Elevator Company, established in 1911 with the assistance of the provincial government, had 230 elevators owned by local farmers, and handled 20 percent of the marketed crop in that province.[21]

In 1914, the GGGC reported that not only were its members getting three or four cents more a bushel that they would not otherwise have got, but they had been "made to feel that they are business men; their interests have been broadened; they have learned the benefits of standing together; and they have become imbued with confidence and determination that have already manifested themselves in a keener interest in business and politics, in intellectual advancement, in improvement of farming methods and in rural bet-

T.A. Crerar (c. 1930)

William Lyon Mackenzie King / Library and Archives Canada C003509

terment." Between 1909 and 1914, the GGGC gave $25,000 to Western farmers' associations and was becoming a political and educational as well as an economic powerhouse.[22]

But even this was not enough for Partridge. His dream was that farmers would unite to create a "co-operative commonwealth" in which the principles of mutual assistance would be applied to the whole of society. In 1910, he started a magazine called the *Grain Growers' Guide*, under the auspices of the GGGC (which also bought a printing plant). Under editor George F. Chipman, the Guide became the bible of Prairie farmers, providing uncoloured news from the world of thought and action, and honest opinions thereon, with the object of aiding our people to form correct views upon economic, social and moral questions, so that the growth in society may continually be in the direction of more equitable, kinder and wiser relations between its members, resulting in the widest possible increase and diffusion of material prosperity, intellectual growth, right living, health and happiness.[23]

It published information on grain prices and agricultural techniques, a women's column edited by Frances Beynon, regular articles denouncing Eastern business and the tariff, frequent contributions from Canadian and American radicals and social reformers, as well as many articles by Partridge himself.[23]

Crerar was meanwhile building on the success of the GGGC to create a national farmers' organization. In 1909, the various grain growers' associations joined with the Dominion Grange to form the Canadian Council of Agriculture (CCA). As a representative of Ontario farmers, Drury had to travel to the founding convention of the CCA on a third-class ticket. But he was so encouraged that in 1913, with the financial support of the GGGC, he, Good, J.J. Morrison, and another man founded the United Farmers of Ontario.

The UFO was formed from the many farmers' clubs, the remnants of the Grange, co-operative societies, self-help groups, and other rural organizations, who could join the new organization while preserving their local autonomy. Its organizing secretary, Morrison, was a dour, fifty-three-year-old farmer who had attended business college, worked as a salesman, and learned trade-union organizing before returning to the family farm in 1900. In parallel, the United Farmers' Co-operative Company Limited was also formed, with W.C. Good as its driving force . By its second meeting in 1916, the UFO had five thousand members and eighty-two new clubs, and it had joined the Canadian Council of Agriculture.[24]

The biggest remaining enemies of farmers (besides the weather) were the banks and the protective tariff. The banks, farmers believed, were the tools of Eastern capitalists; they charged too much, demanded too much collateral, and left all the risks to the farmer. The tariff protected Canadian manufacturing at the expense of the farmer, increasing every cost to him, from implements to transportation to household goods. The farmers rejoiced when Laurier, after a western tour in 1910, negotiated the Reciprocity Treaty in natural products with the United States. They were crushed when Laurier's government was defeated on the issue. Bankers like Sir Edmund Walker might plead in 1917 for "discussion, not animosity, argument not suspicion, and essentially a realization of the guiding principle that we are partners in the work of building up a country for the happiness and prosperity of our children." But how could farmers ever trust the words of an Eastern banker who, with his capitalist friends and urban lackeys, could so control the political system that farmers could never, ever, achieve what they considered essential to their survival?[25]

III

Farmers were no different than other Canadians in seeing the Great War as a crusade for freedom. Many farmers, and their sons, enlisted. But most, like Stead's Gander Stake, saw food production as their indispensible contribution — "They want wheat an' I am helpin' to raise it." Cultivated acreage in the West rose from 9.3 million acres in 1914 to 11.6 million in 1918, and Number One hard wheat rose from less than a dollar a bushel to $2.24. Hog prices went through the roof. Drury never got better prices for his prize lambs. Farmers turned their profits into land, implements, buildings, even gasoline tractors (which proved unreliable). But Western wheat faced fluctuating prices, variable weather, stem rust (1916) and drought (1919). The cost of farm labour soared. With the state controlling food prices and the Board of Grain Supervisors managing the wheat market, the farmer found himself in a familiar position — controls on the price of what he sold, the cost of what he needed skyrocketing, and growing debts at rising interest rates. As consumer prices rose, the once-idealized farmer began to find himself labelled as a "profiteer" and his workers and sons branded as "slackers."[26]

In 1916, the Canadian Council of Agriculture announced a "farmers' platform" and encouraged farmers to support any candidate who would agree to run on it. Its main planks were Reciprocity with the United States; abolition of the tariff on foodstuffs, farm machinery, and other essential items; and reduction of duties on "all the necessities of life." It also proposed a tax on unimproved lands, an end to the "wholesale alienation of natural resources," an inheritance tax on large estates, a graduated personal and corporate income tax, the nationalization of railways, telegraph, and express companies, and votes for women. A number of candidates won on this platform under various banners in the 1917 federal election, including Crerar, who agreed to join the Union Cabinet — not, he told the *Grain Growers' Guide*, as a party man, but "as the representative of organized farmers."[27]

Crerar became a friend of Borden and Rowell, and provided a progressive voice in Cabinet. But he could do little to stop the steep rise in prices of farm machinery, rampant inflation, or the suspension of the "Crowsnest Pass rate" — a fixed freight rate for grain shipped east and farm implements shipped west. Nor could he prevail against the established financial interests and pro-tariff manufacturers who dominated the government. He supported conscription, but he was appalled at the way the government's promise not to conscript farmers' sons was broken in April 1918.[28]

Western farmers took this decision quietly, but in Ontario Morrison organized a mass meeting that voted to send a monster delegation to Ottawa. The fledgling Fermiers unis du Québec also sent a delegation led by the Quebec minister of agriculture. On May 15, 1918, some five thousand farmers were addressed by Crerar, Rowell, and Borden. Their leaders told the ministers that the government could have men or food, but not both. Borden stood his ground. The farmers, he said, would simply have to realize there was a war on. He refused to let the farm leaders address Parliament (as American labour leader Samuel Gompers had done only days before), and police blocked a farmers' delegation when it tried to march on Parliament. The farmers dispersed peacefully, leaving behind a written "Remonstrance," but they were outraged. And as Crerar had feared, there was a backlash among MPs and the urban press — an article by H.F. Gadsby in *Saturday Night* depicting farmers as disloyal hayseeds still rankled Drury and Good fifty years later. Another mass meeting in Toronto, on June 7, with police present to record any subversive statements, heard "[s]corching attacks … on the federal government for its attitude of sangfroid and incivility, and diatribes hurled at the newspapers for their slander mongering and misrepresentation."[29]

By late 1918, Crerar was staying in the Cabinet only to win the war and to try to get whatever reduction he could in the tariff. In November, the CCA issued a new farmers' platform, entitled "The New National Policy," which was a political manifesto even more radical than the Methodist Programme. Besides what they had demanded in 1916, the farmers now called for a more independent role for Canada in foreign affairs, a new world order based on co-operation and social harmony, and the direct involvement of farmers in postwar reconstruction. Soldiers should be demobilized only when the economy could absorb them, given training and assistance, settled on the land "when by training or experience they are qualified to do so," and helped to find jobs, "but not at the expense of the existing labour force." Producer and consumer co-ops should be encouraged, and railway, water, and air transportation, telephone, telegraph, and express systems, all natural power projects, and coal mines, should be publicly owned. The platform called for an end to "government by [O]rder-in-[C]ouncil," reform of the Senate, publication of election expenses and of the ownership of newspapers and periodicals, proportional representation, the initiative, referendum and recall, and opening seats in Parliament "to women on the same terms as men." By early 1919, it was becoming clear that if Crerar and his followers could not get an existing party to adopt this platform, the next step would be to form a third party.[30]

But a powerful opponent to the idea of a third party emerged in the person of Henry Wise Wood of Alberta. Tall, slow of speech, with a bald, dome-shaped head and deep-set eyes that flashed when aroused, Wood was born and raised in Missouri, had trained for the ministry, had owned a ranch, and had been involved in U.S. agrarian politics — which had convinced him that third parties were dead ends for farmers. In 1905, Wood came to Alberta and was soon playing a pivotal role in bringing together

Henry Wise Wood

Glenbow Archives NA-1900-20

squabbling factions to form the United Farmers of Alberta, in creating the Alberta Co-operative Elevator Company, and in creating the United Grain Growers, where he worked closely with Crerar. As a trusted advisor on grain matters, he was even briefly considered for the Union Cabinet.

It is surprising that such a deeply conservative man should have been responsible for unveiling, as he did, beginning in early 1919, ideas that were in their own way as revolutionary as anything the Western Labour Convention was talking about in Calgary. Like his religious and Marxist contemporaries, Wood also saw history as a dialectic, but one between co-operation and competition. Humanity was competitive by nature, he believed, but over time people learned to co-operate in groups. However, these groups then competed with each other for money and power until they, too, learned to co-operate. This process continued until humanity reached the ultimate competition, between nations, which culminated in the Great War. The war had now made it imperative that nations and classes learn to co-operate so that humanity could be "brought into perfect obedience to the true laws of life and become a true social being, operating a perfect civilization."

As a first step, organized farmers should seek representation in Parliament, not as a political party in competition or alliance with others seeking to control the state, but as an occupational group that would then co-operate with all other elected "groups" and convert Parliament into a "Group Government." There were many unanswered questions arising from the system he envisioned. How would individuals function within the "group"? How would groups that were not farmers, plutocrats, or workers organize themselves? How would these groups actually govern the country? But Wood's compelling oratory, building on the hope generated by the war, gained wide support for this uplifting vision, especially in Alberta.[31]

Group government was given a national audience in William Irvine's 1919 book *The Farmers in Politics*. Irvine was a Presbyterian Social Gospel minister who had become a Unitarian, founded a Labour Church, and edited a lively newspaper, the *Nutcracker*, in Calgary. He had helped establish the Non-Partisan League, patterned after an offshoot of the American Socialist Party, which had brought together farmers and labour in North Dakota. Irvine's vision of an inclusive reform movement engaging women, professionals, and intellectuals, as well as farmers and workers, was diametrically opposed to Wood's exclusive focus on farmers. But like his friend Woodsworth, Irvine hoped to unite the reform movement and rescue it from the dead end of Marxism. He therefore adopted Wood's ideas, refined, and moderated them.

Irvine shared Wood's evolutionary (but not his religious) view of history, and his conviction that the "funeral" of the two-party system "is long overdue." In the aftermath of war, he proclaimed, "in church and state, in industry and government, in every department, society is being remodelled upon a democratic and co-operative basis." Where Bolshevism sought to destroy, group government would bring by peaceful evolution "a fully organized co-operative state." A group was neither a mob nor an autocracy, and it did not suppress the rights of the individual. Rather, "a number of people acting on an idea, which, by a synthetic process involving a compounding of the different ideas of all the individuals concerned, is theirs, would be a democracy." Only the farmer could be the catalyst to a co-operative society. "He is both capitalist and labourer. He knows that production is not furthered when war is going on between the two. He sees, also, the hopeless deadlock between organized capital and organized labour in the world of industry and commerce, and is thus led to the discovery of co-operation as the synthesis without which progress cannot be made." Farmers should thus take the lead in seeking representation in Parliament as a group, "so that in bringing to the service of the nation the best knowledge from every group, they may be able, co-operatively, to achieve the highest justice."[32]

By 1919, the long-standing grievances of farmers, the idealization of rural virtue, the resentments engendered by the war, and the vision of a new world born of the war, had combined to create a formidable force seeking social change. "Men and women of the country," said J.J. Morrison, "are thinking beyond their farms and beyond their own community, and are putting their thoughts into operation. They are acting collectively, and that is what organization makes possible." Women were full participants, not as farm wives but as citizens, in the words of the president of the United Farm Women of Ontario, "to work for your motto which we take for our motto, 'Equal opportunity for all, special privileges for none.'"[33]

IV

But the farmers' movement was a spontaneous movement, whose ideas and energy flowed from the grassroots, and it was evolving faster than any of its leaders could direct or control.

All over Ontario, new UFO clubs sprang into existence. The UFO purchased the *Weekly Sun*, renamed it the *Farmer's Sun*, and saw its circulation triple by 1922. Late in 1918, a candidate nominated by the UFO clubs in the remote constituency of Manitoulin defeated a powerful Conservative in a provincial by-election, with only belated support from the central office. Two months later, the same thing happened in another by-election. Drury, Good, and another OAC graduate, Manning Doherty, were tasked to collate "the scattered ideas embodied in resolutions passed by delegates assembled in the annual conventions" into something like a platform for the guidance of candidates. This "platform" was a pastiche of grievances — rural depopulation, the deterioration of rural life, the "unequal rewards of farm and town industry, owing to the dominance ... of privileged urban interests," and the alarming increase in the public debt, which led farmers to "deem it our duty, to ourselves and the Province, to seek independent representation in the Legislature" (there was no mention yet of a party). It called for fiscal prudence; abolishing patronage; facilitation of co-ops; better education in rural districts; "good roads for all rather than high-grade roads for a few"; protection of forest reserves; public control of electricity; encouragement of Prohibition; the initiative, referendum, and proportional representation.[34]

In Alberta, on January 22, 1919, the United Farmers of Alberta convention voted to provide central support to any provincial candidate nominated by 10 percent of the locals in a riding. In May, Wood was forced to allow William Irvine's Non-Partisan League to merge with the UFA — Irvine gave up the idea of a farmer-labour alliance, but got a commitment to political action with a broadly progressive program encompassing urban and professional groups as well as farmers. Wood recovered the initiative in June by elaborating his group government theory in speeches during a by-election, which the UFA candidate won handily. The following month, the UFA convention endorsed group government, and later in the year Irvine published his book popularizing the concept.[35]

In Saskatchewan, in October 1919, a farmer candidate defeated Liberal W.R. Motherwell (who had been the province's agriculture minister for a decade) in a federal by-election. At the other end of the country, the president of the United Farmers of New Brunswick defeated a Union cabinet minister in a federal by-election in November. Founded in April 1919, and assisted by visits from leaders like Morrison, Chipman, Irvine, and Crerar, the UFNB had mushroomed to seven thousand members in more than a hundred branches with a thriving co-op movement. In July 1920, the Nova Scotia United Farmers would return seven MLAs in a provincial election, and in October, the United Farmers of New Brunswick would elect eleven members to the provincial legislature.[36]

In Ottawa, Crerar was waiting for Borden's return from Europe, and the completion of White's budget, which was due in June 1919, before finally deciding what to do next. As Winnipeg moved toward a General Strike, a columnist in *Maclean's* reported that Western farmers were holding almost constant meetings and flooding Crerar and other MPs with telegrams. When Crerar and Borden met in late May, it quickly became apparent that the government could not meet the demands of the farmers, and Crerar resigned on June 7. On June 18, twelve Western Unionists voted for a Liberal amendment to the budget calling for lower tariffs; and Crerar and eight Western Unionists later voted against the budget itself. The election of Mackenzie King as leader of the Liberal Party, with the support of its high-tariff wing, removed the last possibility that the farmers might still support a mainline political party.[37]

Crerar was now the *de facto* leader of a group of eleven MPs. He and his supporters weighed their options. They could bring together the fragments of the western Liberal Party to head off any alliance between radical farmers and socialists. They could create an occupational movement, as Wood wanted, for farmers only. Or they could launch a new political party that would also include moderate labour, women, returned soldiers, and other groups that might accept the New National Policy. As he drifted toward the latter option, Crerar sparred repeatedly with Wood at meetings and in speeches across Western Canada. At a special meeting of the Canadian

Council of Agriculture, in Winnipeg in January 1920, the two men fought to a draw — there would be central support for candidates running on the New National Policy, but no national organization and no leader. On February 26, 1920, Crerar's eleven MPs decided to constitute themselves the parliamentary caucus of the National Progressive Party, with Crerar as leader. But the chance to create a party machinery had been lost.[38]

The United Farmers of Ontario faced the same internal conflict as they struggled to consolidate their victory. Good tried to convince the caucus to offer a grand coalition to the other parties as a step toward group government. When this was rejected and the UFO formed a government, the next logical step would have been to create a political party (with or without Labour). This was certainly Drury's view. He was intelligent, experienced, and confident to the point of arrogance, and his father had once been minister of agriculture in Ontario. He had, like Crerar, run as a Liberal in 1917 (he lost by a significant margin), and (unlike his friend Good) he had little use for "direct democracy," group government, or much of the "platform" he had helped cobble together.

Drury knew that his premiership was a fluke. The UFO had won only about 22 percent of the popular vote and Labour less than 10 percent. The urban establishment was waiting for his government to fall on its face. He picked for his Cabinet the best men he could find among the farmer and Labour members and brought others in from outside — notably Raney as attorney general and Manning Doherty as minister of agriculture. On accepting the premiership, he expressed the hope "that this political movement, which has begun as a class movement, representing farmers and labour, may expand and *broaden out* until it embraces citizens of all classes and occupations and becomes indeed a People's Party." But within weeks he was under attack from forces within the UFO led by Morrison and Agnes Macphail, who criticized his outside appointments and opposed any attempt to build a new party.[39]

In the provincial elections that were approaching in the West, success for the farmers would be no fluke — it would only be a question of what form farmers' governments would take in each province. Wheat prices plunged in 1920 after staying high in 1919. A drought was devastating much of the Prairies. Wartime loans were coming due. In Alberta, membership in the United Farmers doubled between 1919 and 1920. In Saskatchewan, the provincial

Liberal party severed its ties with the national party and faced down an incursion from the Non-Partisan League from the United States. In June 1920, a provincial election in Manitoba resulted in gains by the labour parties and the United Farmers of Manitoba and reduced the Norris government to a minority.

In Alberta, Wood tightened his hold on the UFA, kept its headquarters small, and allowed strategy and policy initiatives to bubble up from the grass roots. Nonetheless, women, religious groups, labour organizations, intellectuals, and professionals rallied to the cause, including Louise McKinney and Irene Parlby. On July 18, 1921, the UFA defeated the moribund Liberals, and then, like the UFO, cast about for a leader. Wood refused to be active in politics, preferring to remain head of the UFA, and Herbert H. Greenfield, a farmer from southern Alberta without any political experience, was appointed premier. The cabinet enjoyed such extensive grass-roots support that the transition to government was surprisingly smooth. In 1925, Greenfield was eased out in favour of J.E. Brownlee, a better-educated and more dynamic leader. With Wood orchestrating from the sidelines, the UFA provided stable and progressive government in Alberta until it was weakened by scandal and defeated by Social Credit in 1935.

In neighbouring Saskatchewan, Liberal Premier William Martin adroitly recruited the strongest members of the Grain Growers and in 1921 called a snap election before the nascent United Farmers of Saskatchewan could get organized. The Liberals became a farmers' party in all but name, and, under Martin's successor, Charles Dunning, enacted progressive legislation including support for co-ops, government ownership of utilities, and social benefits. In Manitoba, Norris was finally unseated in 1922 by the United Farmers of Manitoba under John Bracken, who then provided two decades of stable, socially progressive, and fiscally conservative government.[40]

While farmers could easily capture Western provincial governments, the big issues of the tariff, freight rates, banking, and Eastern capital required action at the federal level. In December 1920, the CCA finally accepted the Progressive parliamentary group as "the present parliamentary exponents of the New National Policy" and endorsed Crerar as its leader — but still without providing much organizational support. On June 27, 1921, Robert Gardiner of the Progressives defeated the Conservative former mayor of Medicine Hat by a landslide in a federal by-election for the seat vacated by the death of Arthur Sifton. In the general election of December 1921, the Progressives won 23 percent of the popular vote and sixty-four seats — thirty-seven in the Prairies, twenty-four in Ontario, one in New Brunswick, and two in British Columbia.[41]

V

This, as it turned out, was the high point for the Progressive Party and, indeed, for the farmers' movement. Their lack of a party organization and constant disputes over their role sapped their energy at the same time as the forces that had driven the movement forward began to subside.

In the Maritimes, farmers' organizations were attacked by forest, fishing, mining, and commercial-export interests. Hard times brought the failure of many co-ops. Their biggest failure was not linking up with more powerful opposition forces such as the Acadians and the labour movement. In Quebec, the promising Fermiers unis, in spite of having the blessing of Bourassa, were fiercely attacked by the nationalist press and conservative clergy — who accused them of either being Bolsheviks or being part of a plot to weaken

Archives of Ontario S332

The farmer-labour government of E.C. Drury
Drury is here pictured with his Cabinet which includes Attorney General Raney and Labour Minister Rollo.

French-Canadian solidarity. Two weeks before the 1921 election, they merged with the conservative Union des cultivateurs, rejected Crerar as leader, issued a less radical manifesto. Still they got only 4 percent of the vote. In 1924, the Union des cultivateurs became the Union catholique des cultivateurs.[42]

The twenty-four Ontario seats the Progressives won in the federal election of December 1921 were actually a disappointment — they had hoped for forty. The fact was that after two years of office Drury's government was coming apart. Morrison's unrelenting attacks on Drury's vision of "broadening out," the independence of the UFO local clubs from the government, the growing rift with a disintegrating Labour party, and even criticism from the *Farmer's Sun* (whose editor was pushed out in 1922 for being too sympathetic to Drury) prevented any party cohesion, much less organization.

The UFO clubs forced the government to back away from raising the school-leaving age, permitting French language schools in eastern Ontario, increasing grants to universities, or accepting an offer from the Massey Foundation to do a Carnegie-style study of the education system. In the United Farmers' Co-operative Company Limited, a battle raged between Good, who believed that the organization should be based on local branches and provide a vehicle for farmers to work together, and its manager, T.P. Loblaw, who wanted to expand along centralized business lines. Much to Drury's chagrin, Loblaw resigned in 1920 to establish a successful chain of grocery stores. And as we have seen, Raney proved an unfortunate choice as attorney general.

The Drury government actually accomplished a great deal: a provincial police force; unemployment insurance; mothers' allowances, minimum wages, and labour laws for women and children; reform of orphanages; new agricultural colleges; the Ontario College of Education; the beginnings of a system of paved highways; a ministry of health; easier credit for farmers, rural schools, and some progress in rural electrification. Many of these measures reflected Drury's own humanitarian beliefs, some were Labour initiatives, and most were broader than the original farmers' agenda — in fact, some, like paved main highways, were directly contrary to the 1919 platform. But he could not overcome the ambivalence of the UFO, whose convention in late 1922 cheered him to the rafters, then the following day passed a motion engineered by Morrison and Agnes Macphail opposing any idea of a new party. By mid-1923, Drury had had enough.

He called an election, and his government was annihilated by the revived Conservatives under Howard Ferguson.[43]

Crerar ran into similar trouble even before the 1921 federal election, when he responded to Mackenzie King's invitation to discuss a possible Liberal-Progressive coalition. Wood at first supported a "measures not men" strategy aimed at shifting the balance within the Liberal party toward lower tariffs, and Drury was quietly supportive. But King quickly made clear that he wanted a merger not an alliance, with Crerar representing agrarian interests around a Liberal Cabinet table as he had done (unsuccessfully) in the Borden government. When word of the discussions leaked out, King denounced any possibility of coalition.

After the election, King was leading a minority government and again approached the Progressives. Wood, Morrison, Macphail, and others threatened to denounce Crerar if he even considered entering a Liberal government. "We are not longing for power as some others have, for its own sake only," said Macphail, "because power without principle is one of the most dangerous things we can have." Under this pressure, Crerar also declined to become the Official Opposition. The Conservatives, he reasoned, would oppose everything the government did anyway; the radical Progressives would oppose anything that would require them to act like a political party; so the only thing he could do was support the Liberals in enacting legislation that served agrarian interests. But by deciding not to have a whip or any party discipline, the Progressives lost any claim to be an alternative government.[44]

The split within the Progressives was widened by the battle over the Canadian Wheat Board. In 1919, the Borden government had moved to dismantle the Board of Grain Supervisors after the British wound up their wartime wheat-trading company. Beset by a chorus of conflicting voices, the government had promised the British fifty to seventy-five million bushels out of an expected Canadian crop of 165 million, and on July 21, trading was reopened on the Winnipeg Grain Exchange. But when the crop was reduced by a severe drought, the British suddenly had a partial corner on the Canadian wheat market. The government was forced to quickly close trading and establish the Canadian Wheat Board to restore order. The Board set its initial payment at $2.15 a bushel — an excellent price, which got better in July 1920, when the Board provided a further interim payment of thirty cents a bushel. But then the United States abandoned its price controls and the Wheat Board refused to accept wheat after August 15. It made a final payment to farmers of eighteen cents per bushel in November, distributed its unspent balance to the provinces, and wound down its operations.

With wheat prices now in free fall, the Progressives were split between those like Wood and Partridge who demanded the reinstatement of the Board, and grain growers like Crerar who argued that this claim for special treatment for wheat farmers was no different from the tariff protection given to manufacturers. Following a royal commission study, the King government brought forward a bill in 1922 to create a very different Wheat Board, one that would be operated by the Prairie provinces and would have no control over railway transport. Manitoba refused to pass the required legislation; Alberta and Saskatchewan could not find qualified people to sit on the board; and the project lapsed.[45]

In the event, the farmers found their own answer, one that got the Progressives off the political hook but also further sapped the momentum of the Western agrarian revolt. In 1923, Aaron Sapiro, a charismatic American who had promoted co-operatives in industries from grapes to tobacco, was in British Columbia advising fruit growers. At the invitation of the grain growers' associations, he toured the Prairie provinces, passing, in the words of one observer, "like a brilliant meteor from point to point, leaving behind him, as it were, a trail of light stretching like the tail of a comet across the heavens." His message was simple — the farmers could control supply and price by pooling their wheat and marketing it themselves. Wood, Partridge, and many of the leaders of the grain growers' organizations quickly signed on. Thus began the wheat pools in the three Prairie provinces, a more risky alternative than a government wheat board, but one controlled by the farmers themselves. By 1926, 140,000 out of a possible 240,000 farmers had signed pool contracts covering 52.2 percent of the wheat crop.[46]

By 1923, King had strengthened his control over his government. Motherwell was named federal minister of agriculture in 1921. Dafoe was offering grudging support for the Liberals, and ties between the federal and Saskatchewan Liberals were restored. Crerar, under constant attack from Wood, and from his fractious and inexperienced MPs, lost patience even before Drury, and resigned on November 10, 1922. A little later, two Progressives crossed the floor to give the King government a working majority. Robert Forke took over as leader of a group that no longer had any pretence of cohesion as a party. Within a year, fourteen of the more radical Progressives had constituted themselves the Ginger Group, and most of the rest began to drift toward the Liberals. In the elections of 1925 and 1926, the Progressives were decimated. The Ginger Group survivors coalesced, with a handful of Labour MPs, into a radical reform caucus, and group government was quietly abandoned.[47]

By the mid-1920s, a fragile rural prosperity returned and between 1926 and 1929 there was a minor boom in wheat prices. By the mid 1920s, the telephone was easing rural isolation, a reliable tractor had been developed, and most farmers had cars or trucks, even if they did without electricity or indoor plumbing. The United States embarked on a policy of protectionism, and even the farmers could see that Canada had no alternative but reciprocity of tariffs — indeed, they now needed protection themselves and assistance in securing access to the U.S. market. Railways and utilities were coming under public control; co-operatives, rural credits, and other supports were provided by Western provincial governments controlled by farmers; and the wheat pools were highly successful — until they ran into difficulty during the Depression.

Perhaps the most decisive factor in weakening the agrarian revolt was simple demographics. As global competition forced prices down after the temporary wartime spike, the drift of farmers from the land continued. In the East, the balance shifted decisively to the cities and towns, and in the West, the number of farms fell between 1921 and 1926. In 1928, C.W. Peterson would write that the glorification of country life was "a threadbare platitude ... a habit — a mere figure of speech." The farm was "generations behind the town in conditions of life," and "the younger generation positively declines to put up with the present economic handicaps and isolation of rural life."[48]

Most farmers had never really been radicals, much less revolutionaries. They deeply resented their domination by Eastern capitalists and manufacturing interests, but they needed the banks and railways to finance and move their crops, and they needed urban and global markets for their produce. They were, as Irvine said, both capital and labour. They could not go on strike. But they could improve their farming techniques through mechanization and increased efficiency, create crop insurance and marketing agencies, and benefit from rural electrification, radio, plumbing, and highways. Once memories of conscription faded, and once they realized that they were as frightened of labour radicalism, urban decadence, and moral laxity as they were resentful of Eastern capitalists, their traditional political loyalties and individualist philosophy reasserted themselves. Drury retired to his farm. Good was part of the Ginger Group but refused to join the CCF. McArthur died in 1924. Crerar returned to the Grain Growers' Association, quarrelled with the wheat pools, became a Liberal cabinet minister in the late 1920s and again from 1935 to 1945, and late in a long life, opposed the social programs of the 1960s as a senator.

Indeed, it would be easy, looking backward from almost a century later, to see United Farmers as an oxymoron and their movement as only the last gasp of agrarian opposition to the inexorable tide of urbanization, industrialization, and modernity. But to do so would be to underestimate both their importance and their lasting achievements.

Farmers' parties would continue to play a role in the politics of the Eastern provinces for a generation. They would control Western provincial governments for much longer — and Western regionalism remains an important element of the Canadian identity today. By the late 1920s, the Ginger Group would move to the left, unite with labour and other progressive forces, and play their part in founding the CCF. The mainstream farmers' organizations would continue to play the non-political roles for which they had been created — managing co-operatives, providing mutual assistance, and advocating the cause of the farmer.

More than any political platform, the United Farmers expressed a strong belief in a way of life. "When will you learn," Aaron Sapiro told Western farmers in 1923, "that you are not dealing with wheat? What you are dealing with is human lives, what your children will eat, what your children will wear, how you will pay the doctor, how you will send them to school, whether you will have taxes to pay for roads, whether you will even have taxes enough to start and pay off the national debt." The United Farmers dreamed of a society that could be more democratic, co-operative, and free, one that valued individual uprightness and growing food and raising children in the pure, open air of the countryside. They made clear that Eastern business dominance was neither just nor permanent. Their values would be woven into the Canadian character long after their political revolt had become a distant memory.[49]

CHAPTER 10

National Reconstruction

"Wake up, Industrial Canada!" cried journalist and editor C.W. Peterson in 1919. "Our nation is in the making at this hour and this is the time for great decisions." The war had brought together "the genius and resourcefulness of Canadian manufacturers and the skill of Canadian labour," wrote Sir John Willison. Now, thought O.D. Skelton, experts should apply these lessons to reconstruction, educate the people, bridge the differences among competing groups, and build a new Canada that would be progressive, prosperous, and socially just. Above all, everyone hoped that Canada would once again grow as it had grown before 1913 — at a rate matched only a few times in human history.[1]

We can see the impact of that spectacular growth in photographs of the large cities of the time. If we need imagination to conjure up the sights and smells of the farm in 1919, we need none to see our modern world reflected in these pictures. Office and warehouse buildings turn the streets into canyons. Tram cars run on tracks set in cobblestones. Motor cars have largely displaced horse-drawn vehicles. Electric and telephone wires festoon a forest of wooden posts. Crowds of people hurry in and out of hotels, offices, and department stores whose windows display a wide variety of newly affordable consumer goods. Perhaps they work at a factory complex sprawling over an acre of land, in a railway workshop, or in one of those office buildings or warehouses, not yet turned grimy by soot. Some may be going home to running water and flush toilets, to food bought at the store and cooked on a gas stove, to read by electric light the daily newspaper reporting events from around the world. The men and women frozen in time

Yonge Street, Toronto, looking north from near King Street, 1920s
The heart of a modern city, in an increasingly urban nation, recovering from war, optimistic about the future.

as they go about their business seem to exude optimism and a belief in continuing progress.

The world that had made that possible was now gone forever. In the decades before 1914, European power, trade, and civilization had reached every corner of the globe, and Canada could find ready markets for its exports, capital for its development, and an endless supply of immigrants. But progress and prosperity had come at a cost. Rapid social and technological change was reshaping the world, destabilizing identities, values and beliefs, altering the very concepts of time and space. The war had taught the grim lesson that industry and science could destroy life as well as enrich it.

The war had also revealed the deficiencies in Canadian industry and finance and the patterns of patronage and corruption that marred its politics. Only when Flavelle's Imperial Munitions Board (IMB) mobilized the best industrial and managerial talent did Canada become an efficient war production machine. By 1918, Canadian factories were producing not only shells but also planes — including the JN-4 "Jenny" (or "Canuck" as it was called in Canada) aircraft — and 350,000 tons of shipping. Base metals, pulp and paper, and forest products were increasingly processed at home, as was steel and the materials of the future — aluminum, nickel, and chemicals. The government had learned war finance on the job, working closely with the Canadian Bankers' Association in the absence of a central bank. It had abandoned the gold standard in 1914, increased the lending power of banks and the currency in circulation by advancing Dominion notes to banks, and got some of this back by selling Victory Bonds. Most people paid no income tax, but those earning $200,000 or more paid 25 percent, and war profits over 25 percent of capital were taxed at 75 percent. These measures had succeeded brilliantly — out of $2,299,000,000 borrowed by the Canadian government, only $195,000,000 was obtained outside Canada.[2]

But now the time of reckoning was coming. Wartime financial measures had produced inflation, which squeezed farmers, workers, and the middle class. The global economic system was in ruins. Railways were bleeding red ink. Social unrest was rife. What would happen when factories had to go back to their old product lines, when the soldiers came home, when prices began to fall, when wages stopped rising, when money was no longer easy and debts had to be paid? Well before the end of the war, Flavelle predicted "a long morning after," when plans made and expectations raised in the hothouse conditions of wartime would start to "look strangely out of proportion."

> I wonder when it is all over, and we take up our tasks, and resume our individual relations, and again become business-getters against the rest of the world, will we have the resource; will we have the money; will we have the willingness to pay through taxes for minimum wages, for sustained labour for every man who wants to work, in the production of goods which will be sold at less than cost to Nations outside?[3]

Canada's industry and trade and its financial systems had changed, and its approach to social welfare and the role of government in the economy would have to change as well in order to adapt to the new challenges of a profoundly altered world. To succeed in competitive markets, warned a leading scientist, Canadians would have to "improve the quality of their products while cutting down costs through the introduction of the best and most advanced methods which can be developed by industrial research." Governments would have to create the new society for which their people had sacrificed. Those who "have been glibly called 'profiteers'" would have to invest in rebuilding business, said James Mavor, with businessmen and workers taking only their fair share of the profits, and no one upsetting the complex but delicate industrial and commercial system. "If we do not mend the machine," warned Leacock, "there are forces moving in the world that will break it." [4]

I

The men who presided over the Canadian economy were a small group of capitalists, living mostly in Toronto and Montreal, with some outliers in Winnipeg, Hamilton, and Halifax. They were mostly Canadian-born Anglo-Celtic Protestants — some with urban and professional backgrounds, but many of them small-town lads with little formal education. They were restless, at times ruthless, visionaries who could see opportunities, master details, recruit experts, and mobilize British capital.

Sir William Mackenzie had begun as a contractor for the CPR, developed street railway and power franchises in Toronto and Winnipeg (with forays into Cuba and Brazil), and built the Canadian Northern into a transcontinental railway. Sir Joseph Flavelle had started as a small grocer, built the William Davies Company into a giant pork exporter, and was a director of the Bank of Commerce, National Trust, Simpson's, and many other expanding enterprises in Toronto. Sir Herbert Holt, who had also begun as a railway contractor, was president of Montreal Light, Heat, & Power, the Royal Bank, and several power and pulp and paper companies, and a director of Stelco, Dominion Textile, Canadian General Electric, Montreal Trust, the CPR, Ogilvie Flour Mills, Canadian Car Company, Sun Life, and dozens of others. Max Aitken had cut his teeth in Halifax; then he moved to Montreal, where in a three-year period he engineered the Steel Company of Canada, Canada Car and Foundry, Dominion Steel and Coal, and Canada Cement mergers, before finally blossoming in England as Lord Beaverbrook. [5]

They knew each other well. Finance Minister Sir Thomas White told an enquiry why he had not acted in 1914 on evidence that Toronto financier

Sir Henry Pellatt was abusing his position as a bank director to borrow more money than he could repay. "When I was General Manager of National Trust Company, I loaned Sir Henry Pellatt money upon securities," he said. "We never sustained a cent of loss and had no apprehension about the man's credit."

They had offices in neo-classical buildings downtown. They lived in sprawling mansions designed by favoured architects with beaux-arts decoration and furnishings, baronial dining rooms that could seat two dozen, and conservatories where a hundred could dance to an orchestra. They travelled in private railway cars and chauffeured limousines, sailed first-class, lodged at ornate hotels, joined exclusive clubs, always with the finest linen, silver, crystal, oak panelling, paintings, tapestries, and carved furniture money could buy. Their lifestyle was evidence of their success, and of the soundness of their enterprises. It was expected of them.[6]

Their watchword was efficiency. Well-managed businesses cut costs, improved products, and made profits. Mergers, together with government regulations, eliminated inefficient competition. Efficiency required clean city governments run by disinterested men who created public health departments, public utilities, harbour commissions, parks, and schools. In the name of improvement, "Progressive" urban reformers could make common cause with socialists like Jimmy Simpson, Frank Spence, and Fred Dixon, and social scientists like James Mavor. At the national level, efficiency translated into state action to conserve the country's natural resources, mobilize its human resources, and improve "the race." Sir Clifford Sifton's quasi-official Commission on Conservation turned out over two hundred publications between 1909 and 1919, on rural land use, forestry, public health, and city planning. "We recognize," wrote a leading town planner for the commission in 1917, "that, in the future, science and clean government must march side by side with enterprise and energy in building up national and individual prosperity." The strength of a nation, he concluded, "depends neither on the physical, intellectual and moral character of its citizens, nor on the stability and freedom of its institutions, nor on the efficiency of its organization, but on the existence of all these things."[7]

Government should promote industry, with tariffs to keep out foreign competition, subsidies and monopoly powers for railways and utilities, and militia to put down strikes. But it should not, as paper-maker Sir William Price argued before the Supreme Court in 1920, restrict "our constitutional right of dealing with whom we choose and of retaining our right of freedom of contract." Businessmen and politicians mixed together easily. Borden, wrote a *Maclean's* columnist in 1918, was "the richest Premier that Canada ever knew — he rather prefers the company of men who make, and know, the value of money." He saw no conflict in playing golf with them, asking their advice, enjoying their company in trips across the Atlantic, or travelling in Mackenzie's private railway car.[8]

And why not? Businessmen were building a nation, raising Canada's standard of living, and defining its "higher life." Flavelle helped reorganize the University of Toronto and build the Toronto General Hospital, funded the Toronto *News* as an experiment in independent journalism, and supported countless charities. Sir Edmund Walker of the Bank of Commerce was an amateur geologist and collector of Japanese prints who funded the Royal Ontario Museum and chaired the National Gallery. They owed their success to the virtues preached from every pulpit — self-discipline, clean living, "work, hard work, intelligent work, and then more work." "There are things which cannot be measured in dollars and cents," said Walker in opposing Reciprocity in 1911. "Such a thing is our national destiny. We must not gamble with our future in the hope of winning some momentary gain."[9]

Walker was, of course, referring to gain by others — in this case farmers. Workers and farmers might well question whether what was good for Walker was good for them. Small businessmen might well see giant corporations and department stores as ruthless destroyers of local industries and small merchants. Businessmen did have to admit that some of their colleagues were a bit of an embarrassment. Pellatt bankrolled the Queen's

Sir Joseph Flavelle (c. 1930)

McCord Museum, Montreal M20111.58

Own Rifles so he could strut his portly figure in a colonel's uniform, and he squandered his fortune on an extravagant Toronto palace called Casa Loma. In his 1914 satire *Arcadian Adventures with the Idle Rich*, Leacock (who was married to Pellatt's granddaughter) depicted florid-faced tycoons plotting mergers, subverting education and religion, desecrating the landscape with tasteless mansions, and taking control of the city and its lucrative utility franchises under the guise of "clean government." He was not laughing when he wrote during the war that the plutocrat seemed "as rapacious and remorseless as the machinery that has made him." "Our notion of 'developing the country'" raged Andrew Macphail, "is to eviscerate it, mining the phosphates and nitrates from the soil under the pretext of farming, ravaging the shores for fish, and felling the forests with ax and fire." Business efficiency, with its passion for organization, "destroys everything fine — religion, friendship, love, education, literature, art, newspapers even — wither and die at the first touch of its breath."[10]

II

As the war ended, many groups of "progressive" business leaders began to consider how to apply the methods of national efficiency to the reconstruction of Canadian society. Foremost among them was the Canadian Reconstruction Association (CRA), which was funded by the Canadian Manufacturers' Association (CMA) though it was often critical of its patron. Its president was Sir John Willison, a journalist skilled at self-promotion, who was well connected in the world of business and politics and with Imperialist circles in London. A blacksmith's son with little formal education, Willison had

Sir John Willison

Yearbook of Canadian Art 1912/13

risen to become the editor of the Toronto *Globe* and a confidant of Laurier. He left in 1905 to edit Flavelle's *Toronto News*, and as an independent journalist managed the propaganda campaign against Reciprocity in 1911. During the war, he headed Ontario commissions on unemployment and housing, and in 1916 he was behind a movement to organize a broad-based national government. From 1918 to 1920, his CRA produced dozens of pamphlets, confidential memos, and major speeches on national reconstruction, including works on technical and higher education, women in the economy, science and research, conservation, and industrial development.

The thrust of Willison's propaganda was that in a competitive world Canada, led by its governments, would have to mobilize its industry, resources, and people as it had done during the war. "Canadian Money, Canadian Made, Should Stay in Canada, For Canadian Trade" was the slogan that appeared on many of its publications. Labour unions should be recognized and Whitley Councils created. Prairie wheat farmers should diversify, mill their crops in Canada, and support industrial growth. Manufacturers in each sector should agree to limit "the number of lines that they will produce," and be encouraged to export. Forget any qualms about monopoly, tariffs, regulation, or restraint on economic freedom. "In the Mother Country," he argued, "the sacred doctrine of individualism is treated with violence; in the United States industrial combination is no longer regarded as the sum of social and political villainy."[11]

Willison was disappointed when he made a trip to the West in 1918, speaking to Canadian Clubs and meeting with Henry Wise Wood, Dafoe, and others, to find that this neo-mercantilist vision would never fly with farmers. He was also at odds with key people in the CMA, like S.R. Parsons, who had no intention of compromising with labour or limiting the freedom of businessmen.[12]

In any case, it was turning out that government intervention in a peacetime economy was an even more difficult thing than organizing a nation for war. In the fall of 1919, the federal government passed legislation providing money to the provinces for housing, roads, health, welfare, and education. But industries that had put aside their own interests to save the nation were no longer prepared to accept regulation or interference. In late 1919, there was chaos in the pulp and paper industry when the government continued a wartime requirement that 15 percent of newsprint production be sold to

Canadians at less than the inflated American price. Because companies varied in what percentage of their production they sold to Canadian consumers, a complex system of offsets was established, which led only to bickering and litigation. In November, Fort Frances Pulp and Paper Company shipped paper to the United States just ahead of an order by the paper regulator to seize it, and Winnipeg newspapers had to briefly cease publication in January 1920.[13]

As inflation soared out of control in 1919, the government created a Board of Commerce with a mandate to study costs and markets and to act as a regulatory tribunal for specific industries. But the board never had enough trained personnel to study more than a few sectors, and it acted as a tribunal on only one commodity — sugar. When the price of Cuban sugar rose sharply in the fall of 1919, the board fixed a retail price. Then it had to make further rulings as the price fluctuated. When the price collapsed in August 1920, the board banned cheap American imports. No one was ever happy. One of the leading sugar men told Willison that he was now "rid of any possible illusions as to what the result of Government control must mean, and I may add, also, entirely satisfied as to the absence of any such quality as gratitude."[14]

The creation of a National Research Council to stimulate and coordinate industrial research fared somewhat better. But soon after its formal establishment in 1918, it began to encounter opposition from some universities, hostility from other science-based government departments, and the skepticism of businessmen like Lord Shaughnessy of the CPR, who wrote to the prime minister in 1920 that "there has not come under my notice one single thing in the way of accomplished results to warrant a fraction of the expenditure that has already been made." In 1921, a bill creating a national research laboratory was killed in the Senate. The NRC had its champions, like Willison, Member of Parliament Hume Cronyn, and a number of progressive businessmen and university professors, and it survived — but it did not get its research lab until the 1930s.[15]

By late 1919, the zeal of the CRA for labour reform and industrial efficiency was waning and it was focusing instead, with the CMA, on the one issue most businessmen, workers, and middle-class Canadians could agree on — the need for a protective tariff. Whatever Crerar and the farmers might say, any minister of finance who wanted to keep his job could no more abolish the tariff than he could advocate that Canada become a colony again. The secretary of the CMA resigned to set up a secret information service to allow manufacturers to respond to negative comments on the tariff and withhold advertising from papers deemed hostile. Manufacturers warned their workers that "economic theories provide neither jobs nor wages. If the worker is to have both without any disastrous interruptions in industrial activity it must be through a continuation of the National Policy which has built up Canada." One of the last CRA pamphlets, published in 1921, was a study showing that "every important country in the world is protecting its own industries and striving to reduce its dependence upon outside sources of supply, and that Protection to-day is established and accepted as the fiscal policy of the nations of the world more generally and firmly than ever before." By then the CRA had run its course and Willison had resigned.[16]

The CRA and the CMA were, in fact, appalled that the tariff should even be open to public discussion and annual debate. No sooner had White's June 1919 budget passed than they began to press for an independent tariff board that would guarantee "a stable tariff which will keep business steady." The CRA distributed some $50,000 to a faction of the Trades and Labour Congress to ensure that its September convention passed resolutions repudiating the OBU and endorsing a tariff commission — without success in the latter case. In 1920, the government did appoint a commission of inquiry, which held hearings across the country. But the following year Prime Minister Meighen finally rejected the demand for a tariff board. Politicians understood better than businessmen that there was no such thing as a "scientific" tariff — it would *always* be a political issue.[17]

III

Besides the tariff, the biggest single issue facing the government in national reconstruction was what to do about an overbuilt and largely bankrupt railway system. The shriek of the train whistle in small towns and farming communities had long symbolized progress. Railways had knit the country together. But they also charged predatory rates, incurred frequent labour strife, and had shaky financing. "For half a century on this continent," said Willison, "the clamour against railways after they have been constructed has been almost as vociferous as the clamour for railways before they were constructed."[18]

The optimism, and the folly, of the Great Boom were epitomized in Laurier's railway policy. Once the CPR was earning a profit, Western farmers wanted a second transcontinental railroad. William Mackenzie and Donald Mann had cobbled some Prairie lines into a profitable network with its terminus at the Lakehead, and in 1903 they announced plans to expand their Canadian Northern Railway (CNoR) into a transcontinental one. The venerable Grand Trunk Railway (GTR), the backbone of central Canada since 1860, also wanted to build a line to the Pacific. Laurier's railway minister wanted any new transcontinental to be state-owned and connected to the Intercolonial, a government railway built in the 1870s to link the Maritimes with the rest of Canada.

Laurier said "yes" to everyone. The Grand Trunk Pacific (GTP), a subsidiary of the GTR, would build west from Winnipeg through the northern Prairies to the Yellowhead Pass, then through empty mountain country to the non-existent seaport of Prince Rupert, British Columbia — with lavish bond guarantees and subsidies. The government would build the National Transcontinental (NTR), west from Quebec City to Winnipeg through the clay belt of northern Quebec and Ontario, and east across the St. Lawrence to join the Intercolonial at Moncton, New Brunswick — and then lease it to the GTP. The Canadian Northern would also get subsidies and loan guarantees to build a link through the Shield between the Lakehead and its eastern lines, and a line west from Edmonton through the Yellowhead and down the Fraser Canyon to Vancouver. By 1914, the Canadian Northern had soaked up $105 million from the federal government and $135 million from six provinces.

This orgy of railway building was one reason for the huge economic expansion of those years — and one reason why it ended in 1913. Hotels, stations, warehouses, and shops sprouted in every large city. Rails were rolled at Algoma Steel. Rival tracks ran side by side through the Yellowhead Pass. The NTR was driven through muskeg and granite. New ports were built, bridges and tunnels constructed. An NTR bridge at Quebec collapsed twice, a CNoR tunnel under Mount Royal in Montreal incurred massive debt, and a landslide caused by CNoR construction in the Fraser

Canyon destroyed the salmon run. The cost was staggering and the boom ended before the railways could show a profit — if indeed they ever could have. In 1913, Borden rammed loans to the Canadian Northern through Parliament, in exchange for 40 percent of its stock. The government, and the Bank of Commerce, now effectively owned this railway. And they *did* own the NTR when the GTP refused to take up its lease.[19]

The war brought a traffic bonanza, but rate controls and rising labour costs ensured that the railways ran at a loss. Railway debt added to the massive borrowing for war. By 1916 the system was in crisis. If the GTP collapsed, it would take down the GTR. The CNoR would take down the Bank of Commerce (whose Toronto backers included the finance minister). The credit of Canada and most of its provinces would be called into question. Lord Shaughnessy of the CPR helpfully offered to take over the whole system if CPR shareholders got a guaranteed return. Instead, the government, led by Borden and Rowell, with support from Flavelle and the Grain Growers, began to explore the possibility of consolidating these railways into a state-owned system. But the CPR, the Bank of Montreal, and the Montreal industrial and financial interests howled with rage. *They* had built the original transcontinental — why should they be confronted with deep-pocketed government railways, rife with corruption and patronage? They conveniently forgot how much they had benefitted from government subsidies, not to mention their cozy relationship with the Conservative Party.

In 1917, a royal commission consisting of Sir Henry Drayton (chair of the Board of Railway Commissioners), an English railway journalist, and the president of the New York Central, recommended that the government take over the CNoR and move toward acquisition of the GTP. The government immediately foreclosed on the Canadian Northern (a commission of arbitration eventually declared its stock to be worth $10 million), and painters began stencilling "Canadian National Railways" on its cars and stations, as well as those of the NTR, the Intercolonial, and some smaller lines. Canadian National, the government decided, would not be operated as a government department, but by trustees, "the same as a private corporation, keeping in view at all times economy and the interests of the shareholders, who of course are the Canadian people." But the GTP was a much bigger problem. If the government foreclosed without forgiving its debts, the GTR would be bankrupt. If it forgave the GTP debt, the GTR's British shareholders would be pleased, but the Canadian taxpayer would be on the hook. The government decided that that decision was best left until after the war.[20]

The crisis came in February 1919, when the GTR, by this time in financial trouble of its own, announced it would no longer pay the interest on its GTP loans. The government appointed the minister of railways and canals as receiver for the GTP and began folding it into Canadian National; and it decided to take over the GTR as well. In the midst of the Winnipeg General Strike, Arthur Meighen — who had become the point man on this as on so many other files — was negotiating with the British directors of the GTR, who were demanding an unrealistic level of compensation. In October 1919, they transferred their shares to the Canadian government on condition that an arbitration tribunal determine their value and manage the railway jointly with the British board. Meanwhile Canadian National was haemorrhaging cash — by 1921, railways alone were costing the country more than its whole government had cost before the war.[21]

The CPR, the Bank of Montreal, and their friends, including the Montreal *Star* and Quebec premier Sir Lomer Gouin, denounced Meighen as a dangerous Western radical. It was one thing to cobble together a state-owned railway from bankrupt Western and Northern lines. It was quite another for that railway to become a powerful competitor in the Eastern heartland. The new CPR president, Sir Edward Beatty, while claiming to welcome competition, deeply resented Canadian National as an affront to free enterprise and the social order, and he accused the government of coercing passengers and shippers to use the "people's railway." In November 1919, Meighen went into the lion's den to address the Montreal Canadian Club. He was not, he said, in favour of public ownership on principle, but if the GTR were allowed to fail it might fall into American hands. Anyway, why should the taxpayers be saddled with unprofitable railways and not have the one that would make the whole system pay? The country had gone on a railway binge. "We are at the point now where an awakening of bitterness follows a night of intoxication; an ebb of retribution now follows in the wake of a flood tide of railway construction."[22]

The arbitration tribunal deliberated. The GTR piled up deficits. In 1921, its directors asked for more time. Instead, the government ended the joint management scheme and appointed a new board, headed by Flavelle, to reorganize the railway as best it could. In September 1921, the majority of the tribunal ruled that the GTR was bound to assume the obligations of the GTP, whose stock had no value. GTR shareholders were outraged. Openly encouraged by the CPR, they fought the decision all the way to the Judicial Committee of the Privy Council in London. In the December 1921 federal election, Montreal business circles got even with Meighen — and with Borden, White, and Flavelle — by supporting Mackenzie King. Only when the GTR appeal was dismissed in late 1922 could the railway be finally folded into Canadian National.[23]

"Canada is now in the railway business," wrote C.W. Peterson. "The people of Canada are on trial. The whole principle of public administration is now about to be discredited or vindicated, as the case may be." Between 1917 and 1922, the interim managers of Canadian National wrestled, surprisingly successfully, with what railway historian D.R. McKay describes as "fitting a head to an octopus." When it was finally incorporated in January 1923, the CNR, with twenty-two thousand miles of track, was the second longest railway in the world. Mackenzie King appointed as its president Sir Henry Thornton, an American who had run the British Great Eastern railroad and been knighted for coordinating railway transport during the war. Over the next decade, Thornton, who combined a zest for all-night parties with exceptional public relations and leadership skills, reduced main-line trackage and the payroll, rationalized management with modern organization and information systems, regularly consulted labour unions, and fought off political interference. At ninety thousand people, the CNR was the largest employer in Canada. It established its headquarters in Montreal and the flamboyant Thornton bought a mansion across the street from the strait-laced bachelor Beatty.[24]

In the late 1920s, the two rival companies went head to head in the last golden age of railways — new and bigger hotels, more steamships, better rolling stock, fourteen-wheel Mountain Class locomotives with the latest technology, and fast trains that broke all speed records rushing Asian raw silk from Vancouver to New York. They competed to recruit immigrants in the hope that a Canada of twenty million people would justify its bloated railway system. Beatty clung to the belief that someday the CPR would take over the CNR, and that Canada would come to its senses, accept once again the leadership of businessmen like himself, renounce "socialist" heresies, and revive its loyalty to the British Empire. Thornton boasted that the "great White Elephant about which such a terrible legend grew up during many years had vanished." This was only true if one ignored its debt, which was one-fifth of the national debt, and which the government refused to write off. When the party ended in 1929, the CNR was near collapse and the CPR was deep in debt, and the "railway mess" would haunt governments for years to come.[25]

IV

Railways were already beginning to face a formidable competitor. By 1919, there were 341,000 cars and trucks registered in Canada.

Railways were highly capitalized, integrated corporations, whose tracks, rolling stock, stations, depots, and workshops had to be all in place before they could operate, much less make money. Privately owned cars and trucks did not need tracks any more than they needed stables or oats; roads could be built as needed; and as the ownership of cars and trucks spread, small businesses like dealerships, gas stations, and auto supply and repair shops sprang up like mushrooms. By 1919, the Ford Model T, a car with many quirks but an affordable purchase price of $500 on a time-payment plan, had put Canadians on wheels. A Prairie farmer recalled that his "was light and it got you over the mud roads in them days and it just spun along. If it broke down, you could fix it with wire and a pair of pliers." When Lucy Maud Montgomery came to Leaskdale, Ontario, in 1911, "cars were still so much of a novelty that we ran to the window to see one going by." By 1918, "half our people have them and there are almost as many cars as buggies at our church Sunday mornings." If the train brought mobility and speed, the car brought personal freedom.[26]

These cars were made by Canadian manufacturers who, after a decade of trial and error, had teamed up with American companies "because with our small and limited outputs it is impossible to carry the tremendous over-head of engineering expenses." Canadians built the carriages and imported American engines, and their fortunes depended on their choice of partner. Gray of Chatham failed in 1924 when Dort of Ohio went out of business. Tom Russell of CCM (a bicycle maker) did better with Willys. Sam Mc-Laughlin of Oshawa did very well with Buick, and Gordon McGregor of Windsor hit the jackpot when he partnered with Henry Ford in 1904. In 1918, McLaughlin sold out to General Motors for $5 million in stock plus the presidency of Canadian General Motors. By 1919, the Canadian auto industry was American-controlled, and the Canadian pioneers had been joined by branch plants wholly owned by Chrysler and Studebaker.[27]

Cars and farm implements were among the few manufactured goods Canada exported in quantity. Canadian protection, plus the Imperial prefer-ential tariff (renewed in 1919), allowed Canadians to manufacture cars with largely American content and export them to the British Empire (except Britain). In the 1920s exports accounted for 50 percent of Ford of Canada's production, 40 percent of GM's, 25 percent of Chrysler's. Ford of Canada established subsidiaries in India, South Africa, Australia, and Malaya, and exported two or three times as many cars as its American parent. Cana-dian sales expanded as cars became more dependable, with better engines and brakes, self-starters, closed cabins, softer suspensions, and (by 1925) balloon tires, and as people upgraded from Model Ts to a wider variety of colours and designs. In 1929, eleven Canadian auto plants employed twelve thousand workers and made two hundred thousand cars. In return for tariff protection, they agreed to source steel, brass tubing, rubber hoses, glass, and upholstery in Canada, and its superior carriage work may have justified Mc-Laughlin's claim that his Buick was "better because it's Canadian."[28]

Petroleum and rubber had become important commodities in the automobile revolution. Oil was now a strategic necessity for the Empire and the federal government supported with bounties the search for secure supplies. But aside from a few wells in Alberta, the remnants of a dying industry in Ontario, and a discovery at Norman Wells in the Northwest Territories in 1920, most crude petroleum refined in Ontario came from Ohio. Imperial Oil dominated the market, with some competition from Shell, S.R. Parsons's upstart British American Oil, and a few smaller players.

As for rubber, Canada's 1919 consumption (twelve thousand tons) was well behind the United States (260,000), but well ahead of most other industrialized countries, and Canada had ready access to raw material within the British Empire. By 1930, Canada was making over four million tires a year. The leaders were Canadian Goodyear (which opened its first plant in 1910 and built a bigger one during the war in New Toronto) and Firestone, which started a branch plant in Hamilton in 1922.[29]

The auto men were a different breed from the elites who ran the banks, railways, and corporations. Because banks at first deemed automobile enterprises too risky, their owners raised capital locally, financed growth from earnings, and were beholden only to their American partners. When McGregor died in 1922, Ford Canada had assets of more than $25 million. Sam McLaughlin built a house in Oshawa that cost twice as much as Flavelle's (he always resented that Flavelle had given him no IMB contracts). Mackenzie King described the auto men he met in 1923 as "the hardest looking lot of manufacturers' promoters I have seen." Only Tom Russell, a university-educated farm boy hired at twenty-four by Flavelle to manage CCM, fitted into the older elites.[30]

Cars quickly took hold in the cities, but driving in the country remained an adventure. Auto clubs put up signposts, published guidebooks, sought protection against careless drivers, and, above all, demanded more and better roads. Canada might claim to have three hundred thousand miles of roads in 1919, but most were only trails and fewer than a thousand miles were paved. As part of national reconstruction, the federal Parliament passed the Canada Highways Act, which gave the provinces $20 million over five years to pay up to 40 percent of the cost of building highways. Ontario planned an eighteen-hundred-mile network, including a concrete road between Toronto and Hamilton and a partly paved main route from Windsor to the Quebec border. By 1930, Canada had eighty thousand kilometres of surfaced roads, of which ninety-two hundred were paved. Most of the early paved highways ran from the major cities to the American border — American tourism was worth $300 million a year — and a cross-Canada highway remained a distant dream. By 1929, six of every ten passenger miles were by private auto, and railway passenger revenue had declined by 20 percent.[31]

Cars reshaped cities. During the 1920s, most city streets were paved, bridges were constructed, bus service to the suburbs was expanded. Suburban houses were built with laneways and garages. Hand-operated gas pumps at the side of a city street gave way to gas stations on corner lots. By the mid-1920s, Imperial and British American were building their own gas stations, designed by architects, offering full service, from tire sales to lubrication, anti-freeze, and washrooms — visible symbols of the growing power of the automobile.

Cars reshaped the countryside. The slogan "Ship by Truck" changed the way farmers got produce to the city and how it was distributed there. Closed cabs and heaters, snow chains and snow-ploughing on major roads meant that driving could be done in all types of weather. Country villages might still resent Sunday drivers and through traffic, but there was money to be made running gas stations, stores, and roadhouses. Villages that had disappeared before the war reappeared as names on the new roadmaps produced by the oil companies. In 1922, over twelve thousand cars used the main Toronto–Hamilton road each day on the Labour Day weekend, and traffic on the Hamilton–Niagara road was almost as heavy.[32]

Cars reshaped all aspects of life and would continue to do so. In particular, they contributed to the new freedom of women and the new mobility of young people. Sometimes the results were less than salutary. When a young girl left to visit an aunt she didn't have, recalled a Prairie farmer, "they would say she's gone visiting a Model T. That meant they figured she'd been knocked up in the back seat of a Model T. Might have been mine. I was always lending it out to the young bucks." Sunday sermons denouncing the car began to replace (or augment) those directed at booze.[33]

Cars required new kinds of regulation. By 1922, all Canadian provinces had decided to drive on the right side of the road, like the Americans. They brought in traffic laws, speed limits, vehicle licenses, and driver training. During the war, policemen appeared at some busy street corners turning a sign that said "stop" or "go," and arresting motorists who did not comply (the first electric traffic light was installed in Toronto in 1925). Provincial police on motorcycles began to patrol highways, enforcing laws and investigating accidents — there were 387 fatalities in Ontario in 1927. Fuel trucks replaced the prewar practice of shipping gasoline in barrels by horse-drawn wagons, and refineries could no longer dump waste products in a nearby swamp. Even pedestrians now had to obey traffic rules — "Reckless walking," said a 1925 editorial in the *Canadian Motorist*, "must be discouraged."[34]

Cars revived the old disputes about the tariff. Why were Canadians paying more for cars than Americans? Why were car manufacturing and related industries concentrated in Ontario? The mayor of Calgary complained that "the whole of the West are grumbling (and have been for years now) at the prices the motor car manufacturers, with the aid of high protection, have been making them pay." In 1926, the King government proposed to reduce the tariff on popular cars from 35 to 20 percent. Sam McLaughlin threatened to close his plants (he backed down when he realized the American parent company would simply move in). Duties were reduced in the late 1920s, but in the Great Depression auto makers were again pleading with the government to raise them. This argument would continue until, and even after, the Auto Pact integrated North American production in 1965.[35]

V

The challenges for governments of creating a state-owned railway system and responding to the automobile revolution were compounded by debates over the regulation and ownership of public utilities. Like the railway question, this issue was not new. When telephone systems, street railways, and electric power production and distribution had been in their infancy in the 1880s and 1890s, cities and towns had been delighted to award long-term franchises to private entrepreneurs. But as utilities began to reshape the urban environment, public opinion changed. By 1914, progressives and urban reformers were portraying the owners of utilities as greedy and anti-social capitalists, like the denizens of the Mausoleum Club in Leacock's *Arcadian Adventures*, who could "hear or almost hear" the roar of the street railway "earning dividends."[36]

By the end of the war, the Western provinces, and many towns, had established government-owned telephone systems. But in Ontario and Quebec, Bell Telephone, a wholly owned subsidiary of the American patent-holder, fought off all attempts at meaningful regulation. Then, in 1919, rising prices forced Bell to appeal to the federal Board of Railway Commissioners for rate increases and permission to issue more stock — and it had to do so again in 1920 and 1921. In return for these increases, the board brought Bell under closer regulation, forced the company to charge a flat rate rather than a per-call tariff, and required that it provide financial information on an ongoing basis.[37]

Far lengthier battles were fought over street railways and electricity, where the central figures were Sir William Mackenzie and Sir Adam Beck. Mackenzie's street railway and electricity franchises in Toronto and Winnipeg brought growth and revenue — in 1914 his street railway paid $122,000 in fees to the city of Winnipeg — but unlike the British-owned BC Electric Railway in Vancouver, which built lines in advance of settlement and enjoyed good relations with the municipalities, Mackenzie seemed to be embroiled in constant legal or political battles over fares, scheduling, and routes (especially into neighbourhoods where aldermen held property). City councils forced fares down — in 1919, Toronto's average fare of 3.3 cents had not changed in almost thirty years and was the lowest in North America.[38]

During the war, street railways faced not only labour disputes and frozen fares but also competition from the automobile. The year 1915 saw the appearance in several cities of jitneys — private cars or trucks that picked people up and took them wherever they wanted to go. There were seven hundred in Toronto by 1917; Winnipeg began to licence them and its mayor even rode them to work. But jitneys caused accidents, they were unregulated, and they cost cities money — in 1919, the Winnipeg street railway could no longer pay the city its fees. By 1918, Winnipeg had shut down the jitneys, in return for a promise by the street railway to improve service, add buses, and upgrade its fleet. The Winnipeg street railway remained in private hands, but in January 1920, Toronto ratepayers voted 21,705 to 2,821 to take over Mackenzie's franchise when it expired in 1921. The city-owned Toronto Transit Company then modernized the system, added buses and suburban trains, and granted itself the 50 percent rise in fares the city had denied to Mackenzie's company in 1919. Cities meanwhile licensed and regulated proper taxi services.[39]

Hydro-electricity had emerged after 1900 as a cheap and plentiful source of power, helping to launch a new industrial revolution. In Quebec, entrepreneurs built generating stations on the mighty rivers of the province for industrial use, and sold the surplus to distribution companies in the cities — for example, the Boston consortium that developed the Shawinigan complex sold electricity to the Montreal Light, Heat, & Power Company headed by Herbert Holt and the Forget family. In Ontario, the privately owned Electrical Development Company (EDC) began to supply power from Niagara to Mackenzie's utilities in Toronto in 1906. By contrast, the City of Winnipeg built its own hydro plant in 1905 (and cut power rates to half of those charged by Mackenzie's generating company). The importance of power for industry as well as urban development generated a demand for public ownership of generation, transmission, and distribution. By 1919, all provinces had some form of public power, except British Columbia and Quebec, where decentralization and abundance reduced pressure for public control.[40]

In Ontario, Adam Beck, a small manufacturer and Conservative MPP from London, was appointed to head the Ontario Hydro-Electric Power Commission in 1906. "Hydro" was intend-
ed to encourage municipalities to establish power commissions, and reduce their dependence on the EDC, by selling to them, at cost, surplus power purchased from American generating companies at Niagara. Beck soon began selling power below cost, with government subsidies, while he used Hydro's regulatory powers to control the rates of private competitors. In 1917, he accused the EDC of "stealing" water from Niagara Falls and got legislation forcing the sale of this "surplus" to Hydro. Hydro began to develop its own power plants, it took over private plants, and it built transmission lines. In 1921, Mackenzie's Toronto electricity company became a public commis-

Sir Adam Beck (c. 1900)

Archives of Ontario Acc 3900 S 292

sion affiliated with Hydro, and most other cities had distribution systems controlled by or affiliated with Hydro. EDC was absorbed in the 1920s, and by 1930, Ontario Hydro was the largest power system in the world.[41]

Beck pushed the concept of the Crown corporation far beyond any previous limits. Electoral defeat in 1919 hardly fazed him. His plans to build the largest generating station in the world at Chippawa on the Niagara River — already racking up huge cost overruns — were well advanced. He was also reviving his scheme, shelved during the war, to build a network of electric, interurban or "radial" railways.

Premier Drury considered Beck "a promoter, a man of great optimism … who can make other people see his vision" but "not the best source from which we can get an unbiased and unimpassioned opinion." Beck was unfazed; he had faced down all previous premiers who attempted to control him and he had even been offered Drury's job. Disputes over Hydro projects added to the pressures on the UFO government and widened the split between the farmers (who opposed them) and labour (which supported them).[42]

Railway and utility promoters, and manufacturers seeking tariffs and subsidies, might control, influence, or manipulate governments. They might resort to the legal system to reduce wages, resist unions, and break strikes. Nonetheless, there was always some competition, political oversight, and a government responsibility to protect the public interest. But as James Mavor pointed out, Beck and Hydro *were* the government. They had access to the deep pockets, regulatory authority, and the legislative power of the state. They could destroy the value of investments, close the courts to challenges, bully competitors and labour, force the municipalities into line, and evade meaningful political control. This, Mavor argued, corrupted the state in a far more insidious way than bribes and patronage from outside — it was power over the people not power for the people.[43]

But Beck was riding a wave of public approval and Mavor, it turned out, was being paid by the private power companies. Beck's major defeat was inflicted not by a political economist, the electorate, or a premier, but by the automobile. In 1920, an Ontario royal commission pronounced radial railways obsolete. When Beck died in 1925, most Ontario radial lines were bankrupt and his vision of an electric interurban railway network had taken its place among the "might-have-beens" of history.

VI

Canadians may well have thought they had dodged a bullet in 1919. They had been saved by the war from a depression. They were saved from the postwar collapse everyone predicted by the demand for Canadian products to feed hungry people and rebuild shattered economies, and by soldiers' gratuities and savings that provided ready cash for consumer spending. Inflation fostered the illusion of growth. Bankers issued dire warnings, but tripled the number of branches across the country. Commercial failures in 1919 were the fewest on record. Unexpected prosperity in 1919 and 1920 made ambitious programs of social reform and national reconstruction seem less urgent.[44]

The bubble burst with brutal suddenness in the summer of 1920. International financial uncertainly, the end of European reconstruction, and the re-emergence of agricultural competitors knocked the bottom out of commodities markets. In one year, the wholesale price index dropped from 288 to 198. Canada's GNP shrank by 20 percent. Commercial failures rose to 2,451 in 1921, then to 3,695 in 1922. The business community had no better answer than Flavelle's echo of the wartime rhetoric of purification. The "old fashioned discipline incident to suffering," he said, would "do good on the whole rather than harm" by alleviating postwar slackness, selfishness, and pleasure-seeking, and reviving the "spirit of service."[45]

The next few years brought blow after blow. Rising American tariffs shut many Canadian products out of the U.S. market. Immigration in the 1920s never came close to the level of the boom years, and a million Canadians departed for the United States. In the Maritimes, shipbuilding collapsed, along with fishing, coal, and steel, and 150,000 people left the provinces. Manufacturing jobs (except in the auto, electrical, and consumer industries) declined. Only Stelco produced the type of steel products required for autos and home appliances. Algoma Steel was constantly seeking assistance. The Nova Scotia steel and coal industries were consolidated by a Montreal syndicate, British Empire Steel Corporation (backed by British financiers, including Lord Beaverbrook, who floated a $100 million stock issue), which then provoked the worst industrial warfare Canada had yet seen. Only when a group under Sir Herbert Holt seized control in 1927 was federal support provided, which propped the company up until the Depression knocked it down again.[46]

The banks had missed the opportunity to replace wartime financial arrangements with something more permanent. E.R. Pease of the Royal Bank had begged Sir Thomas White in 1918 to set up a central bank. But the other banks (especially the Bank of Montreal, which considered itself the *de facto* central bank) considered a central bank a "reckless" experiment that would inevitably succumb to patronage and politics. When prices collapsed in 1921, several banks were only saved by being absorbed by competitors or bailed out by provincial governments. The Home Bank of Toronto did fail in 1923 after years of incompetent and dishonest management, which included loans to Pellatt for real estate ventures and Casa Loma (whose furnishings were sold at auction in 1925, right down to the bathroom scales). There were criminal investigations (two officers went to jail), lawsuits, and grilling of bankers by Progressive MPs from the Banking and Commerce Committee (the grain growers had been heavily invested in the Home Bank). The bankers now decided that they could accept an inspector of banks — but they still balked at the idea of a central bank. By 1928, the thirty chartered banks of 1910 had become ten (albeit with over four thousand branches). Four banks controlled 77 percent of the business, and the Royal Bank, which had started as a small Nova Scotia bank but which had made a series of shrewd acquisitions, was now the largest bank in Canada.[47]

Then, just as commentators were predicting Canada's impending collapse, things got better. By 1925, Sir John Aird, who took over as president of the Bank of Commerce following Walker's death, could tell his shareholders that the country stood on the verge of a new boom in minerals, forestry, and hydro-electricity. Exports rose 67 percent from 1921 to 1928. Cost of living indices finally equalled those from the prewar period, prices stabilized, and wages rose slightly. If there was such a thing as the "roaring twenties" in Canada, it was the last five years of the decade.[48]

New industries produced a new set of leaders: some colourful, like Thornton; some dour, like Herbert Holt, or downright surly, like Sir Harry Oakes; some outsiders, like Sam McLaughlin or Sam Bronfman; some managerial, like Beatty, Russell, and Aird. Many were Canadian branch plant managers reporting to American equity owners and schooled in doctrines of managerial efficiency. International Business Machines, founded in 1917 as the Canadian subsidiary of an American company, which later adopted the same name, passed the $1 million mark in sales by 1919. Even the banks bought adding and cheque-writing machines for the "bank boys." In the later 1920s, there was a new round of corporate mergers as older industries consolidated and newer ones — autos, home appliances, department stores, and consumer services — came to the fore.[49]

As Aird had predicted, the boom was largely propelled by the resource industries of the "Middle North." Forest products, mining, and hydro-electricity required heavy capitalization, advanced technology, railway transport, and the still-new aviation industry. Most of all they needed the co-operation of the provinces, which now became important economic players since (except for the three Prairie provinces until the 1930s) they controlled their natural resources and issued the licences required to exploit them.

New towns, often planned communities with company housing, health centres, schools, stores, and recreation facilities, and with some local farming, began to dot the Middle North. With their growth, the Canadian Shield no longer split Canada in two. Life in these towns could be rewarding, but it also had its drawbacks. The owners lived far away. The bosses were engineers, managers, and accountants. The workers were farmers, foresters, and fishermen, and immigrants catapulted from frontier poverty into affluence — at the price of isolation, dependence on the company, and periodic layoffs, wage cuts, and hardship.[50]

Many of these towns were built around paper mills. Pulp and paper was a product of American mass culture, new technologies that could convert previously worthless trees to newsprint, and provincial leases of two hundred thousand square miles of timber limits by 1929. Production rose from 795,000 tons in 1919 to 2,724,500 in 1929. Overproduction led to the consolidation of firms, which left three large, American-owned companies in control of 55 percent of production and three smaller, Canadian companies holding 26 percent. Reliance on American capital and markets, and failure to diversify products, develop technologies, or build new equipment left the industry vulnerable when the Great Depression hit.[51]

In British Columbia, the giant stands of cedar and fir were more valuable as wood or plywood than as pulp. In 1919, H.R. Macmillan, tired of seeing Canadian lumber exported through the United States, formed a partnership with a British lumber importer and within a few years the thirty vessels of his Canadian Transport Company were carrying B.C. fir around the world, including to Japan and China, with sales rising from $520,000 in 1920 to $5,785,000 in 1928 — about 50 percent of all British Columbia's exports. With the opening of the Panama Canal in 1914, grain and minerals from the Prairie West began to be shipped to Vancouver in preference to the Lakehead. As Canada's Pacific gateway, the manufacturing, processing, and service centre for the booming West Coast, and a warm-weather haven, Vancouver passed Winnipeg as Canada's third-largest city in the early 1920s.[52]

The huge quantities of nickel near Sudbury had become immensely valuable when new refining methods made its development feasible and nickel-steel became an essential war material. The American International Nickel Company swallowed British Mond Nickel after the 1921 recession and controlled 90 percent of production — which more than doubled between 1919 and 1929. Elsewhere, copper, lead, zinc, cobalt, and iron, as well as aluminum, found new uses in construction, manufacturing, automobiles, and electrical machinery and appliances. In the Kootenays, Americans first developed the mines, but after the war, CPR's subsidiary, Cominco, became a big player.

Gold remained the big-ticket item and spectacular discoveries in the Ontario clay belt were joined in the 1920s by mines in Timmins and Red Lake. Smelting of ore was itself a form of manufacturing, and mining became increasingly mechanical, with new processes like Hollinger's process for crushing low grade ore and extracting gold with cyanide.

And this required money, lots of it. Harry Oakes, sitting on what he knew was a bonanza at Kirkland Lake in 1912, was unable to get financing in Toronto, so he sold stock in Buffalo at a discount and paid bills and wages in shares (a Chinese restaurateur who would accept them became fabulously wealthy). By 1921, Oakes was the richest man in Canada. But for every Harry Oakes there was a legion of disappointed prospectors, Toronto investors holding worthless penny stocks, frustrated entrepreneurs always in the wrong place at the wrong time.[53]

These industries all required hydro power and the Middle North had rivers with vast potential. Price Brothers and some other paper companies in Quebec built their own power companies, while others teamed up with private companies in Shawinigan and the Saguenay. Ontario Hydro built a string of northern hydro dams and sent surplus power into its grid. Canada's installed hydro went from twenty-five million horsepower in 1919 to sixty-one million by the end of the decade. Abundant power also stimulated aluminum refining — in 1925, the Aluminum Company of America spun off a Canadian subsidiary, Alcan, to build a refinery at Arvida, Quebec. Hydro-electricity employed machinery, such as turbines and transmission equipment that could be built in Canada, and the increasing electrification of Canadian homes provided markets for copper, rubber, interior wiring and equipment, and a range of products from light bulbs to washing machines.[54]

At the end of the war, Canada had some two thousand pilots trained in the Royal Flying Corps, many more mechanics and ground crew, dozens of aerodromes and flying schools, and scores of surplus Jennies and flying boats made by the IMB. The first trans-Atlantic flight in 1919 and a cross-Canada flight in October 1920, appeared to presage a bright future for civil aviation, but early attempts to establish mail or passenger services quickly folded. Some pilots, like "Wop" May turned to barnstorming at events like the July 1919 Calgary Exhibition, whose posters announced "PASSENGER CARRYING AEROPLANES AND AVIATION STUNTS" along with cattle exhibitions and marching bands. Wing-walking and daredevil flying led inevitably to tragic accidents and to more stringent regulation by the Air Board (established in 1919 to regulate military and civil aviation). By the mid-1920s, air services in Ontario and Quebec were spotting forest fires, mapping lakes and forests, and carrying supplies to isolated people. Wop May could finally make money flying for mining and oil companies and carrying passengers and mail. The golden age of bush flying had begun.[55]

By the mid 1920s, Canada's economic development had apparently resumed its upward trajectory. But the new economy, like the older one, was founded on extractive industries and transportation, dependent on imported capital and foreign markets. The boom-and-bust cycle was compounded by increasingly reckless speculation by the emerging middle class. Mackenzie King, for all his distaste for predatory capitalism, was more *laissez-faire* in his approach to business than Borden had ever been. Some vestiges of wartime government intervention remained, like income taxes, agencies to care for soldiers and their families, a health ministry, new departments and regulations at all levels of government, nationalized railways, and Hydro. But most people seemed to believe that it was better to leave social policy to private agencies; better to allow giant companies to extract resources as long as they did some processing at home; better to let business, for good or ill, be business.[56]

The new economic expansion was fuelled, as the great boom had been also, by optimism. Optimism was reflected in new consumer industries, entertainment, and tourism. It was expressed in a continuing faith in the future of Canada, in new discoveries, in the progress of mankind. On a numbingly cold day in January 1920, Lucy Maud Montgomery and her husband were making their rounds in a Gray-Dort automobile nicknamed "Lady Jane." She was an internationally famous writer whose stories celebrated the idyllic agrarian time of her childhood, and she profoundly regretted what the automobile was doing to that world. But as a Presbyterian minister's wife, she welcomed the ease with which they could now get around their parish — and get out of it. Under mounds of blankets and with a hot brick at her feet, she reflected on the results of the 1919 expeditions to observe the eclipse of the sun off Africa, which had confirmed Einstein's theory of relativity:

> I buried my nose in my collar and forgot the outside world in a series of reflections upon this astounding new discovery of the nature of light made by Einstein which is going to utterly revolutionize most of the beliefs held by scientists for two hundred years. It is a curious thing that this upsetting discovery should come just at a time when almost everything else that made up our old world is being upset, revolutionized, or torn to pieces. The result will probably be in the end a very wonderful era of development in everything.[57]

CHAPTER 11

The Spirit of a Nation

You heard it everywhere in 1919, in conversation, lectures, speeches, sermons, newspapers and magazines: "The war has made Canada a nation." Canada's rapid growth before the war, its triumphs on the battlefield, its contribution to the Imperial war effort, its assertion of nationhood at Paris — all these and more made it seem self-evident that a new Canadian nation would emerge as part of the new world being created by the war.

As with so many other aspects of that vision of a new world, there were conflicts and contradictions. The war had largely suppressed ideas of Canada that did not conform to the dominant Anglo-Canadian worldview. French Canadians had seen their language attacked, their loyalty questioned, and their young men conscripted to fight in a foreign war. When the House of Commons opened in February 1919, Quebec Liberals lost no time in articulating their vision of an independent Canada that included both its founding peoples and was beholden to no other nation or empire. East European immigrants had been labeled "foreigners," disenfranchised, and even interned. *Maclean's* was warning of the "Alien Menace," and the Anglican Bishop of Saskatchewan was railing against re-opening the country's doors to "dirty, stupid, reeking of garlic, undesirable Continental Europeans." They, too, would resist any concept of nationhood that did not include them.[1]

If the war was really to make Canada a nation, and not break it — as it had broken the multi-ethnic empires of Europe — a more tolerant, inclusive, and diverse Canada would have to be imagined. Creating the myths, symbols, and artistic expressions, the culture, sense of common identity,

The Group of Seven Artists, 1920
One of the seven, Franklin Carmichael, is absent from this picture, which was taken at a Toronto Arts and Letters Club luncheon, and there are two guests at the table. This club the centre of the artistic and literary world in Toronto and had counterparts in other large cities.

and civic duty that would express the spirit of such a nation would be the task of its intellectuals, artists, and educators. They would have much to do.

Many people before the war would have agreed with visiting British poet Rupert Brooke who called Canada a "soulless Dominion." Canadians, wrote Leacock, saw the "Unseen Powers riding upon the midnight blast" as "an enormous quantity of horsepower going to waste," the primeval forest as "a first-class site for a saw mill," and "the leaping cataract" as a temptation "to erect a red-brick hydro-electric establishment on its banks and make it leap to some purpose." Painter Arthur Lismer complained that Torontonians could "argue and discourse for hours on the dollar and the ways and means of getting it, but they can't talk on any other subject intelligently." Duncan Campbell Scott, whom Brooke called "the only poet in Canada," was "*thirsty* to talk literature" when Brooke met him in Ottawa. Canada, in Brooke's view, was "a *bloody* place" for such a poet. "Nobody cares if he writes or doesn't."[2]

That picture was beginning to change before the war as some of the country's wealthy men endowed museums, galleries, theatres, academies, and churches, and patronized painters, sculptors, architects, and designers.

Schools, magazines, popular entertainment, and ambitious publishing ventures were beginning to tell Canadian stories and popularize its history. Authors like Leacock, Connor, and Montgomery could build international reputations while residing in Canada. Nonetheless, Lismer recalled that as the war ended "most creative people, whether in painting, writing or music, began to have a guilty feeling that Canada was as yet unwritten, unpainted, unsung."[3]

I

"The difference between 1914 and 1919," recalled Brooke Claxton, "was that by 1919 there were strong bonds of active Canadian sentiment. Canadians were beginning to have a confident pride in themselves and love of their country." Soldiers fighting for the Empire had mingled with British troops and British society, and they had learned that they were a different people and in no way inferior. "We are no longer humble colonials," said A.Y. Jackson. "We've made armies. We can also make artists, historians, and poets."[4]

This new national spirit gave rise during the 1920s to what Claxton called "a Canadian Movement" — a network of personal relationships, religious bodies, galleries, museums, historical societies, scientific, academic, artistic, literary, and cultural organizations, parks and conservation authorities, chambers of commerce, Canadian Clubs, League of Nations societies, service clubs, study and advisory groups — which was "nation-wide, spontaneous, and inevitable" and "cut across political, racial, and social lines." Most of these groups were local bodies, composed of thousands of anonymous individuals "concerned about the same kin[d] of things and working to the same goals though they might take different ways to get there." At the centre of this web were opinion leaders like Dafoe ("perhaps the greatest single force in the Canada of his time"), younger businessmen, politicians, ministers, teachers, philanthropists, and leaders like Graham Spry, Vincent Massey, and Claxton himself. Many were ex-soldiers, educated in Canadian universities, some with post-graduate degrees from Oxford, with a few former Round Tablers, building a nation with the techniques once applied to uniting an Empire.[5]

Vincent Massey drew on his family's wealth to endow Hart House at the University of Toronto, a unique blend of the democratic North American university with an Oxford college, with a theatre, a resident string quartet, an art collection, and a debating society; and his Massey Foundation funded educational and cultural projects. In March and April 1919, anthropologist Marius Barbeau presented the French-Canadian folk music he was recording on Edison wax cylinders in a series of *"Soirées du bon vieux temps"* in Montreal. John Murray Gibbon began making the CPR a major player in preserving and presenting Canadian history in its offices, stations, and advertising, and this example was soon followed by others, including Eaton's and the Hudson's Bay Company.[6]

"The schools are filled to overflowing, colleges and universities beyond all precedent or expectation," wrote University of Toronto president Falconer in 1920. "The air is vibrant with aspiration." High-school texts combined newer selections of Canadian literature with the traditional "heroic" poems and stories. The 1920s were a golden age of history writing, led by George Wrong and his many students and colleagues, who celebrated Canada's liberal democracy, moral and material progress, and evolution to nationhood within the Empire. Wrong's masterpiece, *The Rise and Fall of New France,* was the culmination of a generation of historical writing about the heroic age of French Canada and what American historian Francis Parkman had called the "happy calamity" of its absorption into the British Empire. The second issue of the new *Canadian Historical Review* featured an article on "The Growth of Canadian National Feeling," which pleaded for a sense of nationhood based on common ideals rather than language and race. A Conference on Citizenship and Character Education in Winnipeg in October 1919 brought together speakers such as Falconer, C.W. Gordon, and leading Social Gospellers to seek ways to heal class, ethnic, and religious divisions by uniting Canadians in a common citizenship and renewed national spirit.[7]

There were still echoes of wartime passions, such as the public outcry in 1924 when the winner of a Winnipeg competition to design a war memorial was found to be of German origin. But attacks on French Canada were less frequent and some formerly hostile writers like Castell Hopkins, the Imperialist editor of the *Canadian Annual Review*, were now at pains to acknowledge the contribution of French Canada to the war effort. In 1928, the Ontario and Saskatchewan governments banned a British film on Edith Cavell because it would embitter relations with German Canadians. The emerging master narrative of Canadian nationhood remained British and Christian; it stereotyped aboriginals and excluded Jews and racial minorities; but it was more inclusive of ethnic and linguistic minorities, and it embraced the French fact in Canada.[8]

Canadian Forum, a journal founded in 1920, replaced the older *University Magazine* as a vehicle for social and intellectual commentary, but was far more modernist, nationalist, reformist, and avant-garde — and it promised in its first issue to "trace and value those developments of art and letters which are distinctly Canadian." Popular magazines like *Maclean's* published more Canadian fiction. Publishing houses that had previously been niche players distributing American and British titles began publishing Canadian writers. In 1921, the Canadian Authors' Association was founded to lobby for better copyright protection and tariffs against foreign magazines. Sir Ernest Macmillan (who had written his first symphony as a prisoner of war) produced serious settings of Canadian folk music, and Healy Willan began his career as the father of Canadian church and organ music. The Earl Grey competitions, university drama programs, and, by the late 1920s, the Dominion Drama Festival, anchored an astonishing array of local theatre and amateur musical performances.[9]

The most successful artistic expression of the new national spirit was in painting, where a group of Toronto artists had been exploring new techniques to portray the northern landscape they considered the essence of Canada. Their leading light had been Tom Thomson, who at the time of his death in 1917 was blending bold colours, broad strokes of brush and palette-knife (what a critic called the "hot-mush" style), and minimal forms to capture the stark beauty of Algonquin Park. After the war, his comrades went farther afield, seeking inspiration in giant rocks, wind on water, the bright colours and dappled light of autumn, even in burned forests. In early 1919, Lawren Harris, together with Franz Johnston and J.E.H. Macdonald, showed paintings from a trip to Algoma at the new Art Gallery of Ontario. In November, these three, plus Frederick Varley, Frank Carmichael, Arthur Lismer, and A.Y. Jackson, began planning a show that would also include paintings by Thomson and three Quebec artists. The 1920 exhibition of the Group of Seven, as they called themselves, was the first full flowering of an art that expressed, in the words of poet A.J.M. Smith:

a beauty
of dissonance …
the beauty
of strength
broken by strength
and still strong.

In 1924, the group won an international reputation as part of a Canadian exhibit at the Wembley Exhibition in London.[10]

"The Canadian who does not love keen bracing air, sunlight making shadows that vie with the sky, the wooded hills and the frozen lakes, well, he must be a poor patriot," wrote A.Y. Jackson. Critics in the West pointed out that the Group painted nothing west of Lake Superior. Nor did they only paint landscapes. And there was nothing new about their invocation of the "northern myth," which had inspired not only generations of Canadian painters but also a wide array of poets and intellectuals who celebrated Canadians as a virile "northern race." Nonetheless, there was something about the way the group depicted the land that resonated at home and abroad as uniquely Canadian. By the late 1920s, several of them were painting other parts of Canada, including Quebec, the Atlantic provinces, the Rockies, and the Arctic. They were drawing into their orbit several Quebec painters and Emily Carr, whose remarkable depictions of aboriginal British Columbia were also distinctly Canadian.[11]

But defining and expressing a "Canadian identity" exposed contradictions as often as it promoted unity. Massey himself saw the danger of "artificial Canadianism that is an offence against honest art." There was a deep conflict between younger artists inspired by modernism — those like A.J.M. Smith, who believed that "any subject whatever is susceptible of artistic treatment and that praise or blame is to be conferred after a consideration, not of its moral, but of its aesthetic harmony" — and the older generation, like Duncan Campbell Scott, who denounced art designed "to insult older ideas of beauty … to shock with unwholesome audacities … with the mere malicious design of awakening protest, the more violent the better." In the mid-1920s, rising literary critic W.A. Deacon began to promote "modern" writers like F.P. Grove, Martha Ostenso, and Mazo de la

Roche, and relentlessly criticized older writers like L.M. Montgomery and Ralph Connor, whom he regarded as anachronistic embarrassments — but who nonetheless remained overwhelmingly popular.[12]

The ineffable sorrow that engulfed the nation as a result of the war was beautifully expressed in memorials, church windows, statues, and paintings. These stood as equally important expressions of the Canadian soul as did the artistic depictions of its stark landscape. With only a few exceptions, these works were created in a traditional style — it is hardly surprising, really, that in the aftermath of war most audiences, patrons, and politicians sought art that told a reassuring story in a style they could relate to.

The Dumbells, a troupe formed to entertain soldiers in the trenches, toured to packed houses for a decade. A few wealthy patrons supported the Group of Seven, and Sir Edmund Walker, as chairman of the National Gallery, saw that some of their work was purchased by public institutions; but the private market still favoured the older artists, architects, and designers steeped in the beaux-arts tradition. The avant-garde women painters of the Beaver Hall group despaired of ever seeing their work in the drawing rooms of Montreal. Emily Carr toiled in obscurity, operating a boarding house in Victoria. Most of the younger poets, artists, musicians, and intellectuals shaped by the war — and by the postwar period — would not reach maturity or find a significant audience until late in the decade.[13]

Canadians struggling for new artistic ways to express their identity faced the further disadvantage — if it can be called such — that, unlike European artists seeking to portray the intellectual turmoil and physical horror of a world dislocated by modernity and shattered by war, Canadians remained fundamentally optimistic. Even A.Y. Jackson and F.H. Varley, who as war artists had captured the tragic futility of the Great War, found spiritual affirmation in the grandeur of their country. This optimism partly explains the ease with which Canadians accepted the dynamic American culture that flowed freely across the border, with its novelty, energy, and celebration of life. Intellectuals like Archibald MacMechan lamented that Canada had become a "vassal state" to the United States in accents, cinema, popular newspapers, and magazines — indeed, in habits like chewing gum or buying teddy bears — and continued to consider British films, literature, and criticism the gold standard of high culture. But the emerging younger intellectuals admired America's democratic modernism. "Those colonially-minded persons who think to save us from the flood of Americanism by appealing to English traditions may as well start a campaign to bring back the horse and buggy," wrote Frank Underhill in *Canadian Forum* in 1929.[14]

Canadian newspapers were full of American news articles, comics, fashion, and advertising. Magazines like the *Saturday Evening Post* flooded into Canada, and it was estimated in 1925 that for every Canadian magazine sold eight were imported from the United States. One out of every four pianos sold in Canada was a player piano and music rolls were generally cut in the United States; Victrolas played cylinders and disks that were produced abroad; and Canadian songs and sheet music which had burgeoned during the war were now swamped by American imports. Though radio stations were established in both languages in Montreal in 1920, American radio dominated the Canadian airwaves until one of the nationalist advocacy movements of the 1920s, the Radio League, saw their dream of a Canadian Broadcasting Corporation come to fruition in 1932. Canadians followed with fascination the exploits of Knut Rockne, Babe Ruth, Jack Dempsey, and the Black Sox baseball scandal of 1919. The music they played was jazz, their comedy blackface and vaudeville, their dance the Charleston.[15]

At first it was thought that film would be, in the words of producer Ernest Shipman, a means of "quickening a Canadian national consciousness — the spirit which now finds expression not only in a new and distinctive note in Canadian literature but in a demand for Canadian-made motion pictures, as real and free and wholesome as is Canadian life at its best." In 1920, there were 830 movie houses across the country. Railways and immigration agencies used movies to depict the tourism and agricultural potential of Canada. Travelogues, films of polar expeditions, and stories of Mounties or the heroism of New France, were staples in Canadian films and in American films about Canada. Films were used for recruiting, as well as for Victory Loan and Patriotic Fund campaigns. The federal government and several provinces produced films for education, agricultural, industrial, and scientific use. In 1919, a privately made movie, *The Great Shadow,* depicted the threat of Bolshevism. Shipman's *Back to God's Country* told the story of the daughter of a northern trapper, who communes with the animals of the forest, falls in love, and foils plots to ravish her, all in a stunning natural setting. Ernest Ouimet in Quebec produced *Why Get Married* and other features like *Nanook of the North*. Shipman contracted with Ralph Connor to bring a number of his novels to the screen, and a half-million-dollar studio was built near Trenton, Ontario.[16]

But by 1923 the Canadian feature film industry was all but dead. Most of the movies were produced on a shoestring by men one step ahead of their creditors. *Nanook,* which purported to be a documentary, was fairly successful. But for mainstream cinema, a small country could not match the quality of Hollywood's centralized production, and if a film did not sell in Britain or the United States it could not recoup its costs. By the early 1920s, Hollywood was buying up Canadian film distributors and theatres. Ralph Connor complained that the "peculiar spiritual appeal" of his books was reduced to a "commonplace, wild west, melodramatic, maudlin yarn which will take its place in competition with a thousand other similar and superior yarns for public approval." "If Canadian stories are worthwhile making into films," said American producer Lewis Selznick in 1922, "companies will be sent into Canada to make them."[17]

Hollywood drew the best talent from around the world including a generation of Canadian filmmakers, actors, and producers like Mack Sennett, Mary Pickford, Louis B. Mayer, and Vincent Massey's brother Raymond. There was no public support in Canada for the quota systems other countries used to protect their film industries. Elites might complain that this meant the death of Canadian culture, but for most people it was a sign of cultural maturity. Films brought the world to every small town and were democratic and accessible, just like records and radio — and just like the Carnegie libraries, the local theatre companies playing Shakespeare, or the small-town orchestras and chamber ensembles playing Beethoven. The best young talent from these places might pursue careers in London, Hollywood, or New York — if you were good enough, why not?

Canadians did not become Americans. They absorbed American and British culture, filtered it according to their own values, blended it with their daily experience and their regional and local character, and were beginning to create a layered, diverse, composite, unique identity, albeit with many regional variants. Better communications allowed Canadians to talk to each other across a vast land. Imported American inventions such as service clubs built a sense of community in the small towns of Canada. Rotary alone had sixty-three clubs in Canada by 1923 and a Canadian membership of over forty-one hundred.[18]

Canadians played "American" sports like baseball, golf, basketball, and tennis. But they also had curling rinks in most small towns, and above all they played hockey, participating on everything from pickup squads to professional teams competing for the Stanley Cup. In 1919, the Montreal Canadiens of the National Hockey League played the Seattle Metropolitans of the Pacific Coast Hockey Association for the cup, though the series had to be shortened due to an outbreak of influenza. Across the barriers of culture, language, class, or region, the same dream danced in the heads of young boys all across Canada, falling asleep after an exhilarating day on the frozen river or pond — that they too might one day become an Aurel Joliat, a Howie Morenz, a Joe Malone, a Cyclone Taylor, or a King Clancy.[19]

II

On January 31, 1919, at the Monument-National in Montreal, Canon Lionel Groulx rose to deliver an eagerly awaited speech. The Monument-National was a theatre complex built by the Saint-Jean-Baptiste Society in 1893 on rue Saint-Laurent to be a centre of francophone culture. From its stage the great leaders of French Canada had addressed their nation. Bishops had expounded the providential civilizing mission of French Catholicism in North America. Bourassa had attacked conscription and defended French-language schools in Ontario. Groulx was following in this tradition with a message that was very much a product of the Great War.[20]

Canon Lionel Groulx

Abbé Groulx was a slight, almost ascetic priest in his early forties. He had grown up in a large rural family that had scrimped to provide him with an education. He had studied literature, philosophy, and religion, and become a teacher at a Church-run *collège classique*. From 1906 to 1909 he had studied in Fribourg (Switzerland) and Rome, where he received his doctorate. Repelled by the secularism of republican France, he had been drawn to the deeply conservative philosophies of Charles Maurras and Maurice Barrès. Back in Montreal, he had become a leader of Catholic action groups, a defender of the French language, a poet, charismatic teacher, orator, and — though he had no formal training in the discipline — the first professor of Canadian history at the Université de Montréal.[21]

Groulx had chosen as the title of his speech "If Dollard Were Alive Today." Adam Dollard des Ormeaux had prevented an attack on Montreal by some eight hundred Iroquois with his heroic stand at Long Sault on the Ottawa River in 1660. In the early twentieth century, French-Canadian nationalists had made him into a cult figure. Groulx depicted him as a latter-day medieval knight — along with his sixteen companions, he fasted and prayed to the Virgin Mary all night before taking an oath to die in the defence of her city (Ville-Marie) — and a Canadian patriot who had died for his country when France had deserted it. Dollard's Canada was a land of *seigneurs* and peasants, of mystics and martyrs, not the wilderness of the *coureurs des bois* or the sordid commerce of the fur trade. His Canada would produce heroes as courageous as those who had died in the Great War, when they were fighting for hearth, homeland, and faith.

What would Dollard see if he were alive today? Alas, cried Groulx, he would see a rootless, materialistic people with little of his courage, patriotism, or sacrifice. "No longer would he hear … the confused appeal of a race still to be born, but [instead] the anxious, trembling voice of a people dispersed in all parts of the continent and conscious of the old barbarous coalition closing upon it once again." He would see a war-torn world where "nations have been crazed with mirages of unbridled democracy," duped "under the pretext of being emancipated, to extremes of revolution." He would see "a revolutionary blaze" that "threatens the whole of Europe," whose sparks were falling on North America.

What would he tell them? To recall that "a mere handful of Frenchmen were able to explore and Christianize three-quarters of a continent larger than Europe, that they were able to leave durable memories of France throughout America, and that, having been masters of this territory for a century, they left it, in the end, only as a result of an epic military struggle, wearily dropping their flags grown too heavy with victories." To remember how French Canada had survived 150 years of conquest, "always pushing forward, marking with steeples our conquest of the soil, seizing the rights of the conqueror and forcing him to respect ours, retaining our Christian and French qualities, our language, our faith, our customs, all the elements of our diversity, remaining, finally, in the middle of an immense Anglo-Saxon ocean, an untouchable island built of Catholic and Latin granite." Above all, to see Quebec as *their* country. "The land between Montreal and Tadoussac was, for a long time, the cradle and hearthstone of our race. And in this space, more or less, we were confined after the Conquest; on this territory we lived, suffered, grew, we developed our institutions and our ethnic character."

He would tell them to find new leadership, no longer from soldiers and still less from politicians, but from clerics and intellectuals who would fight, as Dollard had fought, for "the most worthy causes of man: the soul of a race and its past, culture, and faith." Such a leader, he told his audience,

has only to make his intentions and will supernatural through faith; adapt his activities to God's designs; call upon the legions of his glorified ancestors; and immediately, with increased dignity and power, he enters that region where the fates of nations are decided; where, by magnificent pre-ordination, and in response to human prayer, the most generous of divine plans are elaborated. The man of faith who prays as he thinks, acts, speaks, writes, or fights, is no longer a man; he acquires the status of a sublime collaborator in the works of Providence.

"O Commander of the old Fort of Ville-Marie," Groulx concluded,

it is time you were among us! We have such pressing need of a young leader like you, a leader of men. Look, on the frontier where you fell a barbarous throng as menacing as the old threatens our French soul. The work we must now undertake is one of total reconstruction and restoration. Arise, Dollard, and live on your granite pedestal. Summon us, with virile charm, with a hero's accents. We lift toward you our hands quivering like palm leaves, ardent with ambition to serve. Together we shall work for the reconstruction of our family's house. And should you command it, O Dollard, O powerful leader, we are ready to follow you to the supreme holocaust for the defence of our French tongue and our Catholic faith.[22]

Everybody in the audience knew that Groulx was aiming his words at Henri Bourassa, a man he had once admired, but whose star was now in decline. Bourassa had fought for the rights of his people against Imperialism and wartime intolerance, but he believed in Canadian dualism and liberal democracy. He had fought for Catholic control of education, social welfare, and trade unions, and opposed votes for women, but he had also attacked plutocracy and opposed undue interference in politics by ultramontane churchmen. Now English Canadians regarded him as a traitor, and a younger generation of Quebeckers led by Groulx was repudiating his pan-Canadian liberalism. Groulx saw himself as a "lighthouse keeper," guarding French Canada and the Catholic Church against secularism, Anglo-Saxon culture, corrupt politicians, foreign business, Jews, and the *vendus* who collaborated with them.[23]

Groulx's blending of Catholicism, language, and history produced a concept of "race" that was a mirror image of the ideas of some English-Canadian Imperialists. "From the collective acts of our ancestors," he wrote in *Notre Maître le Passé*, "from their resolutions, from their attitudes in daily work as in their gravest hours, develops a special body of thought, a long and perpetual intention which is tradition. History seizes this thought, it disseminates it to the bottom of everyone's soul, it creates the light and the force which orders the numerous activities of a people." Groulx idealized the French-Canadian family as a "masterpiece" of the *ancien régime* and a moulder of its national character, sanctified by the sacrament of marriage, supported by the Church and the law, where sainted mothers (like his own) raised their children in the fear of God.[24]

According to Groulx, French Canadians were a chosen people who survived and prospered only when they kept faith with God and submitted to the divine will. They had been abandoned by France. The British had never stopped trying to crush their language and religion. Confederation had brought not deliverance but renewed bigotry and rule by local sellouts: "traitors — perhaps unwitting — but nevertheless prepared to sacrifice everything, like a herd of wretched sycophants, for the petty glory of a single man, or for party profit." To recover its collective identity and fulfill its divine mission, French Canada would have to rekindle its national spirit, unite as a people, and depend only on itself. This was not separatism, he argued, but a strategy for survival. Canada was coming apart, as were the countries of Europe and the British Empire. If Quebec was not to be sucked into the vortex of American Protestant modernism, it must become, once again, the beacon of hope encouraging French Canadians across North America to survive, to keep the faith.[25]

In 1922, Groulx embodied these ideas in his best-selling novel *L'Appel de la Race,* a book that in some respects resembles those of Ralph Connor. His hero is a French Canadian who has studied at McGill and married an English-speaking Catholic. Then, during the fight over French-language schools in Ontario, guided by his priest, he reads French authors, hears the call of the blood, and eloquently defends his heritage and his people. The breakup of his marriage symbolizes the impossibility of reconciling English and French Canadians even if both are Catholic. Groulx's characters, like Connor's, deliver long, set-piece speeches, but in far more poetic language that evokes the power of history and the beauty of the land.[26]

Following the example of dozens of Catholic youth and nationalist groups before them, Groulx and his followers established an organization, L'Action française, with a journal of the same name, which became in the early 1920s the most vibrant intellectual movement in Quebec. It drew inspiration from the French movement L'Action Française* led by Charles Maurras, which expounded the royalism, extreme conservatism, ultramon-

---

*The French organization is L'Action Française, with a capital "F"; the Quebec organization is L'Action française, with a small "f."

tane Catholicism, and cult of the leader, that marked the European Right during the interwar period. When Groulx went to Europe on sabbatical in 1922, he forged personal and organizational ties with its leaders; afterward, he disseminated its literature in Quebec, and encouraged contact between *québécois* in Paris and L'Action Française members.

L'Action française held yearly seminars on Quebec's national future, urbanization, industry, the economy, culture, and morality, and its members participated in *"semaines sociales"* and other forums. Though they often discussed science and business, it was with a view to using them to promote the prosperity, moral purity, and national identity of French Canadians. The belief that religious intellectuals steeped in history were divinely called to save the nation had an even more magnetic appeal to younger clerics, writers, and teachers in *collèges classiques* than the Protestant vision of "The Lord's Dominion." Groulx had given them pride and confidence in themselves and their homeland, and an alternative to modernism. When Groulx died in 1967, Claude Ryan called him the spiritual father of Quebec.[27]

Though Groulx was a towering figure in the 1920s, there were other schools of thought within the clerical and nationalist tradition. Traditional historians like Thomas Chapais were much closer to Wrong in their interpretation of French Canada's past and its place within Canada and the Empire. Schools of commerce and social science at the Université de Montréal under Édouard Montpetit, and the Association Canadienne-française pour l'Avancement des Sciences led by the botanist Brother Martin Marie-Victorin, combined Catholic tradition with science and progressive learning. Even the majority in the Church and university hierarchies who resisted science and business could see that romanticizing the past, attacking the English, and rejecting modernism was a dead-end. Official Catholic Action and young people's movements were somewhat more progressive and explored a wider range of issues than L'Action française.[28]

And Bourassa was still a force to be reckoned with, though by the early 1920s he had withdrawn from active politics and focused more on religion. To him, Groulx's *"appel de la race"* was indistinguishable from British racism, Orange-Protestant intolerance, and the forces destabilizing Europe, and he rejected the idea that only Quebec was the home of French Canadians. He saw Groulx's fusion of religion and nationalism as distorting Catholicism and its role in society. Groulx resented being lectured to by a layman and responded vehemently, and the two men feuded throughout the 1920s and 1930s.

Bourassa was right in seeing a dark side to L'Action française. Its rhetoric was full of military imagery and fear of the "enemy." It was one thing to deplore the city, alcohol, and modern immorality — that would have found resonance in English-Canadian agrarian and Protestant circles, as well as with Bourassa and most Catholic churchmen. But the shrill attacks on the movies, baseball, Santa Claus, short skirts, American music, and other "foreign" influences often verged on the ridiculous. And on outright bigotry. To Groulx, the French-Canadian "race" was Norman French and Catholic. Indians, Métis, blacks, and Huguenots were secondary; the Irish were all right if they were assimilated; the British were oppressors; and Jews were a "foreign," inassimilable presence in the French-Canadian heartland.[29]

The Jews in Quebec* were blamed for everything from the Russian Revolution to greedy materialism to the decline of racial purity and traditional morality. A Jewish newspaper characterized the extreme anti-Semitism of one Catholic paper as "so distinctly psychopathic that it cannot really bias any of its readers unless they are similarly degenerate and depraved." Only a few concrete actions were ever taken, such as an attempt to ban Jewish vacationers at Sainte-Agathe and an *achat chez nous* campaign to boycott Jewish merchants. But the steady drumbeat of speeches and articles attacking Jews, in religious and nationalist papers and often in the mainstream press, bred fear, which only grew as the prosperous 1920s gave way to the troubled 1930s.[30]

Groulx's most serious setback was delivered by Pope Pius XI, who, troubled by growing nationalist and right-wing influence on the Church in Europe, in 1926 condemned the French L'Action Française as dangerous to the minds of youth. A year passed before L'Action française in Quebec announced this condemnation and changed its own name to L'Action Canadienne-française. Groulx left the editorship of the newspaper and turned his attention to history, where, to his credit, he pioneered in Quebec a more rigorous approach to the use of evidence in the writing of history, which required him to gradually moderate some of his views. But the Pope's action had put paid to any pretension that he, or any other priest obedient to the Church, could don

---

* See Chapter 12.

Dollard's mantle of national leadership. By the 1930s, though he continued to be a revered figure, especially in *collèges classiques*, Groulx's influence was being eclipsed by younger nationalists, some of whom were exploring ideas that increasingly resembled European clerical fascism.[31]

The irony was that Quebec in the 1920s was experiencing unprecedented urban expansion, industrialization, resource development, social progress, and prosperity. French Canada was becoming a more complex society, whose development paralleled the rest of the continent even as it retained its distinct identity. Premiers Gouin (1905–20) and Taschereau (1920–36), while respecting the role of the Church, gradually built a modern provincial government with technical education, health care, and social agencies, and worked to attract investment and development. "We want these industrial centres that spread progress and wealth to proliferate over the territory of our province," Gouin said in 1919. French Canadians did not intend, said Taschereau, to be "a band apart and, like Robinson Crusoes, to live alone and separated on our own island. I will welcome the day when our Province will take the place in the Canadian household which it merits by reason of its riches, its geographical position and all its other elements of greatness."[32]

In Ottawa, younger Quebec Liberals who had been elected when Laurier swept the province in 1917 were asserting Quebec's right to participate in a new, independent Canadian nation. In March 1919, for example, Lucien Cannon responded to yet another attack by an English-Canadian MP on Quebec's enlistment record during the war. "Let us be Canadians," he cried, "let us according to the constitutional spirit of our institutions, represent not merely one county, not merely one province, but represent Canada from the Pacific to the Atlantic." Ernest Lapointe became an indispensible partner to Mackenzie King, who continued Laurier's policy of avoiding conflict between Quebec and the rest of Canada — helped by the fact that few outside Quebec had ever heard of Groulx or L'Action française.[33]

Groulx and his followers were occupying a parallel universe to that other Quebec. Their influence was profound, for they expressed the search for a national destiny that had animated French-Canadian society for generations. But they could never resolve the dilemma expressed in 1920 by Jean-Charles Harvey: "The industrialization of the province of Quebec will inevitably continue, be it by French-Canadians or foreigners.... It would be better that our riches become our property rather than that of our neighbours." During the 1920s and 1930s, French Canadian nationalists too often combined the dream of a rural society with vague ideas of nationalization and corporatism, while Anglo-Canadian and American entrepreneurs reaped the rewards of industrial and resource development. When, in the mid-1930s, the Taschereau government became mired in corruption and fell to a reform movement, Groulx and his followers were bitterly disappointed when Maurice Duplessis — the man they had hoped might be the long-awaited *chef* — hijacked the reform movement, blended Church control of social institutions, moral and social conservatism, support from English business, and authoritarian rule, to clamp a straitjacket on Quebec society that lasted until the Quiet Revolution.[34]

Nationalists had hoped that the Monument-National would be the beating heart of a new, vibrant, francophone Montreal. But even before the Great War, a nationalist writer portrayed rue Saint-Laurent as populated by a "crowd of races hostile to our fate, with its babel of tongues, and our own race represented mainly by its prostitutes of twelve and its young drunkards." In the 1920s, the Monument-National hosted a flourishing avant-garde French theatre, a series of beloved French-Canadian comedians, as well as Chinese performance troupes and some of the finest Yiddish theatre in North America. In succeeding decades, it became a popular burlesque spot. It was saved from the wrecker's ball in the 1970s, declared a historic site, and now houses the National Theatre School of Canada.[35]

III

Late in 1918, a Saskatchewan school inspector published his plan for "Canadianizing" the quarter million "foreigners" who were neither English, French, nor American, nor easily assimilated Germans, Dutch, or Scandinavians. Dr. J.T.M. Anderson, who a decade later would become premier of Saskatchewan (with the tacit support of an anti-Catholic movement that called itself the Ku Klux Klan), warned that the "defects" of Slavic immigrants (which were the "direct results of tyranny") must not be "allowed to enter our national character." But if their children were carefully educated by strict, dedicated teachers, they could be made into good Canadians. J.E. Sisler, principal of a Winnipeg school with a large Ukrainian population, agreed that if "foreigners" were treated "as Canadians and not as aliens, they will be found as good citizens in every way as any people in this country." During 1919, all three Prairie provinces developed citizenship curricula, and the Saskatchewan Department of Education commissioned a film for use in schools called *Nation-Building in Saskatchewan: The Ukrainians.* As wartime passions cooled, Canadians seemed to be more prepared to acknowledge the "foreign" communities living in their midst, and to regard them as potential fellow-citizens.[36]

But that did not mean they had any wish to open the doors to more of them. The Immigration Act of 1919 barred immigration from former enemy countries. It also barred Doukhobors, Mennonites, and Hutterites because of "their peculiar customs, habits, modes of living, and methods of holding property." Immigrants from Europe were required to produce a valid passport, evidence of exemption from military service, and a ticket showing they were making a continuous journey from their country of origin. Two years later, regulations were tightened still further to require prospective immigrants to have $250 in cash ($125 for children) and a visa issued overseas and not at the port of entry — and there were no Canadian visa offices in Eastern Europe. By contrast, the Empire Settlement Act would assist over 130,000 British immigrants to come to Canada.[37]

After the treatment some immigrants from "enemy" countries had received during the war, many were equally ambivalent about whether they wanted to stay. A Polish immigrant recalled his anguished prayer when he was in danger of being sent to a labour camp for being late in reporting to authorities: "Oh God, good God, is there anybody in the world who could talk to the angels on behalf of the Poles…. I am not guilty of anything. I do not owe anyone anything. Austria is not my country." That does not seem to have occurred to Canadian authorities, even when the Allies declared in 1917 that one of their war aims would be the liberation of all the nationalities in the Austro-Hungarian Empire. Ukrainian Bishop Nykyta Budka (who had been branded a traitor in 1914 for a pastoral letter that appeared to advise Ukrainians to be loyal to Austria-Hungary) told Sisler in 1918 that 75 percent of his people would return to the old country after the war. This did not happen, but 150,000 former immigrants did leave Canada in 1919.[38]

Yet most "foreign" immigrants had proven intensely loyal to their new country. They supported the Patriotic Fund and proclaimed their patriotism in mass meetings. Ten to fifteen thousand Ukrainians enlisted by posing as Poles or Russians and several won decorations. In 1916, six Ukrainian newspapers in Alberta issued an "Address to the Canadian People" pointing out that their record of enlistment gave them "the right to ask the Canadian people for better treatment of the Canadian Ukrainians." In Montreal, Italians rioted when *Le Devoir* accused Italy of cowardice for staying out of the war (!), and when Italy joined the Allies in 1915, many went home to fight. The war drove home to immigrant communities that Canada was now their home and they would have to seek, and defend, their place in it. In 1919 three major Italian-Canadian mutual aid societies merged to form the Società Italo-Canadese. In February 1920, several Ukrainian groups came together at Saskatoon to form the Ukrainian People's Council of Canada. Other national communities followed suit.[39]

Why had so many non-British immigrants been encouraged to settle in Canada in the first place? Canadians in the early twentieth century had faced the awesome task of settling an immense land, developing its industries, knitting them together into an economic powerhouse, and building a new nation that would be part of a stronger Empire. Most of the people who would do this would be of British stock. But more were needed. To Clifford Sifton (Laurier's minister of the interior from 1896 to 1905), the "stalwart peasant in a sheepskin coat" from the eastern provinces of the Austro-Hungarian Empire, "born on the soil, whose forefathers have been farmers for ten generations, with a stout wife and a half-dozen children," was the ideal settler for the harsh Canadian Prairies. And if Englishmen, who according to Lord Shaughnessy expected "high wages, a feather bed and a bath tub," would not do the hard, dangerous work at low pay to build the railways, dig the mines, and run the factories, then recruiting companies, railways, and shipping lines would bring in workers from southern and eastern Europe — and from Asia.[40]

By 1914, more than 170,000 Ukrainians, 116,000 Poles, 60,000 Italians, and smaller numbers from Romania, Hungary, Finland, Bulgaria, Lebanon, and Greece, had made their way to Canada, as part of an epic migration from Europe to the New World. Most of these peoples had been ruled for centuries by others. Ukrainians, Poles, and Jews were divided between the Russian and Austro-Hungarian Empires; Finland was part of

Russia; Lebanon was part of the Ottoman Empire, from which Bulgaria and Romania had only recently broken away; Italy had only been united for a generation. Ukrainians from the Austrian province of Galicia belonged to the Uniate or Greek Catholic Church, which combined the Orthodox rites, married priests, and the old Slavonic language with allegiance to the Pope — and 40 percent of the people of that province were Polish and 20 percent Jewish. Ukrainians from Bukovina and Ruthenia belonged to the Ukrainian Orthodox Church and were also intermingled with Jews, Slovakians, and Romanians. "Each little village," said an observer in 1910, "was a tiny world in itself, with its own traditions and ways, its own dress, perhaps even its own dialect. The neighbour from the next town ... is an outsider." Ukrainians were called "Ruthenians," "Galicians," or "Bukovinians" and were often confused with Poles, Russians, and even Jews. Canadians could not always tell who was who, even if they wanted to.[41]

They were poor, but not for the most part primitive peasants — rather they were people made mobile by overpopulation or land reform, with some education, access to a transportation network, and an intense desire to seek a better life. Galician Ukrainians had a long history of local government, political movements ranging from conservative clericalism to progressive radicalism to Marxist socialism, and a tradition of reading halls (*chytalni*), national halls (*narodni domy*), and educational institutions designed to revive their culture and national consciousness. Italians came with trades and skills and a family structure that allowed women and children to contribute to the domestic economy and adapt to change. Those who came first drew others after them, often to settle together.

Ukrainian farmers settled in an arc from southeast Manitoba along the Yellowhead highway to Vegreville, and other nationalities formed enclaves throughout the Prairies. If they could not afford a farm, they worked in Winnipeg or on the railways. Immigrants flooded into eastern cities to work in construction, factories, and new industries like the steel mills of Hamilton. "Little Italies" in Montreal, Toronto, and Vancouver were largely composed of people from a few villages — in Toronto, immigrants from one Sicilian town had a quasi-monopoly of the city's fruit trade. The Finns and others gravitated to mining and forestry in northern Ontario, while Greeks, Lebanese, and Jews found niches as merchants and traders.[42]

Given the size of the influx over a short time, and given the growing concerns about "race" and national character, it is hardly surprising that many Anglo-Canadians had second thoughts. "Canada faces the greatest immigration problem that has ever confronted any nation," a minister told a Presbyterian Church congress in 1913. "One man out of every five who lands on our shores is a foreigner. He comes here with a foreign tongue, foreign ideals, foreign religion, only a mere caricature of religion, with centuries of ignorance and oppression behind him." "Mere herds of the proletariat of Europe," wrote Leacock in 1911, were "fit objects for philanthropic pity but indifferent material from which to build the commonwealth of the future." Frank Oliver, who had replaced Sifton in 1905, declared that immigrants "should not be of such a class and character as will deteriorate rather than elevate the condition of our people and our country at large."[43]

Oliver tried to discourage "foreign" immigrants, but as long as there was land and work, they kept coming. And even our Presbyterian minister admitted that perhaps God had after all sent us these "foreigners" — they had "noble qualities that make for manhood ... which, if properly handled, may help us develop into a great and grand nation." Ralph Connor embodied this faith in his novel *The Foreigner*, in which the children of unsavoury "Galicians" prove that they can become fine Canadians. J.S. Woodsworth, who spent a decade working with immigrants at All Peoples' Mission in Winnipeg, believed that Canadians should "divest ourselves of a certain arrogant superiority and exclusiveness, perhaps characteristic of the English race," and "meet these people half way — seek to sympathize with their difficulties, and to encourage them in every forward movement."[44]

For the immigrants themselves, the challenge of settling in a new country was formidable. Dozens of memoirs recount the long passage on the transatlantic steamer, the occasional friendliness of the immigration officer or policeman, the endless railway journey through a vast countryside, the welcoming parties on station platforms, the doubts about how they could survive in this bleak new land. Farm women shouldered an inhuman workload, often having to clear the land while raising children, keeping language, culture, and faith alive — only to be isolated as husbands and children learned English and adopted new customs. But by the 1920s, the sod hut had given way to the frame house and barns, towns had sprung up with names like Kiew, with a church, a school, and a hall to debate events in the old country and the new, discuss community affairs, and attend concerts or plays.[45]

In the cities, families at first congregated in shabby districts like the north end of Winnipeg, where a 1918 survey revealed tenements housing two to fifteen families each, with about 47 percent living in three rooms or less. Outside observers saw these only as slums. But they were also the portals for immigrants into a new land, where they could converse in the old language while learning the new, develop networks, and find employment. In "Little Italies," people could preserve their own food and culture, even the customs of their native villages. Local intermediaries acted as bankers, suppliers, and employment contractors — some benevolent, like Cyril Genik, the Ukrainian "Czar" in Winnipeg; some exploitative, like Italian labour *padrones* who exacted bribes, kickbacks, and high interest on loans. Newspapers and cultural societies developed a sense of community and projected a voice to the wider world.[46]

Particularly important were churches, with their familiar festivals, fraternal organizations, and schools, which continued to provide cohesion and leadership as they had in the old country. Ukrainian-language novelist Illia Kiriak movingly describes the first visit of a priest to a pioneer village, to bless the graves of their dead, baptize children, solemnise marriages, and instruct the villagers. "They were all hungry for this kind of ministration, like the wayfarer who, after weary miles, halts to refresh himself with a drink of clear, cold water." Ukrainian Catholic Bishop Budka was sent out just before the war in response to a petition to the Pope, to lead his church and train priests. Mainstream Catholics like Poles and Hungarians could be more easily served by the Canadian church, but they still wanted priests who spoke their language and understood their customs. In Quebec, the French-speaking hierarchy initially supported the establishment of Italian churches and schools to keep them within the French-Catholic orbit. By 1921, one-sixth of the total Catholic population of Canada was neither English nor French-speaking.[47]

By the Great War, at least where they were well-established, immigrants had begun to create new communities, blending their sense of possessing the new land with their heritage from the old country. No writer captured this more movingly than Kiriak, a teacher in Ukrainian-language schools (until 1916), then a community cultural leader, poet, and author of a three-volume trilogy *Syny Zemli (Sons of the Soil)*. In one passage, the main character remembers "all the bad times that he and the other settlers had lived through during the first year of their life in the new land. Like a dense fog they had hung heavily over their daily lives, shutting out any sign of hope, which had shone, flickered, and disappeared in the illusory heaven of their dreams." But one day he passes the Cross marking the grave of a friend's son who has died in the new country. "Well friends," he tells his companions, "Canada now for a certainty is becoming our eternal motherland."[48]

The war interrupted regular contact with their places of origin, which were undergoing drastic upheaval. National identities had been nascent when they had left; now delegations from would-be nation-states were pressing on the peacemakers in Paris their claims to independence and territory. Ukrainian factions in the former Russian and Austrian empires united to create a republic in January 1919, which was soon fighting for its life against Bolsheviks and Poles. The new country of Poland tasted defeat in 1920 at the hands of the Bolsheviks, then won additional territory, including large chunks of Belarus and Russian Ukraine. In Italy, Benito Mussolini overthrew the democratic government and established a dictatorship in 1922. As new states began "ethnic cleansing" and fought over boundaries, conflict raged across Eastern Europe. For Canadian immigrant communities, the farms and towns being destroyed were those they had left; the people being killed, displaced, and starved were their friends and relatives. People they had once lived with in relative harmony in their homelands, or as neighbours in Canada, they now saw as enemies.

Competing factions within immigrant communities fought to control newspapers and institutions. In 1919, the Ukrainian Social Democratic Party (USDP) founded the Ukrainian Farmer-Labour Temple Association, which quickly became a popular meeting place, and socialists began to infiltrate student residences, reading clubs, and national halls. Bishop Budka (now in favour with the authorities for providing information about socialists) began expanding Church-supported networks. Nationalist teachers and professionals established a set of non-denominational organizations and newspapers. On December 28, 1918, dissident Uniates and others held the first *sobor* of the Ukrainian Greek Orthodox Church of Canada. The new church would have married priests and orthodox rites, but would elect bishops and place the appointment of priests in the hands of congregations.[49]

These divisions came at a time when ethnic groups most needed unity. In December 1918, the Winnipeg-based Ukrainian Canadian Citizens' Committee (UCCC) brought together most of the Ukrainian organizations to launch a fund-raising campaign to send delegates to Paris — but the pro-Soviet USDP stayed out. On March 27, 1919, one of the Canadians sent by the UCCC, brought the chairman of the Ukrainian delegation in Paris to see Borden. He seemed "a capable, earnest man" Borden told Lloyd George, and added that Canadian Ukrainians "are much concerned to have the Ukraine recognized as an independent state." But despite representations from an Edmonton MP, he did not involve himself further. The Allies still hoped the White Russians would win and the French wanted a strong Poland as an ally against Germany. In the Treaty of Versailles, Poland absorbed not only Galicia but also Ukrainians in former Russian provinces. The Ukrainian Republic was crushed by the Bolsheviks, and Poland soon violated its pledge to respect the rights of its Ukrainian minority. Canadian Ukrainians held mass rallies and wrote petitions, and Canada raised the fate of Ukrainians in Poland at the League in 1921 and again in 1923. But the Ukrainians, and most other East European immigrants, could not overcome the increasing isolationism of Canadians, who were reluctant to involve themselves in events in a far-off corner of Europe that baffled even the Great Powers.[50]

Better times and a renewed demand for labour after 1923 brought the removal of immigration restrictions on "enemy countries" and Mennonites, though other "undesirables" continued to be barred. The Railways Agreement of 1925 allowed the railways to bring in "*bona fide* agriculturalists," and some 185,000 immigrants from Eastern Europe (most of whom were not farmers) entered under this scheme. The biggest inflow was some sixty-eight thousand Ukrainians (by 1941, Ukrainians were the fourth largest ethnic category in Canada) and over fifty thousand Poles (many of whom went on to the United States).[51]

Many of these new arrivals were more educated, nationalist, and politically involved than most of their predecessors. Some elements of the Ukrainian community drifted toward authoritarianism and nationalism, while the USDP and the Farmer-Labour Temple entered open alliance with the Communist Party. When Mussolini ended emigration from Italy in 1925, a vital link with the burgeoning Italian-Canadian community was broken. Political conflict in the old countries provoked divisions within communities in the new, which were often compounded by the propaganda and intelligence-gathering of their consulates.[52]

For "ethnic" Canadians, the Great War marked a turning point, when they came to understand that their place was in Canada, and that events in the old countries now had to take second place to securing acceptance and integration in the new. The mainstream Ukrainian community and its organizations, women's groups, and newspapers opposed extremists of left and right. What Anderson, Sisler, Woodsworth, Connor, and many others had predicted was beginning to work. The school, whether a small country school or the city high school with a stern but sympathetic principal like Sisler, was the means by which a Ukrainian boy like John C. Charyk could learn English and adapt to the ways of his new country.[53]

The process of adjustment was often painful, as young people became alienated from their parents and the old culture. Hungarian-Canadian John Marlyn, in his novel *Under the Ribs of Death,* describes the ordeal of a young boy in Winnipeg, fighting with Canadian boys, conscious of his poverty, ashamed of his parents and their boarders from the old country. In one scene, he describes recent arrivals from Hungary whom he and his

Glenbow Archives NA-2676-6

One-room schoolhouse, Bruderheim, Alberta, 1915
In such schools, farm children got education and immigrant kids became Canadians. Note the map, flags, and pictures of the royal family.

father have dressed up in their best clothes to meet. "They stood there, awkward and begrimed, the men in tight-fitting wrinkled clothes, with their wrists and ankles sticking out, unshaven and foreign-looking, the women in kerchiefs and voluminous skirts and men's shoes ... exactly the way his grandmother looked in that picture in the front room." But his parents, he realizes, have changed. "They used tinned goods sometimes at home now, and store-bought bread when they had enough money. English food was appearing on their table, the English language in their home. Slowly, very slowly, they were changing. They were becoming Canadians."[54]

Immigrants would face discrimination, hazing, and preferential hiring, and some would find the Canadian dream hollow once they had attained it. Girls would face the double challenge of adjusting to the new role of women in Canadian society while facing pressure to conform to old conventions in the name of national survival. Anglo-Canadians would slowly begin to understand and appreciate them — albeit with occasional outbursts of prejudice — and in the West the image of the "melting pot" would begin to replace that of a purely "British" Canada. Some elements of their ethnicity would survive and even find their way into the Canadian mainstream. But "melting" did not mean anything like multiculturalism.[55]

In 1918, Anderson quoted with approval a poem by a "young Ruthenian poet":

> And are you not, O Canada, our own?
> Nay, we are still but holders of thy soil,
> We have not bought by sacrifice and groan
> The right to boast the country where we toil.
>
> But Canada, in Liberty we work till death,
> Our children shall be free to call thee theirs,
> Their own dear land, where, gladly drawing breath,
> Their parents found safe graves, and left strong heirs.

In 1928, a poem by Illia Kiriak expressed similar sentiments, in Ukrainian.[56]

CHAPTER 12

Outsiders

Successive immigration orders and directives in the years after the war made it clear that most Canadians believed that their new nation should be composed of British, French, or at least Northern European "racial stock." They could accept, and eventually integrate, a certain number of Eastern and Southern European immigrants where there was a demonstrated need. But Jews were seen as a race apart, and would face a a widespread undercurrent of anti-Semitism. Chinese, Japanese, East Indians, and even Afro-Canadians who had lived here for generations, would always be defined by the colour of their skin. First Nations people might be romanticized by poets and writers — towns, streets, sports teams, and Boy Scout troops might be named after them — but under the 1876 Indian Act they were wards of the Crown, living on reserves, with no rights as citizens. The idealism engendered by the war encouraged these minorities to hope they might begin to be accepted into the mainstream of the new Canada. But the fears and prejudices it set loose made this considerably more difficult. The multi-racial Canada we know today was still far in the future.

I

On March 26, 1919, two months after Groulx's speech there, 209 delegates gathered at the Monument-National to found the Canadian Jewish Congress. Across the country, twenty-five thousand Jewish Canadians had voted. Twenty-five hundred came to Montreal as observers. Only radical socialists stayed away.

There were bands and children's choirs, streetcars with Jewish and Canadian flags, a reception at city hall, an address by a Cabinet minister, and fraternal greetings from Christian churches and Jews around the world. The congress demanded an open immigration policy and created the Jewish Immigrant Aid Society (JAIS). It elected clothing manufacturer Lyon Cohen as president and Labour Zionist Hannaniah Caiserman as general secretary. It adjourned with the singing of "O Canada" and the Socialist anthem.[1]

In 1919, there were 125,000 Jews in Canada. Every city had a small community, and there were a few farming settlements in Saskatchewan, but the vast majority lived in Montreal (fifty-five thousand), Toronto (thirty-five thousand), and Winnipeg (fifteen thousand), where they made up 7 percent of the population of each city. There had been Jews in Canada for generations, but the majority were recent immigrants from Eastern Europe — the latter being Yiddish-speaking and largely Orthodox. These newcomers settled along St. Urbain Street in Montreal, "The Ward" in Toronto, and Selkirk Street in Winnipeg's North End. Many worked at small trades, as merchants and peddlers, or in the (usually Jewish-owned) clothing industry. Sewing machines in small apartments hummed as wives and daughters did piecework, and workers in garment factories put in long hours at starvation wages. Some of the bitterest labour battles were fought in these "sweatshops."[2]

Benevolent societies, workmen's clubs, Yiddish book clubs, *shuls,* synagogues, libraries, and theatres expressed a rich cultural heritage and were the scenes of intense debates about religion, socialism, and the identity of Jews as a people. Zionism, Theodor Herzl's dream of a Jewish state that would make them respected among nations, had strong support among established Jews like department store owner Archie Freiman of Ottawa and his wife, Lillian, a tireless organizer who had founded Hadassah during the Great War. Many of the newer immigrants were Labour Zionists who believed that any Jewish homeland must be a model of socialist equality. Opposing both was the Workers' Association or Bund, which believed that Jews must build socialism in the communities in which they lived. Conservative rabbis condemned all these secular forms of Zionism — God would send the Messiah to redeem them when their time of exile was fulfilled.[3]

The war had a profound impact on these communities. Established Jews believed that Canada and the Empire had given them a haven of freedom. Five thousand Canadian Jews enlisted and 123 died. But many newer arrivals did not see Russia and Romania, whose persecution they had fled, as allies. Nor did they regard Germany, which had treated its Jews relatively well, or Austria, whose capital was the headquarters of Zionism, as their natural enemies. Regardless of where their affiliation lay, what was true for most was that their friends and relatives were becoming collateral damage — innocent victims of the guns and bombs of all sides in the Great War, and in the national and civil wars that followed it. Between 1914 and 1920 some 250,000 East European Jews died as conscripts and victims of German, Austrian, and Russian armies, White Russian Cossacks, Ukrainian and other nationalists, and Bolsheviks. While established Canadian Jews raised money for the Canadian Patriotic Fund and for Palestine, Labour Zionists in Montreal, Toronto, and Winnipeg formed a Canadian Jewish Alliance in 1915 to raise money for displaced Jews in Europe, and to bring Canadian Jews together in a more left-wing federation which would not be dominated by the older elites.

These differences were largely set aside in 1917 when the Russian Revolution overthrew the hated czarist regime and the British Balfour Declaration promised to promote a Jewish homeland in Palestine after the war. Seven thousand people rallied in support of the Balfour Declaration in Montreal and six thousand in Winnipeg, and visiting Zionist leader David Ben-Gurion recruited some three hundred Canadians to serve with the Jewish Legion being formed to fight with the British in the Middle East. Sam Jacobs was elected to Parliament as a Liberal, promising to work for a Jewish homeland, for increased Jewish immigration, and for a more democratic leadership of the Jewish-Canadian community.[4]

But for Jewish Canadians, the growing hostility to "foreigners" was compounded by anti-Semitism, not only in Quebec but in English Canada and among East European immigrant communities also. Anti-Semitic slurs were common in public discourse and everyone who read English literature knew the stereotypes of Shylock and Fagin. The Winnipeg General Strike was frequently blamed on Jews. The RCMP kept special records on Jews prominent in socialist and labour movements. In the 1920s, editorials in the Toronto *Telegram* asserted that Jews "engage in the wars of no country, but flit from one to another under passports changed with chameleon swiftness, following up the wind the smell of lucre. They are not the material out of which to shape a people holding a national spirit." Toronto Jewish parents complaining that their children should not have to sing Christian hymns were told by a school trustee that Canada was a Christian country and Jews "cannot be citizens of any country except their own — and that is Palestine." Ira MacKay, dean of arts at McGill, was an odious anti-Semite who openly proclaimed that "the Jewish people are of no use to us in this country" and that "as a race of men their traditions and practices do not fit in with a high civilization in a very new country."[5]

Jews were largely excluded from professional jobs, including hospital staff positions; and from resorts, clubs, and restaurants, where "Gentiles only" signs were not uncommon. Property owners often pledged not to sell to Jews — Mackenzie King paid above market price for properties adjoining his Kingsmere estate "to prevent Jews or other undesirable people from getting in." When it found that almost a quarter of its first-year class were Jews (including 40 percent of its medical school), McGill established quotas on Jews in arts, law, and medicine. At Toronto and Queen's, Jews were barred from fraternities. The University of Manitoba imposed some quotas on all "ethnics" in its medical school.[6]

Anti-Semitism was usually directed at Jews in the abstract rather than at individuals. Mackenzie King was a friend of Sam Jacobs. Archie Freiman had broad public support in Ottawa, and Lillian was well connected with political wives. City politicians courted the Jewish vote. Most people, and most other newspapers, found the extreme views of the *Telegram* distasteful, at least when uttered so openly — but discrimination, open or subtle, remained a fact of life for Jewish Canadians. Perhaps, some leaders thought, it was best to keep quiet and enjoy the relative freedom they had. Those who did fight back often found that confronting anti-Semitism was like wrestling with an octopus.[7]

Jewish Canadians were deeply and personally affected by postwar conditions in their former homelands. By 1920, three million Jews were reported to be starving in Eastern Europe, with orphans roaming the countryside "eating such edible wild roots and herbs as were left in a territory." "I have a sister-in-law with three orphans in Warsaw," ran a typical appeal to the JIAS. "Two children of that family have already died of hunger. When they come they will have a good home and will be well taken care of." Public appeals and dozens of meetings raised money for Jewish orphans. The JIAS worked with people on the ground to identify immigrants, fend off corrupt local officials, provide clothing, and organize transport and admission to Canada. Lillian Freiman embraced tattered, anxious, and exhausted Jewish arrivals in Halifax, repeating in her imperfect Yiddish: "*Nisht vein, nisht vein* [don't cry, don't cry]."[8]

Postwar immigration restrictions were designed to block the flow of just such refugees. People who had fled their homes could hardly be expected to have a passport or a ticket from their country of origin. Nor could they get visas in Eastern Europe once the Canadian government decided it would no longer allow British consuls to act on its behalf. Many immigration officers were obstructive and openly anti-Semitic, and new arrivals could be deported on the slightest pretext. In 1921, the JIAS responded to 1,788 cases of detention at the major eastern ports, of which 232 were deported, two died in detention, and twenty-two were further detained. Surely, Caiserman wrote the immigration minister in 1920, he had a right to "expect that the Christian nations of the world would apply the great principles of Christianity in saving an innocent people from annihilation." Mackenzie King, who depended on French-Canadian votes and the support of the Progressives, was no more help. "All our efforts during nearly a year and a half have gone for naught," Sam Jacobs complained to Conservative R.B. Bennett in 1925.[9]

Lillian Freiman tirelessly lobbied the wives of the prime minister and the deputy minister of immigration, with some success — 150 Jewish war orphans were admitted in 1920 (out of one thousand for whom requests were made) and permits for five thousand refugees from Romania were issued "on humanitarian grounds" in 1923. But only three thousand actually entered Canada (and many embarrassed the JIAS by moving on to the United States). When the Canadian Jewish Congress applied to use the remaining allotment to bring in Jews from other parts of Europe, Immigration refused, on the grounds that people who had left Russia with the consent of the authorities were not refugees. It is a tribute to the persistence of the JIAS and the Canadian Jewish community that in spite of restrictive measures and arbitrary enforcement, some four thousand Jews a year still managed to enter Canada between 1921 and 1931. The deputy minister of immigration complained to a parliamentary committee in 1928 that he was being subjected to a "constant hammering from one end of Canada to the other" to admit more Jews. Without the "hammering" things would have been far worse.[10]

This effort was also hampered by divisions within the Jewish-Canadian community — those from Toronto and those from Montreal, established Jews and newcomers — and the adherents to the various forms of Zionism, who sometimes differed widely in their beliefs. Some thought Jewish orphans should be sent to Palestine. Some believed they were better off in the socialist paradise of the Soviet Union. Some asked why funds were being sent to Palestine that could be used in Canada. "Big shots" were accused of favouring their friends. In 1927, criminal charges were brought against two JIAS officials for selling permits and mismanaging funds. The resources required for immigration battles robbed the Canadian Jewish Congress of leadership and energy. It did not meet again until the 1930s, and then under very different circumstances.[11]

The immediate priority for most Canadian Jews in the 1920s, as with other immigrant communities, was to shake off their memories of oppression and get ahead in the new country. As they prospered, many moved uptown. By the 1930s, new leaders like the Bronfmans were endowing hospitals, sports facilities, summer camps, charities, synagogues, and culture, and, with the aid of political leaders Sam Jacobs and Abe Heaps of Winnipeg, were revitalizing the CJC.

Above all, they wanted education for their children. In Montreal, where schools were controlled by Catholic and Protestant boards, Jews constituted 40 percent of Protestant enrolment by 1914. Some Protestants wanted to impose quotas, while Jewish parents demanded representation on the school board and the hiring of Jewish teachers. In the late 1920s, "downtowners," fought a bitter battle in the legislature and the courts for a separate Jewish school system, against opposition from the "uptowners," the Catholic Church, and the Protestant board. They lost, and for two generations Jews in Quebec continued to be "Protestants." In Toronto and Winnipeg, schools in heavily Jewish districts were more accommodating. In fact, Jewish Canadian children received excellent instruction from

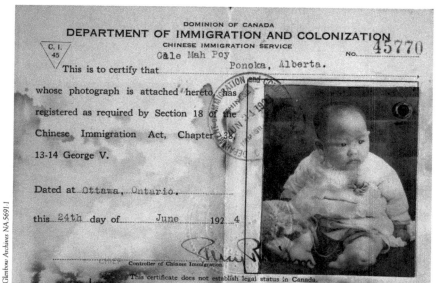

Chinese Canadian family, Cardston Alberta, 1920s

A Chinese-Canadian family is dressed in their best clothes for a portrait, blending old and new customs and dress. But as the card registering the birth of Gale Mah Poy shows, Chinese Canadians remained outsiders to the Canadian mainstream.

dedicated teachers in schools like Harbord Collegiate in Toronto, Baron Byng in Montreal, and St. John's in Winnipeg, and a Toronto study found that where they were 80 percent of the enrolment, they excelled academically.[12]

Twelve-year-old David Lewis arrived in Montreal in1922 from a *shtetl* in modern Belarus to join an uncle who owned a garment factory. The small flat was paradise and the city was huge after the small village. His hardworking father accepted wage labour by day and discussed Bundist politics at night. Inspired by excellent teachers, David mastered English by reading *The Old Curiosity Shop* with an English-Yiddish dictionary and moved through four grades in a year. By 1928, he was at McGill, excelling in academics, debating, co-founding a literary journal with his friend the poet A.M. Klein, and deeply engaged in socialist politics. In 1932, he was awarded a Rhodes Scholarship (at his interview, he told Sir Edward Beatty that as prime minister he would nationalize the CPR). Lewis, an architect of the CCF and leader of the NDP, was but one of many younger Jewish Canadians who, in spite of quotas and prejudice, would advance in future years to careers in the professions, labour unions, politics, business, the arts, and learning.[13]

But the short-term challenge remained daunting. In the Great Depression, anti-Semitism became more, not less, prevalent, and not only in Quebec. Jewish immigration stopped altogether in 1931. Refugees from Hitler's Germany were turned away, in spite of desperate efforts by socialist MP Abe Heaps, the CJC, and sympathetic Anglo-Canadians. "None is too many," was the mordant response when the deputy minister was asked how many Jews Canada should take. It would be several decades yet before Jewish Canadians could feel that they were fully accepted as part of the mainstream of Canadian life.[14]

II

J.S. Woodsworth was only repeating a belief common in the English-speaking world when he wrote in 1909 that Chinese, Japanese, and East Indians "cannot be assimilated." So was Sir Edmund Walker (who was considered sympathetic to Afro-Canadians) when he told a group of their leaders in 1916 that they were the "closest of all people to aboriginal man" and could not hope "to jump to the front in one or two or three generations." Few people believed the warning in Hilda Glynn-Ward's 1922 novel, *The Writing on the Wall*, that the Chinese and Japanese were plotting to make British Columbia an Oriental province, but no one seems to have questioned her sanity. Social reformers were as likely as white supremacists to associate gambling, opium dens, white-slave rings, disease, and filth with Chinatown, or to regard "coloured" men as a potential menace to white women. Racial epithets were frequently seen in print and heard in common speech.[15]

In actual fact, the percentage of these racial minorities in the Canadian population at the end of the war — less than 1 percent and shrinking — was the lowest it had been in a generation. There were eighteen thousand Afro-Canadians, where there had been twenty-two thousand at Confederation. There were just under forty thousand Chinese, thirty-seven thousand of them single men. There were about a thousand Sikhs, so few that one man recalled that in the 1920s he was the only Sikh kid in school and he knew of only three Sikh women in Vancouver. Only the Japanese community, at sixteen thousand, was growing, with a birth rate several times the Canadian average. But white British Columbians remembered that in 1911 one person in ten in the province had been of Asian origin, and few doubted there would be a flood if the gates were ever opened again.[16]

One-third of Afro-Canadians were descendants of Loyalists who lived on small farms in Nova Scotia or in poor urban communities like Africville in Halifax. Another third, descendants of fugitive slaves from the United States, lived on farms or in villages in southwestern Ontario. The remainder were scattered in cities and towns, in a few Prairie communities of recent immigrants (mostly from Oklahoma), and in Cape Breton, where West Indians had been brought in to work in the coal mines (most left after the war). The larger communities had distinctive cultural identities based on their American traditions, their determined and continuing drive for education and self-improvement, their African Methodist and Baptist churches, and their schools, newspapers, and community organizations.[17]

Chinese labourers had been recruited in two provinces near Hong Kong in the nineteenth century for mining and railway-building in British Columbia. They had expected to make money and go back to their families, but most never made enough. By 1920, 40 percent of Chinese Canadians lived east of the Rockies, where they dominated the restaurant and laundry trades in Prairie towns. In the large cities, they settled in Chinatowns, such as in Vancouver where the Sun Yat-sen Gardens are now, along Fan Tan Alley in Victoria, and in smaller ones in Toronto and Montreal. The Chinese Benevolent Association, local businessmen, agents, and a secret society, the CKT or Freemasons, managed relief, schools, and liaison with mainstream institutions — often competing fiercely for control of their communities and influence in the wider society.[18]

Japanese immigrants had come in a few large waves (six thousand in 1906–07 alone) from fishing and agricultural provinces (as well as some via Hawaii) to work in canning factories. Two-thirds had gone back, but those who stayed began sending for wives and families, including "picture brides." By 1919, they held half the fishing licenses in British Columbia; many more fished for canneries; and about a thousand Chinese and Japanese owned or leased twenty-seven thousand acres of the best farmland and supplied 90 percent of the fresh produce for the city markets of Vancouver.

The Sikhs also came from a small region and a few villages in India, also in a few waves, and also with the intention of making money and then going back. Most of those who stayed found employment in the forest industries or became small entrepreneurs. They were highly adaptable, and they had a network of organizations and entrepreneurs to find jobs and get settled. Most Japanese and Sikhs lived within forty miles of Vancouver.[19]

Most Canadians could accept, even welcome, small racial minorities within their communities, though there were strict rules regarding status and little interracial marriage. Canadians were proud of having been the terminus of the Underground Railroad. They believed their missionaries were bringing civilization to Africa and Asia. They shuddered at news of lynchings in the southern United States, or the race riots that tore Chicago and Washington D.C. apart in the summer of 1919. And they needed immigrant labour: the Chinese, said one B.C. woman, "are generally abused, yet everyone employs them."[20]

But it was a different story where large minority communities could be portrayed as threatening jobs, living standards, public health, or moral and racial purity. Labour unions were constantly complaining about cheap Asian labour. Victoria segregated its schools in 1922 so that Chinese boys would not "corrupt" white girls. Several provinces had laws forbidding Chinese restaurants or laundries from hiring white women. The Nova Scotia Education Act of 1918 allowed separate schools for Afro-Canadian children. In 1919, a court upheld the right of a Montreal theatre to require "coloured" people to sit in the balcony. "The management of a theatre may impose restrictions and make rules as to the place which each person should occupy during a representation," read the judgment. "Therefore, when a coloured man, bearer of a ticket of general admission, wants to take a seat in a part of the House which he knows is by a rule of the manager prohibited to a coloured person, he cannot complain if he is refused admission."[21]

The American experience, said a petition signed in 1911 by three thousand people in Alberta, showed "that negroes and whites cannot live in proximity without the occurrence of revolting lawlessness and the development of bitter race hatred." Why would anyone want to bring this problem to Canada, much less the "Yellow Peril" of Asia? "In the Orient, at our doors, there are eight hundred million Asiatics," said British Columbia MP H.H. Stevens "— and mark you I care not how high a value they place on their civilization — it is distinct in all its features from that which we hold dear. Eight hundred millions — the least tremor from that source would unquestionably swamp us by weight of numbers." British Columbia, Borden vowed in 1907, would be "a British and Canadian province, inhabited and dominated by men in whose veins runs the blood of those great pioneering races which built up and developed not only Western but Eastern Canada."[22]

British Columbia repeatedly enacted measures to limit the immigration of Asians and force them out of any niche they managed to occupy. British Columbia and Saskatchewan were allowed to disenfranchise Asians in 1908 (an action that also denied them the federal vote). In 1884, the Canadian government enacted a Chinese Head Tax — $10 initially, then $50 in 1885, $100 in 1900, and $500 by 1904 — which allowed railways to bring in labour but made it virtually impossible for Chinese men to send for their families. The immigration of Sikhs was shut off in 1908 by a requirement that they must have continuous passage from India (there were no direct passenger routes to Canada). Canadian immigration officers used every artifice to discourage African-American farmers from homesteading in the Canadian West, without actually banning them (African-Canadians, after all, could vote).[23]

In 1907, when a mob organized by the Asiatic Exclusion League rampaged through Vancouver's Chinese and Japanese districts, an investigation by Mackenzie King led to compensation for the Chinese and a "gentleman's agreement" with Japan limiting immigration to five hundred a year. Sikhs, however, were British subjects who could fight in the courts and appeal to Imperial authorities. But in 1914, the *Komagata Maru*, a ship chartered by an Indian businessman to bring Sikhs from Calcutta, was held by Canadian authorities in Vancouver harbour for six months. The Sikhs repulsed attempts to board or supply the ship, conditions deteriorated, a court rejected their case, the vessel was escorted out to sea by the fledgling Canadian navy, and all but a handful of the Sikhs returned to India.[24]

Yet in spite of all this, African, Chinese, and Japanese Canadians generally supported the war and many volunteered for service. "Justice has not been dealt us in every pursuit in life in Canada," wrote an African-Canadian editor in 1916. But if the war was being fought for Justice, then "in unity let us prove our worth to the country and the Empire. Let us show we stand for justice, and we really know what it means. If we work together our united efforts will count for something, and whatever position we gain will prove a lasting credit to the progress of our race."[25]

Although there were no formal restrictions on African-Canadian enlistment, many local commanders refused to accept them and the Chief of the Defence Staff reported that "the average white man will not associate with them on terms of equality." "This is not for you fellows," an officer told a group of fifty African-Canadians in Sydney, Nova Scotia, "this is a white man's war." By 1916 a military desperate for recruits was willing to put such reservations aside. Japanese men rejected by B.C. units enlisted in other provinces, and one intrepid Chinese-Canadian ranch hand from Kamloops rode on horseback to Calgary to sign up. Chinese Canadians were recruited as labourers (and in 1919 some labourers from China returning from the front escaped in Victoria and vanished into the local community). About a thousand African-Canadians joined combat units including the 106th Battalion. The No. 2 Construction Battalion (Coloured), recruited in Nova Scotia, went to France on a separate transport ship, then joined the Canadian Forestry Corps. The construction battalion performed valiantly under fire and several African-Canadian combat soldiers won decorations.[26]

Enlistment did little to improve the treatment of minority races in a country at war. Workers in British Columbia protested that Chinese and Japanese men were taking their jobs, until the war made jobs plentiful. There was a riot at the camp in Kinmel in January 1919 when an African-Canadian sergeant arrested a white man and placed him in the custody of a "coloured" escort. African-Canadian soldiers were airbrushed out of official histories. Japanese veterans sarcastically declared that they did not wish the vote if this would "have an evil influence or prejudice the welfare of the country for whose liberties we have fought." Veterans from minority races were eventually enfranchised, but the Dominion Elections Act of 1920, which gave women (including Quebec women) the vote in federal elections, specifically excluded those disenfranchised by a province "for reasons of race." When Wee Hoy Louie, one of the few Chinese Canadians who had served at the front, was refused a business licence in 1923 because of his race, he mailed his uniform and medals to Mackenzie King. The prime minister wrote a personal letter of apology and the licence was granted.[27]

After the war, measures were put in place to reduce Asian immigration to virtually nil. In December 1919, in response to Indian pressure at the Paris Peace Conference, Canada agreed to allow Indian officials to interview prospective family-class immigrants for final Canadian approval, and permitted Indians who had gone back to India to return to Canada within six years. But Mackenzie King resisted demands at subsequent Commonwealth conferences that he enfranchise Indians or open the door further, and fewer than five hundred Sikhs were admitted during the 1920s. The Japanese quota was lowered in 1920 to 150 a year. Then, in 1922, H.H. Stevens introduced a bill in Parliament to replace the hated Chinese Head Tax by a total ban on *all* Chinese immigration. Under the Chinese Immigration Act, only twenty-four Chinese would be legally admitted to Canada between July 1, 1923, and its repeal in 1947. During those years, Chinese Canadians would celebrate Dominion Day as "Humiliation Day," closing businesses and staying home.[28]

The 1920s saw thousands of individuals like Wee Hoy Louie and their families struggling to build lives, and small communities striving to define their identities, within a society that was usually indifferent and sometimes hostile. For thousands of single Chinese men dreaming of "tiles over one's head and soil under one's feet," life in Canada remained isolated and lonely. For Afro-Canadians like sixteen-year old Carrie Best, experiences like the race riot in New Glasgow, Nova Scotia, in 1919 were rare but unforgettable. Less rare was the summary rejection of her challenge two decades later to segregated seating in a local movie theatre, by a judge for whom her mother had worked as a domestic. Japanese Canadians could not vote, their participation in the B.C. fishery was restricted, and they were for the most part unable to enter the professions. As Japan became a Pacific power in the 1930s, and as the Japanese community in British Columbia became larger and more prosperous, much of the hostility previously directed at the Chinese was turned on them. After the Japanese attack on Pearl Harbor in 1941, they were expelled and their property was seized.[29]

At the same time, the war had decisively changed conditions in the homelands of Asian immigrants, who often still had wives and families there. Sikhs had not rushed to enlist, despite their martial past, because many were influenced by the *Gadr* society which advocated Indian independence. Half of them left after the war, many to perish in futile revolts in the Punjab. The Chinese Revolution of 1911, led by Sun Yat-sen, found resonance in Canada as well. Sun's party, the Kuomintang (KMT),* soon had branches across the country and became a bitter rival of the Freemasons as a benevolent society. The KMT was among the "foreign" organizations banned in 1918, but once the ban was lifted it held a national convention in late 1919 and established a central headquarters in Vancouver. Even African Canadians, though they were not recent immigrants, were nonetheless affected by events in the United States, where the National Association for the Advancement of Coloured People rejected the teaching of Booker T. Washington — get education, prove your worth, integrate into the society — in favour of a more militant assertion of identity and opposition to racism. (A similar Canadian association formed in 1924 had limited influence.)[30]

The war made these communities, like other immigrants, realize that, whatever obstacles they faced, they needed to find a way to make a future in Canada. Younger, Canadian-educated Chinese leaders led the fight against the 1923 immigration regulations and successfully challenged school segregation in Victoria. They began to work with Canadian authorities to stem

---

* Today spelled Guomindang.

the opium trade, and the enforcement of health and safety regulations began to make Chinatowns safer and more welcoming communities, which white Canadians began to enter. In dozens of cities and towns, Chinese-Canadian families put down roots, and Chinese restaurants became meeting places where, through the ritual of food, communities could begin to understand each other. Among Japanese-Canadians, the first-generation *Issei* clung to older customs but their Canadian-born children, the *Nisei*, spoke English, became Christian, adopted Canadian customs, including smaller, nuclear families, built prosperous businesses and expected to participate fully in Canadian society — which made their expulsion in 1942 the more unjust and tragic.[31]

Many Afro-Canadians joined the postwar migration to the cities. They found niche occupations as maids, cleaners, laundresses, waiters, janitors, barbers, and labourers. A prized job was working as a waiter or porter on passenger trains, which provided a decent income, travel, and independence within a work environment where a black man had a defined and respected role. Because the national railways were headquartered in Montreal, African Canadians, and immigrants from the United States and the West Indies, formed an urban enclave where the Bell Centre and Bonaventure Station are now. It, too, became a meeting place, one where white Canadians could begin to encounter jazz music and other elements of what until then had been an alien culture.[32]

And although prejudice on the part of the Canadian majority remained strong, the war brought the first faint stirrings of change, among churches, intellectuals, and politicians. Canadians, Woodsworth told the House of Commons in 1927, needed to "overcome the prejudices which we have against men of other races," and recognize that "there are many

Archives of Ontario F 1075.13 H1718

Japanese-Canadian kids in Vancouver, 1927

more things in common between the different races than things which separate us, and the apparent divergences are not so great as sometimes we
imagine." Influential Ontarians, including Sir Adam Beck, supported the
Canadian Association for the Advancement of Coloured People. There was
strong, if minority opposition, from the churches and CCF to the mistreat-
ment of Japanese Canadians in British Columbia. Carrie Best, like many
other members of minority communities, would persevere; she would become an important civil rights leader, and she would receive the Order of
Canada. In 1988, the Canadian government would apologize to Japanese
Canadians, and in 2006 it would apologize for the Chinese Head Tax.[33]

III

In August 1919, fifty thousand people at the Canadian National Exhibition in
Toronto cheered as the Prince of Wales pinned military decorations on Frank
Pegahmagabow, an Ojibwa from Parry Island Reserve. "Sturdy, well set up and
with soldierly brevity, he thanked his future sovereign," gushed a local newspaper. In an official account of the war, Duncan Campbell Scott, the poet who
was deputy minister of Indian Affairs, lauded the "unselfish loyalty, gallant-
ry, intelligence, resourcefulness, and efficiency displayed by Indians," which
would herald "an increasingly honourable and useful part in the history of a
country that was once the free and open hunting-ground of their forefathers."[34]

Thirty-five hundred First Nations men had gone to war — on some
reserves virtually all the young men had enlisted. Many had done so in
fulfillment of their treaty obligation to their ally, the king. They had served
in forestry, labour, and railway battalions; and in fighting units, where they
were especially valued as snipers. When Henry Norwest, a Métis from Saskatchewan, was killed in August 1918, his comrades wrote on his grave
marker, "It must have been a damned good sniper that got Norwest." Lieutenant Cameron Brant of the Six Nations was killed leading a charge at Second Ypres. Olympic runners Joe Keeper from Manitoba and Tom Longboat
of the Six Nations served as dispatch runners; Longboat was twice wounded
and Keeper won a Military Medal. Some three hundred were killed in action; many more fell victim to TB and other respiratory diseases.[35]

But once they got back to their reserves, the rhetoric counted for little. One Alberta Blood recalled his pride when his band celebrated his return with a Sun Dance. But another veteran was refused permission for a similar ceremony. "You have been forbidden to hold the Sun Dance," said an Indian Affairs official. "It's part of the Indian religion and it's no damn good." "I went to the war," replied the veteran. "I have fought for you and for all those who sat in this office during the war. I have the right to ask you to give us back our Sun Dance." Indian Affairs finally allowed the dance as long as no Indians attended from other reserves — they did anyway and the RCMP looked the other way.[36]

Unlike all other returning soldiers, the programs for Indian veterans were administered by the Indian Affairs Department. Under a 1919 amendment to the Indian Act, lands were set aside on reserves for resettlement of Indian soldiers, with loans secured on the properties of the reserve (whether the band agreed or not). But these loans were only for farmers — not very practical for the Mohawk in Muskoka who was refused a loan in 1920 for a wood-sawing machine. Access to veterans' doctors, hospitals, and other benefits required the consent of the Indian agent.[37]

Of the land acquired for other veterans by the Soldier Settlement Board, eighty-five thousand acres in the West was Indian* land — "far in excess of what they are utilizing now for productive purposes," said Interior Minister Arthur Meighen. Much of this land had been leased during the war to white farmers as part of a "Greater Production" scheme, under which First Nations had also grown food on reserves. Indian Affairs did block some proposed sales, and it held the million dollars from the sale in trust, but more Indian land was sold between March 1919 and March 1920 than during any other period.[38]

Frank Pegahmagabow returned to his reserve with physical injuries and mental trauma, and applied for a farm loan. His Indian agent vetoed the application. Frank, he said, could be a labourer, fire ranger, or guide, but he was "not very well balanced and does not make good at anything and I am afraid he will be the same in his farming venture." Pegahmagabow could indeed be outspoken and erratic, but his real crime was to demand respect. His frequent

---

* The term "Indian" is used in places in this chapter because it was the common, and legal, term at the time. Inuit were not covered by the Indian Act, and Metis were not recognized at all.

letters to politicians were routinely referred to Indian Affairs for non-action. When he was elected band chief, his Indian agent repeatedly blocked his proposals and eventually engineered his ouster. When he was finally able to get a disability pension, he could only get at this money through the Indian agent. Despite his treatment as a veteran, like so many other old soldiers, "Peggy" was only really in his element when he could meet old chums, dress up in uniform with his medals, and participate in militia exercises.[39]

In 1919, there were an estimated 110,000 status Indians, about thirty thousand Métis, and about three thousand Inuit. "Indians" comprised many nations and cultures. In the East, there were well-established reserves, including the Six Nations near Brantford, which had a history of interacting with the wider community, and could boast champion lacrosse teams and celebrities like poet Pauline Johnson and marathoner Tom Longboat. In the West, the Plains Indians, except for some successful ranchers in Alberta, were still struggling to adjust to a sedentary agrarian life. The British Columbia Coastal tribes had a long history of political and cultural sophistication, and they had built stable economies based on fishing and work in canning factories and forest industries. In the Rocky Mountains, the Shield, and the North, Indians still followed their traditional way of life. Further north, the Inuit had for years had contact with traders and whalers in the Arctic, as well as missionaries, scientists, and explorers. This contact was limited, however. In spite of claims by explorer Vihjalmur Stefansson that the Arctic was "friendly," and his appeals that Canadians should lead the "northward course of empire," Canada had done little to assert real control over the Far North and few Canadians ever ventured into the Arctic.[40]

Indians had once been essential trading partners and military allies of the rival imperial powers. Canadians believed, with some truth, that in contrast to the Americans they had been just and fair in their treatment of Indians. But few white Canadians saw the treaties as the Indians saw them — solemn pacts between nations to share the land. Instead, they saw them as tools to manage the Indians. Under the Indian Act, Indians were pushed onto reserves, their traditional governments were replaced by elected councils, and the Indian Affairs department controlled every aspect of their lives. Indians who were "educated and of good character" could become full citizens, but only if they gave up all their rights as Indians — there was no in-between. "If one were to deal with wards in the same way as he would deal with citizens," said Meighen, "he would not be dealing with wards at all." Only 250 Indians had been enfranchised by 1920.[41]

This treatment was justified by the widespread belief that aboriginal people represented an early stage of human evolutionary development — like the Indian described by Scott as "still wild as a lynx, with all the lore and instinct of his race undimmed." Historians like Wrong and Leacock depicted them as childlike, improvident, undisciplined "savages" who could never have possessed or developed the land. Scott's poems depict a noble race, well adapted to the wilderness but doomed to perish with its passing. A member of a royal commission used less poetic language to inform B.C. chiefs in 1913 that "a strong race had supplanted a weaker" and they would simply have to accept the inevitability of progress. "Culturally," wrote government anthropologist Diamond Jenness in the conclusion to his massive 1932 study, *The Indians of Canada*, "they have already contributed everything that was valuable for our own civilization beyond what knowledge we may still glean from their histories concerning man's ceaseless struggle to control his environment."[42]

Scott shaped Indian policy from 1913 to 1932. The son of a clergyman, an accomplished pianist and poet, he had aspired to be a doctor but had been forced instead to take a job in the Indian department. Unlike other men of letters, who used their Ottawa civil service jobs as sinecures, Scott climbed to the top of the bureaucratic ladder. There was, however, a permanent tension between the romantic poet who sought to protect the vanishing Indian, and the politically astute, class-conscious, sharp-elbowed administrator who treated all opposition as an attack on his authority. Late in life, Scott claimed that he was bound by "the law which I did not originate and which I never tried to amend in the direction of severity." But during his tenure, there were few

Duncan Campbell Scott

Library and Archives Canada C003187

Indian laws or policies which he did not originate or approve.[43]

Scott believed that Canada had the same duty to Christianize, civilize, and uplift its Indians that the Empire had toward all other "backward" races. But Indians were not some far-off subject people. They were integral to Canada's history, and would be part of its future. They must therefore be removed from their "savage" state, placed on reserves, protected from exploitation by the baser elements of Canadian society. Then they must be guided gradually through the stages of development until they could take their place as citizens in the Canadian commonwealth. The objective, as Scott told a parliamentary committee in 1920, was "to continue until there is not a single Indian in Canada that had not been absorbed into the body politic, and there is no Indian question, and no Indian Department."[44]

Given the wide gulf between how Indians and European Canadians saw themselves and each other, such policies were bound to produce pernicious results. No one beyond a handful of frontier missionaries and enlightened Indian agents even considered the possibility that traditional Indian culture might be able to adapt to modernity, much less that they should be consulted about it. "As well might the Christian or civilized parent allow his children to follow uncurbed the dictates of the blind promptings of their own unregenerate human nature and grow up the outcasts of society," said Indian Affairs official Hayter Reed, "as leave an ignorant savage to determine his own course for himself." "I have never heard one Indian even hint at conserving anything," wrote naturalist Jack Miner. "You cannot do anything for the Indians, nor have anything for the Indians, unless you control the Indians."[45]

Reserves became, in the words of Jenness, an "apartheid system" which enhanced Indians' dependence and encouraged others to treat them with contempt. Indian farmers could not borrow money, buy equipment, or sell their produce, except with permission from Indian Affairs. Their birth rate in the 1920s was double the Canadian average, but their death rate was four times and infant mortality more than twice the national average — indeed, in the 1920s the Indian population reached its lowest ebb. Instead of the "medicine chest" promised by treaty, they too often got inadequate care by missionaries and infrequent visits from doctors. Doctors, in turn, were frustrated by the traditional belief in dancing and spirits and the claim that the hospital was filled with ghosts. "If their diet was deficient," recalled Jenness, "their health poor, their housing unsatisfactory, it was the fault of the white man, they said, and the white man's government should set things right."[46]

The Sun Dance and the Thirst Dance of Western Indians were outlawed. Old Chief Thunderchild, who had been at Big Bear's side when the Western treaties were negotiated, wondered why the white man had "no respect for the religion that was given to us, when we respect the faith of other nations." To Scott, these ceremonies were only "senseless drumming and dancing." He refused to allow Indians to dance in costume at an early version of the Calgary Stampede, fearing that this would only exploit them and delay assimilation. Under political pressure, his department relented, and throughout the 1920s, Indians served as guides, story-tellers, and tourist attractions — with Indian agents constantly pleading for tighter restrictions. The RCMP finally contented themselves with ensuring that Sun Dances were orderly and that no liquor was consumed at them.[47]

The potlatches sacred to B.C. Coastal Indians were banned because, in the words of a Methodist missionary, "all the objects or advantages to be secured by good government, are frustrated by this very demoralizing custom." In 1922, potlatchers in Alert Bay were told they would go to jail unless their fellow villagers surrendered all their potlatch gear. "The scow came around from the cannery and put in at the village to pick up the big pile of masks and headdresses and belts and coppers — everything we had for potlatching," a young Kwakiutl recalled. "Our old people who watched the barge pull out from shore with their masks on it said: 'There is nothing left now. We might as well go home.' When we say 'go home,' it means to die." The government paid $145.50 for these treasured possessions, which were shipped to museums in Ottawa, Toronto, and New York.[48]

Nor would education be the pathway into the white man's world for Indians that it would be for "foreign" children. There were well-established schools on Eastern reserves, and Western chiefs demanded the schools they were promised by treaty. But Indian Affairs believed that the first duty of Indian schools was to "civilize" children, and the best way to do this was by taking them from their homes, suppressing their Indian identity, replacing "pagan superstition" with "moral laws," and transforming them — like the children in widely circulated "before and after" photographs — into men and women who could perform "useful" roles as craftsmen, farmers, and domestics. The best and cheapest means of doing this was to fund Christian mission schools with per capita grants. Residential, mission, and industrial schools were consolidated in 1923 into a system that by 1928 comprised eighty-three schools — over half run by the Catholics (Oblates), with a smaller number run by the Anglicans, the United Church, and the Presbyterians. An amendment to the Indian Act in 1920 made school attendance compulsory between ages seven and fifteen.[49]

Two generations later, the Canadian government, and several churches, would apologize for what happened in these residential schools. The worst atrocities would occur later in the history of residential schools, but even in the early 1920s there were reports of sexual abuse, bullying, overwork, and cruelty. Children used to gentle discipline and observational learning entered a world of strange ideas taught in a foreign tongue and enforced with corporal punishment. For more than half the day, boys worked in the fields and shops while girls did cleaning and cooking. In a myriad of ways, including in chapel, Indian children were taught that their old ways were sinful. "We believed it," recalled a student. "So we came out having different ideas and a different outlook on what we were about." Bad diet, overcrowding, and poor care produced an appalling death rate, especially from TB. During the 1918 influenza epidemic, the principal of the Red Deer Industrial School, after expressing his outrage at the lack of medical attention, informed the Department of Indian Affairs that the victims had been buried with proper economy, two in a grave. Dr. H.P. Bryce, in a 1922 booklet, *The Story of a National Crime,* accused Indian Affairs of "manslaughter on a vast scale." Many graduates went back to their reserves like returned soldiers, leaving a world they hated for another to which they no longer belonged. "I know I blamed my parents for putting me there because I felt they didn't want me. And I blamed the [S]isters and the [F]athers that they were trying to take something away from me," recalled one. "I felt I was beginning to have hate."[50]

In the early 1920s, many Indian children escaped this experience. There were day schools on or near many reservations, especially in Eastern Canada, and the system did not reach the Maritimes until 1928. Some children ran away or did not attend school at all. Some bands, like the Six Nations, the Anishinabeg at Shoal Lake, or the B.C. Coastal tribes, had enough power to ensure adequate conditions and have bad teachers removed. Indian children defied authority with the variety of subversive acts all schoolchildren excel in. Many retained positive memories of good schools that allowed visits from relatives and trips home, and dedicated Christian teachers who learned their language, founded youth clubs, and looked after their welfare. W.W. McLaren, principal of the Birtle School in Manitoba, believed that Indians were as important to Canada's future as "an equal number of Galicians, Jews, or any other race, and I felt that if we were to weld out of many peoples one truly Christian nation, the moral welfare of the Indian deserved the best I could give as much as any other race."[51]

Scott was confident that Indian soldiers coming back from the war, who had "witnessed the many wonders and advantages of civilization," would not want to return to the "weird and picturesque ceremonies of potlatches and Sun Dances and native languages." The time was ripe to encourage Indians who did not follow "the Indian mode of life" to apply for enfranchisement. Frustrated when a 1918 amendment to the Indian Act did not produce the desired result, Scott brought forward another amendment in 1920, which would allow Indian Affairs to initiate the process of enfranchisement without the consent of the individual, in cases where "continuance of wardship was no longer in the interests of the public or the Indians."[52]

As with so many other things, Scott completely misread the Indians. They had mingled with soldiers and other Indians from across Canada; they had been treated with respect; they had voted; they had taken responsibility. They had a new pride in their identity *and* a desire to be citizens of Canada. When the proposed amendments were greeted with a firestorm of opposition, the government referred them to a parliamentary committee. Scott did not inform the majority of bands, who in his judgement would be "opposed to the Bill or any Government measure, unless they saw some immediate profit, financial or otherwise, without any outlay on their part." But those who did appear left no doubt where they stood. If they were civilized enough to be enfranchised, asked the Six Nations, why were they not intelligent enough to be consulted about it? Why, asked the Allied Tribes of British Columbia, could Indians not be given citizenship while keeping their lands and status? The amendment passed in June 1920, but no one was enfranchised under its provisions, and in 1922 it was repealed by the King government.[53]

Scott could face down most opposition, like "Chief Thunderwater," whose Council of Indians had attracted support among the Iroquois during the war until he was exposed as an Afro-American from Cleveland. But he could not so easily brush aside Lieutenant Frederick Loft (Onondeyoh), an educated Mohawk from the Six Nations reserve. An Anglican and an active Liberal, Loft had a patronage appointment at the Ontario Asylum, and was married to a wealthy Toronto real estate broker.

Loft had helped with recruitment of Indians during the war, then lied about his age in 1917 (he was 55) to accept a commission in the Canadian Forestry Corps. His experience overseas convinced him that "Indians, from one end of the Dominion to the other, are sadly strangers to each other; we have not learned what it is to co-operate and work for each other as we should." By working together, they could free themselves "from the domination of officialdom and from being ever the prey and victims of unscrupulous means of depriving us of our lands and homes and even ... the rights we are entitled to as free men under the British flag." Loft toured reserves, organising the League of Indians of Canada, which held its first congress near Sault Ste. Marie in September 1919. Subsequent congresses were held in the West where the league gained strong support and attracted fifteen hundred people to its meeting in Alberta in 1922. Edward Ahenakew, an Anglican minister, was elected president for Western Canada.[54]

Canada, Department of National Defence/Library and Archives Canada PA007439

If Indian Affairs had shown the "sympathy, encouragement, and assistance" Loft pleaded for in his manifesto, history might have been different. But in late 1919, RCMP commissioner Perry warned that the league was causing "considerable unrest" in the West. Scott advised his minister to give Loft "a good snub." Loft was trying to live off his fellow Indians, Scott charged. He had "some education" and "an attractive personal appear-

F.O. Loft

ance," Scott allowed, but at the end of the day Loft was, Scott felt, "a shallow, talkative individual," who "looked very well in a uniform" and was "cunning enough to evade any active service, and I do not think his record in that regard is a very good one." (In fact, Loft was paying the bills of the league from his pocket, had the same level of education as Scott, and had been kept from the front because of his age — which was the same as Scott's.)[55]

Scott initiated the process of enfranchising Loft under the 1920 amendment. He instructed Indian agents not to permit any use of band funds for the league, and to use "pass laws" to prevent Western Indians from leaving their reserves to attend meetings. He asked the RCMP to investigate Loft's background (they found nothing subversive), ramped up his network of informers on reserves, and asked the police to infiltrate league meetings in 1920 and 1921. In 1926, Loft had to take his wife to Chicago for her health. When he returned in 1929, only the League of Western Indians, led by Ahenakew, had survived. In 1931, Loft abruptly resigned when the RCMP were preparing to prosecute him for raising money to take a legal challenge to the Judicial Committee of the Privy Council. The Western League collapsed when Ahenakew's bishop ordered him to cease his activities. Loft died in 1934.[56]

A different approach was taken by Deskaheh (Levi General), a Cayuga from the Six Nations reserve who wanted a return to traditional religion and government. He had opposed raising a Six Nations battalion except in response to a direct appeal from "their brother, Chief Ka-rah-kon-tye" (Governor General His Royal Highness Prince Arthur, the Duke of Connaught). He led the opposition to setting aside reserve land for veterans, as well as the 1920 amendment to the Indian Act. He then championed a petition to the governor general, demanding a judgment from the Supreme Court that the Six Nations was a sovereign nation and so was not governed by the Indian Act. When this claim was rejected by Canadian courts, Deskaheh took it to London, where he was rebuffed by the Colonial Office. Two years later, the Six Nations applied for Iroquois membership in the League of Nations. Though he spent a year in Geneva (funded by a Swiss NGO) and got a sympathetic hearing, British and Canadian diplomacy thwarted any attempt to put the matter on the League agenda.

Deskaheh's campaign was part of an ongoing struggle within the Six Nations between traditionalists like himself and modernists like Loft (who told Mackenzie King that the Iroquois were subjects of the Crown "in no degree differing from the acknowledged and accepted status of other Indians of Canada"). Chronic unrest on the reserve, culminating in an armed confrontation when the RCMP desecrated a burial ground while attempting to enforce Prohibition, led in 1923 to the appointment of a royal commission which *inter alia* recommended that the Six Nations Council be elected. Deskaheh lost his position as Iroquois spokesman and settled in New York State, where he was promoting the idea of a sovereign, cross-border Iroquois Confederacy when he died in 1925.[57]

A third source of postwar opposition was the Allied Tribes of British Columbia. The federal government had taken over responsibility for Indian Affairs when British Columbia joined Confederation in 1871, but only a handful of treaties were in place. For four decades, Indian Affairs tried to negotiate new treaties, establish reserves, and open land for settlement and railways, against the opposition of successive provincial governments to any recognition of aboriginal title. When the Grand Trunk Pacific crossed Indian lands in 1912, an Indian Rights Association was formed to demand that the courts adjudicate this question once and for all.

Indian Affairs and the provincial government agreed to establish a royal commission — not to consider aboriginal title, but only to determine the size, number, and location of reserves. In 1916, it recommended that 482 new reserves be created, consisting of 87,291 acres of relatively poor land, but the commission also recommended that 47,058 acres of good land be "cut off" from existing reserves, with the proceeds to be divided between the province and the federal government (in trust for Indians). The Coastal reserves were pitiably small (after all, fishing people did not need land!), reserves in the interior were moved away from settlement, and Indian Affairs consolidated its control over B.C. Indians.[58]

In 1919, the Allied Tribes united the various B.C. nations, rejected the royal commission report, and announced their intention to take the case to London. In 1920, the federal government responded with an act that authorized Indian Affairs to implement the commission's recommendations "notwithstanding any provisions of the Indian Act to the contrary." But in

1921 the Judicial Committee of the Privy Council, ruling on a totally different (Nigerian) case, found that aboriginal title was a pre-existing right that
could only be extinguished by agreement. A Canadian Order-in-Council was
issued in 1924 giving force to the commission's recommendations. The Allied
Tribes petitioned for a joint parliamentary committee in 1925, as a first step
to taking their case to London. In 1927, this committee recommended they
be given $100,000 in place of annuities, and that no further claims be accept-
ed. The government quickly enacted these measures, and then amended the
Indian Act to make it an offence for Indians or their representatives to solicit
funds to fight legal cases (this was the law Loft was accused of violating). The
Allied Tribes disbanded and the Depression halted further activity.[59]

Further to the north, a boom in the fur trade during the war and the
discovery of oil at Norman Wells had sparked interest in negotiating a new
treaty to open the North West Territories for resource development. As in
previous negotiations, commissioners travelled from one Dene village to
another, signing up bands and paying treaty money. Many Dene people
were reluctant to sign, but most hoped that, like the Prairie Indians half a
century earlier, they would retain some rights to their lands and preserve
their old way of life while being assisted in the transition to the new. Treaty
11, completed in July 1921, allowed Indians to pursue their traditional
activities until land was needed for development, but gave them no real
control over or profit from resource development.[60]

On February 5, 1919, news of the Armistice reached the Albany mission on James Bay; the news was followed a few days later by a service of
thanksgiving. The church was "decorated with all the Flags available & it
looked quite National, nearly everyone was present." More than four years
before, men had paddled and walked for days to enlist in a war far across
the ocean. A few had become heroes; others would never again see the forests and lakes of their homeland. For most Canadian Indians, the war had
brought only a lost opportunity. "The Native people talked about going to
war for their children and their future," recalled the son of a veteran from
Attawapiskat. "I have never seen my father bring anything back or get those
things that he was promised."

Indian Affairs redoubled its commitment to policies that were clearly
not working. An "atmosphere of mingled apathy and discontent settled

on the reserves," recalled Jenness, "and it was the apathy that dominated." Meanwhile, the public rested content in the illusion that Indians, as portrayed in the poetry of Scott, the histories of Wrong, the paintings and pageants, the anthropological studies chronicling a vanishing culture, were being gently led into civilization.[61]

But the war *had* produced recognition of their contribution to the war effort, an alternative vision and leadership that would inspire future First Nations activists, and a few authentic Native voices. Edward Ahenakew was educated in a mission school, ordained as an Anglican minister in 1910, travelled as a missionary by canoe and dogsled to remote communities, and published a monthly magazine in Cree. After influenza ravaged his people, he studied medicine for three years until his health collapsed. Recovering at the camp of Chief Thunderchild from 1921 to 1923, Akenahew faithfully recorded the sayings of the old wise man. He also created fictional stories of "Old Keyam," which in Cree means "what does it matter?" Keyam is a man who "tried to fit himself to the new ways; he had thought that he would conquer; and he was defeated instead." Through this character, Akenahew expressed the anguish of First Nations people struggling to adapt to the modern world, not by becoming white people but by seeking "in our changed conditions to attain the same proficiency that our fathers showed in their day and in their lives." And he also expressed their sense of loss. "The sun has set upon those days, but the heart of our nation still mourns for them, still weeps behind the closed door-flaps of the tepee. The council fires have gone out, the voice of the Indian is not heard, the ploughshare of the settler has long since turned the over-grown paths that the buffalos followed."[62]

CHAPTER 13

Return to Normalcy?

Tens of thousands of silent mourners lined the route on February 22, 1919, as the hearse passed through the snowy streets of Ottawa. "No measure of national respect that could be offered was lacking in the State funeral which was accorded the dead leader," reported the *Canadian Annual Review*. Forty-five thousand people had filed slowly past the catafalque in the great hall of the Victoria Museum, the temporary home of Parliament since the 1916 fire. In debates in the House of Commons, dozens of members from all parties had paid tribute to his legacy. Condolences had poured in from across the country, from the leaders of the Empire, and from the king. A requiem Mass had been said by the papal legate. Businessmen had begun to raise $30,000 for a monument in Notre Dame Cemetery.[1]

All this was not for some hero of the Great War, but for Sir Wilfrid Laurier, who months before had been deserted by much of his party and vilified in English Canada. Yet the memory of his leadership in the golden days of the Great Boom, his "attractive and magnetic" character, his eloquence in both languages, the way he seemed to personify what Canada could be, made him even now a revered figure — a man who three months before his death could still inspire young Liberals with his message that "faith is better than doubt and love is better than hate." He had been a member of Parliament since just after Confederation and his passing marked the end of an era. Borden in Paris expressed his "great shock" at the death of a political opponent with whom he had always felt a personal bond. Former followers who had become adversaries, like White, Rowell, Bourassa, Willison, and Sifton, were unstinting in their respect. Arthur Meighen (who could have benefited from Laurier's skill in managing people) took his nine-year-old daughter with him when he paid his respects. "You're too young to understand," he told her, "but I want you to be able to say that you saw one of the finest men I have ever known."[2]

Borden was also a weary man. "I should be very happy to return to Canada," he wrote in his diary as he boarded his ship for home in May 1919, "were it not for politics." Like many people in his country, he was torn between a desire to complete his task, to ensure that the world that emerged from the war would fulfill the dreams for which it had been fought, and a growing longing for peace after the great struggle, rest

Mackenzie King and Sir Wilfrid Laurier (1910)
The universe as Mackenzie King wanted it to unfold, and as, eventually, it did. This picture was likely taken on King's camera. The "Young Protégé" prepares to don the mantle of the "Old Leader," his political father-figure – who does not look entirely comfortable with the idea.

after superhuman exertion, respite from political conflict and social upheaval, a return to something like a normal life.[3]

I

Borden had known even as the war was ending that if his Union coalition were to survive and manage successfully the many challenges before it, he would have to weld his team of rivals into a united political party. With one of the strongest Cabinets in Canadian history, he could afford to be absent in Paris with three of his top ministers, while White, Meighen, Rowell, Calder, and others implemented his ambitious agenda at home. With their leader dead and their party in disarray, the Liberals provided weak and inconsistent opposition. But they still controlled Quebec and they were slowly beginning to revive in the rest of the country. Some Conservative ministers resented the prominent positions given to Unionist Liberals, and Robert Rogers was gathering support among the rank and file for reviving the old Conservative machine and the politics of patronage. Crerar and some Western members were all but out the door. Unionist Liberals were considering their options if the coalition broke down.

Borden had shouldered a killing workload all through the war, managing with a small staff and a few colleagues a stunning range of issues, events, and people. With his focus on winning the war at any cost, and faced with an array of seemingly intractable problems, it was difficult for him to tolerate bickering, selfishness, or pettiness, much less to concern himself about the long-term future of his party. He had departed for Europe with a certain sense of relief. He was in his element in Paris, hobnobbing with great men, remaking the world, being treated with the respect he and his country deserved.[4]

But if there were to be a Union party, Borden's leadership was essential. The alternative, as Meighen had written him in December 1918, was for the coalition to remain "a government at large, the sport of every sniper, of every liar and of every disappointed partisan." The longer Borden stayed in Paris, the more urgent became the pleas from his Cabinet, and the demands from the opposition, that he come home and take command — and the more impatient he became with them. "If Parliament reaches the conclusion that Union Government has served its purpose and should no longer be continued," he bluntly, and unfairly, told them, "I do not know that any of us have the right to complain."[5]

When Borden finally returned to Canada in May 1919, he found himself confronting the Winnipeg General Strike, the railway question, galloping inflation, social unrest, and soldiers' resettlement and pensions; he also had to deal with the creation of the Department of Health and the Bureau of Commerce, try to manage the ratification of the Treaty of Versailles, and secure support for Canada's role in the Empire and the League of Nations. On top of all of that, there was the management of a seemingly endless list of reconstruction measures from housing to highways, trade to technical education, science to immigration. His immediate priority was to shore up his agrarian wing, with or without Crerar, and he did at least succeed in keeping Calder and some other Western Unionists in the fold. White was finally allowed to retire and was replaced at Finance by Sir Henry Drayton. Simon Tolmie, a Liberal Unionist from British Columbia, was brought into Cabinet, and some other ministers were shuffled. The coalition continued, resolutely and competently, to address the many problems of the postwar.[6]

In June, Borden made his most concerted attempt to create a Union party, one with a platform that would recognize the legitimate aspirations of labour, repeal the "repressive and restrictive measures necessitated under war conditions," adopt a fiscal policy to develop Canadian resources, promote industries, control profits, and harmonize the conflicting regional interests, and develop "constitutional relations within the Empire." Such a party would need to attract conservative Quebeckers as well as win back the West. In July, Borden, with Drayton and Foster, took a "vacation" cruise down the St. Lawrence. He and Drayton played golf at Murray Bay with retiring Quebec premier Sir Lomer Gouin, with U.S. ex-President Taft making up the foursome. He visited Ernest Lapointe and other religious, political, and financial leaders. The message he got was clear. No credible Quebecker would join any Union government unless some dramatic concession were made, like restoring French-language schools in Ontario — which Ontario premier Hearst quickly made clear was not going to happen. At the same time, Rowell was receiving a similar message in the West — nothing a government controlled by Eastern business interests could offer would placate even moderate agrarians. And everyone was waiting to see what would happen at the Liberal convention in August that would elect a successor to Laurier.[7]

At this point, Borden seemed to recognize that building a new party was more than he was physically or temperamentally prepared to undertake. In August, he accompanied the Prince of Wales through the Maritimes and Quebec. September was taken up with the special session of Parliament to ratify the Treaty of Versailles (in the middle of which Borden was felled by an attack of grippe). It was not until October 1919 that Borden once again met his caucus to review the policy of the government and plan for the future. Several senior ministers wanted to follow White into retirement. Liberal Unionists saw the window closing on their future. Borden realized that he was "very tired." He went on a holiday in the United States. His ministers simultaneously urged him to rest and peppered him with messages. Borden returned to Ottawa in November, long enough to again shuffle his Cabinet so that more ministers could retire, and then his doctors (to his own evident relief) told him that he too must retire.[8]

If he had, the Union party might have had a chance. But as his coalition began to lose members, cohesion, and direction, his colleagues were convinced that Borden was the only one who could hold it together. They proposed that he "retain the Premiership and take a vacation of a year," and Borden unwisely accepted. In December, he set out on a tour that included visiting Havana, travelling to England with Lord Jellicoe, and visiting his old friends from the Paris Peace Conference, then vacationing with his wife in North Carolina. Acting Prime Minister Foster, aging and with his wife near death, now had to take charge of a Cabinet "launched on a troubled sea without a chart, compass or captain." Rowell signalled his intention to retire whenever Borden did. Wherever he could be reached, Borden was pestered with requests for urgent advice.[9]

Borden arrived back in Ottawa in May 1920, assisted Drayton with his budget (which continued wartime taxes in the face of the daunting war debt), and completed the work of dismantling the autocratic wartime powers his government had wielded. The War Measures Act had been allowed to lapse at the end of 1919. A general amnesty had been proclaimed for those who had avoided conscription. In March 1920, the government introduced the Dominion Franchise Act, which was extensively studied in a parliamentary committee. A number of Opposition amendments were accepted. The final act, which came into force on July 1, 1920, not only undid the electoral rigging of 1917, but gave the franchise to most Canadians, created a chief electoral officer, and provided for standardized voters' lists and polling practices. Then, in June, after further medical advice, he told the caucus that he was through. After renaming itself the National Liberal and Conservative Party, and passing resolutions endorsing the policies of the Union government, the caucus asked Borden to select his successor after consultation with MPs, ministers, and "prominent Canadians."[10]

There were really only two candidates. Sir Thomas White was "the most capable Minister of Finance the Dominion has seen since Confederation, and he was as disinterested as he was able," wrote Willison. White had many friends and the confidence of the business community and the Cabinet. Arthur Meighen was a Scots-Irish Ontarian who had studied mathematics at the University of Toronto when Mackenzie King was taking a degree in political economy, and had then moved to Manitoba where he became a prominent lawyer. He had a brilliant mind, an exceptional ability to argue a brief, an immense capacity for work; and he had managed almost every major domestic file since 1917. He had the support of the back bench.

Meighen, thought Flavelle, was

> clever, destructive in debate, crushing in criticism, but there it ends. No one possessed of such qualities can command heart loyalty.... He is by qualification intended for first lieutenant, in place of commander-in-chief. He should be the fighting mate of a big, simple, human man, who would win the affection and command the respect of his party. He is the terrier who worries the other fellow, the auditor who discovers mistakes in the man of constructive imagination.[11]

But White's wartime ordeal as finance minister and his stint as acting prime minister had cured him of any desire for the top job, even when Flavelle offered to raise a private endowment to make him financially secure. Borden presented White's name to the governor general so he could

then urge the caucus to rally behind Meighen when White turned it down. On July 10, 1920, Meighen — now publicly revealed as Borden's second choice — became prime minister, with the daunting task of building from a disintegrating coalition a party he could lead into battle, while confronting a hostile Quebec and the emerging Progressives, and dealing with an economy slipping into recession.

"So ended for the time being my public life of twenty-four years," Borden

Arthur Meighen

wrote in his memoirs, "during which, doubtless, I had made many mistakes but in which I had always striven to do my duty as God gave me to see it." Borden quietly assumed the mantle of elder statesman, a stolid, proud man, who had led his country through the severest trial of its history. His achievement was impressive by any measure, as were the accomplishments of his postwar government, even without his presence. But his Union coalition had smashed the old party system and it effectively ended with his retirement.[12]

II

Mackenzie King learned of Laurier's death on a lecture trip in Ohio. Catching the first train home, he stopped off in Toronto to consult political friends, then headed back to Ottawa. "This begins a new chapter in my life," he wrote in his diary, "a chapter of great responsibilities & I believe great opportunities. Had Sir Wilfrid lived there is no question that his guiding hand would have secured me the leadership of the Liberal Party at the Convention in June. In his death I lose a political father as well as a great leader."[13]

A month earlier, he had written in his diary that 1919 would be "a year of momentous decisions so far as my own life is concerned, a year of momentous decisions in the history of the world." He had been a high-flying deputy minister and Cabinet minister under Laurier. During the war, he had won an international reputation for his labour relations work with the Rockefellers. As a consultant for some of the largest American corporations, he had thoroughly delved into the details of management, investigated conditions in the workplace, and skilfully brought the parties together to find solutions. All this time he had kept his residence in Canada, had been part of a Liberal policy team, and had been one of the few prominent English-speaking Liberals willing to run (unsuccessfully) as a Laurier Liberal in the 1917 election.[14]

The Mackenzie King contemporaries saw in 1919 was not the stodgy, unpleasant man he became during his long years in power, nor the "mother's boy in the lonely room" of the Dennis Lee poem, "with his dog, his medium and his ruins." King at forty-five was a sociable, religious man who loved dancing, horseback riding, swimming, walking, and his country estate — not everyone's cup of tea perhaps, but a man with influential friends in three countries, an income of over $22,000 (over $300,000 today), and bright prospects ahead of him. He could take a full-time position with the Rockefellers at $30,000 a year, providing advice and influencing the spending of millions of dollars. He could become the director of the Carnegie Foundation at $25,000 a year (with $100,000 more if he wrote Carnegie's biography), overseeing the disbursement of the income from a $150 million endowment, with the opportunity "to meet the best people of the world, to be in touch in a commanding way with the affairs of the world on the subjects which I have most at heart, industrial peace, international peace, social well-being." But he concluded that he would "rather serve my own country than any other land…. My desire, my inclination, is all for politics."[15]

King published the results of his work for the Rockefellers in late 1918 in a five-hundred-page tome called *Industry and Humanity*, which sold ten thousand copies in its first four editions in Canada. King's book, like so many others, was a study in historical evolution, tracing the growth of big industry and big labour and the resulting need for the modern state to control their relations. But he went further, borrowing his terms from Louis Pasteur, to develop socio-historical "laws" of "Peace, Work and Health," and "Blood and Death." Modern states had mobilized industrial power and vast populations for war, he argued; now all elements of human activity "must substitute Faith for Fear" and be grounded in "a belief in an underlying order which presupposes between individuals, not conflict, but [a] community of interest in all that pertains to human well-being." King believed his book was a major contribution not only to industrial relations but to a new social order "at a crisis in the world's affairs when it is most needed and most likely to be of real & enduring service."[16]

Before his death, Laurier had worked to draw Liberals who had supported conscription but not joined the government back into the party. The most prominent of these was W.S. Fielding, a seventy-year-old former premier of Nova Scotia who had been finance minister from 1896 to 1911 and the author of Reciprocity. Laurier had announced his intention to retire, and a convention was scheduled for June to draft a platform and elect a new leader — a first in Canadian political history. When he died, the caucus rescheduled the convention for August and chose a dour Nova Scotian named Daniel D. Mackenzie as interim leader.

Mackenzie proclaimed that there was a light in the window for other Liberals who wished to come back. But how many would? The federal party in the West had been shattered by conscription and the agrarian revolt. The Ontario party was split among Rowell's Unionists, Laurier loyalists, and those, like Drury, who had gone to the United Farmers. In Quebec, a reformist wing led by Ernest Lapointe was challenging the high-tariff, pro-business Gouin-Taschereau machine. Many Liberals would not welcome back people they believed had betrayed their leader, and many former Liberals would never again embrace a party that in their view had let the country down in its hour of greatest need.

When King got back to Ottawa, he was unpleasantly surprised to find that he was not being asked to be a pall-bearer at Laurier's funeral, and that Laurier, according to his widow, had preferred that Fielding succeed him. Undaunted, King quietly lined up his support, negotiated the termination of his work for the Rockefellers, and put himself in the public eye with speeches on "The Four Parties to Industry" in the major Eastern cities.

Then, astonishingly, he kept his remaining commitment to the Rockefellers, to examine labour conditions in Britain. Between May 15 and July 20, he met a wide range of political contacts in England and studied Whitley Councils. He visited battlefields in France, talked with General Currie (whom he fawningly admired), and reflected on the Christ-like sacrifice of those who "in His name have left all to take up their cross and follow after Him, that mankind might be saved." He was visiting British social reformer Violet Markham at her country home when church bells announced the signing of the Treaty of Versailles. The two friends "spoke of the new consecration which one so keenly felt to the cause of peace and righteousness throughout the world." He was so completely out of touch that if his secretary had not booked him on an earlier ship than planned he would have been late for the convention.[17]

Once home, King continued his strategy of appearing indifferent, still waiting to see how the convention would shape up. The Liberals had decided that there would be no campaigning at the convention. But there would be debates on policy resolutions on the tariff (moderate protection with preference to Britain and a nod to Reciprocity, duty-free farm equipment and other machinery for primary production); autonomy (no centralized Imperial control, any change in Canada's status to be approved by Parliament); and labour and industry (a radical blueprint for social security and labour reform). As chair of the labour and industry committee, King could address the convention, and he brilliantly used the opportunity to burnish his credentials as a social reformer and bring the delegates to their feet with a paean to Laurier. His progressive ideas, his professed belief in lower tariffs, his position on Canadian autonomy, and, above all, his loyalty to Laurier, won him the support of Lapointe and his Quebec delegates. After winning a narrow victory over Fielding on the fifth ballot on August 7, 1919, he recorded: "it is right, it is the call of duty. I have sought nothing, it has come. It has come from God.... It is to His work I am called, and to it I dedicate my life."[18]

"The people want clean & honest govt., ideals in politics, a larger measure of Social Reform," wrote King as he began his life as Liberal leader. "I am unknown to the people as yet, but they will soon know & will recognize. The Liberal Party will yet rejoice in its entirety at the confidence they have placed in me." In the short term, the prospects of this did not seem bright. Gouin and Fielding saw no need to defer to him. He needed the old party bosses and business support more than they needed him. Lapointe and his followers would have to be kept happy, loyal, and patient. King would also have to woo the moderate agrarian leaders, or at least avoid conflict with them. He had to resist the hard-liners who wanted to purge the party of all who had not remained loyal to Laurier. And he had to seek a seat in Parliament. He decided to choose a P.E.I. riding to avoid offense to any regional blocs.[19]

Flavelle (who had actually read and admired King's book) was as critical of King as he had been of Meighen. "He is clever, he has many high ideals, he works hard; but, generally speaking, for one reason or another, men do not trust his judgment, and perhaps some of them do not trust his disinterestedness, not in the sense that he is dishonest or dishonourable, but that he is so self-centred that he is unable to lose himself, and all his actions are more or less coloured by the limitations imposed in men possessed of an over supply of self-consciousness." In his first parliamentary session, in 1920, King performed badly; he was outshone by his older rivals, and showed his insecurity by responding to criticism of his war record with speeches extolling his wartime contribution in industrial relations and social peace. Meighen delighted in sneering at his "demagogic platitudes" on the duty of members to the people, which "I venture in all humility to suggest every hon. member of this House was thoroughly aware of, thoroughly conscious of, long before the House received this rather nauseating reminder from the hon. gentleman."[20]

In the second half of 1920, these two new leaders (with Crerar emerging as a third) began to recreate their parties. King and Meighen had detested each other since university. They were shaped by opposing elements of their Presbyterian heritage. Each believed he was chosen by God for greatness, and that hard work, rectitude, and service were virtues in themselves. Meighen would never have invoked Christ the way King did constantly in his diaries. His was an intellect sharpened to a point, unstinting in its pursuit of truth, and fearless in his defence of the social and political order against greedy and unscrupulous people who would disrupt it. King was an intuitive thinker, whose belief that he was guided from the spirit world allowed him to claim support for his instincts — and also helped to justify his hypocrisy and cunning. King relished Violet Markham's characterization of him as a "Knight of the Holy Spirit," fighting for the little man against the big interests, bringing harmony where there had been conflict. He understood the complexity of Canada, appreciated power and how to use it, and knew that people were emotional as well as rational beings and that politics was not a courtroom.

Meighen staked his party's future on returning to its Conservative base. He believed he could persuade people across the country to return not "to old conditions but to old time sanity of thought and action, to get back to our old high standards of living and character — standards handed down to us by our forebears." Canadians, he argued repeatedly, had "been living for the last six years in a highly abnormal and artificial age, and the sooner we get to normal conditions the better it will be for all of us." It was time to stop "mentally chasing rainbows, striving for the unattainable"; time for people to get ahead "in the old fashioned way by hard honest intelligent effort"; time to bring an end to "dangerous doctrines taught by dangerous men, enemies of the State" which "poison and pollute the air."[21]

But he carried immense baggage, which he would not repudiate. He had been the author of conscription — "I did it because I thought it was right." He had been the champion of railway nationalization — that, too, was right, he believed, whatever the Montreal interests might say. His position at the Imperial Conference of 1921 was also right, even if it outraged old-time Tories. King, on the other hand, kept Gouin and his business constituency in the fold by advocating a "tariff for revenue," and he had the field to himself as the champion of labour against the man who had crushed the Winnipeg General Strike, and of farmers against this renegade Westerner and his high-tariff cronies.

Meighen decided to call an election in the fall of 1921. "If I can get the people of this country to see that the issue is Protection or no Protection, the battle will be won," he proclaimed. He attacked the Progressives as a "class" party, called their tariff policy "madness," accused radical labour of "Bolshevism," and promised farmers a "voluntary" wheat board. King dodged all these issues and, even when three-cornered contests threatened Liberal victories, kept the lines open to Crerar and Drury to ensure they would direct their fire at Meighen. The slogan *"Écrasons Meighen, c'est le temps"* summed up the attitude of most French Canadians. King ended his campaign with a call for an administration "prepared to avoid the extremes of reaction and radicalism," committed to "that co-operation between citizens of all occupations and callings which is necessary not less to a due consideration of particular needs than to the advancing of interests held in common, and which, moreover, is an absolute essential of national unity."[22]

The election of December 6, 1921, was a landmark in Canadian political history. Under the supervision of Chief Electoral Officer Oliver Mowat Biggar and seventy-five thousand quickly trained election officials, it was smooth, efficient, and fair. The electorate was the largest ever. The Liberals, with 118 seats, had risen from the dead as a national party, winning seats in every province but Alberta, but they failed to win a majority. The Conservatives won only fifty seats and were shut out in Quebec, Prince Edward Island, Nova Scotia, and the three Prairie provinces, and Meighen lost his own seat. The Progressives won sixty-four ridings, with seats in British Columbia, the Prairie provinces, and Ontario, as well as one in New Brunswick. J.S. Woodsworth and William Irvine were elected as Independent Labour candidates.[23]

In forming his government, King wrote his brother, his long-term objective was "not a coalition, but a coalescence of Liberal and Progressive forces" into "a new, strong, vigorous, united, solid Liberal Party, representative of the will and the wish of the great body of the people." After weeks of negotiations, King got a commitment from the Progressives — fatal to them as it turned out — that they would not form the Official Opposition and would support the government when they agreed with its policies. Fielding was given Finance and Lapointe stood aside in favour of Gouin at Justice. King kept External Affairs and Privy Council for himself. W.R. Motherwell and Charles Stewart (the former premier of Alberta) were the key Western figures.[24]

Slowly and patiently, King worked to strengthen his hold on his government. He defused Maritime discontent by satisfying some of their demands, and began discussions with the Western premiers on giving their provinces control over natural resources. He lowered tariffs somewhat, arguing that high American tariffs made it impossible for him to do more. By 1924 he had sidelined Gouin and Fielding, Lapointe was becoming his trusted Quebec lieutenant, and he was picking up support among ex-Progressives. But the economy was in recession and he had done little about the social programs promised in the 1919 Liberal platform.

Meighen's relentless attacks, and a reviving conservative mood as prosperity returned, reinvigorated his party, and the Progressives remained as a third force. In the 1925 election, the Conservatives secured 116 seats, the Liberals 104, the Progressives twenty-four, the remaining seats being occupied by three Labour members and a couple of independents.[25]

Mackenzie King might have been a one-term prime minister but for a series of events that can only be briefly recounted here. With his faith that the Progressives and Labour were really "Liberals in a hurry," King decided to carry on as a minority government with their support (in return for enacting old age pensions). A year later, the Customs Scandal* led to his defeat, and King asked Governor General Lord Byng (who had

---

* See Chapter 6.

commanded the Canadian Corps at Vimy) for a dissolution. Instead, Byng asked Meighen to form a government, which soon fell. In the election that followed, King won a smashing majority by decrying Byng's actions as Imperial interference in Canadian affairs. It would be King, not Meighen, who would preside over the 1927 Diamond Jubilee, and — after a time in the wilderness during the worst of the Depression — it would be King who would lead the country out of Depression and into World War II. In the days of victory following the war, it would be King who would begin the process of creating a modern welfare state.

Politics at the federal level had returned to something like "normalcy," with two major parties bringing together different regions and interests in broad coalitions to compete for power. But there had also emerged a permanent third force, a "Ginger Group" of radical agrarians and socialists that would in the 1930s form the base of the CCF and later the NDP. Provinces were now more powerful economic players, having control over their natural resources (except for the three Prairie provinces until the 1930s), and being the front-line providers of social programs. A new generation of leaders had emerged, shaped by the war and conscious of the need to heal and unite the nation. Perhaps most important, democracy itself had been revived. A wartime coalition elected on a rigged vote, authoritarian government by Orders-in-Council under the War Measures Act, and the isolation of French Canada, had all come to an end. The expanded electorate, more educated and less wedded to party allegiances, the more professional conduct of elections, and the beginnings of a professional civil service, had permanently changed the political process that had dominated the country before the war.

III

In 1923, Douglas Durkin, a Manitoba teacher who had gone to New York to seek his fortune as a writer, published *The Magpie*, a novel about Craig Forrester, a war hero returning to Winnipeg in 1919. Forrester has been sustained in the trenches by his belief that his sacrifice would produce a better world. Instead, he finds that few others share his idealism and most want only to restore the worst aspects of the world he hoped the war would sweep away.

The book is peopled with characters who represent the conflicting forces in a city whose optimistic modernity conceals religious doubt, social and economic dislocation, class conflict, and struggles for power. Forrester's wife is a "new" woman who only wants to fit into her social class. Her father is a businessman who loves art, wants to do right by his workers, but opposes unions and sides with employers during the General Strike. A rabble-rousing labour militant and a brutal enforcer brought in by the employers are both men without principles who use the strike for their own advancement. Forrester's old army sergeant is the epitome of the respectful underclass, who only wants to return to his house, garden, and faithful, long-suffering wife — but when he dies, she is soon laughing and drunk with another man. The Methodist minister is adept at furnishing the upper classes with the right prayer for the right occasion. And there is a feminist war widow, who finds new life with her lover, a Russian straight out of Tolstoy who despises both bosses and strikers and proclaims that only moral regeneration will save the world.

Forrester believes that as a trader at the Winnipeg Grain Exchange he is benefitting humanity by providing food to hungry people. But his chief rival is a speculator only seeking quick wealth — and worse, his rival makes off with his wife. Defeated and disillusioned, Forrester flees Winnipeg and his broken dreams for a life in the country with his childhood sweetheart, a sculptor.[26]

The Magpie is not a particularly good novel, but it does provide a fascinating portrayal of the ideals and forces that swept over Winnipeg, and Canada, in 1919 and the months that followed. Forrester embodies the hope, shared in so many different ways by the diverse people we have met in this book, that the war would create a new Canada in this "time such as there never was before." But he encounters a hard truth. People do not "regenerate." Old orders are never swept away — at least not peacefully. Things are never quite made new. Forrester cannot define his beliefs; he has no idea how to bring the new world about; he does not accept that others might have ideals and dreams that clash with his. He is bound to be disillusioned.

"When I knew of the declaration of war," James Mavor wrote in his memoirs, "I said to myself, 'The world has altered.' I was wrong. The world is the same old world; only a few revolutions have occurred; a few dynasties have toppled; only a few frontiers have been altered; only millions of men have fallen; only mountains of debt have been incurred; only a few countries have been devastated — yet the world spins on its axis just the same; and I doubt if the war has made any radical change in the world of men." President Falconer did not share Mavor's world-weary cynicism, but did confess to being "chastened" and "less confident as to the triumphant advance of the human race over all obstacles to the goal of its perfection." Few Canadians could avoid some disillusionment with a postwar reality that could never have measured up to wartime hopes.[27]

Between the Armistice in 1918 and the federal election of 1921, a great storm of pent-up energy roared through Canada, cleansing and destroying, whirling dust and dreams into the air, until it blew itself out with the violence of its conflicting forces. Its power frightened Canadians, as did the actual results of some of the changes they thought they had wanted. They were exhausted by the social divisions, the rancorous debate, the constant upheaval. Above all, they had become bone-weary of being told by the likes of Professor John MacNaughton that what was needed was "to change our minds, to repent, to say, it is my sin, my selfishness that had made all this terrible sacrifice necessary." The desire for a "new spirit" had given way to a desire to get on with life, and if that meant the very materialism and hedonism that the war had been sent to purge, well, so be it. By 1924, the *Canadian Forum* was complaining of "a cold detachment towards questions of social justice."[28]

Hundreds of thousands of young men struggled with an experience of war that had changed their psyches and worldview forever. Families ached with the memory of lost sons, husbands, and fathers. The economy crashed between late 1920 and 1923. Canadians retreated from Europe, the world, and the Empire into the safety of North America. Belief in traditional religion declined, the United Church became a powerful but increasingly conservative institution in English Canada, and the Catholic Church took a nationalist and conservative turn in Quebec. Prohibition failed and took much of the energy of the Social Gospel with it. Pensions, unemployment insurance, health insurance, and other social security measures dreamed of in the postwar receded into the distance; budgets were cut for health and social welfare; and the old philosophy of means tests and grudging charity replaced the belief that a government that had sent its soldiers to die must also help its people to live. Labour was in retreat. The agrarian revolt and the idea of Group Government petered out. Emancipated women became modern homemakers. Some Quebec intellectuals rejected any role in a Canadian nation. Other minorities remained excluded from the national mainstream.

But it would be far from the truth to suggest that the postwar brought only discord and disillusionment, or that the great dreams of a better world were abandoned in a mad rush to "normalcy." The achievements of a young country in responding to the war and its aftermath had been remarkable; and although much had been abandoned, much remained.

Independent status within a new Commonwealth, the beginnings of a more inclusive Canadian identity, and the reassertion by French Canadians of a political role within Canada, were important steps forward. Many of the reforms that the war had brought — votes for women; public ownership of railways and utilities, roads and housing; control of the sale and consumption of alcohol; health ministries, child welfare, and assistance to families; a professional public service; income tax — were by the mid-1920s simply accepted as normal. The Social Gospel lived on within the United Church, in social agencies, and in secular social scientists and government "experts." The rise of the middle class, modern communications, the integration of newcomers, and the memory of the comradeship of the trenches were producing a more egalitarian society. Farmers' movements had produced permanent change in the governance of the Western provinces and their role in Confederation; and in the labour movement, there remained an impulse toward radical reform that flickered but refused to die.

Even the desire to get on with life was itself a reaction to the war, and the young Canadians who formed organizations for nation-building, portrayed their country in art and literature, went back to school, embarked on new careers, started new families, made new discoveries, or built new businesses, were finding concrete ways to realize their visions of a new world.

Despite its much longer wartime experience, Canada never descended into the postwar hysteria, bombings, strikes, riots, and persecution that marked the Red Scare in the United States, nor did it experience the violence and lawlessness of American Prohibition, or the extreme fundamentalism of its Bible Belt. There was no "lost generation" of sensitive young men as depicted by American writers, shattered by the hypocrisy of those who had led them to war, finding meaning only in a stoic devotion to a code of duty. There was jazz, and life, and fun, but no "jazz age." Canadians avoided the social and intellectual upheaval of Britain in the early twenties, and, though they mourned the loss of many of their best young men, they were never haunted by the destruction of their next generation of leaders at the Somme. There was no Canadian artistic portrayal of the war to match the horrifying images of Otto Dix in Germany, no Canadian equivalent of the nihilistic, despairing philosophies of Europe. Nor, except in Quebec, was there the aggressive anti-modernism that marked the European Right.

Nationalists like Skelton and Lapointe maintained a continuing vigil against attempts by British Imperialists to embroil Canada in overseas wars, and the publication of documents and reminiscences cast doubt on whether British motives had been altogether pure. But, outside of Quebec at least, few would have shared the belief common among American intellectuals that the war had been a Great Betrayal. The British connection remained strong. And though some flirted with pacifism in the 1930s, when another war broke out, most Canadians — this time without any illusions about what war would be like — nonetheless knew that they must again rise to the defence of freedom.

Poet and professor F.R. Scott (son of Canon Scott) wrote in 1931 that the "failure of the beatific visions of the 'reconstruction' period, on top of the intellectual ferment caused directly by the war" had produced among the younger intellectuals "a shifting of beliefs the like of which had probably not been experienced in Christendom since the Renaissance." He was probably overstating his case as far as Western civilization was concerned. He was certainly doing so in respect of Canada. Looking back from a world mired in depression and drifting toward war, he and others might well regard the twenties as a "lost" decade of failure and disillusionment. But seen from any other perspective, they were a dynamic era of progress and change.

There were of course many Canadians who were disillusioned and critical, many who experimented with new ideas and values in response to the war, many who were influenced by cross-currents of thought sweeping through the Western world. But most also rejoiced in the advances of science, medicine, culture, and material prosperity, and they continued to believe in the future of their country and the progress of humanity. Falconer's depiction of a chastened, skeptical maturity seems better to convey the mood of the 1920s in Canada than either Mavor's wholesale disillusionment or the popular stereotype of the "roaring twenties."[29]

The stress of war on a young country, and the vision of a new world after the war, produced hope, fear, and intolerance, and shook to the core Canada's sense of itself, its beliefs, for a time even democracy itself. The story we have told is full of drama, and the people we have met are remarkable and varied, and both belie any lingering suspicion that Canadians are a dull and stodgy people.

But it is too easy to overlook the other, and more important part of the story — that in spite of having the dice heavily loaded against it by its youth, vastness, regionalism, and the resulting centrifugal forces seemingly written into its DNA, in spite of all the conflict, intolerance, and clashing visions magnified by the ordeal of war, in spite of the many outside forces, ideas, and impulses acting on it, Canada survived and prospered as a nation and managed to restore its social equilibrium and political stability. In the end, the values of compromise and continuity, social cohesion and tolerance, liberty combined with respect for authority and tradition, which Canadians had learned through a long history of having to accommodate differences, re-asserted themselves. Most Canadians were not ready for social revolution, nor for endless conflict and hatreds, nor for a more adventurous role in a troubled world. They restored their commitment to the middle way and gradual change, and the optimistic outlook that had suited them during their boom years and sustained them in the Great War.

Still, Scott was right about one thing — the world had changed forever. Nothing could ever be the same again, and Canadians knew it. "Normalcy" for most Canadians was not a desire to turn back the clock, nor a repudiation of any impulse toward change or reform. It was, rather, a quest for balance between the old and the new, between hopes and reality, between conformity and diversity, between getting on with life and keeping faith with those who had sacrificed for a better world, between pride in growing up and a desire to hold on to as much of their innocence as they could.

Epilogue: July 1, 1927

Mackenzie King has been fussing like a mother hen over every detail of the ceremonies that will take place on Parliament Hill to celebrate the Diamond Jubilee of Confederation. The Golden Jubilee had passed uncelebrated during the dark days of wartime. The Diamond Jubilee, in a time of peace and prosperity, will display the pride and confidence of a united and independent Canada.[1]

The celebrations have been conceived by the "nationalist network," especially the Canadian Clubs; the "Canadian movement," Claxton will recall, is "at work in every field." A blue-ribbon national committee staffed by nationalists like Graham Spry has supervised sub-committees comprising business, universities, and organizations like Vincent Massey's National Council of Education. With only a few months to prepare, it has spent $250,000 to produce guidebooks, speeches, and materials for local celebrations. It has distributed 180,000 copies of *Sixty Years of Canadian Progress,* lavishly illustrated and crammed with statistics depicting the growth of Canada and its "strong and permanent recovery" after the war. It has produced a documentary film shown in theatres across the country. It has funded thousands of medals and prizes for editorials, essays, poems, and speeches, and a copper plaque for each school. It has encouraged pageants that involve a broad range of people in depicting the approved national narrative. The CPR has taken out full-page ads, and other businesses have followed suit with displays, advertising, and sponsorship of local events, contests, and prizes. Through the superhuman efforts of a committee of telephone and telegraph companies, railways, and radio stations led by

The Diamond Jubilee of Confederation, Ottawa, July 1, 1927, Parliament Hill, Ottawa
A large choir organized for the occasion sings in front of the official podium, under the newly completed Peace Tower.

Thomas Aherne of Ottawa, a makeshift system has been cobbled together to feed the Ottawa ceremonies to twenty-two radio stations across Canada, and to London and New York.[2]

Now the great moment has come. Forty thousand people have gathered on the lawn of Parliament Hill, many under silk parasols on this brilliant sunny day, and thousands more are in the surrounding streets and on top of buildings. King, the governor general, and other dignitaries sit on a platform decorated with maple leaves and Union Jacks and the dates 1867 and 1927. As the hands of the clock on the new Peace Tower (the scaffolding has been taken down only days earlier) strike twelve, there is a trumpet fanfare, the booming of the noon gun, and the tall, courtly governor general, Lord Willingdon (who has replaced the ill-fated Byng), pushes a button that sends a signal to a young man seated in cramped quarters in the tower. The first notes of the newly installed fifty-three-bell carillon ring out, followed by "O Canada" and "The Maple Leaf Forever."

King has spent days preparing his speech and has cried as he writes about the tragic loss of sixty thousand young Canadians. He points out that the tower, planned as a Tower of Victory, will, instead, be called the Peace Tower. He quotes the popular hymn "O Valiant Hearts":

Who to your glory came
Through dust of conflict and through battle-flame;
Tranquil you lie, your knightly virtue proud,
Your memory hallowed in the land you loved.

As with the design of the National War Memorial, he has taken special care to downplay the glory of war and stress sorrow, sacrifice, and faith in future progress under God.[3]

The Ottawa celebrations go on all day. Lady Willingdon has planted a Confederation maple. Messages are read out from the king, the British prime minister (the Prince of Wales and the British PM will visit Canada in August), the premiers of the other Dominions, and the leaders of other governments in the League of Nations. A message from the premier of Ontario and the mayor of Toronto is delivered by Boy Scout runners who have carried it in relays — and Scouts, Girl Guides, Cadets, and school children in red sashes, are everywhere. At three o'clock there is another ceremony, with another speech by King, which outlines Canada's national progress and its emergence among the nations of the world. There are speeches by French and English-speaking politicians, two Senators who are sons of Fathers of Confederation. Actress Margaret Anglin, who is the daughter of a former House Speaker and was born in the parliamentary precincts, reads a commissioned poem by Bliss Carman.* The daughter of Sir George-Étienne Cartier lays a wreath at her father's statue and King lays a wreath at the new statue of Laurier. A thousand-voice choir sings patriotic songs and the band of the Governor General's Foot Guards plays martial music. At dusk, a massive float parade rolls through the city, bringing alive the sixty years of Canadian progress. The governor general gives a dinner for representatives of the Dominions. In the evening, the Peace Tower is illuminated and much of the earlier program is repeated. At midnight, the massed choirs sing "God Save the King," and at one o'clock Ottawa trundles happily off to bed.

Great care has been taken to ensure that the ceremonies fully reflect the French fact in Canada. The post office has issued the first ever bilingual stamp. The national committee has encouraged local committees to include

---

* Carman was one of four "poets of the confederation," who had, beginning in the 1880s, given literary voice to the new nation. The others were Archibald Lampman, Charles G.D. Roberts, and Duncan Campbell Scott.

the French words in the singing of "O Canada." On Parliament Hill, Sir Lomer Gouin reads the original Confederation resolution expressing the desire of the Fathers to build a new nation. Senator and historian T.C. Chapais takes direct aim at Groulx when he says that "the little homeland, nearer, more intimate and beloved … does not preclude love of country. On the contrary, the first sentiment is the most solid foundation of the other and gives it warmth and force." Senator Dandurand's plea for a bilingual Canada is followed by the singing of "Vive la Canadienne." The radio commentaries are in both languages.

And every effort is made to include the newer immigrants. The national committee has suggested that local pageants include their traditional songs and dances, with children in modern dress symbolizing their successful integration into Canadian society. The organizers will report that these children entered essay contests "on an equality with the children of Canadian-born, and in many cases the children of the newer Canadians made a splendid showing." They will conclude that the Jubilee has healed differences and dispelled prejudices and that "New Canadians" "joined enthusiastically in the celebrations, helped materially toward their success … and demonstrated their attachment to their adopted homeland."[4]

Saturday, July 2, is a day of athletic events, picnics, essay contests, prizes, and public celebrations. Charles Lindbergh — the most famous man in the world since his solo flight across the Atlantic two months ago — flies into Ottawa with seven military planes. The crowd is stunned into silence when two planes clip wings and a pilot falls to his death in a vain attempt to bail out. At a state dinner to honour the new U.S. ambassador,* King speaks of the creation of a Canadian diplomatic service but assures his audience that such direct representation in other countries "simply means increased co-operation within the British Empire."

Sunday, July 3, is designated as a day of Thanksgiving, and in Ottawa the governor general presides over a religious service. Lindbergh's pilot is given a public funeral, with the flag on the Peace Tower at half mast, the carillon playing the funeral march, and Lindbergh swooping down in his plane to drop flowers as Mounties escort the casket to Union Station.

---

* His official title was "Envoy Extraordinary and Minister Plenipotentiary." The United States and Canada began to formally designate their envoys to each other as "Ambassador" in 1943.

All across the country there are historical pageants and parades, outdoor concerts, picnics, baseball games, egg-and-spoon races, family outings, water regattas, and street parties. In Toronto, one hundred thousand people watch a massive float parade. In Winnipeg, a huge parade with twenty-two bands works its way through the city and a community picnic draws fifty thousand people. The climax is a huge tableau of "Canada standing in the midst of the nations she had gathered to be her people" with "Canada" represented by a granddaughter of Sir John A. Macdonald. In St. Boniface, a pageant celebrates the arrival of La Vérendrye, with Indians in costume re-enacting the friendly meeting of the two peoples. In Montreal, Dominion Day and Saint-Jean-Baptiste Day celebrations are combined, with float parades celebrating the four-hundred-year history of Quebec. On Sunday, in churches across the country, and around war memorials, thousands of clergy give thanks for Canada's good fortune and pray that the country might be worthy of this blessing.

In two hundred cities and towns, thousands of people hear the events in Ottawa broadcast on radio with remarkable clarity. "On the morning, afternoon and evening of July 1," King writes, "all Canada became, for the time being, a single assemblage, swayed by a common emotion, within the sound of a single voice.… Hitherto to most Canadians Ottawa has seemed far off, a mere name to hundreds of thousands of our people, but henceforth all Canadians will stand within the sound of the carillon and within hearing of the speakers on Parliament Hill." Listening in Toronto to "O Canada" on the radio from the capital, a *Canadian Forum* editor muses on the possibility that the Jubilee might inspire Canadians to new heights of artistic endeavour, intellectual achievement, and national service. In 1928, the government will appoint a Royal Commission on Broadcasting under John Aird, which will lead in 1932 to the creation of the CBC.[5]

Of course, the local celebrations do not always portray the approved national narrative. Indian Affairs has refused to allocate funds for "unproductive" celebrations on reserves, but the national committee believes that it is "highly desirable … that as many First Canadians as possible take a prominent part in the observance of the Jubilee." So, Indians are encouraged to participate in pageants in neighbouring communities, where they appear in costume in depictions of the Heroic Age, as faithful allies who will surrender their land and give way to civilization — and celebrations in residential schools depict the same message. But as Indian Affairs officials have feared, by dressing in traditional costumes they have been able to celebrate their own identity, as have "foreign" immigrants.[6]

In Toronto, the emphasis is on Loyalism and the development of a British society. In Montreal, a gathering in Jeanne Mance Park, advertised as an *"examen de conscience national,"* attracts twenty thousand people. Its main speaker, Henri Bourassa, argues that Confederation has not always worked well and pleads for a new dedication to a nation based on two founding races, truly autonomous, in thrall neither to bigotry nor imperialism, which can confront the evils of industrialism and modernity — his message, which is also a rejection of Groulx, is misunderstood and criticized in the English press. Many a Sunday sermon agrees with the *Canadian Forum* that there are still hungry children and a host of unsolved problems. There is little labour presence (though Tom Moore is on the national committee), and radical journals attack the celebration as the glorification of an evil system. At Canning, Nova Scotia, flags fly at half-mast carrying on the old grudge against Confederation. Chinese Canadians stay home, as they do every year on this day.[7]

While Canadians celebrate in 1927, most of the rest of the developed world also basks in peace, prosperity, and an outpouring of cultural achievement and scientific discovery. In the United States, *Showboat* is the culmination of a remarkable generation of Broadway musical writers and jazz composers. *Steppenwolf* by Herman Hesse, *Amerika* by Franz Kafka, *The Bridge of San Luis Rey* by Thornton Wilder, *Elmer Gantry* by Sinclair Lewis, *Death Comes for the Archbishop* by Willa Cather, and *To The Lighthouse* by Virginia Woolf are the latest novels to express the modernist spirit, while *Seated Woman* by Picasso, *Picture with Ornamental Background* by Matisse, and *Radiator Building, New York* by Georgia O'Keeffe are breaking new ground in art and design. *The Jazz Singer* is the first major "talking" motion picture. Mazo de la Roche wins the $10,000 *Atlantic Monthly* prize for her novel *Jalna*, which will become a popular series that for two generations will, together with *Anne of Green Gables,* define Canada in the minds of millions around the world.

The Peace Bridge is the latest symbol of Canada-U.S. commerce and friendship. Borden Dairies introduces homogenized milk; Wonder Bread makes its first appearance in balloon-decorated packages; Gerber begins making prepared baby foods; German scientists develop a pregnancy test;

Lindbergh makes his famous flight; Babe Ruth hits sixty home runs. In Germany, twenty-seven-year-old Werner Heisenberg formulates the uncertainty principle, whose quantum mechanics will rewrite the laws of physics. In China, the discovery by a Canadian of Peking Man sheds further light on the origin and evolution of the human species.

In France and Belgium, the line of trenches, which had once been considered for a ceremonial road, is now filled in and grassed over. Farmers still unearth shell fragments, unexploded ordnance, and body parts, but there is little outward sign that millions of men once lived like rats and slaughtered each other with industrial thoroughness. The Cloth Hall at Ypres still lies in ruins, but a memorial arch has been built at the Menin Gate, on whose walls are carved the names of fifty-five thousand soldiers from Canada and other parts of the Empire who perished before Ypres (many thousands more are memorialized at Tyne Cot near Passchendaele). Beginning on November 11, 1929, the "Last Post" will be sounded at the Menin Gate every evening at eight o'clock, a tradition that, except for the years 1940 to 1944, continues to this day.

At the Mons city hall and at the church where George Kilpatrick preached his sermon, plaques commemorate the liberation by Canadians, and George Lawrence Price rests in the only Commonwealth Cemetery shared between German and British dead. The first stones from a reopened Roman quarry are beginning to arrive for Walter Allward's memorial at Vimy. At St. Julien, where Canadian soldiers repulsed a gas attak in 1915, a statue that will come to be known as *The Brooding Soldier* stands guard with arms reversed, solemnly contemplating the tragedy of the past and the uncertainty of the future.* In dozens of beautiful and peaceful cemeteries across France and Belgium, thousands of Canadians sleep in corners

Last resting place of George Lawrence Price, St. Symphorien, Mons, Belgium

---

* The image of the "brooding soldier" is used on the cover and at the beginning of each chapter.

of foreign fields that are forever Canada.[8]

"Canada has hit her stride," proclaims E.R. Beatty. From our vantage point in history we may see this as foolishly optimistic. We, of course, have the advantage of looking back on the Diamond Jubilee, just as those who celebrated it could look back on the idyllic days before August 1914. *We* know that "normalcy" will turn out to be an illusion. *We* know that in a little over two years, debt, overcapitalization, an unbalanced, largely un-regulated economy, and the folly of believing that a bubble market would rise forever, will plunge the country and the world into a Great Depression. *We* know that within a dozen years another generation of young men and women will be going back to fight in Europe. We might even feel justified in looking on their Sunday School picnics, ice-cream festivals, sports and pageants, speeches and sermons, Union Jacks and essay contests, with the same foreboding that Thomas Gray felt two centuries earlier as he looked on Eton College boys at play:

> Yet ah! Why should they know their fate?
> Since sorrow never comes too late,
>   And happiness too swiftly flies,
> Thought would destroy their paradise.
> No more: where ignorance is bliss,
>   'Tis folly to be wise.[9]

History can, after all, only be written after the present has become the past. The future is always shrouded in mystery; it is a place of infinite possibilities, where Schrödinger's Cat is both dead and alive. The fate that awaits these happy people of 1927 is no more pre-ordained than that an assassin's bullet in Sarajevo would precipitate the most terrible conflict in the history of the world. In a myriad of ways, from the celebration of enterprise to the small achievements of ordinary people finally able to own a home, pay for a farm, or send a child to school, they have every reason to be optimistic about a world made new. It is their hopes and dreams, their prejudice and tolerance, their courage and illusions, the lives they lived, the children they raised, and the country they shaped, that are their legacy to us.

Timeline

1911

Sep. 21   Robert Borden's Conservatives, with Quebec nationalists, defeat Laurier's Liberals, who have governed since 1896.

1913

May 29   Senate vetoes $3 million contribution for battleships for Imperial Navy.

1914

Mar. 3–5   Social Service Congress in Ottawa brings together churches, agencies, and scholars to discuss range of social issues.

Aug. 4   Canada enters Great War as Britain declares war on Germany and Austria-Hungary.

Aug. 18–22   Special session of Parliament passes War Measures Act, establishes Canadian Patriotic Fund.

1915

Apr. 22   Canadian contingent in Second Battle of Ypres faces gas attack; six thousand casualties in week-long engagement.

Nov. 15   Imperial Munitions Board under Flavelle established to manage Canadian military production and procurement.

Nov. 22   First domestic war loan (renamed "Victory Loan" in 1917) issued.

Dec. 8   Dr. John McCrae's poem "In Flanders Fields" published in London magazine *Punch*.

1916

Jan. 4   Borden drafts, then retracts, letter protesting lack of consultation about the war.

Jan. 12   Order-in-Council increases Canadian Expeditionary Force to 500,000 men.

Jan. 28   Women given right to vote in Manitoba.

Feb. 3–4   Parliament Buildings in Ottawa burn to the ground.

Feb. 8   Life of Parliament extended for one year.

Mar. 14   Women given right to vote and hold office in Saskatchewan.

Apr. 19   Women given the right to vote and hold office in Alberta.

Jun. 3   Board of Pension Commissioners established.

1916   (Cont'd)

Jun. 30   Royal commission recommends new reserves for B.C. Indians.

Jul. 13   Royal commission on railways appointed (report will favour nationalization).

Nov. 10   Order-in-Council establishes price controls.

    Sir Sam Hughes resigns as minister of militia.

Nov. 30   United Farmers of Alberta, Farmers' Co-operative Elevator Company, and Manitoba Grain Growers Association amalgamate to form United Grain Growers.

Dec. 6   Canadian Council of Agriculture publishes Farmers' Platform (endorsed by affiliate organizations in 1917).

Dec. 7   David Lloyd George becomes British prime minister.

Dec. 11   Saskatchewan government abolishes liquor stores (Ontario, Alberta, and Manitoba institute Prohibition in 1916).

1917

Jan. 18   Soldiers' Settlement Act passed.

Mar. 15   Russian czar abdicates; provisional government formed under Kerensky, pledges to keep Russia in the war.

Mar. 20   Imperial War Cabinet convenes in London.

Apr. 5   Women get right to vote and hold office in British Columbia.

Apr. 6   United States enters war.

Apr. 9–12   Battle of Vimy Ridge.

Apr. 10–13   Great War Veterans' Association founded in Winnipeg.

Apr. 12   Women get right to vote in Ontario, but not to hold office.

Apr. 16   Resolution IX of Imperial War Conference calls for "continuous consultation" among Dominions and for constitutional conference after the war.

Jun. 7   Louise McKinney in Alberta becomes first woman MLA.

Jun. 19   General Arthur Currie assumes command of Canadian Corps.

Aug. 20   Income Tax Act passed.

Aug. 29   Military Service Act passed.

    Act to nationalize Canadian Northern Railway passed.

Sep.   Trades and Labour Congress supports conscription, agrees to support Labour candidates in coming federal election.

Sep. 20   Military Voters Act and Wartime Elections Act give overseas soldiers and their female relatives the vote, disenfranchise Canadians from enemy countries.

Oct. 6   Parliament dissolved; Union coalition formed.

Nov.   Ordnance Agreement allows United States to make war purchases in Canada through Imperial Munitions Board.

Nov. 2   Balfour Declaration states British government would "view with favour the establishment in Palestine of a national home for the Jewish people."

Nov. 7   Bolsheviks under Lenin overthrow Russian government.

    Canadians take Passchendaele.

Dec. 6   Halifax Explosion destroys most of downtown.

Dec. 17   Borden's Unionists win overwhelming election victory.

1918

Feb. 4	Canadian War Mission in Washingtoh established under Lloyd Harris, the representative of IMB in Washington.
Feb. 6–11	War Trade, War Purchasing, Food Boards established.
Feb. 21	Department of Soldiers' Civil Re-establishment created.
Mar. 3	Treaty of Brest-Litovsk signed between Soviet Russia and Germany.
Mar. 28–Apr. 1	Conscription riots in Quebec City — five killed as soldiers fire on crowds.
Apr. 1	Interprovincial shipments of liquor prohibited by federal government.
Apr. 17	House of Commons told in secret session that Allied armies face possible defeat.
Apr. 20	Men aged between twenty and twenty-two called to military service.
Apr. 26	Women get right to vote in Nova Scotia.
May 2	Winnipeg power and light workers strike; May 7, teamsters strike; May 16, telephone operators join strikers; May 21, railway workers also go on strike.
May 15	Five thousand in Ottawa protest breach of promise not to conscript farmers' sons.
May 24	Civil Service Act requires appointments be made by Civil Service Commission — loopholes and patronage remain.
May 24	Act gives women, except for Native Canadians and some Asians, federal vote as of January 1, 1919.
Jun. 7	Mass meeting of farmers in Toronto protests treatment of farmers' delegation in Ottawa.
Jun. 22	Second national registration for military draft.
Jun. 30	William Ivens founds Labour Church in Winnipeg.
Jul. 27	Killing of Socialist Ginger Goodwin leads to Vancouver riots.
Aug.	Serious influenza outbreaks in Brest, Sierra Leone, Boston.
Aug. 8	Breakthrough at Amiens begins "Hundred Days" of rapid victories.
Aug.– Sep.	C.H. Cahan investigates Bolshevist agitation, reports "widespread unrest."
Sep.	TLC Congress in Quebec elects Tom Moore as president; defeats radicals.
	Influenza outbreaks in Quebec, Niagara, Halifax, Toronto, Montreal, and military hospitals.
Sep. 28	Orders-in-Council ban fourteen organizations, including Social Democratic Party, ethnic socialist parties, and Kuomintang.
Oct.	Flu spreads across Western Canada as troops are transported to West Coast.
Oct. 1	Order-in-Council bans books, newspapers, and publications in enemy languages.
Oct. 2	Public Safety Branch of Department of Justice formed under C.H. Cahan.
Oct. 2–17	Tenth General Conference of Methodist Church adopts Methodist Programme.
Oct. 11	Order-in-Council regulates wartime labour, prohibits strikes, lockouts.
Oct. 24	United Farmers of Ontario win by-election.
Oct. 27	Four thousand Canadian soldiers arrive in Vladivostok, Russia.
Oct. 28	Lloyd George informs Borden of peace talks with Germany.
Nov.	Flu peaks in Winnipeg, Calgary, and Vancouver, spreads to North and rural areas.
Nov. 7	Canadian trade mission under Lloyd Harris established in London.

1918   (Cont'd)

Nov. 8   Borden leaves for New York to embark for England.

Nov. 10   Canadians enter Mons.

Nov. 11   Armistice signed with Germany.

Nov. 15   Repatriation Committee of Cabinet formed.

Nov. 19   Federal-provincial conference agrees on postwar measures for soldiers' resettlement and employment, as well as for education, housing, roads.

Nov. 20–   Imperial War Conference in London prepares for Paris Peace Conference;
Dec. 31   Borden demands greater voice for Dominions and direct representation in conference.

Nov. 29   Canadian Council of Agriculture adopts "New National Policy."

Dec.   Flu abates in most parts of Canada, except the North.

            Mackenzie King publishes *Industry and Humanity.*

Dec. 13   Canadian troops begin two months of occupation of Cologne area of Germany.

Dec. 17   Near-mutiny of Canadian troops near Nivelles.

Dec. 18   Government institutes War Services Gratuity.

Dec. 20   Canadian National Railways formed from CNoR and Government Railways.

Dec. 22   Meeting at Walker Theatre, Winnipeg, gives three cheers for Russian Revolution.

            Sam McLaughlin completes sale of McLaughlin Carriage Company to General Motors, creates General Motors of Canada.

Dec. 28   Dissident "Uniates" found Ukrainian Greek Orthodox Church of Canada.

1919

Jan.   Canadian troops leave Germany, begin crossing to camps in England.

Jan. 4   Borden opens exhibition of Canadian war art in London.

Jan. 5–17   Imperial War Conference moves to Paris, becomes British Empire Delegation.

Jan. 10   Socialist meeting in Winnipeg is followed by attacks by returned soldiers.

Jan. 16   Eighteenth Amendment to U.S. Constitution ratified, prohibiting manufacture and sale of intoxicating liquors.

Jan. 18   Peace Conference begins in Paris.

Jan. 22   United Farmers of Alberta vote to support any provincial candidate nominated by 10 percent of locals in a riding.

Jan. 31   Groulx delivers speech "If Dollard Were Alive Today" in Montreal.

Feb.   Soldiers begin to return from overseas in large numbers.

            Federated Women's Institutes of Canada founded in Winnipeg.

Feb.   Allied Tribes of British Columbia reject 1916 royal commission report.

Feb. 1   Grand Trunk Pacific defaults on debenture payments, placed in trusteeship.

Feb. 6–11   Seattle General Strike.

Feb. 17   Winston Churchill demands Bolshevism be "strangled in its cradle" — Borden resists call for more troops.

            Death of Sir Wilfrid Laurier.

Feb. 17   "Calgary Resolution" demands bonus of $2000 for soldiers who served overseas.

1919 (Cont'd)

Feb. 26– Jul. 7	Parliament in five month session: establishes Department of Health and Board of Commerce; amends Soldiers' Settlement Act to provide financial aid and land; amends Immigration Act to exclude anarchists, enemy aliens, and illiterates over the age of fifteen; agrees to pay provinces 50 percent of cost of technical education and $20 million for highways; makes prohibition of interprovincial trade in liquor permanent; allows women to derive citizenship in their own right and to hold office.
Mar. 4	Sam Hughes attacks General Currie's actions at Mons in House of Commons.
Mar. 4–5	Canadian soldiers riot in Kinmel, Wales.
Mar. 13	Borden presents paper to British Empire Delegation criticizing Article X of League of Nations Covenant.
	Western Labour Conference in Calgary decides to form One Big Union.
Mar. 25	British House of Commons passes Imperial Preferential tariff which *inter alia* favours Canadian exports of cars and farm machinery within the Empire.
Mar 27	Canadian Jewish Congress convenes in Montreal.
	Canadian Ukrainians call on Borden in Paris.
Mar.–Apr.	Second wave of Spanish flu.
	Mackenzie King gives speeches on "Four Parties to Industry."
Apr.	Withdrawal begins of Canadian troops from Siberia, all home by June.
Apr. 9	Royal Commission on Industrial Relations (Mathers Commission) established.
Apr. 10	Referendum in Quebec approves sale of beer and wine.
Apr. 16	Sir Thomas White requests Borden ask British to send cruiser to Vancouver.
Apr. 17	Women in New Brunswick granted right to vote.
May	"Chaplains' message" to leading Protestant churches calls for renewal, asks message be read in churches first Sunday in June.
May 1	May Day brings widespread labour disturbances in United States.
	Two thousand workers walk off job at Vulcan Iron Works, Winnipeg.
May 6	Wilson, Clemenceau, Lloyd George declare Canada eligible for membership in League of Nations Council.
May 7	Peace treaty presented to Germans.
	Henry Wise Wood publishes article advocating UFA enter politics not as third party but as an occupational "group."
May 13	Winnipeg Trades and Labour Council votes in favour of general strike.
May 14	Borden leaves Paris, arrives in Halifax May 25.
May 15	Winnipeg General Strike begins.
	Mackenzie King arrives in Britain.
May 16	Winnipeg's major newspapers shut down.
May 22	Commons passes resolution requesting Crown no longer give titles to Canadians.
May 29	Borden and Crerar meet.
	Germans criticize harshness of treaty, are told no changes can be made.
May 31	Most Canadian soldiers have returned from Europe.
May 31– Jun. 5	March of returned soldiers in Winnipeg supports strike; soldiers march on legislature June 2; parades prohibited by mayor on June 5.
Jun. 2	Home of U.S. attorney general Mitchell Palmer bombed.
Jun. 3	General strike of twelve thousand workers in Vancouver; other sympathetic strikes from Victoria to Amherst, Nova Scotia.

1919   (Cont'd)

	Winnipeg strikers ban milk and bread delivery.
Jun. 4	One Big Union officially launched in Calgary.
Jun. 5	Finance minister White introduces budget retaining tariffs, some increased taxes.
Jun. 5–6	Criminal Code amended to include "seditious conspiracy"; Immigration Act amended to allow deportation of "any person" advocating overthrow of government.
Jun. 6	Air Board established to control military and civilian aviation.
	Crerar resigns as minister of agriculture.
	Canadian National Railways incorporated.
Jun. 9	Most Winnipeg police are dismissed.
Jun. 14	British pilots Alcock and Brown make first non-stop transatlantic flight.
Jun. 16	Proposed settlement in Winnipeg metal trades rejected.
Jun. 16–17	Strike leaders arrested in Winnipeg.
Jun. 17	Canadian soldiers assault police station at Epsom, England.
Jun. 18	Twelve Western MPs vote for budget amendment calling for lower tariffs.
Jun. 21	Winnipeg Strike leaders charged with seditious conspiracy, freed on bail.
	"Bloody Saturday" in Winnipeg, two people killed.
Jun. 25	Winnipeg strike ends.
Jun. 28	Peace treaty signed with Germany, A.L. Sifton and C.J. Doherty sign for Canada.
	Anglo-French Treaty exempts Canada from obligation to defend France, unless Parliament consents.
Jul.	Immigration Board hearing for Winnipeg "foreign" defendants.
	Senate rejects Canada Temperance Act.
Jul. 1	Report of Mathers Royal Commission calls for recognition of labour unions.
Jul. 7	Department of Health established.
Jul. 17–27	Borden takes "holiday" trip down St. Lawrence, consulting Quebec leaders; Rowell visits the West.
Jul. 19	Peace Day celebrated throughout the Empire.
Jul. 20	Mackenzie King embarks for Canada.
Jul. 21–Aug. 14	Preliminary hearing for Winnipeg strike leaders on charge of seditious conspiracy.
Jul. 27–Aug. 3	Race riots in Chicago, Washington D.C., and other American cities.
Jul. 31	Canadian Wheat Board replaces Board of Grain Supervisors.
Jul.–Aug.	Strike at Davie shipyards, Quebec, condemned by Catholic Church.
Aug.	Leacock publishes "The Tyranny of Prohibition."
Aug. 5–7	Liberal convention elects Mackenzie King leader.
Aug. 17	Sir Arthur Currie arrives at Halifax.
Aug. 21–Oct. 27	Prince of Wales visits Canada.
Aug. 27	Borden refuses Great War Veterans' Association demand for $2,000 bonus.
Sep.	Leacock publishes series of newspaper articles, subsequently collected in book form in 1920 as *The Unsolved Riddle of Social Justice*.
	TLC convention attacks radicalism, opposes Prohibition.

1919 (Cont'd)

Sep. 1– Nov. 10	Special session of Parliament.
Sep. 2–4	League of Indians of Canada meets near Sault Ste Marie.
Sep. 7	Veterans meeting in Toronto hears Harry Flynn advocate force to achieve demands.
Sep. 10	Treaty of Saint-Germain-en-Laye with Austria agreed on; Britain signs for Empire.
	Lodge Committee, after weeks of hearings, reports on Treaty of Versailles to U.S. Senate, demanding fourteen amendments.
Sep. 12	Canada ratifies peace treaty with Germany.
Sep. 14	C.H. Cahan reports there is revolutionary movement in Canada.
Sep. 15–20	National Industrial Conference held in Ottawa.
Sep. 19– Oct. 31	Parliamentary committee under Calder hears demands from many witnesses for bonus and other benefits, government refuses.
Sep. 26	Paper Tribunal fixes export price for newsprint.
Oct.	Drought reduces wheat crop in prairie West.
Oct. 3– Nov. 26	Borden takes holiday in United States.
Oct. 15	Shares of Grand Trunk Railway transferred to Canadian government.
Oct. 20	United Farmers of Ontario win forty-four seats, Labour eleven; together they form government.
	Ontario votes for Prohibition in referendum.
Oct. 27	Saskatchewan farmers' candidate defeats W.R. Motherwell in federal by-election; farmers' candidate in New Brunswick wins federal by-election.
Oct. 28	Volstead Act becomes law, having been passed by U.S. House and Senate over veto of President Wilson.
Nov.	"Forward Movement" in Protestant churches begins.
Nov.–Dec.	Lord Jellicoe visits Canada, promoting Canadian navy within Imperial fleet.
Nov. 5	Meighen defends railway policy to Montreal Canadian Club.
Nov. 6	Robson Commission reports Winnipeg Strike not a revolution — not made public.
Nov. 11	Two-minutes' silence observed throughout the Empire.
Nov. 19	U.S. Senate rejects Treaty of Versailles and League of Nations.
Nov. 27	Treaty of Neuilly ends war with Bulgaria; Britain signs for Empire, including Canada.
Dec.	Canada agrees to allow officials of the government of India to interview family class immigrants.
Dec. 1	First Silver Crosses awarded to mothers of fallen soldiers.
Dec. 3	Government votes $23 million to help home ownership.
Dec. 14	Caucus convinces Borden to take leave instead of resigning.
Dec. 18	Winnipeg strike leader Bob Russell convicted of seditious conspiracy, sentenced to two years.
Dec. 20	General amnesty for prisoners still in jail for evading conscription.
Dec. 31	War Measures Act expires.

1919   (Cont'd)

Books published in 1919	Ralph Connor, *The Sky Pilot in No Man's Land*; John A. Stevenson, *Before the Bar: Prohibition — pro and con*; Ellen Mary Knox, *The Girl of the New Day*; W.C. Good, *Production and Taxation in Canada*; John MacCrae, *In Flanders Fields*; Peter MacArthur, *The Red Cow and Her Friends*; C.W. Peterson, *Wake Up, Canada*.

1920

Jan.	"Palmer raids" in United States result in arrest of hundreds of radicals, seize "evidence" of Bolshevik conspiracy.
Jan. 1	Under revised Canada Temperance Act (November 1919), federal prohibition of trade in liquor ends.
Jan. 2	Borden leaves on extended rest trip.
Jan. 6	Special conference of Canadian Council of Agriculture agrees to support candidates running on New National Policy.
Jan. 8	Board of Commerce issues first of several orders regulating price of sugar.
Jan. 10	League of Nations formed in Geneva.
Jan. 16	Eighteenth Amendment (Prohibition) comes into force in United States.
Jan. 20–25	United Farmers of Alberta convention endorses group government.
Feb.	Forward Movement in Protestant churches holds week-long fundraising campaign.
Feb. 1	RCMP established.
Feb. 9	Ukrainian People's Council formed in Saskatoon.
Feb. 16	Winnipeg strike leader Fred Dixon acquitted on charge of seditious libel; case against J.S. Woodsworth does not proceed.
Feb. 26	New Centre Block of Parliament Buildings opened.
	Eleven MPs constitute themselves as National Progressive Party.
Mar. 27	Winnipeg strike leaders Queen, Ivens, Johns, Pritchard, Armstrong convicted of seditious conspiracy; Bray convicted on a common nuisance charge; Heaps acquitted.
Mar. 29	Report of Robson Committee on Winnipeg General Strike made public.
Apr. 10	Helen MacMurchy becomes director of Child Welfare Division, Department of Health.
May 7	Art Gallery of Ontario holds its first Group of Seven exhibition.
May 10	Canada announces it will appoint minister in Washington.
May 12	Borden returns to Ottawa.
	Appointment of Sir Arthur Currie as principal of McGill.
May 14	*Canadian Forum* founded.
Jun. 4	Treaty of Trianon with Hungary; Britain signs for Empire, including Canada.
Jun. 16–17	Debate on militia estimates; drastic cuts in military budgets.
Jun. 28	Dominion Elections Act passed, comes into force on July 1.
Jun. 29	Manitoba elects twelve farmer, nine labour, and two socialist MLAs, including four imprisoned strike leaders and Rev. A.E. Smith — Norris government reduced to minority.
Jul. 1	Amendments to Indian Act require aboriginal parents to send children to school; allow Indian Affairs to ban hereditary rule of bands; allow for involuntary enfranchisement of any status Indian.

1920 (Cont'd)

Indian Affairs Settlement Act gives federal government power to implement 1916 Royal Commission on B.C. Indian land claims.

Borden announces resignation; Union caucus forms "National Liberal and Conservative Party"; Rowell resigns.

Jul. 10   Arthur Meighen becomes prime minister.

Jul. 27   Twelve farmer and labour MLAs elected in Nova Scotia.

Aug. 10   Treaty of Sèvres ends war with Ottoman Empire; Britain signs for the Empire, including Canada.

Aug. 31   Canadian Wheat Board terminates operations.

Sep.   Prices begin to fall, economy commences downward slide.

Sep. 1   Drayton Commission on the Tariff begins hearings across the country.

Oct.   Ukrainian republic collapses after defeat by Bolsheviks.

Oct. 1   Ontario legislation on minimum wages, mother's allowances, workmen's compensation comes into force.

Oct. 7–17   First trans-Canada flight from Halifax to Vancouver.

Oct. 9   Nine farmers, two labour members elected to New Brunswick legislature.

Oct. 16   Oil discovered at Fort Norman on Mackenzie River.

Oct. 20   British Columbia voters approve government sale of liquor.

Oct. 25   Three Prairie provinces and Nova Scotia vote to go "dry."

Nov. 2   Warren G Harding elected U.S. president on platform of "Normalcy."

Nov. 4   Sugar prices collapse on Montreal market, begin free-fall.

Nov. 15–
Dec. 18   First meeting of League of Nations at Geneva. Rowell makes speech attacking European diplomacy.

Dec. 1   OIC requires immigrants to have $250 to enter Canada.

British Columbia Liberal government re-elected; three Labour MLAs elected.

Dec. 6   CCA accepts Progressive parliamentary group led by Crerar as "parliamentary exponents of the New National Policy."

Dec. 20   "Luxury taxes" in place since the war are quietly removed

Books
published
in 1920   Salem Bland, *The New Christianity*; Stephen Leacock, *The Unsolved Riddle of Social Justice*; William Irvine, *The Farmers in Politics*; Dr. Helen MacMurchy, *The Almosts*.

1921

Jan. 1   Toronto ratepayers approve takeover of Mackenzie's street railway.

Feb. 14–
Jun. 4   Parliament in session.

Mar. 3   *Canadian Mother's Book* published, 150,000 copies distributed by end of 1921.

Mar. 12   Canadian Authors' Association formed.

Mar. 18   Treaty of Riga ends war between Soviet Union and Poland and Ukraine.

Apr. 18   Ontario referendum votes province "dry."

Jun. 1   Communist Party of Canada founded at secret meeting in barn in Guelph, ON.

Jun. 9   Saskatchewan elects Liberal government under William Martin.

Jun. 27   Progressive Robert Gardiner wins federal by-election in Medicine Hat.

Jun. 27–
Jul. 1   Imperial Conference debates Anglo-Japanese Treaty.

1921 (Cont'd)

Jul. 17	Treaty 11 opens Dene land in NWT to resource development.
Jul. 18	United Farmers of Alberta under Greenfield win provincial election; Irene Parlby becomes first woman cabinet minister; Nellie McClung elected for Liberals.
Sep.	Arbitration board rules GTR is responsible for debt of GTP, whose shares are valueless.
Sep. 24	Confédération des travailleurs catholiques du Canada founded.
Nov. 8	Willison resigns as CRA president.
Nov. 11	Remembrance Day becomes yearly event; poppy introduced as symbol of remembrance, with proceeds of sales to wounded veterans.
Nov.12– Feb. 6 (1922)	Washington Conference on Naval Disarmament establishes naval limits among Britain, USA, Japan, France, and Italy, and arrangements regarding China.
Dec.	First seminar of L'action française discusses economy.
Dec. 6	Federal election returns 118 Liberals, sixty-four Progressives (including Agnes Macphail), fifty Conservatives, and two Labour MPs (including Woodsworth).
Dec. 28	Chippawa generating station opened, largest in the world.
Books published in 1921	Vilhjalmur Stefansson, The Friendly Arctic; Lucy Maud Montgomery, Rilla of Ingleside; Ralph Connor, To Him That Hath; Salem Bland, The New Christianity.

1922

Feb. 11	Discovery of insulin at University of Toronto.
Mar. 11	Gordon McGregor dies; Ford Canada has assets of more than $25 million.
Apr.	Ten thousand Ukrainian Canadians march in Winnipeg to demand that government support creation of independent Ukraine.
Apr.–May	Deskaheh goes to London to plead case for Iroquois sovereignty.
May	Marie Gérin-Lajoie appeals to International Union of Catholic Women's Leagues in Rome, which rules women's suffrage is subject to approval of bishops.
May 3	Women given the vote in P.E.I.
May 12	Royal Canadian Navy reduced to three small ships on each coast.
Jun. 11	Nanook of the North premiers in New York.
Jun. 28	National Defence Act brings all services under one minister.
Jul. 18	United Farmers of Manitoba government elected; six Labour MLAs also elected.
Sep. 15	British government requests assistance for its forces in Chanak, Turkey.
Sep. 18	King says response to British request must be decided by Parliament.
Sep. 19	U.S. Fordney-McCumber Tariff passed, highest rates in U.S. history.
Oct. 4	Paul Matoff murdered in Bienfait, Saskatchewan.
Oct. 22	Mussolini marches on Rome, establishes fascist state in Italy.
Nov. 10	Crerar resigns as leader of Progressive Party.
Dec. 30	Union of Soviet Socialist Republics formed; includes Ukrainian SSR.
Books published in 1922	Frederick Philip Grove, Over Prairie Trails; Canon F.G. Scott, The Great War As I Saw It; Canon Lionel Groulx, L'Appel de la Race; Dr. Peter Bryce, The Story of a National Crime, being an appeal for Justice to the Indians of Canada (pamphlet); Hilda Glynn-Ward, The Writing on the Wall.

1923

Jan.	Immigration Order establishes four orders of priority: British; north European; south and east European; Jews, Blacks, and Orientals.
Mar. 2	Halibut Treaty first international agreement signed by Canada on its own.
Jun. 25	Howard Ferguson's Conservatives defeat United Farmers of Ontario.
Jul. 1	Chinese Immigration Act prohibits Chinese immigration.
Jul. 5	Strike begins at Sydney Steel; will last two years.
Aug. 17	Home Bank fails; bankruptcy followed by commission of enquiry and criminal prosecutions of two of its officers — Pellatt is ruined.
Aug. 23	Harding, first U.S. president to visit Canada, dies on visit to Alaska.
Oct. 19	Alberta Wheat Pool opened in Calgary.
Oct. 22	At Imperial Conference, King insists final statement declare Commonwealth a gathering of autonomous Dominions.
Books published in 1923	Douglas Durkin, *The Magpie*; Dr. Alan Brown, *The Normal Child: Its Care and Feeding*.

1924

Apr. 25	Wembley Exhibition opens in London with Group of Seven paintings.
Oct. 23	Ontario referendum supports prohibition by narrow majority.

1925

Jun. 10	United Church of Canada inaugurated.
Sep. 7	Senator Raoul Dandurand elected president of the League of Nations Assembly, calls Canada a "fireproof house."
	Railway Agreement allows railways to recruit agricultural immigrants.
Oct. 29	Federal election returns 116 Conservatives, 101 Liberals, twenty-four Progressives, four Independents. King continues as prime minister, with minority government.
Nov. 10	Wheat yield of 423 million bushels is largest to date.
Nov. 25	Unity Conference in Winnipeg establishes Royal Canadian Legion.

1926

Feb. 2	Customs scandal ends Mackenzie King's minority government.
Jun. 28	King asks Governor General Lord Byng to dissolve the House; Byng refuses and sends for Meighen — Meighen government falls on July 2.
Sep. 14	Liberals win election, alleging Byng interfered in Canadian affairs.
Nov. 18	Balfour Report declares Dominions equal, united by common allegiance to the Crown, and freely associated as the British Commonwealth of Nations.
Dec. 1	Ontario voters give Ferguson mandate to repeal Prohibition.
Dec. 29	Pope condemns *L'Action Française*.

1927

Jul. 1–3	Canada celebrates Diamond Jubilee of Confederation.

Cast of Main Characters

Ahenakew, Rev. Edward (1885–1961): Born on Poundmaker Reserve; educated Prince Albert, Saskatoon, Wycliffe College, Toronto; Anglican missionary; author of Cree-English dictionary, *Voices of the Plains Cree*; leader of League of Western Indians.

Aird, Sir John (1885–1938): Succeeded Sir Edmund Walker as president of Bank of Commerce (1924–29); chaired royal commission that recommended establishing the CBC.

Aitken, Max, Lord Beaverbrook (1879–1964): Halifax financier; moved to Montreal, engineered corporate mergers; moved to London (1910), became Lord Beaverbrook; press baron; British minister of information in World War I, minister of war production in World War II.

Anderson, J.T.M. (1878–1946): School inspector in Saskatchewan; recommended education to assimilate immigrants; Conservative leader in 1922, premier (1929–34).

Andrews, Alfred J. (1865–1950): Lawyer; mayor of Winnipeg (1898–1900); organized Citizens' Committee during the General Strike; lawyer for Bronfman family.

Beatty, Sir Edward (1877–1943): Lawyer; president of CPR (1918–43); chancellor of Queen's University, then McGill (1921–43).

Beck, Sir Adam (1857–1925): Manufacturer; mayor of London; MPP (1906–19, 1923–25); chair, Ontario Hydro (1906–25); built

Chippawa generating station; made Hydro largest public power system in world; unsuccessfully advocated radial railways.

Beynon, Frances (1884–1951): Winnipeg feminist; women's columnist for *Grain Growers' Guide;* opposed war; left Canada 1918; wrote autobiographical novel, *Aleta Dey.*

Bird, Will (1891–1984): Enlisted after his older brother killed; after 1923 became journalist and writer of novels, memoirs, stories, history, and travel books; in 1930s, was voice of veterans.

Bland, Salem (1859–1950): Social Gospel minister; teacher at Wesley College Winnipeg (1900–17); prime author of Methodist programme (1918); wrote *The New Christianity;* leading voice for social reform and liberal theology within United Church.

Borden, Sir Robert (1854–1937): Nova Scotia corporate lawyer; Conservative leader (1900), prime minister (1911–20); led Canada through World War I, formed Union government in 1917, asserted Canadian nationhood at Paris; supported internationalism in 1920s.

Bourassa, Henri (1868–1952): Left Laurier cabinet over Boer War (1899), founded Ligue nationaliste (1903), *Le Devoir* (1910); Catholic critic of capitalism; anti-imperialist, advocated Canadian nation based on duality; opposed conscription; critical of Canon Groulx.

Bray, Roger E. (dates unknown): Butcher, lay Methodist preacher, socialist; came to Winnipeg from England in 1903; opposed war but enlisted in 1916; leading organizer of soldiers during Winnipeg General Strike; imprisoned; gardener and CCF organizer in British Columbia.

Bronfman, Sam (1891–1971): With his Saskatchewan family, converted their hotel chain into liquor business; supplied American bootleggers; moved to Montreal, built Seagram's into world-famous brand; prominent Jewish leader, benefactor, advocate for immigration.

Bruchési, Archbishop Louis Joseph Napoléon Paul (1855–1939): Archbishop of Montreal (1897–1939); conservative cleric, asserted Church authority in all aspects of social policy.

Cahan, Charles H. (1861–1944): Montreal lawyer; promoted investments in Latin America; warned of Bolshevism (1919); ran for Conservative leadership (1927); minister in cabinet of R.B. Bennett (1930–35).

Caisserman, Hannaniah (1884–1950): General secretary of Canadian Jewish Congress; Labour Zionist; promoted Jewish immigration; political candidate; author.

Calder, J.A. (1868–1956): Liberal minister and deputy premier in Saskatchewan (1905–17); Union cabinet minister and key Western Canada political figure (1917–21); Conservative senator (1921–56).

Cassidy, Harry (1900–1951): Dean of Social Work, University of Toronto; involved with early CCF, then Liberal Party, in Ontario; his 1943 study was basis for modern social welfare system.

Chapais, (Sir) Thomas C. (1858–1946): Son of a father of Confederation; journalist; Conservative member of Quebec Legislative Council; senator (1919–46); professor of history at Laval (1907–34); president of Canadian Historical Association; delegate to League of Nations; minister in Duplessis government (1944); knighted (1935).

Chown, Samuel Dwight (1853–1933): Methodist minister; secretary, Department of Temperance and Moral Reform (1902), general superintendent (1910); declined to be first moderator of United Church as gesture to Presbyterians.

Christie, Loring (1885–1941): Nova Scotia–born Harvard Law graduate; served with U.S. Department of Justice; External Affairs legal advisor (1913–24); Round Tabler; joined private sector in Britain and Canada; rejoined External Affairs (1935), ambassador to United States (1939–41).

Church, Tommy (1870–1950): Conservative politician; mayor of Toronto (1915–21), MP (1921–30, 1934–50); noted for outspoken, populist style.

Claxton, Brooke (1898–1960): Soldier, lawyer, part of "nationalist network" in 1920s; minister of health and welfare (1944–46), minister of national defence (1946–54).

Cohen, Lyon (1868–1937): Born in Poland, came to Montreal, 1871; founded Freedman Company and Canadian Export Clothiers; with Sam Jacobs founded *Canadian Jewish Times*; president, Canadian Jewish Congress (1919); organized Jewish Immigrant Aid Services.

Connor, Ralph: (See Gordon, Charles W.)

Creighton, William B. (1864–1946): Methodist minister, editor *Christian Guardian*; supporter of Social Gospel and war effort; in 1920s supported League of Nations and internationalism.

Crerar, Thomas (1876–1975): President, Manitoba Grain Growers (1910); Union minister of agriculture (1917–19); led Progressive Party (1920–22); cabinet minister in King Liberal governments (1929–30, 1935–45); Liberal senator (1945–66).

Currie, Sir Arthur (1875–1933): Victoria real estate agent and militia officer; one of best generals in Imperial armies, commanded Canadian Corps (1917–19); principal of McGill (1920–33); sued journalist for libel in 1928 after it was charged he wasted lives at Mons.

Dafoe, John Wesley (1866–1944): Influential editor of *Winnipeg Free Press;* Western liberal; opposed French schools; supported conscription; opposed centralized Empire, supported internationalism; key nationalist intellectual, confidant of political leaders.

Dandurand, Senator Raoul (1861–1942): Quebec lawyer; senator (1898–1942); advisor to Mackenzie King; delegate to League of Nations, president of Assembly (1925).

Deskaheh (Levi General) (1873–1925): Cayuga from Six Nations; proponent of traditional Long House culture; in 1923–24, pleaded before League of Nations for recognition of Iroquois sovereignty; died at Tuscorora Reserve, New York State.

Dixon, Fred (1881–1931): Socialist, elected to Manitoba legislature in 1914; opposed conscription; acquitted of seditious libel after Winnipeg Strike; elected to legislature in 1921 as independent labour member, resigned in 1923.

Doherty, Charles J. (1855–1931): Montreal lawyer, professor, judge; minister of justice (1911–21); delegate to Paris Peace Conference; opposed Article X there and at first League Assembly in 1921; signed Versailles treaty for Canada; opposed labour radicalism.

Durkin, Douglas (1884–1967): Winnipeg literature professor; became writer in New York (1921), wrote novel *The Magpie* (1923); helped Martha Ostenso write *Wild Geese* (1925).

Drayton, Sir Henry (1869–1950): Toronto lawyer; chair, Board of Railway Commissioners (1912–19); headed royal commission on Canadian Northern (1917); finance minister (1919–21); ran for Conservative leadership (1927); appointed to Liquor Control Board of Ontario (1928).

Drury, E.C. (1878–1968): Farmer; co-founder of United Farmers of Ontario (1913); defeated as Liberal (1917); premier of Ontario (1919–23); prohibitionist; ran unsuccessfully as Progressive in federal elections in late 1920s; wrote history and memoirs.

Falconer, Sir Robert (1867–1943): Presbyterian scholar; president, University of Toronto (1907–32); wrote *Idealism in National Character* (1920), *Pastoral Epistles* (1937).

Fielding, William Stevens (1848–1929): Liberal premier of Nova Scotia (1886–96); minister of finance under Laurier (1896–1911) and King (1921–25); author of Reciprocity agreement (1911); supported conscription (1917); defeated by King for Liberal leadership (1919).

Flavelle, Sir Joseph (1858–1939): Toronto capitalist; president, William Davies Company; founded Toronto *News*; Methodist philanthropist, active in University of Toronto and founding Toronto General Hospital; chair, Imperial Munitions Board (1916–18); accused of profiteering; advised Borden on railway policy, chaired Grand Trunk Railway (1921).

Foster, Sir George 1847–1931): minister in cabinets of seven Conservative prime ministers from Macdonald to Meighen; delegate to Paris Peace Conference 1919; acting prime minister (1920); senator (1921–31).

Freiman, Archibald (1880–1944): Ottawa department store owner; with wife, Lillian (organizer of Hadassah), supported immigration and Zionism; fought anti-Semitism; supported Jewish relief during World War II.

Gérin-Lajoie, Marie Lacoste (1867–1945): Quebec feminist, suffragist, social reformer, self-taught legal expert, and professor; co-founder Fédération nationale Saint-Jean-Baptiste.

Good, William C. (1876–1967): Agrarian reformer; educated at University of Toronto, and Ontario Agricultural College; co-founder of United Farmers of Ontario; Progressive MP (1921–25), Ginger Group (1924); president, Co-operative Union of Canada (1921–45).

Gordon, Charles W. (Ralph Connor) (1860–1937): Winnipeg minister, Social Gospeller, served as chaplain in war; moderator of Presbyterian Church (1921); as Ralph Connor, wrote best-selling novels on themes ranging from prohibition to immigration, labour, and war.

Gouin, Sir Jean Lomer (1861–1929): Liberal premier of Quebec (1905–20); supported business and investment, modernized government; federal justice minister (1921–24).

Gray, James H. (1906–1998): Messenger, Winnipeg Grain Exchange (1922), trader, freelance writer, reporter; editor; published memoirs and books on Western Canadian history.

Groulx, Canon Lionel (1878–1967): Priest; studied for doctorate in Switzerland and Rome; professor of Canadian history at Université de Montréal; through writings including *L'Appel de la Race* and *l'Action française* advocated Quebec clerical nationalism; influenced a generation of Québecois intellectuals, clerics, and nationalists.

Hague, Dyson (1857–1935): Evangelical Anglican, lecturer at Wycliffe College, Toronto; one of the authors of *The Fundamentals*; advocated return to traditional doctrines within his church.

Harris, Lawren (1885–1970): Member of farm implement manufacturing family; Canadian painter, key force behind Group of Seven; later paintings of Arctic broke new ground.

Harris, Lloyd (1867–1925): Businessman from farm implement manufacturing family; Liberal MP (1908–11); headed Canadian trade missions in Washington and London; attended Paris Peace Conference to promote trade and relief after the war.

Hatch, Harold Clifford (1884–1946): Distiller; bought Gooderham and Worts (1923), Hiram Walker (1927), Corby's (1935); exported into United States during and after Prohibition; later, thoroughbred horse racer and pioneer in Niagara wine industry.

Heaps, Abraham Albert (1885–1954): Upholsterer, came to Winnipeg from Britain (1911); Labour alderman (1917–25); arrested after General Strike and acquitted; elected as Labour MP (1925); founding member of CCF; pressed for Jewish immigration in 1930s.

Holt, Sir Herbert (1856–1941): Railway contractor; president, Royal Bank of Canada, Montreal Light, Heat & Power, and director of 250 companies; key member of Montreal financial community and seen, especially by French Canadians, as ruthless face of capitalism.

Hughes, James Laughlin (1846–1935): (Brother of Sir Sam); educator, inspector of Toronto schools; Orangeman; advocated military training, kindergarten, votes for women (his wife was a suffragist and his daughter a socialist and pacifist).

Hughes, Sir Sam (1853–1921): Orangeman, editor, politician, soldier; minister of militia (1911–16); anti-French rhetoric, erratic behaviour, and fiascos like that involving the Ross rifle led to his dismissal from Cabinet; attacked Currie after his son was denied command of a Canadian division.

Hughes, William "Billy" (1862–1952): Nationalist coalition prime minister of Australia (1915–23); noted for being acerbic; changed parties five times and was expelled from three; took on Woodrow Wilson at Paris over German colonies.

Hutton, Maurice (1856–1940): Professor of Classics at University of Toronto (1880–1928); principal of University College (1900–28); much-admired teacher, writer and speaker.

Irvine, William (1885–1962): Presbyterian Social Gospel minister, became Unitarian, founded Labour Church in Calgary; socialist but joined H.W. Wood in advocating group government; Labour MP (1921–25), member of Ginger Group; a founder of CCF.

Ivens, William (1878–1957): Methodist minister; opposed conscription; established Labour Church; edited strikers' newspaper during Winnipeg General Strike; convicted of seditious libel; elected to Manitoba legislature (1920); later joined CCF.

Jackson, Alexander Young (A.Y.) (1882–1974): Painter; war artist; member of Group of Seven.

Jacobs, Samuel (1871–1938): Lawyer; MP (1917–38); co-founded *Jewish Times*; fought anti-Semitism and discrimination; pressed for Jewish immigration, especially in 1930s.

Jenness, Diamond (1886–1969): New Zealand-born anthropologist, member of Stefansson Arctic expedition (1913); recruited from Oxford to Canadian Natural History Museum; did ground-breaking studies of Inuit and Indians; disagreed with policies of Indian Affairs.

Johns, Richard (1889–1970): Socialist leader of OBU; convicted of seditious conspiracy after Winnipeg General Strike; became industrial arts teacher and leading technical educator.

Kavanagh, John Patrick Marcus (1879–1964): B.C. Socialist and OBU leader; joined Communist Party (1921); in 1925 moved to Australia and became leading Communist there.

Ketchen, General (1872–1959): From British military family, came to Canada (1894); NWMP; lieutenant in Boer War, brigadier-general in CEF (1915–18), retired as major-general (1929); Manitoba MLA (Conservative, 1936–45), Leader of Opposition (1941–50).

Kilpatrick, Thomas (1857–1930): Scottish Presbyterian professor; his son George was also a church leader; padre during World War I; leader in the United Church.

King, William Lyon Mackenzie (1874–1950): Studied political economy at Toronto, Chicago, Harvard (Ph.D.); deputy minister (1900–08) and minister (1908–11) of labour; adviser to Rockefellers (1915–19); Liberal candidate (1917); *Industry and Humanity* (1918); Liberal leader (1919); longest serving prime minister in Canadian history (1921–25; 1926–30; 1935–48).

Kiriak, Illia (1888–1955): Ukrainian immigrant trained as a teacher in Ukrainian-language schools; writer, poet, scholar; wrote fictional trilogy *Sons of the Soil* in Ukrainian.

Knox, Ellen Mary (1858–1924): Evangelical Anglican; educated at Oxford and Cambridge; principal, Havergal School for girls (1894–1924).

Lapointe, Arthur (1895–1960): From Saint-Ulric, Quebec; station agent; soldier in 22nd Regiment; Liberal MP (1935–45).

Laurier, Sir Wilfrid (1841–1919): Lawyer; MP (1874–1919); promoted tolerance and language rights, opposed clerical interference in politics, elegant and eloquent in both languages; as prime minister (1896–1911), presided over economic boom until defeated on naval and Reciprocity issues; opposed conscription; Liberals shattered in 1917 election.

Leacock, Stephen (1869–1955): Born in England, raised on Ontario farm; educated, Upper Canada College, University of Toronto (languages); Ph.D. (Chicago, political economy); McGill professor, social commentator; best-selling humorist in English (1910–25); wrote over sixty books, including *Sunshine Sketches of a Little Town* (1912).

Lismer, Arthur (1885–1969): Painter; trained in England and Belgium, came to Canada (1911); taught in Halifax (1916–19); one of the Group of Seven.

Loft, Frederick O. (Onondeyoh) (1861–1934): Mohawk from Six Nations; Liberal; Ontario civil servant; militia officer; served overseas; organized League of Canadian Indians (1919).

Mackenzie, Sir William (1849–1923): Built street railways in Toronto and Winnipeg; with Donald Mann built Canadian Northern into transcontinental railway; by 1917, CNoR was bankrupt and was taken over by CN; in 1921, his Toronto street railway was taken over by the city.

Mackinney, Louise (1868–1931): Schoolteacher; elected Alberta MLA (1917); defeated as UFA candidate (1921); one of "Famous Five" in "Persons Case."

MacMurchy, Dr. Helen (1862–1953): Pioneer woman doctor, public health expert; Ontario Inspector for the Feeble-minded; director, Maternal and Child Welfare, Department of Health (1920–34); originated Little Blue Books; in 1949 voted one of ten leading female physicians in world.

MacMurchy, Marjory (1870–1938): (Sister of Helen); journalist; author of *The Woman — Bless Her* (1916), *The Canadian Girl at Work* (1919); head, women's department, Canadian Reconstruction Association; served on various public commissions; second wife of Sir John Willison (1926).

Macphail, Sir Andrew (1864–1938): Professor of medicine at McGill; founded *University Magazine;* essayist with conservative views; novelist; joined medical corps, wrote its official history.

Macphail, Agnes (1890–1954): Schoolteacher; first woman MP (Progressive, 1921); opposed its evolution into a party; member of Ginger Group (1924); joined, then left, CCF; later Ontario CCF MPP.

Marie-Victorin, Brother Martin, (born Joseph-Louis Conrad Kirouac (1885–1944): Pioneer of botanical study in Quebec; professor, researcher, collector of biological specimens.

Massey, Raymond (1896–1983): (Brother of Vincent); educated, Toronto and Oxford; artillery officer in WWI and Siberia; actor on both London and New York stage; long career in film and TV (best known as Dr. Gillespie in *Dr. Kildare* series); wrote memoirs.

Massey, Vincent (1887–1967): Educated at Toronto and Oxford; Round Tabler; secretary to Repatriation Committee; endowed Hart House at Toronto; headed family educational foundation;

Liberal candidate; ambassador to United States and high commissioner to Britain; chaired Massey Commission on Culture; first Canadian-born governor general; endowed Massey College at Toronto.

Mavor, James (1854–1925): Scottish-born professor of political economy at Toronto; wrote economic history of Russia; helped bring Doukhobors to Canada; opposed public ownership of utilities; world traveller with wide circle of friends.

May, "Wop" (1896–1952): World War I flying ace; barnstormer, pioneer bush pilot; organized air training and RCAF Search and Rescue in World War II.

McArthur, Peter (1866–1924): Educated, University of Toronto; writing career in New York and London; returned to his farm (1908); as "sage of Ekfrid," wrote hundreds of articles, collected in books, about animals, rural living, and extolling "common man" against "the interests."

McClung, Nellie (née Moodie) (1873–1951): Leading novelist and essayist, gained fame with *Sowing Seeds in Danny* (1908); campaigner for prohibition, women's suffrage; moved to Alberta (1914); Alberta MLA (1921–25); one of "Famous Five" in "Persons Case."

McGregor, Gordon (1873–1922): As president of family wagon company, secured rights to manufacture Ford cars in Canada (1904); established subsidiaries in Australia, New Zealand, South Africa; by 1922, seven out of every ten cars sold in Canada were Fords.

McLachlan, James Bryson (1869–1937): Scottish-born leader of bitter Cape Breton coal strikes in 1920s; convicted of seditious libel in 1923; member of Socialist Party of Canada, then Communist party (1921); radical labour leader and political candidate in 1930s.

McLaughlin, Sam (1971–1972): Converted carriage factory in Oshawa to produce cars with engines from Buick, sold to GM (1918); president of General Motors Canada.

McNeil, Grant (1892–1976): Served in military overseas; secretary of Great War Veterans' Association (1918–25); MP from Vancouver for CCF (1935); later CCF national organizer; B.C. MLA.

Meighen, Arthur (1874–1960): Educated at University of Toronto (mathematics); Manitoba lawyer; MP (1908–27); as cabinet minister managed key issues in Union government, including conscription, veterans' resettlement, railway nationalization, Winnipeg General Strike; prime minister (1920–21, 1926); senator (1932–42); unsuccessful comeback as Conservative leader in 1942 ended in defeat.

Montpetit, Édouard (1881–1954): First Paris-trained political economist in Quebec; founded École des sciences sociales (1920); secretary-general; dean of social science, law teacher at University of Montreal and at affiliated École des hautes études commerciales.

Montgomery, Lucy Maud (1874–1942): World-famous author of *Anne of Green Gables* (1908); published twenty novels set in Prince Edward Island; as wife of Presbyterian minister, lived in Leaskdale and Norval, Ontario.

Moore, T. Albert (1860–1940): Methodist minister; secretary of evangelism and social service committees; with Presbyterian J.G. Shearer, led campaigns for Lord's Day observance, prohibition, and social reform; moderator of the United Church (1932–34).

Moore, Tom (1878–1943): Carpenter, came from England (1909); president Trades Union Congress (1918–35, 1938–43); fought off challenge from socialists and One Big Union.

Morrison, James J. (1861–1936): Leader of co-operative movement; co-founder and general secretary of United Farmers of Ontario; opposed UFO becoming a party, alliance with labour, and other Drury policies; continued as leader of UFO into 1930s.

Motherwell, William Richard (1860–1943): Saskatchewan agricultural pioneer; leader in grain growers' movement; provincial minister of agriculture (1905–17); defeated for federal Parliament (1919), elected (1921); minister of agriculture (1921–30).

Murphy, Emily (1868–1933): Alberta feminist; popular writer under name "Janey Canuck"; police magistrate; in *The Black Candle* (1922), painted sensational (and racist) picture of drug trade; one of "Famous Five" in "Persons' Case."

Norris, Tobias C. (1861–1936): Liberal premier of Manitoba (1915–22); enacted votes for women, Prohibition, workmen's compensation, abolished French language schools; dealt with Winnipeg General Strike; defeated by United Farmers of Manitoba (1922).

Oakes, Sir Harry (1874–1943): American-born promoter of Kirkland Lake gold mine, became immensely wealthy and moved to Bahamas; murdered under mysterious circumstances.

Oliver, Edmund H. (1882–1935): B.A., M.A., Ph.D.; principal of St. Andrew's Theological College, Saskatchewan (1905); padre in World War I; moderator of the United Church (1930–32).

Parlby, Irene (1888–1965): Immigrated from England 1896; president, United Farm Women of Alberta (1916–19); Alberta MLA (1921–35); one of the "Famous Five" in "Persons Case."

Parsons, Silas R. (1853–1932): President, British-American Oil; Methodist opponent of Social Gospel; president of Canadian Manufacturers' Association; proponent of high tariffs and opponent of labour unions.

Partridge, Edward Alexander (1862–1931): Agrarian reformer and visionary, founded Grain Growers' Grain Company (1906); *Grain Growers' Guide* (1908); advocated government ownership of elevators and "co-operative commonwealth"; supported wheat pools.

Pease, Edson R. (1856–1930): Built Royal Bank into largest in Canada; as president of Canadian Bankers Association instrumental in organizing wartime finance; unsuccessfully advocated for central bank.

Pegahmagabow, Francis (1891–1952): Ojibwa from Parry Sound reserve; most decorated First Nations soldier of WWI; native rights activist; band chief (1921–24).

Pellatt, Sir Henry (1859–1939): Toronto stockbroker and financier; colonel of Queen's Own Rifles; made fortune in electricity, railways, real estate; spent most of it on Casa Loma in Toronto; ruined when real estate ventures failed; died virtually penniless.

Perry, Bowen (1860–1956): Commissioner of North West Mounted Police (1900–20), and of RCMP (1920–23); after military and legal training, joined NWMP, served in Northwest Rebellion (1885); recommendations led to establishment of RCMP; monitored radical activity.

Peterson, Charles Walter (1868–1944): Journalist, edited business and agriculture journals; author of many articles and books, including *Wake Up, Canada* (1919).

Pidgeon, George (1872–1971): Theology professor (1909–15); minister of Bloor Street church, Toronto (1916–48); moderator of Presbyterian Church (1923–25) and United Church (1925–26); co-founded Canadian Council of Churches (1945), World Council of Churches (1946).

Pritchard, William (1888–1981): British-born B.C. socialist, organizer of OBU; address to jury at trial for seditious conspiracy after Winnipeg General Strike a masterly exposition of socialism; reeve of Burnaby; B.C. CCF leader in 1930s; left for California; returned in 1960s.

Queen, John (1882–1946): Cooper, came to Winnipeg from Scotland (1906); socialist alderman (1916–19); General Strike leader; elected to Manitoba legislature while in prison (1921); leader, Independent Labour Party (1923–35); mayor of Winnipeg (1934–36, 1937–42).

Raney, William E. (1859–1933): Lawyer; attorney-general in UFO government (1919–23); enforced Prohibition and attacked gambling; leader of UFO (1925); after electoral defeat in 1926, appointed to Supreme Court of Ontario (1927).

Robertson, Gideon(1874–1933): Telegraphist; trade unionist; senator (1917–33); minister of labour in Union (1918–21) and R.B.

Bennett (1930–32) governments; played key role in wartime labour negotiations and Winnipeg General Strike.

Rogers, Robert (1864–1936): Manitoba Conservative known as master of machine politics and patronage in provincial (1900–11) and federal (1911–17) governments; dropped from Cabinet in 1917; defeated for party leadership in 1927.

Rollo, Walter (1875–1956): Hamilton labour leader and health; Labour Party Ontario MPP (1919–23); minister of labour and health; solid achievements as minister but could not unite caucus or prevent farmer-dominated government from enacting some measures opposed by labour.

Rowell, Newton Wesley (1867–1941): Lawyer, Methodist, prohibitionist, Ontario Liberal leader (1911–17); Union cabinet minister (1917–20); supporter of League of Nations; co-chair of Rowell-Sirois Commission on Canadian federalism (1937–41).

Russell, Robert Boyd (1889–1964): Machinist, came to Winnipeg from Scotland (1911); socialist; leader in OBU and Winnipeg General Strike; imprisoned; defeated in provincial (1920) and federal (1921) elections; led OBU until 1950s.

Russell, Thomas A. (1877–1940): B.A., political economy (Toronto); protégé of Flavelle, president of Canada Cycle and Motor Company (1901); began making cars; key figure in war production for IMB; partnership with Willys (1915); in 1930s revitalized Massey-Harris.

St-Pierre, Arthur (1885–1959): Journalist, parliamentary correspondent; co-founder of l'École sociale populaire (1911); social science professor, University of Montreal (1922–52).

Scott, Duncan Campbell (1862–1947): Man of letters, musician, deputy minister of Indian Affairs (1913–32); one of the "Confederation Poets" in 1880s and 1890s; pursued a policy of assimilating Indians; president of Royal Society of Canada (1921–22).

Shearer, John G. (1859–1925): Presbyterian minister; crusader against prostitution and for prohibition and moral purity; with T.A. Moore, established the Social Service Council of Canada (1913); his focus shifted increasingly from moral to social reform during the war.

Sifton, Arthur (1858–1921): (Brother of Sir Clifford); jurist; premier of Alberta (1910–17), enacted Prohibition, women's suffrage, labour legislation and other reforms; joined Union Cabinet in 1917; attended Paris Peace Conference and signed the treaty for Canada.

Sifton, Sir Clifford (1861–1925): Manitoba lawyer, businessman; opposed bilingual schools; as federal minister of interior (1896–1905), brought East European immigrants to Canada; chaired Commission on Conservation (1909–18); his newspapers included the *Free Press*.

Simpson, James (1873–1938): Printer; trade unionist; long-time Toronto socialist city councillor; first CCF mayor of Toronto (1935); a leader of the Ontario Labour Party, which entered a coalition with UFO in 1919; fought Communists in 1920s; devout Methodist.

Skelton, Oscar Douglas (1878–1941): Professor of political economy; student of socialism; frequent commentator; biographer of Laurier; advisor to Mackenzie King; as under-secretary for external affairs (1925–41), built the Canadian foreign service.

Smith, Albert E. (1871–1947): Methodist Social Gospel minister; founded Labour Church in Brandon (1919); socialist MLA (1920–22); joined Communist Party (1925), loyal Stalinist.

Spence, Francis Stephens (1879–1917): Key Ontario figure in Dominion Alliance for the Suppression of the Liquor Traffic; national president (1912–17); succeeded in Ontario by brother, Ben Spence, who was more militant in demanding stringent prohibition measures in 1920s.

Stevenson, John A. (1883–1970): Educated in Scotland and at Oxford; wrote for *Free Press* and Toronto *Star*; Canadian correspondent of the London *Times* (1926–40); editorial writer for *Globe and Mail*, and *Saturday Night*; gained reputation for integrity and skill.

Taschereau, Louis-Alexandre (1867–1952): Liberal premier of Quebec (1920–36); opposed agrarian conservatism, advocated business and resource development; modernized government; scandals and party revolt destroyed party and led to Duplessis government.

Thornton, Sir Henry (1871–1933): President of Canadian National Railways (1923–32); after a career in U.S. railways, reorganized the British system during the war; modernized the CNR; his flamboyant lifestyle made him enemies, and after a scandal the government forced his resignation in 1932.

Underhill, Dr. Fred (1858–1936): British-trained doctor; pioneer public health officer in Vancouver; directed the fight against the Spanish flu.

Van Passen, Pierre (1895–1968): Dutch pacifist; came to Canada to study theology; served during the war; moved to United States; as journalist covered Middle East conflicts, war in Ethiopia, African slave trade, Spanish Civil War; wrote two books of memoirs.

Varley, Frederick (1881–1969): British artist, came to Canada in 1912; enlisted, serving as war artist (1918); painted searing pictures; member of Group of Seven.

Walker, Sir (Byron) Edmund (1848–1924): President, Canadian Bank of Commerce (1907–24); art collector and palaeontologist; key figure with University of Toronto, National Gallery of Canada, Champlain Society, Art Gallery of Ontario, Royal Ontario Museum.

White, Sir Thomas (1866–1955): Managing director, National Trust; key Toronto capitalist; joined Conservatives over Reciprocity in 1911; finance minister (1911–20); organized war finance; acting prime minister (1918–19); turned down prime ministership in 1920.

Willison, Sir John (1856–1927): Editor of *Globe*, then Toronto *News* (1902); organized publicity against Reciprocity (1911); Round Tabler; president, Canadian Reconstruction Association (1918–21); independent journalist and friend of political figures in Canada and Britain.

Winch, Ernest (1879–1957): Immigrated from Britain (1909); joined Social Democratic Party; president, Vancouver Trades and Labour

Congress (1918); co-founder, Independent Labour Party and CCF; MLA in British Columbia (1933–57).

Winning, James (dates unknown): Scottish-born bricklayer, came to Winnipeg in 1906; alderman; president of Trades and Labour Council during General Strike; served on Manitoba Minimum Wage Board (1918–41).

Wood, Henry Wise (1860–1941): American-born farm leader; organized grain growers and co-op elevators; dominated United Farmers of Alberta; advocated "group government."

Woodsworth, James S. (1874–1942): Methodist Social Gospeller; super-intendent of All Peoples' Mission Winnipeg (1907–15); opposed World War I; resigned ministry; arrested during Winnipeg General Strike; elected Independent Labour MP in 1921; first leader of the CCF (1933); in 1939 opposed Canada's entry into World War II.

Wright, Sarah Rowell (1862–1930): (Sister of N.W. Rowell); key figure in temperance, women's rights, and education move-ments; noted speaker and writer; president, Dominion WCTU, and executive of a host of other organizations, including world WCTU in 1920s.

Wrong, George M. (1860–1948): Professor at Wycliffe College, Toronto, then professor of history at University of Toronto; as the "father of Canadian history," he started the Champlain Society and wrote many books, including *The Rise and Fall of New France*; a liberal Imperialist, also an evangelical Anglican minister.

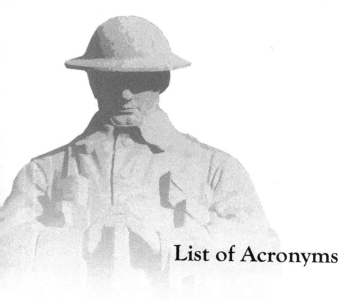

List of Acronyms

AFL	American Federation of Labour
CAR	*Canadian Annual Review of Public Affairs*
CCA	Canadian Council of Agriculture
CMA	Canadian Manufacturers' Association
CNoR	Canadian Northern Railway
CPR	Canadian Pacific Railway
CRA	Canadian Reconstruction Association
DCER	*Documents on Canadian External Relations*
DSCR	Department of Soldiers' Civil Re-establishment
EDC	Electrical Development Company
GGGC	Grain Growers' Grain Company
GTR	Grand Trunk Railway
GTP	Grand Trunk Pacific Railway
GWVA	Great War Veterans' Association
ILO	International Labour Organization
IMB	Imperial Munitions Board
IWC	Imperial War Cabinet
IWW	International Workers of the World
JIAS	Jewish Immigrant Aid Society
JCPC	Judicial Committee of the Privy Council
KMT	Kuomintang, today spelled Guomindong
MLA	Member of Legislative Assembly (provincial parliaments)
MPP	Member of Provincial Parliament (Ontario)

NTR	National Transcontinental Railway
OBU	One Big Union
RNWMP	Royal North-West Mounted Police
SDP	Social Democratic Party of Canada
SPC	Socialist Party of Canada
TLC	Trades and Labour Congress
UFA	United Farmers of Alberta
UFNB	United Farmers of New Brunswick
UFO	United Farmers of Ontario
USDP	Ukrainian Social Democratic Party
UCCC	Ukrainian Canadian Citizens' Committee
WCTU	Women's Christian Temperance Union
WTLC	Winnipeg Trades and Labour Congress

Acknowledgements

I want to express gratitude to those who have read chapters, offered comments and advice, and most of all, encouraged me to continue in this endeavour, especially Ramsay Cook, Roy Culpeper, Gerry Friesen, John Hilliker, Adriaan de Hoog, Margaret MacMillan, Donald B. Smith, and David Staines.

I want also to acknowledge the kindness of many archivists and librarians who have gone above and beyond in helping me to obtain images: Alix McEwen and other staff at Library and Archives Canada; Adria Lund of the Glenbow Archives; Sharon Foley of the Archives of Manitoba; Elizabeth Mathew of United Church Archives; Marnee Gamble of the University of Toronto Archives; Christine Sommerfeldt of Ontario Archives; Mélissa Tremblay of the McCord Museum; Sharon Anderson of the City of Toronto Archives; Kathryn Harvey and Paul Slack of the University of Guelph; Sally Keefe-Cohen, literary agent for the Heirs of L.M. Montgomery; Debra Latcham, archivist of Havergal College, Toronto; and Janet Mason, the archivist of Timothy Eaton Memorial Church — and all those who assisted them.

And of course, my thanks to Kirk Howard, Beth Bruder, and especially my editor, Dominic Farrell; they and all the other energetic and dedicated people at Dundurn Press made this book a reality and its production a pleasure.

I acknowledge the kindness of those who have allowed me to quote from copyrighted works: Norm Christie of CEF Books for Will Bird's *Ghosts Have Warm Hands;* the Heirs of L.M. Montgomery, Inc.; Professor Mary Rubio, and Oxford University Press for L.M. Montgomery's published journals;* Joan Champ of the Western Development Museum for her online article on the 1918 influenza epidemic; Gordon Goldsborough of the Manitoba Historical Society for permission to use the cartoon of A.J. Andrews, which he kindly scanned for me; and for the archives and collections that have granted permission to use pictures and images, which are detailed in the captions.

Above all, my wife, Carolyn, for her many suggestions, editorial assistance, and for putting up with me through this long process of creation. Of course, all the *bêtises* that remain — and they are undoubtedly legion — are my responsibility alone.

* *L.M. Montgomery* is a trademark of the Heirs of L.M. Montgomery, Inc.; *Anne of Green Gables* and other indicia of "Anne" are trademarks and Canadian official marks of the Anne of Green Gables Licensing Authority Inc.

Notes

To keep this book to a manageable size the Notes have not been included in the print edition. They are included in the electronic version, and may also be accessed at the author's website, *www.alanbowker.ca* or at the publisher's website, *www.dundurn.com*.

Bibliography

Additional references on specific subjects appear in the Notes, which are included in the electronic version of this book, or are available from the author's website, *www.alanbowker.ca* or the publisher's website, *www.dundurn.com*.

Abella, Irving. *The Canadian Labour Movement, 1902–1960.* Ottawa: Canadian Historical Association, 1975.

———. *A Coat of Many Colours: Two Centuries of Jewish Life in Canada.* Toronto: Key Porter Books, 1990.

Abella, Irving, and Harold Troper. *None Is Too Many.* Toronto: Lester and Orpen Dennys, 1983.

Acton, Janice, Penny Goldsmith, and Bonnie Shepard, eds. *Women at Work: Ontario, 1850–1930.* Toronto: Women's Press, 1974.

Adachi, Ken. *The Enemy That Never Was: A History of the Japanese Canadians.* Toronto: McClelland & Stewart, 1976.

Ahenakew, Edward. *Voices of the Plains Cree.* Edited by Ruth M. Buck. Regina: Canadian Plains Research Center, 1995.

Airhart, Phyllis D. "Condensation and Heart Religion: Canadian Methodists as Evangelicals, 1884–1925." In *Aspects of the Canadian Evangelical Experience,* edited by G.A. Rawlyk, 91–105. Montreal and Kingston: McGill-Queen's University Press, 1997.

———. *Serving the Present Age: Revivalism, Progressivism, and the Methodist Tradition in Canada.* Montreal and Kingston: McGill-Queen's University Press, 1992.

Akenson, Donald H., ed. *Canadian Papers in Rural History.* Multi-volume. Gananoque, ON: Langdale Press, 1988–92.

Allen, Richard. *The Social Passion: Religion and Social Reform in Canada 1914–28.* Toronto: University of Toronto Press, 1973.

———. "The Triumph and Decline of Prohibition." In *Documentary Problems in*

Canadian History. Vol. 2, *Post-Confederation,* edited by J.M. Bumsted, 185–214. Georgetown, ON: Irwin-Dempsey, 1969.

Anctil, Pierre. "Interlude of Hostility: Judeo-Christian Relations in Quebec in the Interwar Period, 1919–39." In *Antisemitism in Canada: History and Interpretation,* edited by Alan Davies, 135–66. Waterloo, ON: Wilfrid Laurier University Press, 1992.

———. *Saint-Laurent: Montréal's Main.* Montreal: Montreal Museum of Archaeology and History, 2002.

Anderson, J.T.M. *The Education of the New-Canadian: A Treatise on Canada's Greatest Educational Problem.* London and Toronto: J.M. Dent & Sons, 1918.

Anderson, Kay. *Vancouver's Chinatown: Racial Discourse in Canada, 1875–1980.* Montreal and Kingston: McGill-Queen's University Press, 1991.

Angus, Ian. *Canadian Bolsheviks: The Early Years of the Communist Party of Canada.* Montreal: Vanguard, 1981.

Armour, Moira, and Pat Staton. *Canadian Women in History: A Chronology.* Toronto: Green Dragon Press, 1990.

Armstrong, Christopher, and H.V. Nelles. "Contrasting Development of the Hydro-Electric Power of the Montreal and Toronto Regions, 1900–1930." In *Canadian Capitalism: Essays in Business History,* edited by Douglas McCalla, 167–89. Toronto: Copp Clark Pittman, 1990.

———. *Monopoly's Moment: The Organization and Regulation of Canadian Utilities, 1830–1930.* Philadelphia: Temple University Press, 1987.

Armstrong, Elizabeth. *The Crisis of Quebec, 1914–18.* New York: AMS Press, 1967.

Avery, Donald. *Dangerous Foreigners: European Immigrant Workers and Labour Radicalism in Canada, 1896–1932.* Toronto: McClelland & Stewart, 1979.

———. "Divided Loyalties — The Ukrainian Left and the Canadian State." In *Canada's Ukrainians: Negotiating an Identity,* edited by Stella Hryniuk and Lubomir Luciuk, 271–87. Toronto: University of Toronto Press, 1991.

Azoulay, Dan. *Hearts and Minds: Canadian Romance at the Dawn of the Modern Era, 1900–1930.* Calgary: University of Calgary Press, 2011.

Bacchi, Carol Lee. *Liberation Deferred? The Ideas of English-Canadian Suffragists, 1877–1918.* Toronto: University of Toronto University Press, 1983.

Bacic, Jadranka. *The Plague of the Spanish Flu: The Influenza Epidemic of 1918 in Ottawa.* Bytown Pamphlets 63. Ottawa: Historical Society of Ottawa, 1998.

Badgley, A. *Ringing In the Common Good: The United Farmers of Ontario, 1914–1926.* Montreal and Kingston: McGill-Queen's University Press, 2000.

Balan, Jars. "The Populist Patriot: Illia Kiriak." In *Re-Imagining Ukrainian Canadians: History, Politics, and Identity,* edited by Rhonda L. Hinther and Jim Mochoruk, 129–72. Toronto: University of Toronto Press, 2011.

Balawyder, Aloysius. *The Winnipeg General Strike*. Toronto: Copp Clark, 1964.

Barman, Jean. *The West Beyond the West: A History of British Columbia*. Revised edition. Toronto: University of Toronto Press, 1996.

Barry, John M. *The Great Influenza: The Epic Story of the Deadliest Plague in History*. New York: Viking, 2004.

Béland, H.S. "The Returned Soldier." *Annals of the American Academy of Political and Social Science* 107 (May 1923): 267–72.

Bélanger, Damien-Claude. *Prejudice and Pride: Canadian Intellectuals Confront the United States, 1891–1945*. Toronto: University of Toronto Press, 2011.

Beloff, Max. *Imperial Sunset*. Vol. 1, *Britain's Liberal Empire, 1897–1921*. London: Methuen, 1969.

Bercuson, David. *Confrontation at Winnipeg: Labour, Industrial Relations, and the General Strike*. Revised edition. Montreal and Kingston: McGill-Queen's University Press, 1990.

———. *Fools and Wise Men: The Rise of the One Big Union*. Toronto: McGraw-Hill Ryerson, 1978.

———. "Organized Labour and the Imperial Munitions Board." *Relations industrielles/Industrial Relations* 28 (July 1973): 602–16.

Berger, Carl. *Imperialism and Nationalism, 1884–1914: A Conflict in Canadian Thought*. Toronto: Copp Clark, 1969.

———. *The Sense of Power: Studies in the Ideas of English-Canadian Imperialism, 1867–1914*. Toronto: University of Toronto Press, 1970.

Bernier, Jacques. *Disease, Medicine and Society in Canada: A Historical Overview*. Ottawa: Canadian Historical Association, 2003.

Best, Carrie. *That Lonesome Road: The Autobiography of Carrie Best*. New Glasgow, NS: Clarion, 1977.

Bird, W.R. *Ghosts Have Warm Hands: A Memoir of the Great War, 1916–1919*. Nepean, ON: CEF Books, 1997.

Bissell, Claude. *The Young Vincent Massey*. Toronto: University of Toronto Press, 1981.

Blanchard, Jim. *Winnipeg's Great War: A City Comes of Age*. Winnipeg: University of Manitoba Press, 2010.

Bland, Salem. *The New Christianity: or the Religion of the New Age*. Introduction by Richard Allen. Toronto: University of Toronto Press, 1973.

Bliss, Michael. *A Canadian Millionaire: The Life and Times of Sir Joseph Flavelle, Bart., 1858–1939*. Toronto, Macmillan, 1979

———. *A Living Profit: Studies in the Social History of Canadian Business, 1883–1911*. Toronto: McClelland & Stewart, 1974.

———. "The Methodist Church and World War I." *Canadian Historical Review* 49, No. 3 (September 1968): 213–33.

———. *Northern Enterprise: Five Centuries of Canadian Business*. Toronto: McClelland & Stewart, 1987.

Borden, Robert. *Canadian Constitutional Studies: The Marfleet Lectures, University of Toronto, October 1921*. Oxford: Oxford University Press, 1922.
———. *Robert Laird Borden: His Memoirs*. Vol. 2, *1916–1920*. Toronto: McClelland & Stewart, 1969.

Bothwell, Robert. *Loring Christie: The Failure of Bureaucratic Imperialism*. New York: Garland Publishing, 1988.

Bothwell, Robert, Ian Drummond, and John English. *Canada 1900–1945*. Toronto: University of Toronto Press, 1987.

Bowker, Alan, ed. *Stephen Leacock Social Criticism: The Unsolved Riddle of Social Justice and Other Essays*. Toronto: University of Toronto Press, 1995.

Bramadat, Paul, and David Seljak, eds. *Christianity and Ethnicity in Canada*. Toronto: University of Toronto Press, 2008.

Broadfoot, Barry. *Next-Year Country: Voices of Our Prairie People*. Toronto: McClelland & Stewart, 1988.

Brown, Lorraine. *Two Hundred Years of Tradition: The Story of Canadian Whisky*. Toronto: Fitzhenry and Whiteside, 1994.

Brown, Michael. *Jew or Juif? Jews, French Canadians, and Anglo-Canadians, 1759–1914*. Philadelphia, New York and Jerusalem: Jewish Publication Society, 1987.

Brown, Robert Craig. *Robert Laird Borden: A Biography*. Vol. 2, *1914–1937*. Toronto: Macmillan, 1980.
———. "'Whither are we being shoved?' Political Leadership in Canada During the Great War." In *War and Society in North America: Papers Presented at the American Association for Canadian Studies Meeting, Montreal, Fall, 1970*, edited by J.L. Granatstein and Robert Cuff, 104–19. Toronto: Thomas Nelson, 1971.

Brown, Robert Craig, and Ramsay Cook. *Canada, 1896–1921: A Nation Transformed*. Toronto: McClelland & Stewart, 1974.

Brown, Robert Craig, and M.E. Prang. *Canadian Historical Documents*. Vol. 3, *Confederation to 1949*. Scarborough, ON: Prentice-Hall, 1966.

Brunet, Michael. "Lionel Groulx (1878–1967): historien national." In *Québec Canada Anglais: Deux itinéraires un affrontement*, 65–76. Montréal: Éditions HMH, 1968.

Buchignani, Norman, and Doreen M. Indra, with Ram Srivastiva. *Continuous Journey: A Social History of South Asians in Canada*. Toronto: McClelland & Stewart, 1985.

Buckner, Philip, ed. *Canada and the British Empire*. Oxford: Oxford University Press, 2008.

Buitenhuis, Peter. *The Great War of Words: British, American, and Canadian Propaganda and Fiction, 1914–1933*. Vancouver: University of British Columbia Press, 1987.

Bumsted, J.M. *The Peoples of Canada: A Post-Confederation History*. Toronto: Oxford University Press, 2004.

———. *The Winnipeg General Strike of 1919: An Illustrated History*. Winnipeg: Watson-Dwyer, 1994.

Burley, Kevin H. *The Development of Canada's Staples, 1867–1939: A Documentary Collection*. Toronto: McClelland & Stewart, 1970.

Burnet, Jean R., with Howard Palmer. *Coming Canadians: An Introduction to the History of Canada's Peoples*. Toronto: McClelland & Stewart, 1988.

Campbell, Peter. *Canadian Marxists and the Search for a Third Way*. Montreal and Kingston: McGill-Queen's University Press, 1999.

Canadian Annual Review of Public Affairs, 1918. Edited by J. Castell Hopkins. Toronto: Canadian Annual Review Publishing Company, 1919 [*CAR 1918*].

Canadian Annual Review of Public Affairs, 1919. Edited by J. Castell Hopkins. Toronto: Canadian Annual Review Publishing Company, 1920 [*CAR 1919*].

Canadian Annual Review of Public Affairs, 1920. Edited by J. Castell Hopkins. Toronto: Canadian Annual Review Publishing Company, 1921 [*CAR 1920*].

The Canadian Annual Review of Public Affairs, 1927–28. Toronto: The Canadian Review Company, 1928 [*CAR 1927–28*].

Carter, Sarah. *Lost Harvests: Prairie Indian Reserve Farmers and Government Policy*. Montreal and Kingston: McGill-Queen's University Press, 1990.

Cassel, Jay. "Public Health in Canada." In *The Theory of Public Health and the Modern State,* edited by Dorothy Potter, 276–311. Amsterdam and Atlanta, GA: Editions Rodopi, 1984.

Cavell, Janice, and Jeff Noakes. *Acts of Occupation: Canada and Arctic Sovereignty, 1918–1925*. Vancouver: University of British Columbia Press, 2010.

Champ, Joan. "The Impact of the Spanish Influenza Epidemic on Saskatchewan Farm Families, 1918–1919." Research paper written as background information for the creation of the 2005 "Winning the Prairie Gamble" exhibit at the Western Development Museum. *http://olc.spsd.sk.ca/de/saskatchewan100/researchpapers/WDM/1918%20Spanish%20Flu.pdf*.

Charyk, John C. *Syrup Pails and Gopher Tails: Memories of the One-Room School*. Vancouver and Toronto: Douglas and McIntyre, 1983.

Chennells, David. *The Politics of Nationalism in Canada: Cultural Conflict since 1760*. Toronto: University of Toronto Press, 2001.

Christie, Nancy. *Engendering the State: Family, Work, and Welfare in Canada*. Toronto: University of Toronto Press, 2000.

Christie, Nancy, and Michael Gauvreau. *Christian Churches and their Peoples, 1840–1965: A Social History of Religion in Canada*. Toronto: University of Toronto Press, 2010.

———. *A Full-Orbed Christianity: The Protestant Churches and Social Welfare in Canada, 1900–1940*. Montreal and Kingston: McGill-Queen's University Press, 1996.

Clark, S.D. *The Canadian Manufacturers Association: A Study in Collective Bargaining and Political Pressure.* Toronto: University of Toronto Press, 1939.

Cleverdon, Catherine. *The Woman Suffrage Movement in Canada.* Introduction by Ramsay Cook. Toronto: University of Toronto Press, 1974.

Clippingdale, Richard. *The Power of the Pen: The Politics, Nationalism, and Influence of Sir John Willison.* Toronto: Dundurn, 2012.

Collier, Richard. *The Plague of the Spanish Lady: The Influenza Pandemic of 1918–19.* London: Atheneum, 1974.

Comacchio, Cynthia. *The Infinite Bonds of Family: Domesticity in Canada, 1850–1940.* Toronto: University of Toronto Press, 1999.

———. *"Nations are Built of Babies": Saving Ontario's Mothers and Children, 1900–1940.* Montreal and Kingston: McGill-Queen's University Press, 1993.

Con, Harry, *et al. From China to Canada: A History of the Chinese Communities in Canada.* Toronto: McClelland & Stewart, 1982.

Cook, Ramsay, ed. *The Dafoe-Sifton Correspondence, 1919–1927.* Manitoba Record Society Publications 2. Altona, MB: D.W. Friesen and Sons, 1966.

———, ed. *French-Canadian Nationalism: An Anthology.* Toronto: Macmillan, 1969.

———. *The Politics of John W. Dafoe and the Free Press.* Toronto: University of Toronto Press, 1963.

Cook, Ramsay, and Wendy Mitchinson, eds. *The Proper Sphere: Women's Place in Canadian Society.* Toronto: Oxford University Press, 1976.

Cook, Sharon Anne. *"Through Sunshine and Shadow": The Women's Christian Temperance Union, Evangelism, and Reform in Ontario, 1874–1930.* Montreal and Kingston: McGill–Queen's University Press, 1995.

Cook, Sharon Anne, Lorna McLean, and Kate O'Rourke, eds. *Framing Our Past: Canadian Women's History in the Twentieth Century.* Montreal and Kingston: McGill-Queen's University Press, 2001.

Cook, Tim. *Shock Troops: Canadians Fighting in the Great War, 1917–18.* Toronto: Viking, 2008.

Cosentino, Frank. *Afros, Aboriginals, and Amateur Sport in Pre–World War I Canada, 1900–1914.* Ottawa: Canadian Historical Association, 1998.

Coutts, Ian. *Brew North: How Canadians Made Beer and Beer Made Canada.* Vancouver: Greystone Books, 2010.

Crerar, Adam. "Ontario and the Great War." In *Canada and the First World War: Essays in Honour of Robert Craig Brown,* edited by David Mackenzie, 230–71. Toronto: University of Toronto Press, 2005.

Crerar, Duff. *Padres in No Man's Land: Canadian Chaplains and the Great War.* Montreal and Kingston: McGill-Queen's University Press, 1995.

Crosby, Alfred W. *America's Forgotten Pandemic: The Influenza of 1918.* New York: Cambridge University Press, 1989.

Cross, Michael S., and Gregory S. Kealey. *Readings in Canadian Social History.* Vol. 4, *The Consolidation of Capitalism, 1896–1929.* Toronto: McClelland & Stewart, 1986.

Crowley, Terry. *Agnes Macphail and the Politics of Equality.* Toronto: James Lorimer, 1990.

Crysdale, Stewart. *The Industrial Struggle and Protestant Ethics in Canada: A Survey of Changing Power Structures and Christian Social Ethics.* Toronto: Ryerson Press, 1961.

Cuff, R.D., and J.L. Granatstein. *Ties That Bind: Canadian-American Relations in Wartime from the Great War to the Cold War.* Toronto and Sarasota, FL: Samuel Stevens Hakkert, 1977.

Cupido, Robert. "Appropriating the Past: Pageants, Politics, and the Diamond Jubilee of Confederation." *Journal of the Canadian Historical Association* 9, No. 1 (1998): 155–86.

———. "The Medium, the Message, and the Modern: The Jubilee Broadcast of 1927." *International Journal of Canadian Studies* 26 (Fall 2002): 101–23.

———. "Sixty Years of Canadian Progress: The Diamond Jubilee and the Politics of Commemoration." In *Canadian Identity: Region, Country, Nation,* edited by Caroline Andrew, Will Straw, and J-Yvon Thériault, 19–33. Montreal: Association for Canadian Studies, 1988.

Danysk, Cecilia. *Hired Hands: Labour and the Development of Prairie Agriculture, 1880–1930.* Toronto: McClelland & Stewart, 1995.

Davies, Alan, ed. *Antisemitism in Canada: History and Interpretation.* Waterloo, ON: Wilfrid Laurier University Press, 1992.

Davis, Donald F. "Dependent Motorization: Canada and the Automobile to the 1930s." In *Canadian Capitalism: Essays in Business History,* edited by Douglas McCalla, 191–215. Toronto: Copp Clark Pittman, 1990.

Dawson, R. Macgregor. *Mackenzie King: A Political Biography, 1874–1923.* Toronto: University of Toronto Press, 1958.

Dempsey, L. James. "The Indians and World War One," *Alberta History* 31, No. 3 (Summer 1983): 1-8.

———. *Warriors of the King: Prairie Indians in World War I.* Regina, SK: Canadian Plains Research Center, 1999.

Denison, Merrill. *The Barley and the Stream: The Molson Story.* Toronto: McClelland & Stewart, 1955.

Dick, Lyle. *Farmers Making Good: The Development of Abernethy District, Saskatchewan, 1880–1920.* Second edition. Calgary: University of Calgary Press, 2008.

Dickason, Olive Patricia, with William Newbigging. *A Concise History of Canada's First Nations.* Second edition. Toronto: Oxford University Press, 2010.

Dickin, Janice. "Pale Horse/Pale History: Revisiting Calgary's Experience of the Spanish Influenza, 1918–19." In *In Harm's Way: Disasters in Western*

Canada, edited by Anthony Rasporich and Max Foran, 41–68. Vancouver: UBC Press, 2004.

Documents on Canadian External Relations. Vol. 1, *1909–1918.* Ottawa: Queen's Printer, 1967 [*DCER 1*].

Documents on Canadian External Relations. Vol. 2, *Paris Peace Conference, Paris, 1919.* Ottawa: Queen's Printer, 1969 [*DCER 2*].

Documents on Canadian External Relations. Vol. 3, *1919–1925.* Ottawa: Information Canada, 1970 [*DCER 3*].

Drummond, Ian M. *Progress Without Planning: The Economic History of Ontario from Confederation to the Second World War.* Toronto: University of Toronto Press, 1987.

Drury, E.C. *Farmer Premier: The Memoirs of E.C. Drury.* Toronto: McClelland & Stewart, 1966.

Dumont Micheline, *et al. Québec Women: A History.* Translated by Roger Gannon and Rosalind Gill. Toronto: The Women's Press, 1987.

Durkin, Douglas. *The Magpie.* Introduction by Peter E. Rider. Toronto: University of Toronto Press, 1974.

Eayrs, James. *In Defence of Canada: From the Great War to the Great Depression.* Toronto: University of Toronto Press, 1964.

Edwardson, Ryan. *Canadian Content: Culture and the Quest for Nationhood.* Toronto: University of Toronto Press, 2008.

Endicott, Stephen. *James G. Endicott: Rebel Out of China.* Toronto: University of Toronto Press, 1980.

English, John. "Political Leadership in the First World War." In *Canada and the First World War: Essays in Honour of Robert Craig Brown,* edited by David Mackenzie, 76–95. Toronto: University of Toronto Press, 2005.

Ewenchuk, Michael. *Reflections and Reminiscences: Ukrainians in Canada, 1892–1992.* Winnipeg: M. Ewenchuk, 1995.

Fahrni, Magda, "'Elles sont partout …' Les femmes et la ville en temps d'Épidemie Montréal, 1918–20." *Revue d'histoire de l'Amérique française* 58, No. 1 (2004): 67–85.

Fahrni, Magda, and Esyllt W. Jones, eds. *Epidemic Encounters: Influenza, Society, and Culture in Canada, 1918–20.* Vancouver: University of British Columbia Press, 2012.

Fairbairn, Gary. *From Prairie Roots: The Remarkable Story of the Saskatchewan Wheat Pool.* Saskatoon, SK: Western Producer Prairie Books, 1982.

Falconer, Robert. *Idealism in National Character: Essays and Addresses.* Toronto: University of Toronto Press, 1920.

Ferguson, Barry. *Remaking Liberalism: The Intellectual Legacy of Adam Shortt, O.D. Skelton, W.C. Clark, and W.A. Mackintosh, 1890–1925.* Montreal and Kingston: McGill-Queen's University Press, 1993.

Fleming, R.B. *The Railway King of Canada: Sir William Mackenzie, 1849–1923.* Vancouver: University of British Columbia Press, 1991.

Fleming, R.B., ed. *The Wartime Letters of Leslie and Cecil Frost.* Waterloo, ON: Wilfrid Laurier University Press, 2007.

Forbes E.R., and D.A. Muise, eds. *The Atlantic Provinces in Confederation.* Toronto: University of Toronto Press; and Fredericton, NB: Acadiensis Press, 1993.

Francis, Daniel. *Seeing Reds: The Red Scare of 1918–1919: Canada's First War on Terror.* Vancouver: Arsenal Pulp Press, 2010.

Francis, R. Douglas, and Howard Palmer, eds. *The Prairie West: Historical Readings.* Second edition. Edmonton: University of Calgary Press, 1992.

Fraser, Brian J. *The Social Uplifters: Presbyterian Progressives and the Social Gospel in Canada, 1875–1915.* Waterloo, ON: Wilfrid Laurier University Press, 1988.

Friesen, Gerald. "Bob Russell's Political Thought: Socialism and Industrial Unionism in Winnipeg, 1914 to 1919." In *River Road: Essays on Manitoba and Prairie History,* 121–46. Winnipeg: University of Manitoba Press, 1996.

———. *The Canadian Prairies: A History.* Toronto: University of Toronto Press, 1987.

———. "'Yours in Revolt': Regionalism, Socialism, and the Western Canadian Labour Movement." *Labour/Le Travailleur* 1 (1976): 139–57.

Gagan, David, and Rosemary Gagan. *For Patients of Moderate Means: A Social History of the Voluntary Public General Hospital in Canada, 1890–1950.* Montreal and Kingston: McGill-Queen's University Press, 2002.

Gatenby, Greg, ed. *The Wild is Always There: Canada Through the Eyes of Foreign Writers.* Toronto: Knopf, 1993.

Gauvreau, Michael. *The Catholic Origins of Quebec's Quiet Revolution.* Montreal and Kingston: McGill-Queen's University Press, 2005.

———. *The Evangelical Century: College and Creed in English Canada from the Great Revival to the Great Depression.* Montreal and Kingston: McGill-Queen's University Press, 1990.

Gauvreau, Michael, and Ollivier Hubert, eds. *The Churches and Social Order in Nineteenth- and Twentieth-Century Canada.* Montreal and Kingston: McGill-Queen's University Press, 2006.

Gerus, O.W., and J.E. Rea. *The Ukrainians in Canada.* Ottawa: Canadian Historical Association, 1985.

Gidney, Catherine. *A Long Eclipse: The Liberal Protestant Establishment and the Canadian University, 1920–1970.* Montreal and Kingston: McGill-Queen's University Press, 2004.

Glazebrook, G.P. de T. *Canada at the Paris Peace Conference.* Toronto: Oxford University Press, 1942.

———. *A History of Transportation in Canada.* Vol. 2, *The National Economy, 1867–1936.* Toronto: McClelland & Stewart, 1964.

Glynn-Ward, Hilda. *The Writing on the Wall: Chinese and Japanese Immigration to*

BC, 1920. Introduction by Patricia Roy. Toronto: University of Toronto Press, 1974.

Good, W.C. *Farmer Citizen: My Fifty Years in the Canadian Farmers' Movement.* Toronto: Ryerson Press, 1958.

———. *Production and Taxation in Canada; From the Farmers' Standpoint.* Toronto: J.M. Dent, 1919.

Gordon, Charles. "The New State and the New Church." In Allen, Richard. "The Triumph and Decline of Prohibition." In *Documentary Problems in Canadian History.* Vol. 2, *Post-Confederation,* edited by J.M. Bumsted, 192–93. Georgetown, ON: Irwin-Dempsey, 1969.

Graham, Roger. *Arthur Meighen. A Biography.* Vol. 1, *The Door of Opportunity.* Toronto: Clarke Irwin, 1960.

———. *Arthur Meighen, A Biography.* Vol. 2, *And Fortune Fled.* Toronto: Clarke Irwin, 1963.

Granatstein, J.L. *Canada's Army: Waging War and Keeping the Peace.* Toronto: University of Toronto Press, 2002.

Granatstein, J.L., and J.M. Hitsman. *Broken Promises: A History of Conscription in Canada.* Toronto: Oxford University Press, 1977.

Gray, James H. *Booze: The Impact of Whisky on the Prairie West.* Toronto: Macmillan, 1972.

———. *The Boy from Winnipeg.* Toronto. Macmillan, 1970.

———. *The Roar of the Twenties.* Toronto: Macmillan, 1997.

Grescoe, Audrey, and Paul Grescoe, eds. *The Book of War Letters: 100 Years of Private Canadian Correspondence.* Toronto: McClelland & Stewart, 2003.

Groulx, Lionel. "If Dollard Were Alive Today." In *French-Canadian Nationalism: An Anthology,* edited by Ramsay Cook, 188–201. Toronto: Macmillan, 1969.

Gutkin, Harry, and Mildred Gutkin. *Profiles in Dissent: The Shaping of Radical Thought in the Canadian West.* Edmonton: NeWest, 1997.

Gwyn, Sandra, ed. *Tapestry of War: A Private View of Canadians in the Great War.* Toronto: HarperCollins, 1992.

Haig-Brown, Celia. *Resistance and Renewal: Surviving the Indian Residential School.* Vancouver: Arsenal Pulp Press, 1988.

Hallowell, Gerald. *Prohibition in Ontario, 1919–1923.* Toronto: Ontario Historical Society, 1972.

Hayes, Adrian. *Pegahmagabow: Life-Long Warrior.* Toronto: Blue Butterfly, 2009.

Heron, Craig. *Booze: A Distilled History.* Toronto: Between the Lines, 2003.

———. ed., *The Workers' Revolt in Canada, 1917–1925.* Toronto: University of Toronto Press, 1998.

Hewitt, Steve. *Riding to the Rescue: The Transformation of the RCMP in Alberta and Saskatchewan, 1918–1939.* Toronto: University of Toronto Press, 2006.

Hillmer, Norman, and J.L. Granatstein. *Empire to Umpire: Canada and the World to the 1990s.* Toronto: Copp Clark Longman, 1994.

Hinther, Rhonda L., and Jim Mochoruk, eds. *Re-Imagining Ukrainian Canadians: History, Politics, and Identity.* Toronto: University of Toronto Press, 2011.

Hryniuk, Stella, and Lubomir Luciuk, eds. *Canada's Ukrainians: Negotiating an Identity.* Toronto: University of Toronto Press, 1991.

Humphries, Mark Osborne. "The Horror at Home: The Canadian Military and the 'Great' Influenza Pandemic of 1918." *Journal of the Canadian Historical Association* 16, No. 1 (2005): 235–60.

———. *The Last Plague: Spanish Influenza and the Politics of Public Health in Canada.* Toronto: University of Toronto Press, 2013.

———. "The Limits of Necessity: Public Health, Dissent, and the War Effort During the 1918 Influenza Pandemic." In *Epidemic Encounters: Influenza, Society, and Culture in Canada, 1918–20,* edited by Magda Fahrni and Esyllt W. Jones, 21–47. Vancouver: UBC Press, 2012.

———. "Points of Infection: The First World War and the Origins of the 1918 Influenza Pandemic," *War in History* 21, No. 1 (2014): 55–81.

———, ed. *The Selected Papers of Arthur Currie: Diaries, Letters, and Report to the Ministry, 1917–1933.* Waterloo, ON: LCMSDS Press of Wilfrid Laurier University, 2008.

———. "War's Long Shadow: Masculinity, Medicine, and the Gendered Politics of Trauma, 1914–1939." *Canadian Historical Review* 91, No. 3 (September 2010): 503–31.

Hutton, Maurice. "Militarism and Anti-Militarism." *University Magazine* 12 (April 1913): 179–96.

———. "To the Graduating Class of University College." *Torontonensis* 21 (1919): 12.

Irvine, William. *The Farmers in Politics.* Introduction by Reginald Whitaker. Toronto: McClelland & Stewart, 1970.

Isitt, Benjamin, *From Victoria to Vladivostok: Canada's Siberian Expedition, 1917–19.* Vancouver: University of British Columbia Press, 2010.

———. "Mutiny from Victoria to Vladivostok, December 1918." *Canadian Historical Review* 87, No. 2 (June 2006): 223–64.

James, Norman. *The Autobiography of a Nobody.* Toronto: J.M. Dent, 1947.

Janigan, Mary. *Let the Eastern Bastards Freeze in the Dark: The West Versus the Rest Since Confederation.* Toronto: Knopf, 2012.

Jenness, Diamond. "Canada's Indians Yesterday. What of Today?" In *As Long as the Sun Shines and Water Flows: A Reader in Canadian Native Studies,* edited by Ian L. Getty and Antoine S. Lussier, 158–63. Vancouver: University of British Columbia Press, 1983.

———. *The Indians of Canada.* Ottawa: National Museum of Canada, 1932.

Johnston, Charles M. *E.C. Drury: Agrarian Idealist.* Toronto: University of Toronto Press, 1986.

Johnston, Hugh M. *The East Indians in Canada.* Ottawa: Canadian Historical Association, 1984.

———., ed. *The Pacific Province: A History of British Columbia.* Vancouver and Toronto: Douglas & McIntyre, 1996.

Jones, David, and Ian MacPherson, eds. *Building Beyond the Homestead: Rural History on the Prairies.* Calgary: University of Calgary Press, 1985.

Jones, Esyllt W. *Influenza 1918: Disease, Death, and Struggle in Winnipeg.* Toronto: University of Toronto Press, 2007.

Kealey, Linda, ed. *A Not Unreasonable Claim: Women and Reform in Canada, 1880s–1920s.* Toronto: Women's Press, 1979.

Keillor, Elaine. *Music in Canada: Capturing Landscapes and Diversity.* Montreal and Kingston: McGill-Queen's University Press, 2006.

Kelly, Ninette, and Michael Trebilcock. *The Making of the Mosaic: A History of Canadian Immigration Policy.* Toronto: University of Toronto Press, 1998.

Kelm, Mary-Ellen. "Flu Stories: Engaging With Disease, Death, and Modernity in British Columbia, 1918–19." In *Epidemic Encounters: Influenza, Society, and Culture in Canada, 1918–20,* edited by Magda Fahrni and Esyllt W. Jones, 167–79. Vancouver: University of British Columbia Press, 2012.

Kerr, Donald, and Deryck W. Holdsworth, eds. *Historical Atlas of Canada.* Vol. 3, *Addressing the Twentieth Century, 1891–1961.* Toronto: University of Toronto Press, 1990.

Keshen, Jeffrey A. *Propaganda and Censorship During Canada's Great War.* Calgary: University of Alberta Press, 1996.

King, Ross. *Defiant Spirits: The Modernist Revolution of the Group of Seven.* Vancouver and Toronto: Douglas and McIntyre, 2010.

King, William Lyon Mackenzie. "Diaries, 1893–1950." Library and Archives Canada. Accessed online via *www.bac-lac.gc.ca/eng/discover/politics-government/prime-ministers/william-lyon-mackenzie-king/Pages/search.aspx.*

———. *Industry and Humanity: A Study in the Principles Underlying Industrial Reconstruction.* Introduction by David Jay Bercuson. Toronto: University of Toronto Press, 1973.

Kinnear, Mary. "'Do You Want Your Daughter to Marry a Farmer?' Women's Work on the Farm, 1922." In *Canadian Papers in Rural History.* Edited by Donald H. Akenson, 6: 137–53. Gananoque, ON: Langdale Press, 1988.

Kiriak, Illia. *Sons of the Soil.* Winnipeg: St. Andrew's College in Winnipeg, 1983.

Klempa, William, ed. *The Burning Bush and a Few Acres of Snow: The Presbyterian Contribution to Canadian Life and Literature.* Ottawa: Carleton University Press, 1994.

Knowles, Valerie. *Forging Our Legacy: Canadian Citizenship and Immigration, 1900–1970.* Ottawa: Public Works and Government Services Canada, 2000.

———. *Strangers at Our Gates: Canadian Immigration and Immigration Policy, 1540–1997.* Toronto: Dundurn, 1997.

Knox, Ellen, *The Girl of the New Day*. Toronto: McClelland & Stewart, 1919.

Kottman, Richard N. "Volstead Violated: Prohibition as a Factor in Canadian-American Relations." *Canadian Historical Review* 43, No. 2 (June 1962): 106–26.

Kramer, Reinhold, and Tom Mitchell. *When the State Trembled: How A.J. Andrews and the Citizens' Committee Broke the Winnipeg General Strike*. Toronto: University of Toronto Press, 2010.

Kulchyski, Peter, Don N. McCaskill, and David Newhouse, eds. "'A considerable unrest': F.O. Loft and the League of Canadian Indians." *Native Studies Review* 4 (1988): 95–107.

———. *In the Words of Elders: Aboriginal Cultures in Transition*. Toronto: University of Toronto Press, 1999.

Lackenbauer, P. Whitney. "Soldiers Behaving Badly: CEF Soldiers 'Rioting' in Canada During the First World War." In *The Apathetic and the Defiant: Case Studies of Canadian Mutiny and Disobedience, 1812–1919*, edited by Craig Leslie Mantle, 195–260. Toronto: Dundurn, 2012.

Lai, David C. *Chinatowns: Towns Within Towns in Canada*. Vancouver: University of British Columbia Press, 1988.

Lavigne, Marie, Yolande Pinard, and Jennifer Stoddart. "The Fédération nationale Saint-Jean-Baptiste and the Women's Movement in Quebec." In *A Not Unreasonable Claim: Women and Reform in Canada, 1880s–1920s*, edited by Linda Kealey, 71–87. Toronto: Women's Press, 1979.

Leacock, Stephen, "Democracy and Social Progress." In *The New Era in Canada: Essays Dealing With The Upbuilding of the Canadian Commonwealth*, edited by J.O. Miller, 13–33. Toronto: J.M. Dent, 1917.

———. "Greater Canada: An Appeal." In *Stephen Leacock Social Criticism*, edited by Alan Bowker, 3–11. Toronto: University of Toronto Press, 1995.

———. "Our National Organization for War." In *The New Era in Canada: Essays Dealing With The Upbuilding of the Canadian Commonwealth*, edited by J.O. Miller, 409–21. Toronto: J.M. Dent, 1917.

———. "The Unsolved Riddle of Social Justice." In *Stephen Leacock Social Criticism*, edited by Alan Bowker, 71–145. Toronto: University of Toronto Press, 1995.

Letters from the Front, Being a Record of the Part Played by the Officers of the Bank in the Great War, 1914–1919. Vol. 1. [Toronto]: Canadian Bank of Commerce [1920].

Lévesque, Andrée. *Making and Breaking the Rules: Women in Quebec, 1919–1939*. Toronto: McClelland & Stewart, 1994.

Levine, Allan. *The Exchange: 100 Years of Trading Grain in Winnipeg*. Winnipeg: Pegius Publishing, 1987.

———. *King: William Lyon Mackenzie King: A Life Guided by the Hand of Destiny*. Vancouver: Douglas & McIntyre, 2011.

Levitt, Joseph. *Henri Bourassa — Catholic Critic.* Ottawa: Canadian Historical Association, 1977.

Lewis, David. *The Good Fight: Political Memoirs, 1909–1958.* Toronto: Macmillan, 1981.

Li, Peter. *The Chinese in Canada.* Second edition. Toronto: Oxford University Press, 1998.

Linteau, Paul-André, René Durocher, and Jean-Claude Robert. *Quebec: A History, 1867–1929.* Translated by Robert Chodos. Toronto: James Lorimer, 1983.

Lipton, Charles. *The Trade Union Movement of Canada, 1827–1959.* Montreal: Canadian Social Publications, 1968.

Livesay, J.F.B. *Canada's Hundred Days: With the Canadian Corps from Amiens to Mons, Aug. 8–Nov. 11, 1918.* Toronto: Thomas Allen, 1919.

Lupul, Manoly R., ed. *A Heritage in Transition: Essays in the History of Ukrainians in Canada.* Toronto: McClelland & Stewart, 1982.

Lux, Maureen. *Medicine That Walks: Disease, Medicine, and Canadian Plains Native People, 1880–1940.* Toronto: University of Toronto Press, 2001.

———. "'The Bitter Flats': The 1918 Influenza Epidemic in Saskatchewan." *Saskatchewan History* 49, No. 1 (Spring 1997): 3–14.

MacDougall, John. *Rural Life in Canada: Its Trend and Tasks.* Introduction by Robert Craig Brown. Toronto: University of Toronto Press, 1973.

MacDowall, Laurel Sefton, and Ian Radforth, eds. *Canadian Working Class History: Selected Readings.* Toronto: Canadian Scholars' Press, 1992.

MacIntosh, Robert. *Distant Drummers: Banking and Politics in Canada.* Toronto: Macmillan, 1991.

MacKay, Donald. *The People's Railway: A History of Canadian National.* Vancouver and Toronto: Douglas and McIntyre, 1992.

Mackenzie, David, ed. *Canada and the First World War: Essays in Honour of Robert Craig Brown.* Toronto: University of Toronto Press, 2005.

MacMillan, Margaret. "Canada and the Peace Settlements." In *Canada and the First World War: Essays in Honour of Robert Craig Brown,* 379–408. Toronto: University of Toronto Press, 2005.

MacPherson, Ian. *Each For All: A History of the Co-operative Movement in Canada, 1900–1945.* Toronto: Macmillan, 1979.

Mantle, Craig Leslie, ed. *The Apathetic and the Defiant: Case Studies of Canadian Mutiny and Disobedience, 1812–1919.* Toronto and Kingston: Dundurn and Canadian Defence Academy, 2007.

Mar, Lisa Rose. *Brokering Belonging: Chinese in Canada's Exclusion Era, 1885–1945.* Toronto: University of Toronto Press, 2010.

Marchildon, Gregory P. *Profits and Politics: Beaverbrook and the Gilded Age of Canadian Finances.* Toronto: University of Toronto Press, 1996.

Mardiros, Anthony. *William Irvine: The Life of a Prairie Radical.* Toronto: James Lorimer, 1979.

Marrus, Michael. *Mr Sam: The Life and Times of Samuel Bronfman.* Toronto: Penguin, 1991.

Marshall, David B. "Methodism Embattled: A Reconsideration of the Methodist Church and World War I." *Canadian Historical Review* 66, No. 1 (1985): 48–64.

———. *Secularizing the Faith: Canadian Protestant Clergy and the Crisis of Belief, 1850–1940.* Toronto: University of Toronto Press, 1992.

Martin, Joe. *Relentless Change: A Casebook for the Study of Canadian Business History.* Toronto: University of Toronto Press, 2009.

Marunchak, Mykhaolo. *Ukrainians in Canada: A History.* Winnipeg: Ukrainian Free Academy of Sciences, 1988.

Massey, Raymond. *When I Was Young.* Toronto: McClelland & Stewart, 1976.

Masters, D.C. *The Winnipeg General Strike.* Toronto: University of Toronto Press 1950.

Mathieson, William D., ed. *My Grandfather's War: Canadians Remember the First World War, 1914–1918.* Toronto: Macmillan, 1981.

McArthur, Peter. *The Best of Peter McArthur.* Selected and introduced by Alec Lucas. Toronto: Clarke Irwin, 1967.

McCalla, Douglas, ed. *The Development of Canadian Capitalism: Essays in Business History.* Toronto: Copp Clark Pittman, 1990.

McClung, Nellie. *In Times Like These.* Introduction by Veronica Strong-Boag. Toronto: University of Toronto Press, 1972.

———. *The Next of Kin: Those Who Wait and Wonder.* Toronto: Thomas Allen, 1917.

———. *The Stream Runs Fast: My Own Story.* Toronto: Thomas Allen, 1945.

McCormack, A. Ross. *Reformers, Rebels, and Revolutionaries: The Western Canadian Radical Movement.* Toronto: University of Toronto Press, 1977.

McDowall, Duncan. *Quick to the Frontier: Canada's Royal Bank.* Toronto: McClelland & Stewart, 1993.

McGinnis Dickin, Janice. "The Impact of Epidemic Influenza: Canada, 1918–1919." In *Medicine in Canadian Society: Historical Perspectives,* edited by S.E.D. Shortt, 447–77. Montreal and Kingston: McGill-Queen's University Press, 1981.

McGowan, Mark. *The Waning of the Green: Catholics, the Irish, and Identity in Toronto 1877–1922.* Montreal and Kingston: McGill-Queen's University Press, 1999.

McGregor, F.A. *The Fall & Rise of Mackenzie King: 1911–1919.* Toronto: Macmillan, 1962.

McIntosh, Dave. *The Collectors: A History of Canadian Customs and Excise.* Toronto: NC Press, 1984.

McKay, Ian. *Reasoning Otherwise: Leftists and the People's Enlightenment in Canada, 1890–1920.* Toronto: Between the Lines, 2008.

———. "The 1910s: The Stillborn Triumph of Progressive Reform." In *The*

Atlantic Provinces in Confederation, edited by E.R. Forbes and D.A. Muise, 192–229. Toronto and Fredericton: University of Toronto Press and Acadiensis Press, 1993.

McKay, Ian, and Suzanne Morton. "The Maritimes: Expanding the Circle of Resistance." In *The Workers' Revolt in Canada, 1917–1925,* edited by Craig Heron, 43–86. Toronto: University of Toronto Press, 1998.

McKillop, A.B. *A Disciplined Intelligence: Critical Inquiry and Canadian Thought in the Victorian Era.* Montreal and Kingston: McGill-Queen's University Press, 2001.

———. *Matters of Mind: The University in Ontario, 1791–1950.* Toronto: University of Toronto Press, 1994.

McLaren, Angus. *Our Own Master Race: Eugenics in Canada, 1885–1945.* Toronto: Oxford University Press, 1990.

McNaught, Kenneth. *A Prophet in Politics: A Biography of J.S. Woodsworth.* Toronto: University of Toronto Press, 1959.

McNaught, Kenneth, and David Bercuson. *The Winnipeg General Strike.* Don Mills, ON: Longmans, 1974.

Miller, Ian Hugh Maclean. *Our Glory and Our Grief: Torontonians and the Great War.* Toronto: University of Toronto Press, 2002.

Miller, J.O. *The New Era in Canada: Essays Dealing with the Upbuilding of the Canadian Commonwealth.* Toronto: J.M. Dent, 1917.

Miller, J.R. *Lethal Legacy: Current Native Controversies in Canada.* Toronto: McClelland & Stewart, 2004.

———. *Reflections on Native-Newcomer Relations: Selected Essays.* Toronto: University of Toronto Press, 2004.

———. *Shingwauk's Vision: A History of Native Residential Schools.* Toronto: University of Toronto Press, 1996.

———. *Skyscrapers Hide the Heavens: A History of Indian-White Relations in Canada.* Toronto: University of Toronto Press, 1989.

Milloy, John S. *A National Crime: The Canadian Government and the Residential School System, 1879 to 1986.* Winnipeg: University of Manitoba Press, 1999.

Mitchell, Tom. "A.J. Andrews to Arthur Meighen: Winnipeg General Strike Correspondence." *Manitoba History* 24 (Autumn 1992), accessed online at *www.mhs.mb.ca/docs/mb_history/24/generalstrikecorrespondence.shtml.*

———. "'Repressive Measures': A.J. Andrews, the Committee of 1,000, and the Campaign Against Radicalism after the Winnipeg General Strike." *Left History* 3, Nos. 2/4 (Fall 1995/Spring 1996): 133–67.

———. "'To Reach the Leadership of this Revolutionary Movement': A.J. Andrews, the Canadian State, and the Suppression of the Winnipeg General Strike." *Prairie Forum* 18, No. 2 (Fall 1993): 239–55.

Morris, Peter. *Embattled Shadows: A History of Canadian Cinema, 1895–1939.* Montreal and Kingston: McGill-Queen's University Press, 1978.

Morton, Desmond. "The Cadet Movement in the Moment of Canadian Militarism, 1909–1914." *Journal of Canadian Studies* 13, No. 2 (Summer 1978): 56–68.

———. *Fight or Pay: Soldiers' Families in the Great War.* Vancouver: University of British Columbia Press, 2004.

———. "'Kicking and Complaining': Demobilization Riots in the Canadian Expeditionary Force, 1918–19." *Canadian Historical Review* 61, No. 3 (1980): 334–60.

———. *A Military History of Canada.* Fourth edition. Toronto: McClelland & Stewart, 1999.

———. *When Your Number's Up: The Canadian Soldier in the Great War.* Toronto: Random House, 1993.

———. *Working People: An Illustrated History of the Canadian Labour Movement.* Montreal and Kingston: McGill-Queen's University Press, 1998.

Morton, Desmond, and Glenn Wright. *Winning the Second Battle.* Toronto: University of Toronto Press, 1987.

Morton, Suzanne. *Ideal Surroundings: Domestic Life in a Working-Class Suburb in the 1920s.* Toronto: University of Toronto Press, 1995.

Morton, W.L. *The Progressive Party in Canada.* Toronto: University of Toronto Press, 1950.

Moss, Mark. *Manliness and Militarism: Educating Young Boys in Ontario for War.* Toronto: Oxford University Press, 2001.

Naylor, James. *The New Democracy: Challenging the Social Order in Industrial Ontario, 1914–1925.* Toronto: University of Toronto Press, 1991.

Nelles, H.V. *The Politics of Development: Forests, Mines, and Hydro-Electric Power in Ontario, 1849–1941.* Toronto: Macmillan, 1974.

Nerbas, Don. *Dominion of Capital: The Politics of Big Business and the Crisis of the Canadian Corporation, 1914–1947.* Toronto: University of Toronto Press, 2013.

Norrie, Kenneth, Douglas Owram, and J.C. Herbert Emery. *A History of the Canadian Economy.* Fourth Edition. Toronto: Thomson Nelson, 2008.

Novak, Dagmar. *Dubious Glory: The Two World Wars and the Canadian Novel.* New York: Peter Lang, 2000.

O'Keefe, Betty, and Ian Macdonald. *Dr. Fred and the Spanish Lady: Fighting the Killer Flu.* Surrey, BC: Heritage House, 2004.

Oliver, Michael. *The Passionate Debate: The Social and Political Ideas of Quebec Nationalism, 1920–1945.* Montreal: Véhicule Press, 1999.

Oliver, Peter. *G. Howard Ferguson, Ontario Tory.* Toronto: University of Toronto Press, 1977.

Oreskovich, Carlie. *Sir Henry Pellatt: The King of Casa Loma.* Toronto: McGraw-Hill Ryerson, 1982.

Ormsby, Margaret. *British Columbia: A History.* Toronto: Macmillan, 1958.

Palmer, Howard. *Patterns of Prejudice: A History of Nativism in Alberta.* Toronto: McClelland & Stewart, 1982.

———. "Reluctant Hosts: Anglo-Canadian Views of Multiculturalism in the Twentieth Century." In *Readings in Canadian History: Post-Confederation*, sixth edition, edited by R. Douglas Francis and Donald Smith, 116–30. Toronto: Nelson, 2002.

———. "Strangers and Stereotypes: The Rise of Nativism, 1880–1920." In *The Prairie West: Historical Readings*, second edition, edited by R. Douglas Francis and Howard Palmer, 308–34. Calgary: University of Calgary Press, 1992.

Palmer, Howard, and Tamara Jeppson Palmer, eds. *The Peoples of Alberta: Portraits of Cultural Diversity*. Saskatoon: Western Producer Prairie Books, 1985.

Parr, Joy, ed. *Childhood and Family in Canadian History*. Toronto: McClelland & Stewart, 1982.

Penner, Norman, ed. *Winnipeg 1919: The Strikers' Own History of the Winnipeg General Strike*. Second edition. Toronto: James Lorimer, 1975.

Perin, Roberto, and Franc Sturino, eds. *Arrangiarsi: The Italian Immigration Experience in Canada*. Montreal: Guernica, 1989.

Peterson, C.W. *Wake Up, Canada! Reflections on Vital National Issues*. Toronto: Macmillan, 1919.

Pettigrew, Eileen. *The Silent Enemy: Canada and the Deadly Flu of 1918*. Saskatoon: Western Producer Prairie Books, 1983.

Phillips, Howard, and David Killingray, eds. *The Spanish Influenza Epidemic of 1918–19: New Perspectives*. London: Routledge, 2003.

Phillips, Paul. *No Power Greater: A Century of Labour in BC*. Vancouver: BC Federation of Labour, 1967.

Pomeyrols, Catherine. "Les intellectuels nationalistes québécois et la condamnation de l'Action française." *Vingtième Siècle. Revue d'histoire*, No. 73 (janvier–mars 2002): 83–98.

Potestio, John, and Antonio Pucci, eds. *The Italian Immigrant Experience*. Thunder Bay, ON: Canadian Historical Association, 1988.

Potvin, Rose, ed. *Passion and Conviction: The Letters of Graham Spry*. Regina: Canadian Plains Research Centre, 1992.

Prang, Margaret. *N.W. Rowell, Ontario Nationalist*. Toronto: University of Toronto Press, 1975.

Prentice, Alison, *et al. Canadian Women: A History*. Second edition. Toronto. Harcourt Brace Jovanovich, 1996.

Prince, Robert S. "The Mythology of War: How the Canadian Daily Newspaper Depicted the Great War." Ph.D. thesis, University of Toronto, 1998.

Quiney, Linda. "'Rendering Valuable Service': The Politics of Nursing During the 1918–19 Influenza Crisis." In *Epidemic Encounters: Influenza, Society, and Culture in Canada, 1918–20*, edited by Magda Fahrni and Esyllt W. Jones, 48–69. Vancouver: University of British Columbia Press, 2012.

Radecki, Henry, with Benedykt Heydenkorn. *A Member of a Distinguished Family: The Polish Group in Canada*. Toronto: McClelland & Stewart, 1976.

Ramirez, Bruno. *The Italians in Canada*. Ottawa: Canadian Historical Association, 1989.

Ramkalawansingh, Ceta. "Women During the Great War." In *Women at Work: Ontario, 1850–1930,* edited by Janice Acton, Penny Goldsmith, and Bonnie Shepard, 261–303. Toronto: Women's Press, 1974.

Rawlyk, G.A., ed. *Aspects of the Canadian Evangelical Experience.* Montreal and Kingston: McGill-Queen's University Press, 1997.

———. *The Canadian Protestant Experience, 1760 to 1990.* Burlington, ON: Welch Publishing, 1990.

Ray, Arthur. *I Have Lived Here Since the World Began: An Illustrated History of Canada's Native People.* Toronto: Lester/Key Porter, 1996.

Rea, J.E. *T.A. Crerar: A Political Life.* Montreal and Kingston: McGill-Queen's University Press, 1997.

———. *The Winnipeg General Strike.* Toronto: Holt Rinehart Winston, 1973.

Read, Daphne, ed. *The Great War and Canadian Society.* Toronto: New Hogtown Press, 1974.

Rennie, Bradford James. *The Rise of Agrarian Democracy: The United Farmers and Farm Women of Alberta, 1909–1921.* Toronto: University of Toronto Press, 2000.

Richling, Barnett. *In Twilight and In Dawn: A Biography of Diamond Jenness.* Montreal and Kingston: McGill-Queen's University Press, 2012.

Roberts, Barbara. *Whence They Came: Deportation from Canada, 1900–1935.* Ottawa: University of Ottawa Press, 1988.

Robertson, Heather. *Driving Force: The McLaughlin Family and the Age of the Car.* Toronto: McClelland & Stewart, 1995.

Robertson, Ian Ross. *Sir Andrew Macphail: The Life and Legacy of a Canadian Man of Letters.* Montreal and Kingston: McGill-Queen's University Press, 2008.

Robertson, Kirsty. "The Canadian War Art Collection." In *Under Fire: the Canadian Imagination and War,* edited by Lorne Shirinian, 51–64. Kingston, ON: Blue Heron Press, 2004,

Rolph, William Kirby. *Henry Wise Wood of Alberta.* Toronto: University of Toronto Press, 1950.

Roy, Patricia. *The Oriental Question: Consolidating a White Man's Province, 1914–41.* Vancouver: University of British Columbia Press, 2003.

Rubio, Mary, and Elizabeth Waterston, eds. *The Selected Journals of L.M. Montgomery.* Vol. 2, *1910–1921.* Toronto: Oxford University Press, 1987.

Rudin, Ronald. *Making History in Twentieth-Century Quebec.* Toronto: University of Toronto Press, 1997.

Rumilly, Robert. *Henri Bourassa: la vie publique d'un grand Canadien.* Montreal: Èditions Chantecler, 1953.

Rutherdale, Robert. *Hometown Horizons: Local Responses to Canada's Great War.* Vancouver: University of British Columbia Press, 2005.

Schull, Joseph. *100 Years of Banking in Canada; A History of the Toronto-Dominion Bank.* Toronto: Copp Clark, 1958.

Scott, Duncan Campbell. "The Canadian Indians and the Great World War." In *Canada in the Great War: An Authentic Account of the Military History of Canada From the Earliest Days to the Close of the War of the Nations*. Vol. 3, *Guarding the Channel Ports*, Various Authorities, 283–328. Toronto: United Publishing, 1919.

Seager, Allen, and David Roth. "British Columbia and the Mining West: A Ghost of a Chance." In *The Workers' Revolt in Canada, 1917–1925*, edited by Craig Heron, 231–67. Toronto: University of Toronto Press, 1998.

Semple, Neil. *The Lord's Dominion: The History of Canadian Methodism*. Montreal and Kingston: McGill-Queen's University Press, 1996.

Sharpe, Robert J. *The Last Day, The Last Hour: The Currie Libel Trial*. Toronto: The Osgoode Society, 1988.

Shortt, Adam, and Arthur G. Doughty, eds. *Canada and Its Provinces: A History of the Canadian People and Their Institutions*. 23 vols. Toronto: Glasgow, Brook, 1914.

Shortt, S.E.D., ed. *Medicine in Canadian Society: Historical Perspectives*. Montreal and Kingston: McGill-Queen's University Press, 1981.

Smith, Donald B. "Deskaheh," *Dictionary of Canadian Biography* online: *www. biographi.ca/EN/009004–119.01–e.php?id_nbr=8103*.

———, "Loft, Frederick Ogilvie." *Dictionary of Canadian Biography* online: *www.biographi.ca/EN/009004–119.01–e.php?id_nbr=8419*.

Socknat, Thomas B. *Witness Against War: Pacifism in Canada, 1900–1945*. Toronto: University of Toronto Press, 1987.

Speisman, Stephen, "Antisemitism in Ontario: The Twentieth Century." In *Antisemitism in Canada: History and Interpretation*, edited by Alan Davies, 113–34. Waterloo, ON: Wilfrid Laurier University Press, 1992.

Spence, Ruth. *Prohibition in Canada: A Memorial to Francis Stephen Spence*. Toronto: Dominion Alliance (Ontario Branch), 1919.

Stacey, C.P. *Canada and the Age of Conflict: A History of Canadian External Policies*. Vol. 1, *1867–1921*. Toronto: Macmillan, 1977.

———. *Canada and the Age of Conflict: A History of Canadian External Policies*. Vol. 2, *1921–1948: The Mackenzie King Era*. Toronto: University of Toronto Press, 1981.

Stackhouse, Jr., John, *Canadian Evangelicalism in the Twentieth Century: An Introduction to its Character*. Toronto: University of Toronto Press, 1993.

Staples, Melville H. *The Challenge of Agriculture: The Story of the United Farmers of Ontario*. Toronto: Morang, 1921.

Stead, Robert. *Grain*. Toronto: McClelland & Stewart, 1969.

Stevenson, John A. *Before the Bar: Prohibition — Pro and Con*. Toronto: J.M. Dent, 1919.

Strange, Carolyn, and Tina Loo. *Making Good: Law and Moral Regulation in Canada, 1876–1939*. Toronto: University of Toronto Press, 1997.

Strong-Boag, Veronica. "The Girl of the New Day: Canadian Working Women in the 1920s." In *Readings in Canadian Social History.* Vol. 4, *The Consolidation of Capitalism, 1896–1929,* edited by Michael S. Cross and Gregory S. Kealey, 131–64. Toronto: McClelland & Stewart, 1986.

———. "Intruders in the Nursery: Childcare Professionals Reshape the Years One to Five, 1920–1940." In *Childhood and Family in Canadian History,* edited by Joy Parr, 160–78. Toronto: McClelland & Stewart, 1982.

———. *"Janey Canuck": Women in Canada, 1919–1939.* Ottawa: Canadian Historical Association, 1994.

———. *The New Day Recalled: Lives of Girls and Women in English Canada, 1919–1939.* Toronto: Copp Clark Pitman, 1988.

———. "Pulling in Double Harness or Hauling a Double Load: Women, Work, and Feminism on the Canadian Prairie." In *The Prairie West: Historical Readings,* second edition, edited by R. Douglas Francis and Howard Palmer, 401–23. Calgary: University of Calgary Press, 1992.

———. "'Wages for Housework': Mothers' Allowances and the Beginnings of Social Security in Canada." *Journal of Canadian Studies* 14, No. 1 (Spring 1979): 24–34.

Sturino, Franc. *Forging the Chain: A Case Study of Italian Migration to North America, 1880–1930.* Toronto: Multicultural History Society of Ontario, 1990.

Swainson, Donald, ed. *Historical Essays on the Prairie Provinces.* Toronto: McClelland & Stewart, 1970.

Swyripa, Frances. *Wedded to the Cause: Ukrainian Canadian Women and Ethnic Identity 1891–1991.* Toronto: University of Toronto Press, 1993.

Tan, Jin, and Patricia Roy. *The Chinese in Canada.* Ottawa: Canadian Historical Association, 1985.

Taubenberger, Jeffery K., and Daniel M. Morens. "1918 Influenza: The Mother of All Pandemics." *Emerging Infectious Diseases* 12, No. 1 (May 1979). Accessed online via *www.cdc.gov/ncidod/EID/vol12no01/05–0979.htm.*

Taylor, Graham D. *The Rise of Canadian Business.* Toronto: Oxford University Press, 2009.

Taylor, John Leonard. *Canadian Indian Policy During the Interwar Years, 1918–1939.* Ottawa: Indian and Northern Affairs, 1984.

Thompson, John Herd. "'The Beginning of Our Regeneration': The Great War and Western Canadian Reform Movements." *Historical Papers* [Canadian Historical Association] (1972): 227–246.

———. *Ethnic Minorities During Two World Wars.* Ottawa: Canadian Historical Association, 1991.

———. *Forging the Prairie West: The Illustrated History of Canada.* Toronto: Oxford University Press, 1998.

———. *The Harvests of War: The Prairie West, 1914–1918.* Toronto: McClelland & Stewart, 1978.

Thompson, John Herd, and Stephen J. Randall. *Canada and the United States: Ambivalent Allies.* Athens, GA and London: University of Georgia Press, 1994.

Thompson, John Herd, with Allen Seager. *Canada, 1921–1939: Decades of Discord.* Toronto: McClelland & Stewart, 1985.

Tippett, Maria. *Art in the Service of War: Canada, Art, and the Great War.* Toronto: University of Toronto Press, 1994.

———. *Making Culture: English-Canadian Institutions and the Arts Before the Massey Commission.* Toronto: University of Toronto Press, 1990.

Titley, E. Brian. *A Narrow Vision: Duncan Campbell Scott and the Administration of Indian Affairs in Canada.* Vancouver: University of British Columbia Press, 1986.

Traves, Tom. "The Development of the Ontario Automobile Industry to 1930." In *Progress Without Planning: The Economic History of Ontario from Confederation to the Second World War,* edited by Ian M. Drummond, 208–23. Toronto: University of Toronto Press, 1987.

———. *The State and Enterprise: Canadian Manufacturers and the Federal Government, 1917–1931.* Toronto: University of Toronto Press, 1979.

Trofimenkoff, Susan Mann. *Abbé Groulx: Variations on a Nationalist Theme.* Vancouver: Copp Clark, 1973.

———. *L'Action française: French-Canadian Nationalism in the Twenties.* Toronto: University of Toronto Press, 1976.

———. *The Dream of Nation: A Social and Intellectual History of Quebec.* Toronto: Gage, 1983.

———, ed. *The Twenties in Western Canada: Papers of the Western Historical Society Conference, 1972.* Ottawa: History Division of the National Museum of Man, 1972.

Tulchinsky, Gerald J. *Canada's Jews: A People's Journey.* Toronto: University of Toronto Press, 2008.

Valverde, Mariana. *The Age of Light, Soap, and Water: Moral Reform in English Canada, 1885–1925.* Toronto: McClelland & Stewart, 1991.

Vance, Jonathan. *Death So Noble: Memory, Meaning, and the First World War.* Vancouver: University of British Columbia Press, 1997.

———. *A History of Canadian Culture.* Toronto: Oxford University Press, 2009.

———. *Maple Leaf Empire: Canada, Britain, and Two World Wars.* Toronto: Oxford University Press, 2012.

Van Passen, Pierre. *Days of Our Years.* New York: Hillman-Curl, 1939.

Veatch, Richard. *Canada and the League of Nations.* Toronto: University of Toronto Press, 1975.

Vigod, Bernard. *The Jews in Canada.* Ottawa: Canadian Historical Association, 1984.

Vipond, Mary. "Best Sellers in English Canada, 1899–1918: An Overview." *Journal of Canadian Fiction* 24 (1979): 96–119.

————. *The Mass Media in Canada*. Toronto: James Lorimer, 1989.

————. "National Consciousness in English-Speaking Canada in the 1920s: Seven Studies." Ph.D. Thesis, University of Toronto, 1974.

————. "The Nationalist Network: English Canada's Intellectuals and Artists in the 1920s." *Canadian Review of Studies in Nationalism* 5 (Spring 1980): 32–52.

Voisey, Paul. *Vulcan: The Making of a Prairie Community*. Toronto: University of Toronto Press, 1988.

Wade, Mason. *The French Canadians, 1760–1967*. Vol. 2, *1911–1967*. Toronto: Macmillan, 1968.

Walden, Keith, ed. *The Papers of Harry Cassidy and Beatrice Pearce: The Courtship Years, 1917–1925*. Toronto: The Champlain Society, 2009.

Walker, James W. St. G. "Race and Recruitment in World War I: Enlistment of Visible Minorities in the Canadian Expeditionary Force." *Canadian Historical Review* 70, No. 1 (March 1989): 1–26.

————. *Racial Discrimination in Canada: The Black Experience*. Ottawa: Canadian Historical Association, 1982.

————. *The West Indians in Canada*. Ottawa: Canadian Historical Association, 1984.

Ward, Peter. *The Japanese in Canada*. Ottawa: Canadian Historical Association, 1982.

————. *White Canada Forever: Popular Attitudes and Public Policy Toward Orientals in British Columbia*. Montreal and Kingston: McGill-Queen's University Press, 2002.

Wardhaugh, Robert A. *Mackenzie King and the Prairie West*. Toronto: University of Toronto Press, 2000.

Warsh, Cheryl Krasnick, ed. *Drink in Canada: Historical Essays*. Montreal and Kingston: McGill-Queen's University Press, 1993.

Weintraub, Stanley. *A Stillness Heard Round the World: The End of the Great War, November 1918*. New York: Oxford University Press, 1985.

Whitaker, Reg. *Canadian Immigration Policy*. Ottawa: Canadian Historical Association, 1991.

Wigley, Philip. *Canada and the Transition to Commonwealth: British-Canadian Relations, 1917–26*. Cambridge: Cambridge University Press, 1977.

Wilson, Barbara M., ed. *Ontario and the First World War, 1914–1918: A Collection of Documents*. Toronto: The Champlain Society, 1977.

Wilson, J. Donald, Robert M. Stamp, and Louis-Philippe Audet, eds. *Canadian Education: A History*. Scarborough, ON: Prentice-Hall, 1970.

Winegard, Timothy. *For King and Kanata: Canadian Indians and the First World War*. Winnipeg: University of Manitoba Press, 2012.

Winks, Robin W. *The Blacks In Canada: A History*. Second edition. Montreal and Kingston: McGill-Queen's University Press, 1997.

Wood, Louis Aubrey. *A History of Farmers' Movements in Canada*. Introduction by Foster J.K. Griezic. Toronto: University of Toronto Press, 1975.

Woodsworth, J.S. *My Neighbour.* Introduction by Richard Allen: Toronto: University of Toronto Press, 1972.

———. "Nation-Building." *University Magazine* 16, No. 1 (February 1917): 85–99.

———. *Strangers Within Our Gates.* Introduction by Marilyn Barber. Toronto: University of Toronto Press, 1972.

Wright, Robert A. "The Canadian Protestant Tradition, 1914-1945." In *The Canadian Protestant Experience 1760 to 1990,* edited by G.A. Rawlyk, 139–97. Burlington, ON: Welch Publishing, 1990.

———. *World Mission: Canadian Protestantism and the Quest for a New International Order, 1918–1939.* Montreal and Kingston: McGill-Queen's University Press, 1992.

Zaslow, Morris. *The Northward Expansion of Canada, 1914–1967.* Toronto: McClelland & Stewart, 1988.

Zucchi, John. *History of Ethnic Enclaves in Canada.* Ottawa: Canadian Historical Association, 1998.

———. *Italians in Toronto: Development of a National Identity, 1875–1935.* Montreal and Kingston: McGill-Queen's University Press, 1988.

Index

Other Books by Alan Bowker

On the Front Line of Life: Stephen Leacock:
Memories and Reflections, 1935–1944
Alan Bowker, ed.

In the last decade of his life, Leacock turned to writing informal essays that blended humour with a conversational style and ripened wisdom to address the issues he cared about most — education, literature, economics, Canada and its place in the world — and to confront the joys and sorrows of his own life. With an introduction that sets them in the context of his life, thoughts and times, these essays reveal a passionate, intelligent, personal Leacock, against a backdrop of Depression and war, finding hope and conveying the timeless message that only the human spirit can bring social justice, peace, and progress.

Other History Books from Dundurn

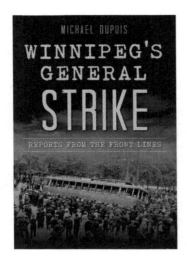

Winnipeg's General Strike: Reports from the Front Lines
Michael Dupuis

A strike gripped Winnipeg from May 15 to June 26, 1919. Some twenty-five thousand workers walked out, demanding better wages and union recognition. Red-fearing opponents insisted labour radicals were attempting to usurp constitutional authority and replace it with Bolshevism. Newspapers like the *Manitoba Free Press* claimed themselves political victims and warned of Soviet infiltration. Supporters of the general sympathetic strike like the *Toronto Daily Star* maintained that strikers were not Reds; they were workers fighting for their fair rights. What was really happening in Winnipeg? In an information age dominated by newspapers and magazines, the public turned to reporters and editors for answers.

VISIT US AT
Dundurn.com
@dundurnpress
Facebook.com/dundurnpress
Pinterest.com/dundurnpress